Did you know that the earth is spinning at incredible speed? It's been spinning so fast for so long that all the edges have been worn down and it's gotten round.

—Tsugumi Ohba

I published my first manga series in the school newspaper when I attended Higashi-Yamanoshita elementary school, class 3 in the third grade. It was a strange manga where the hero transformed into a disposable pocket warmer when he was in trouble.

D1052474

Tsugumi Ohba

Born in Tokyo, Tsugumi Ohba is the author of the hit series *Death Note*. His current series *Bakuman₀* is serialized in *Weekly Shonen Jump*.

Takeshi Obata

Takeshi Obata was born in 1969 in Niigata, Japan, and is the artist of the wildly popular SHONEN JUMP title *Hikaru no Go*, which won the 2003 Tezuka Osamu Cultural Prize: Shinsei "New Hope" award and the 2000 Shogakukan Manga award. Obata is also the artist of *Arabian Majin Bokentan Lamp Lamp*, *Ayatsuri Sakon*, *Cyborg Jichan G.*, and the smash hit manga *Death Note*. His current series *Bakuman₀* is serialized in *Weekly Shonen Jump*.

Volume 3

SHONEN JUMP Manga Edition

Story by **TSUGUMI OHBA**
Art by **TAKESHI OBATA**

Translation & Adaptation | **Tetsuichiro Miyaki**
Touch-up Art & Lettering | **James Gaubatz**
Design | **Fawn Lau**
Editor | **Alexis Kirsch**

Printed in the U.S.A.

Published by VIZ Media, LLC
P.O. Box 77010
San Francisco, CA 94107

10 9 8 7 6 5 4 3 2 1
First printing, February 2011

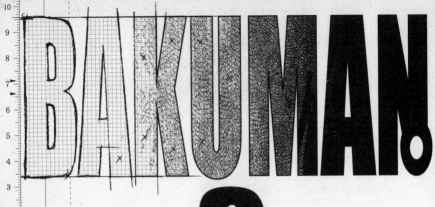

BAKUMAN.

3

DEBUT and IMPATIENCE

STORY BY

TSUGUMI OHBA

ART BY

TAKESHI OBATA

MAN。バクマン。 vol. 3

*These ages are from May 2009.

EIJI
Nizuma

A prodigy who received the Tezuka Award at just age 15. He's in the same age group as Moritaka and Akito.

Age: 16

KAYA
Miyoshi

Miho's best friend who thinks Akito has a crush on her.

Age: 15

AKITO
Takagi

Aspiring manga writer. An extremely smart guy who gets the best grades in his class. A cool guy who becomes very passionate when it comes to manga.

Age: 15

MIHO
Azuki

A girl who dreams of becoming a voice actress. She promised to marry Moritaka under the condition that they not see each other until their dreams come true.

Age: 15

MORITAKA
Mashiro

Aspiring manga artist. An extreme romantic who believes that he will marry Miho Azuki once their dreams come true.

Age: 15

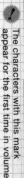

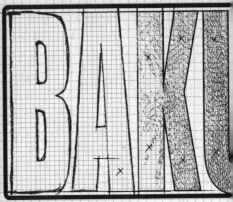

STORY In order to attain the glory that only a handful of people can, two young men decide to walk the rough "path of manga" and become professional manga creators. This is the story of a great artist, Moritaka Mashiro, a talented writer, Akito Takagi, and their quest to become manga legends!

4
5
1
3
2

The characters with this mark appear for the first time in volume 3.

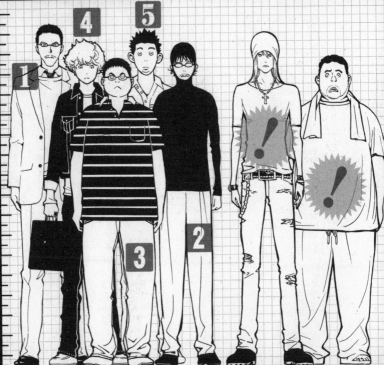

WEEKLY SHONEN JUMP
Editorial Office

1 Editor in Chief Sasaki	Age: 46
2 Deputy Editor in Chief Heishi	Age: 41
3 Soichi Aida	Age: 34
4 Yujiro Hattori	Age: 27
5 Akira Hattori	Age: 29

The Editors of *Weekly Shonen Jump*.

SHINTA Fukuda

A rookie manga artist whom the editorial office has high hopes for. He has twice won a prize in the Tezuka Award. He works as Nizuma's assistant while trying to get his own series.

Age: 19

TAKURO Nakai

A veteran assistant who received a monthly award around 10 years ago. He still hasn't given up his dream to become a manga artist.

Age: 33

BAKUMAN. Vol.3

(DEBUT AND IMPATIENCE)

CONTENTS

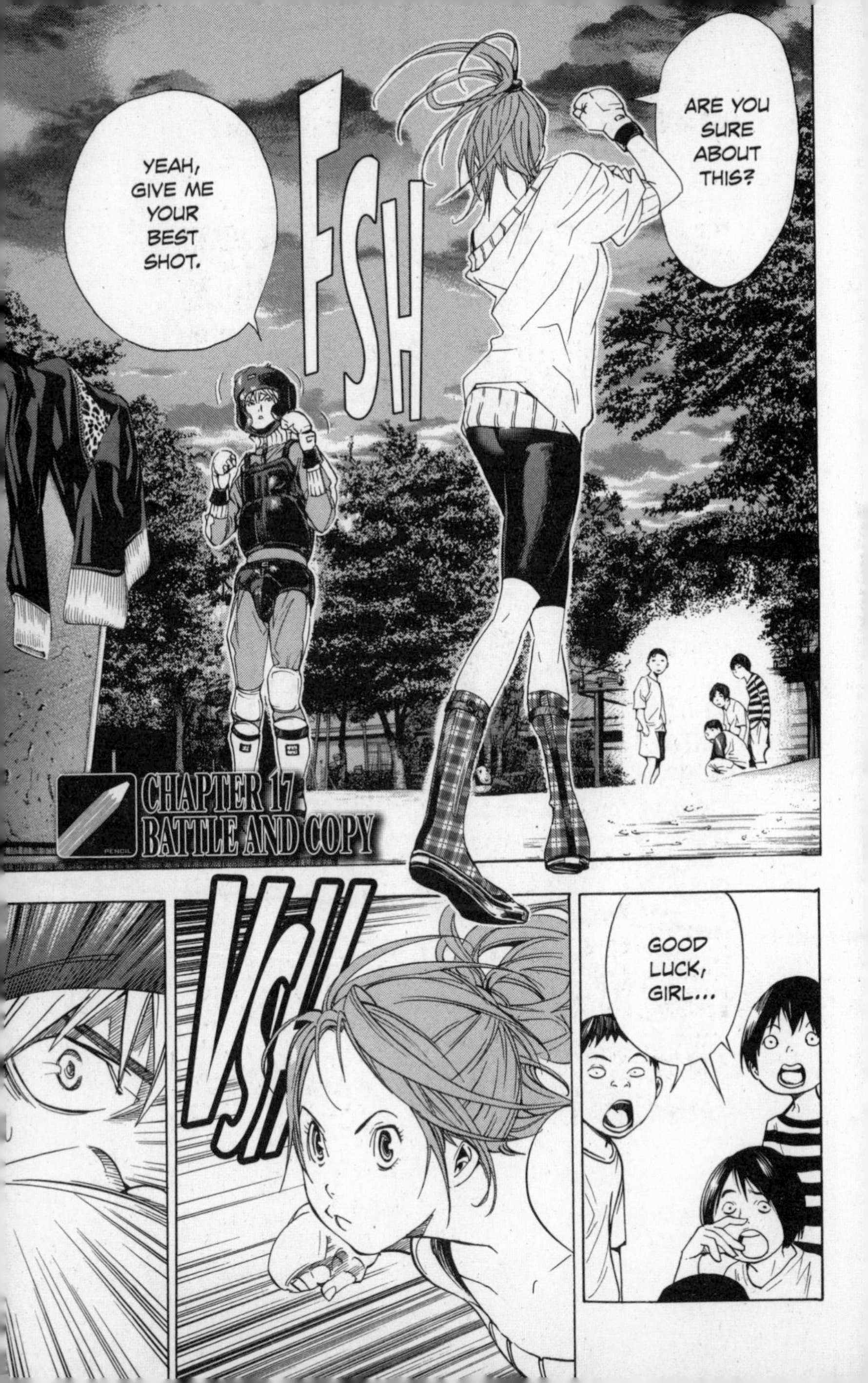
ARE YOU SURE ABOUT THIS?
YEAH, GIVE ME YOUR BEST SHOT.
FSH
CHAPTER 17 BATTLE AND COPY
GOOD LUCK, GIRL...

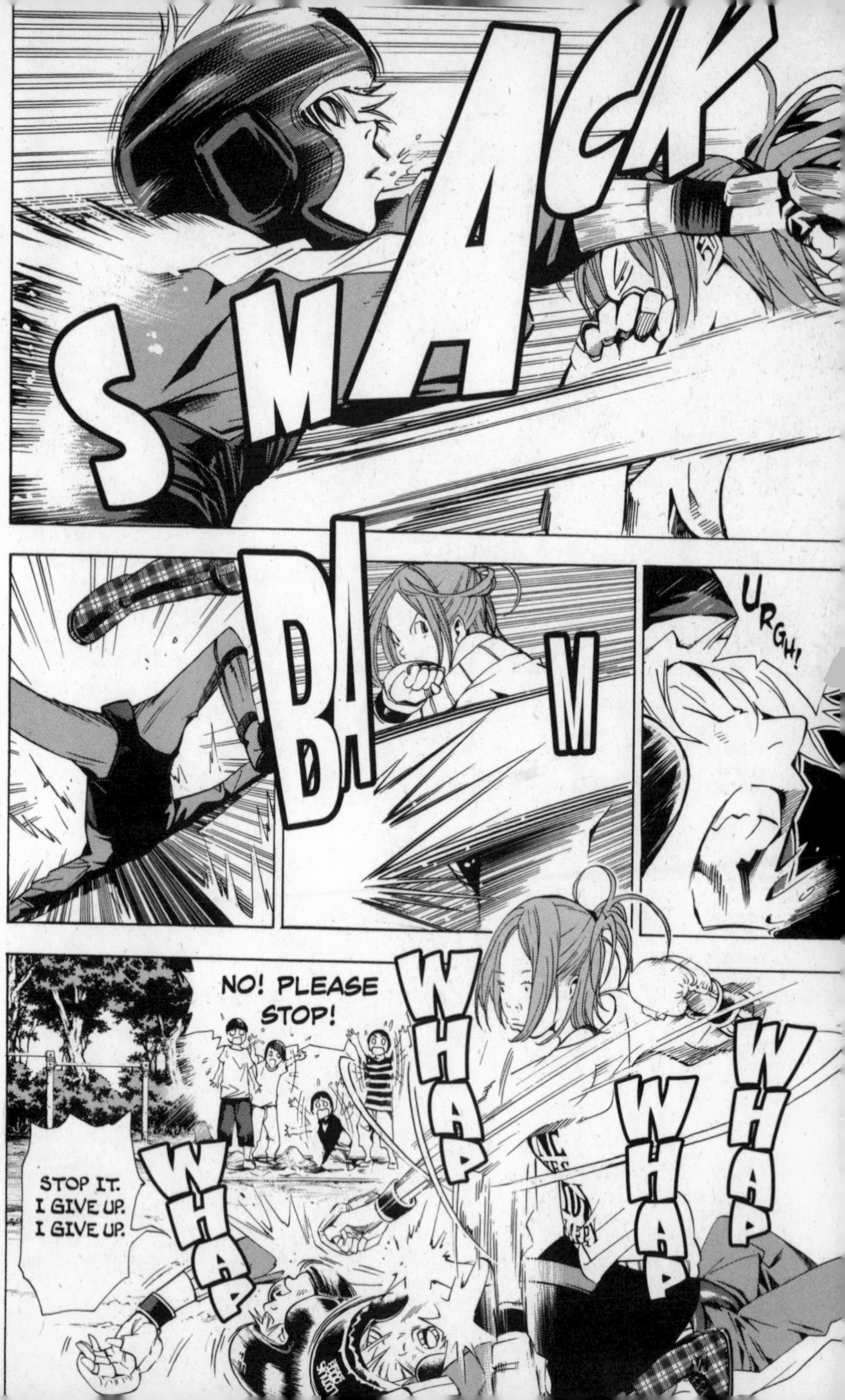
SMACK
URGH!
BADAM
WHAP
WHAP
WHAP
NO! PLEASE STOP!
WHAP
STOP IT. I GIVE UP. I GIVE UP.

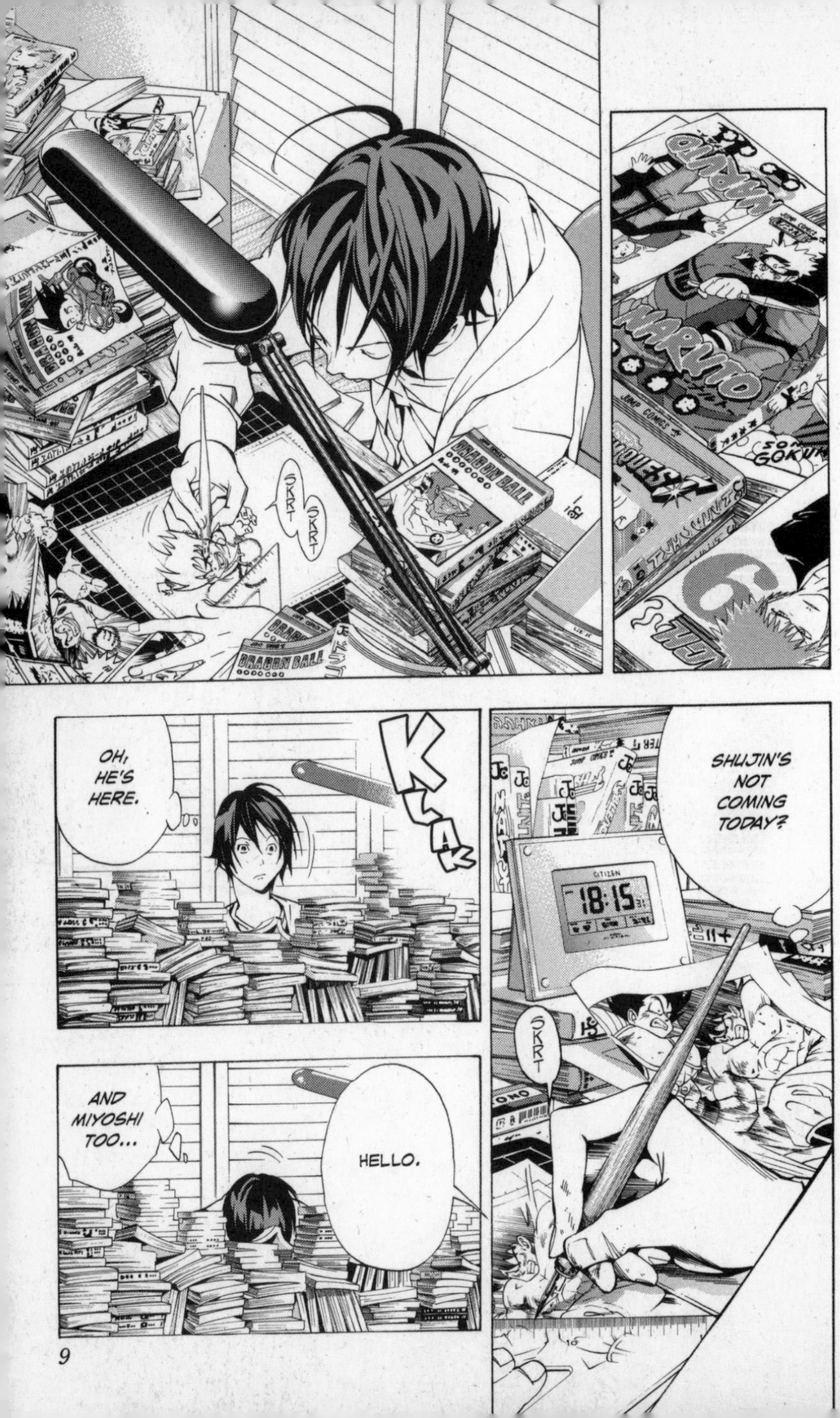
NARUTO
SKRT SKRT
DRAGON BALL
SHUJIN'S NOT COMING TODAY?
SKRT
OH, HE'S HERE.
KLAK
AND MIYOSHI TOO...
HELLO.

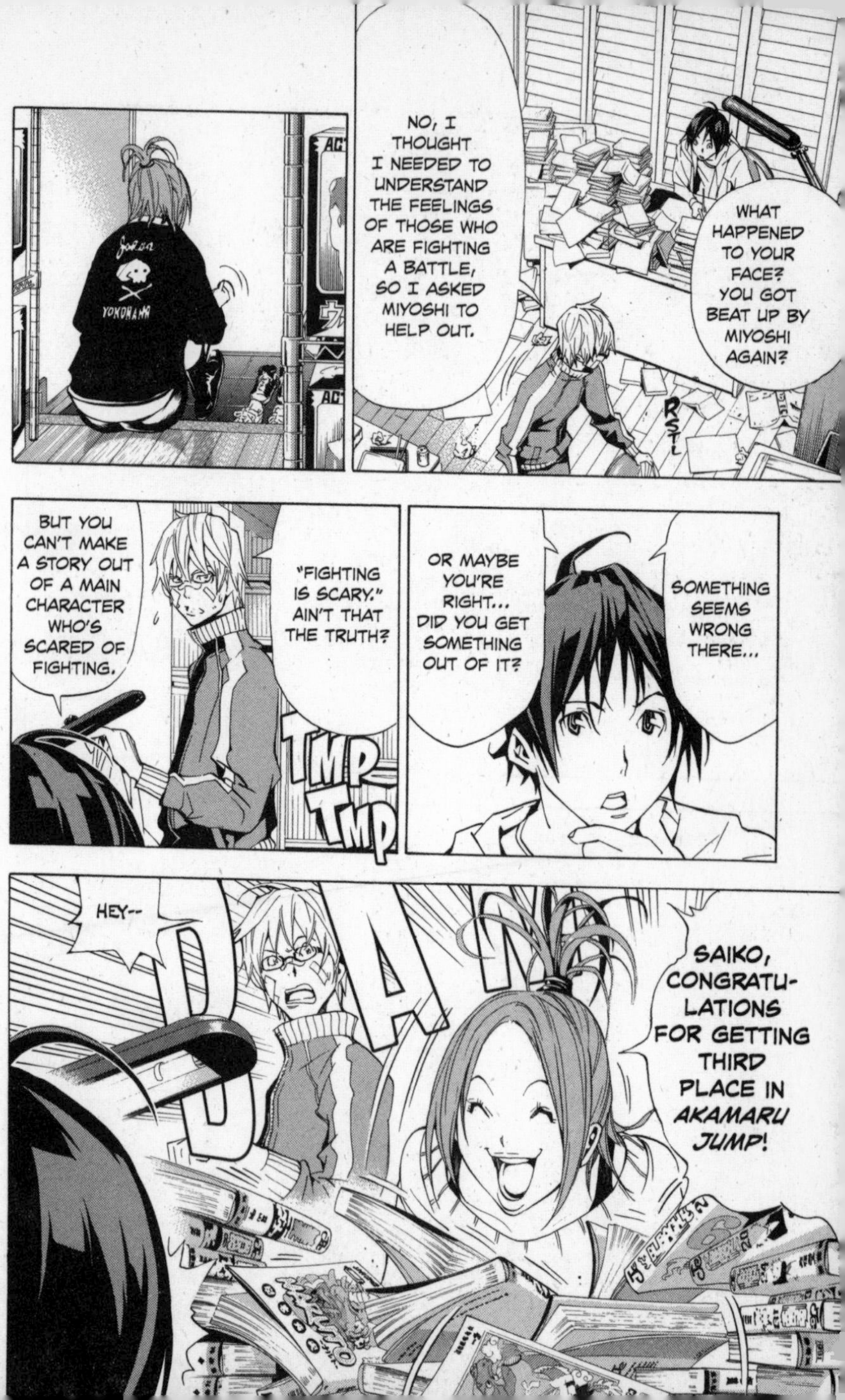
WHAT HAPPENED TO YOUR FACE? YOU GOT BEAT UP BY MIYOSHI AGAIN?
RSTL
NO, I THOUGHT I NEEDED TO UNDERSTAND THE FEELINGS OF THOSE WHO ARE FIGHTING A BATTLE, SO I ASKED MIYOSHI TO HELP OUT.
SOMETHING SEEMS WRONG THERE...
OR MAYBE YOU'RE RIGHT... DID YOU GET SOMETHING OUT OF IT?
"FIGHTING IS SCARY." AIN'T THAT THE TRUTH?
TMP TMP
BUT YOU CAN'T MAKE A STORY OUT OF A MAIN CHARACTER WHO'S SCARED OF FIGHTING.
SAIKO, CONGRATULATIONS FOR GETTING THIRD PLACE IN *AKAMARU JUMP*!
HEY--

READ THIS WAY

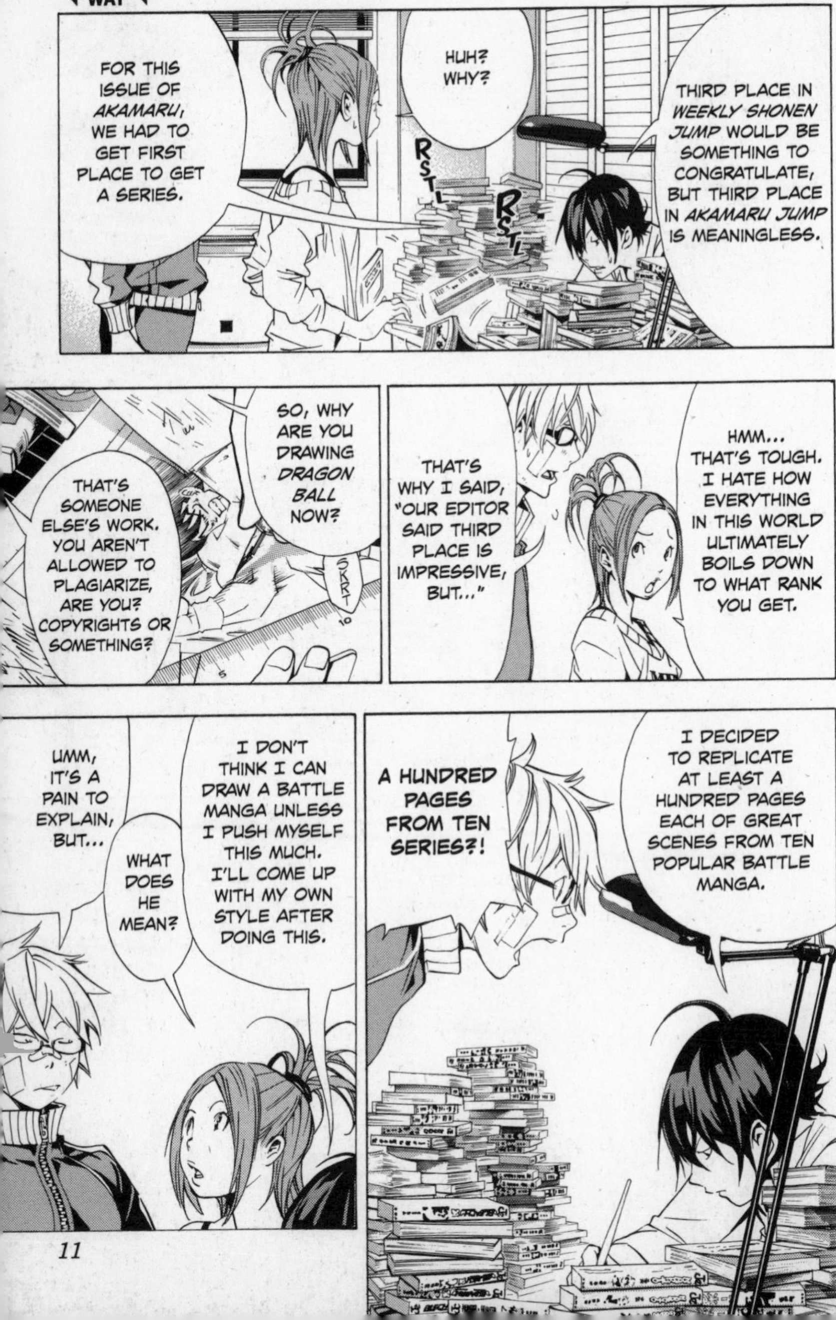
THIRD PLACE IN *WEEKLY SHONEN JUMP* WOULD BE SOMETHING TO CONGRATULATE, BUT THIRD PLACE IN *AKAMARU JUMP* IS MEANINGLESS.
HUH? WHY?
RSTL
RSTL
FOR THIS ISSUE OF *AKAMARU*, WE HAD TO GET FIRST PLACE TO GET A SERIES.
HMM... THAT'S TOUGH. I HATE HOW EVERYTHING IN THIS WORLD ULTIMATELY BOILS DOWN TO WHAT RANK YOU GET.
THAT'S WHY I SAID, "OUR EDITOR SAID THIRD PLACE IS IMPRESSIVE, BUT..."
SO, WHY ARE YOU DRAWING *DRAGON BALL* NOW?
SKRT
THAT'S SOMEONE ELSE'S WORK. YOU AREN'T ALLOWED TO PLAGIARIZE, ARE YOU? COPYRIGHTS OR SOMETHING?
I DECIDED TO REPLICATE AT LEAST A HUNDRED PAGES EACH OF GREAT SCENES FROM TEN POPULAR BATTLE MANGA.
A HUNDRED PAGES FROM TEN SERIES?!
I DON'T THINK I CAN DRAW A BATTLE MANGA UNLESS I PUSH MYSELF THIS MUCH. I'LL COME UP WITH MY OWN STYLE AFTER DOING THIS.
WHAT DOES HE MEAN?
UMM, IT'S A PAIN TO EXPLAIN, BUT...

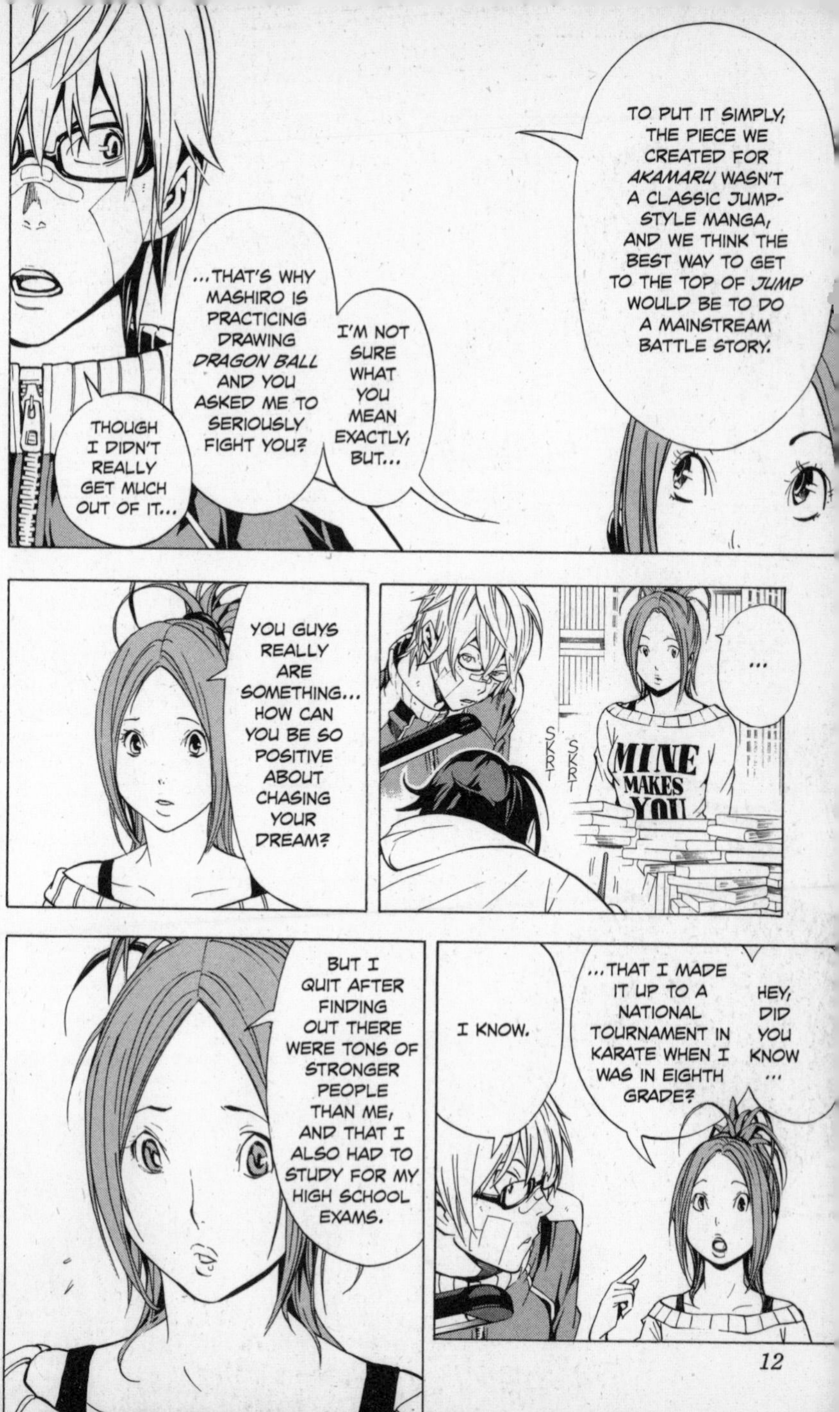
TO PUT IT SIMPLY, THE PIECE WE CREATED FOR AKAMARU WASN'T A CLASSIC JUMP-STYLE MANGA, AND WE THINK THE BEST WAY TO GET TO THE TOP OF JUMP WOULD BE TO DO A MAINSTREAM BATTLE STORY.
I'M NOT SURE WHAT YOU MEAN EXACTLY, BUT...
...THAT'S WHY MASHIRO IS PRACTICING DRAWING DRAGON BALL AND YOU ASKED ME TO SERIOUSLY FIGHT YOU?
THOUGH I DIDN'T REALLY GET MUCH OUT OF IT...
...
SKRT
SKRT
MINE MAKES YOU
YOU GUYS REALLY ARE SOMETHING... HOW CAN YOU BE SO POSITIVE ABOUT CHASING YOUR DREAM?
HEY, DID YOU KNOW ...
...THAT I MADE IT UP TO A NATIONAL TOURNAMENT IN KARATE WHEN I WAS IN EIGHTH GRADE?
I KNOW.
BUT I QUIT AFTER FINDING OUT THERE WERE TONS OF STRONGER PEOPLE THAN ME, AND THAT I ALSO HAD TO STUDY FOR MY HIGH SCHOOL EXAMS.

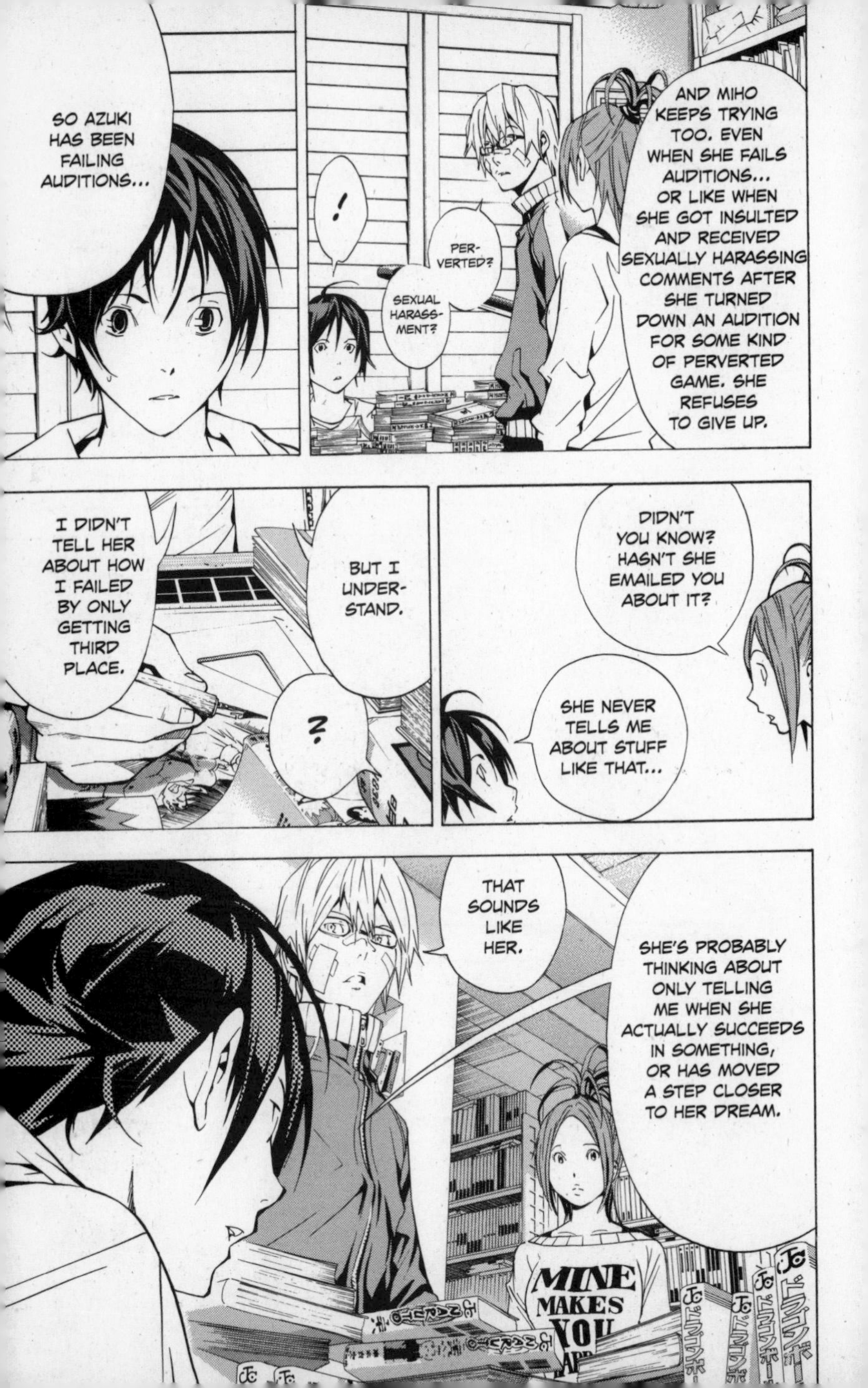

AND MIHO KEEPS TRYING TOO. EVEN WHEN SHE FAILS AUDITIONS... OR LIKE WHEN SHE GOT INSULTED AND RECEIVED SEXUALLY HARASSING COMMENTS AFTER SHE TURNED DOWN AN AUDITION FOR SOME KIND OF PERVERTED GAME. SHE REFUSES TO GIVE UP.
PER-VERTED?
SEXUAL HARASS-MENT?
!
SO AZUKI HAS BEEN FAILING AUDITIONS...
DIDN'T YOU KNOW? HASN'T SHE EMAILED YOU ABOUT IT?
SHE NEVER TELLS ME ABOUT STUFF LIKE THAT...
I DIDN'T TELL HER ABOUT HOW I FAILED BY ONLY GETTING THIRD PLACE.
BUT I UNDER-STAND.
?
THAT SOUNDS LIKE HER.
SHE'S PROBABLY THINKING ABOUT ONLY TELLING ME WHEN SHE ACTUALLY SUCCEEDS IN SOMETHING, OR HAS MOVED A STEP CLOSER TO HER DREAM.
MINE MAKES YOU

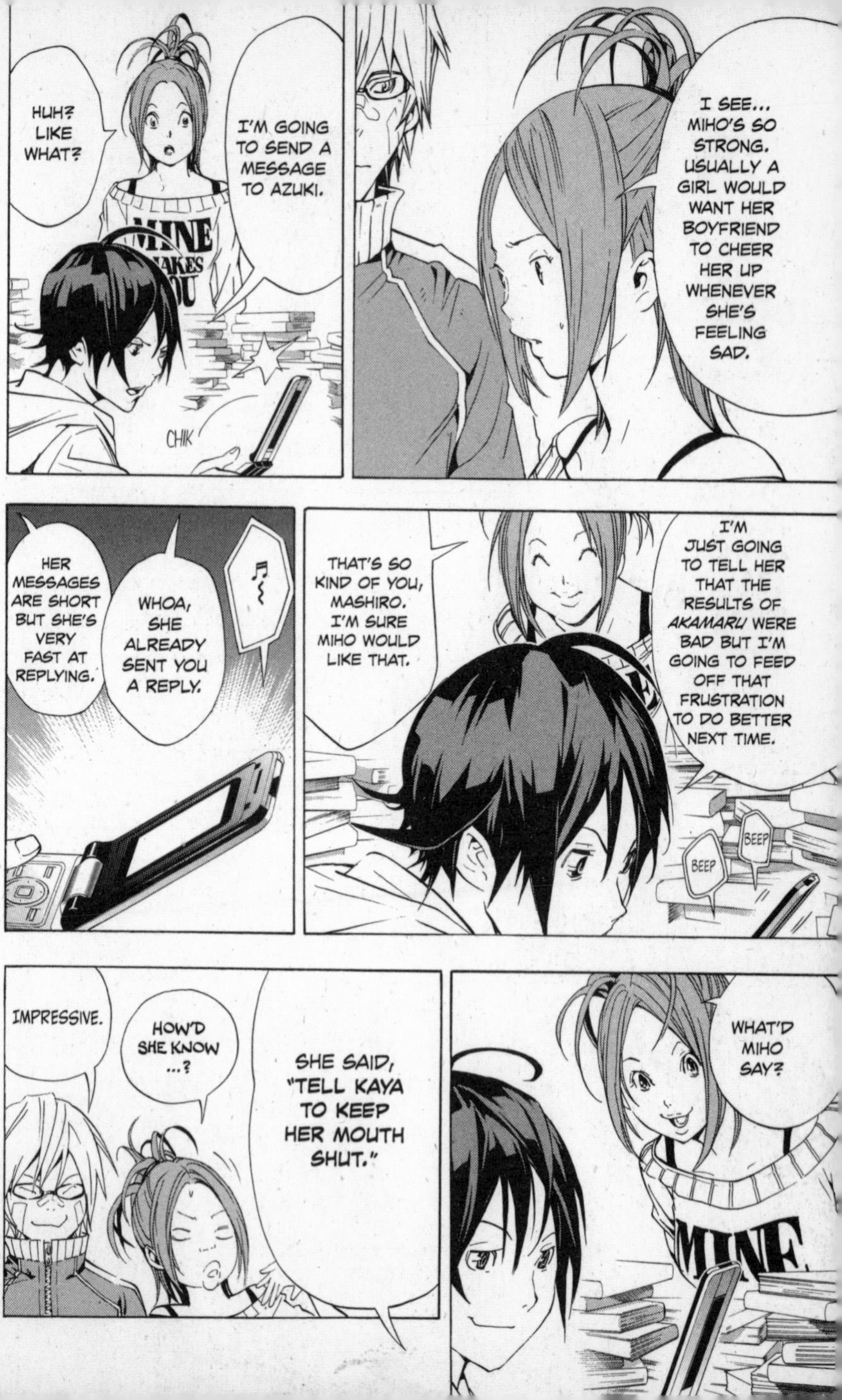
I SEE... MIHO'S SO STRONG. USUALLY A GIRL WOULD WANT HER BOYFRIEND TO CHEER HER UP WHENEVER SHE'S FEELING SAD.
I'M GOING TO SEND A MESSAGE TO AZUKI.
HUH? LIKE WHAT?
CHIK
I'M JUST GOING TO TELL HER THAT THE RESULTS OF *AKAMARU* WERE BAD BUT I'M GOING TO FEED OFF THAT FRUSTRATION TO DO BETTER NEXT TIME.
THAT'S SO KIND OF YOU, MASHIRO. I'M SURE MIHO WOULD LIKE THAT.
BEEP
BEEP
♪~
WHOA, SHE ALREADY SENT YOU A REPLY.
HER MESSAGES ARE SHORT BUT SHE'S VERY FAST AT REPLYING.
WHAT'D MIHO SAY?
SHE SAID, "TELL KAYA TO KEEP HER MOUTH SHUT."
HOW'D SHE KNOW ...?
IMPRESSIVE.

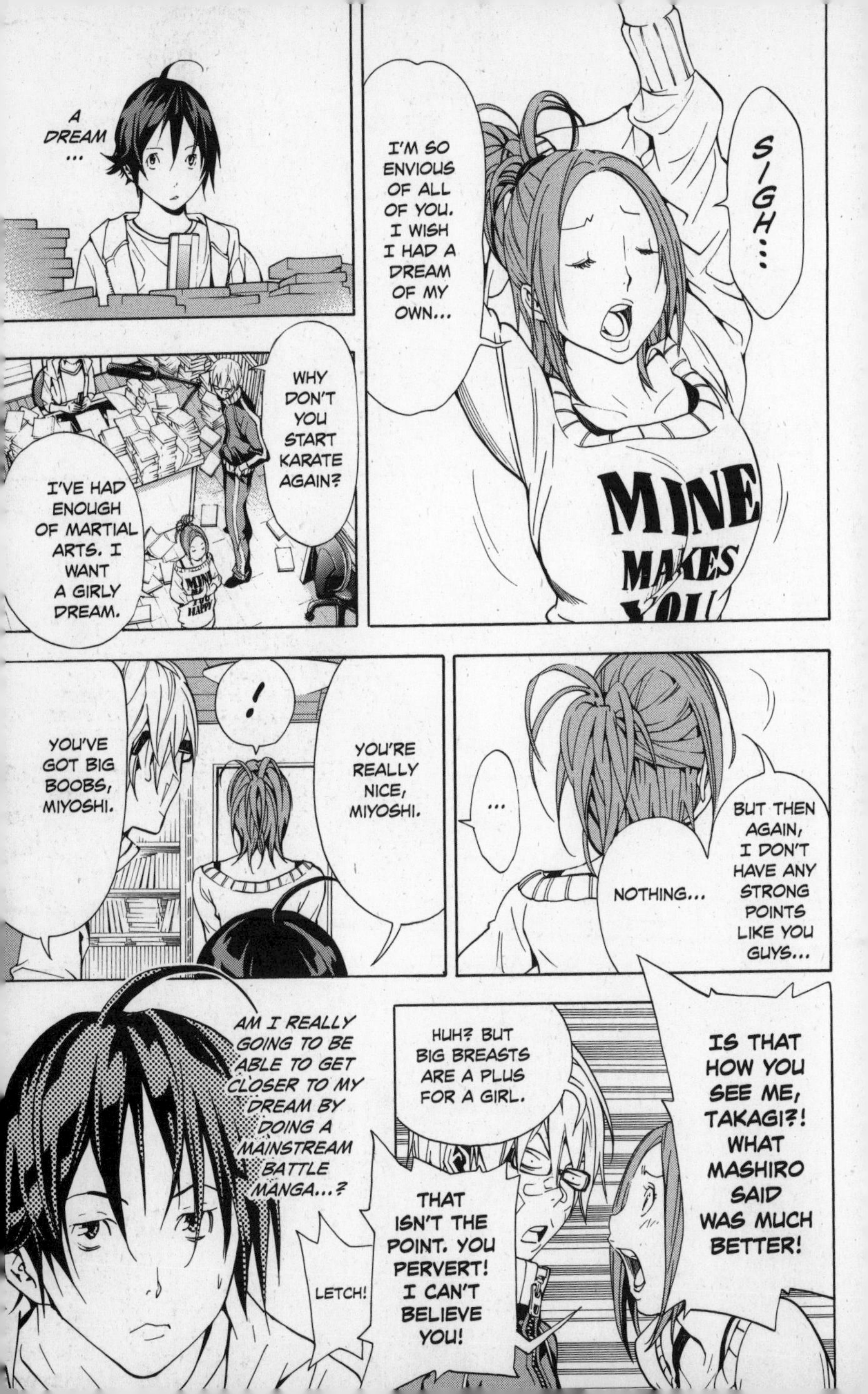
SIGH...
I'M SO ENVIOUS OF ALL OF YOU. I WISH I HAD A DREAM OF MY OWN...
MINE MAKES YOU
A DREAM...
WHY DON'T YOU START KARATE AGAIN?
I'VE HAD ENOUGH OF MARTIAL ARTS. I WANT A GIRLY DREAM.
BUT THEN AGAIN, I DON'T HAVE ANY STRONG POINTS LIKE YOU GUYS...
...
NOTHING...
YOU'RE REALLY NICE, MIYOSHI.
!
YOU'VE GOT BIG BOOBS, MIYOSHI.
IS THAT HOW YOU SEE ME, TAKAGI?! WHAT MASHIRO SAID WAS MUCH BETTER!
HUH? BUT BIG BREASTS ARE A PLUS FOR A GIRL.
THAT ISN'T THE POINT. YOU PERVERT! I CAN'T BELIEVE YOU!
LETCH!
AM I REALLY GOING TO BE ABLE TO GET CLOSER TO MY DREAM BY DOING A MAINSTREAM BATTLE MANGA...?

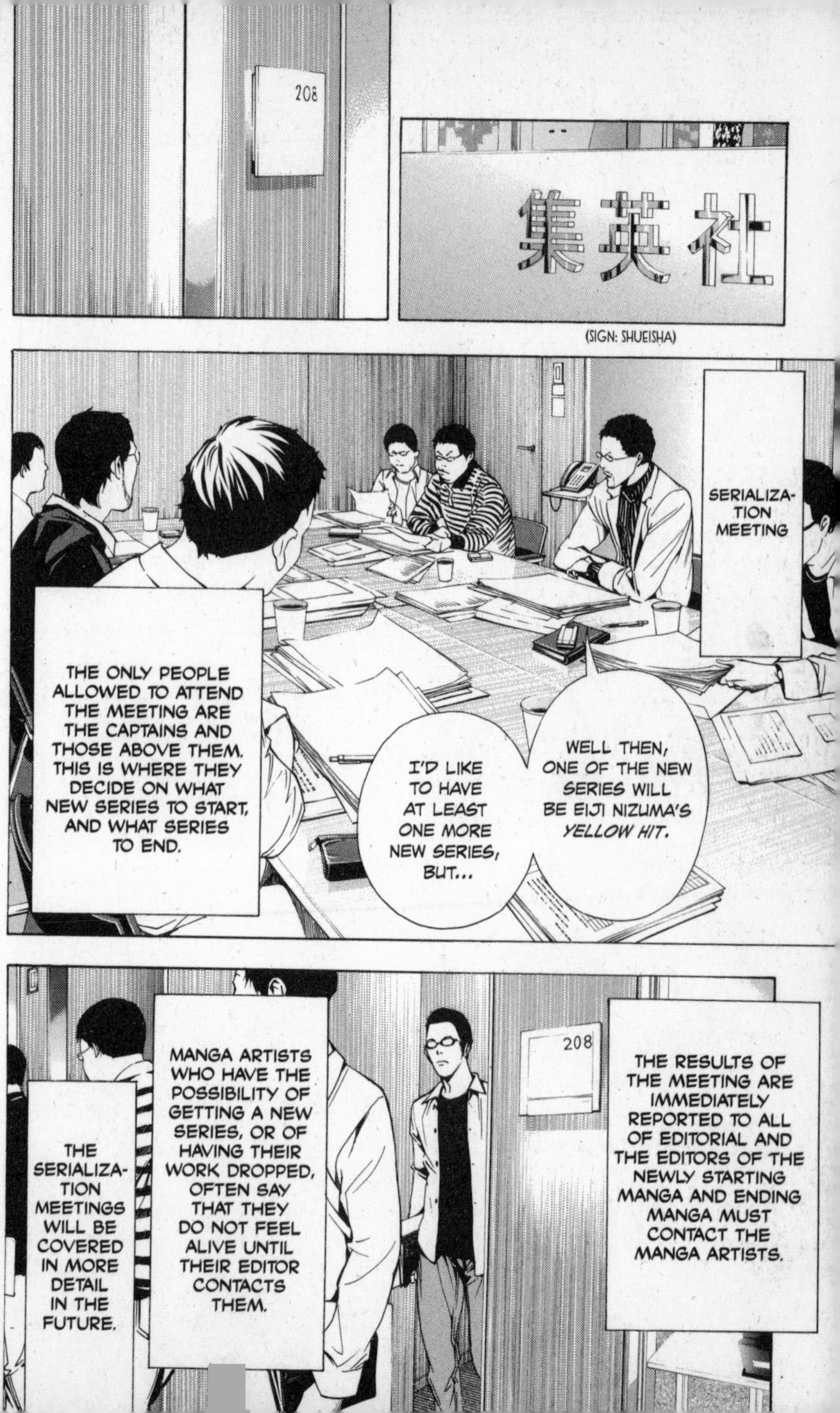
集英社
(SIGN: SHUEISHA)
208
SERIALIZATION MEETING
WELL THEN, ONE OF THE NEW SERIES WILL BE EIJI NIZUMA'S *YELLOW HIT*.
I'D LIKE TO HAVE AT LEAST ONE MORE NEW SERIES, BUT...
THE ONLY PEOPLE ALLOWED TO ATTEND THE MEETING ARE THE CAPTAINS AND THOSE ABOVE THEM. THIS IS WHERE THEY DECIDE ON WHAT NEW SERIES TO START, AND WHAT SERIES TO END.
THE RESULTS OF THE MEETING ARE IMMEDIATELY REPORTED TO ALL OF EDITORIAL AND THE EDITORS OF THE NEWLY STARTING MANGA AND ENDING MANGA MUST CONTACT THE MANGA ARTISTS.
208
MANGA ARTISTS WHO HAVE THE POSSIBILITY OF GETTING A NEW SERIES, OR OF HAVING THEIR WORK DROPPED, OFTEN SAY THAT THEY DO NOT FEEL ALIVE UNTIL THEIR EDITOR CONTACTS THEM.
THE SERIALIZATION MEETINGS WILL BE COVERED IN MORE DETAIL IN THE FUTURE.

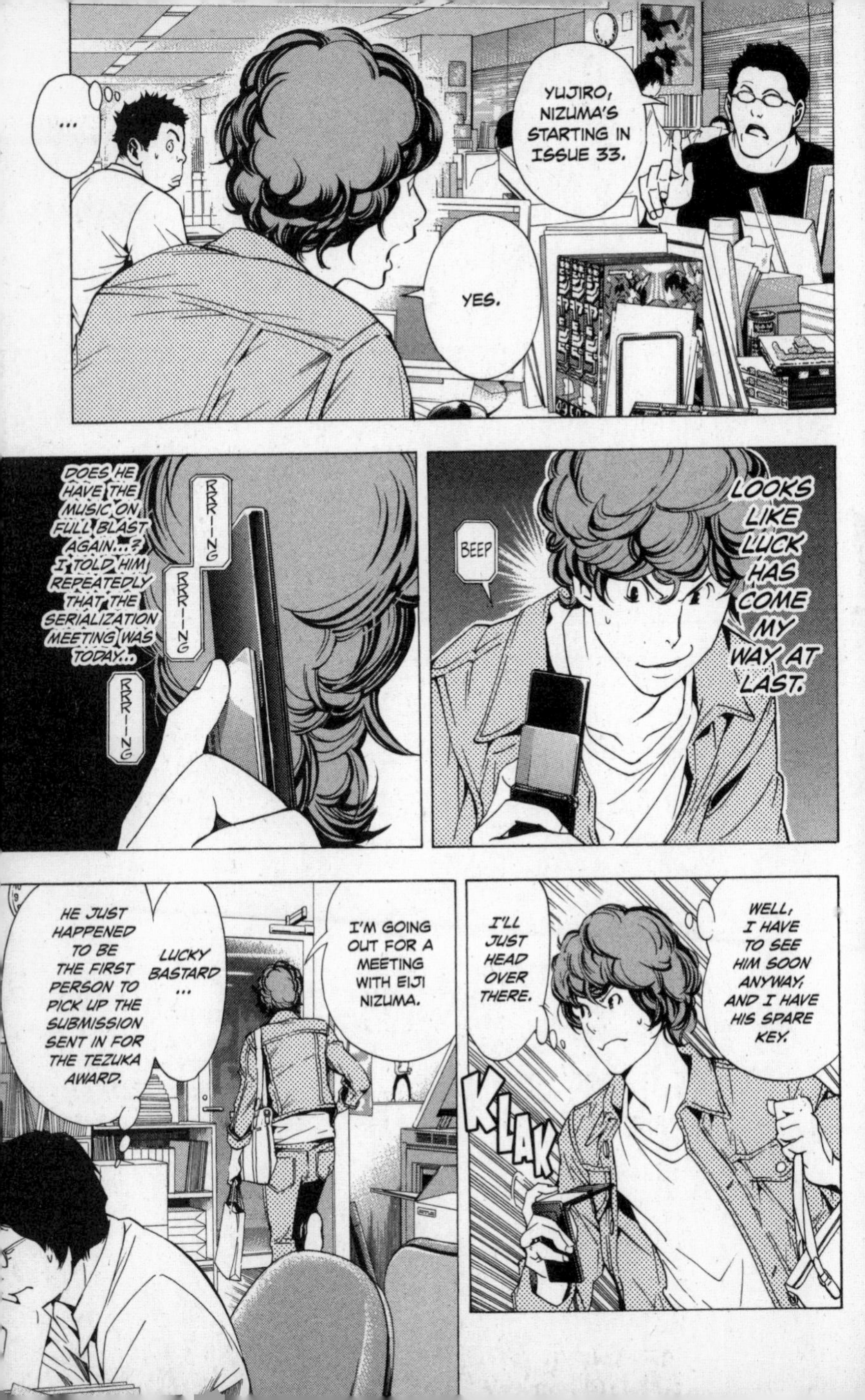
YUJIRO, NIZUMA'S STARTING IN ISSUE 33.
YES.
...
LOOKS LIKE LUCK HAS COME MY WAY AT LAST.
BEEP
RRRING
RRRING
DOES HE HAVE THE MUSIC ON FULL BLAST AGAIN...? I TOLD HIM REPEATEDLY THAT THE SERIALIZATION MEETING WAS TODAY...
RRRING
WELL, I HAVE TO SEE HIM SOON ANYWAY, AND I HAVE HIS SPARE KEY.
I'LL JUST HEAD OVER THERE.
KLAK
I'M GOING OUT FOR A MEETING WITH EIJI NIZUMA.
LUCKY BASTARD ...
HE JUST HAPPENED TO BE THE FIRST PERSON TO PICK UP THE SUBMISSION SENT IN FOR THE TEZUKA AWARD.

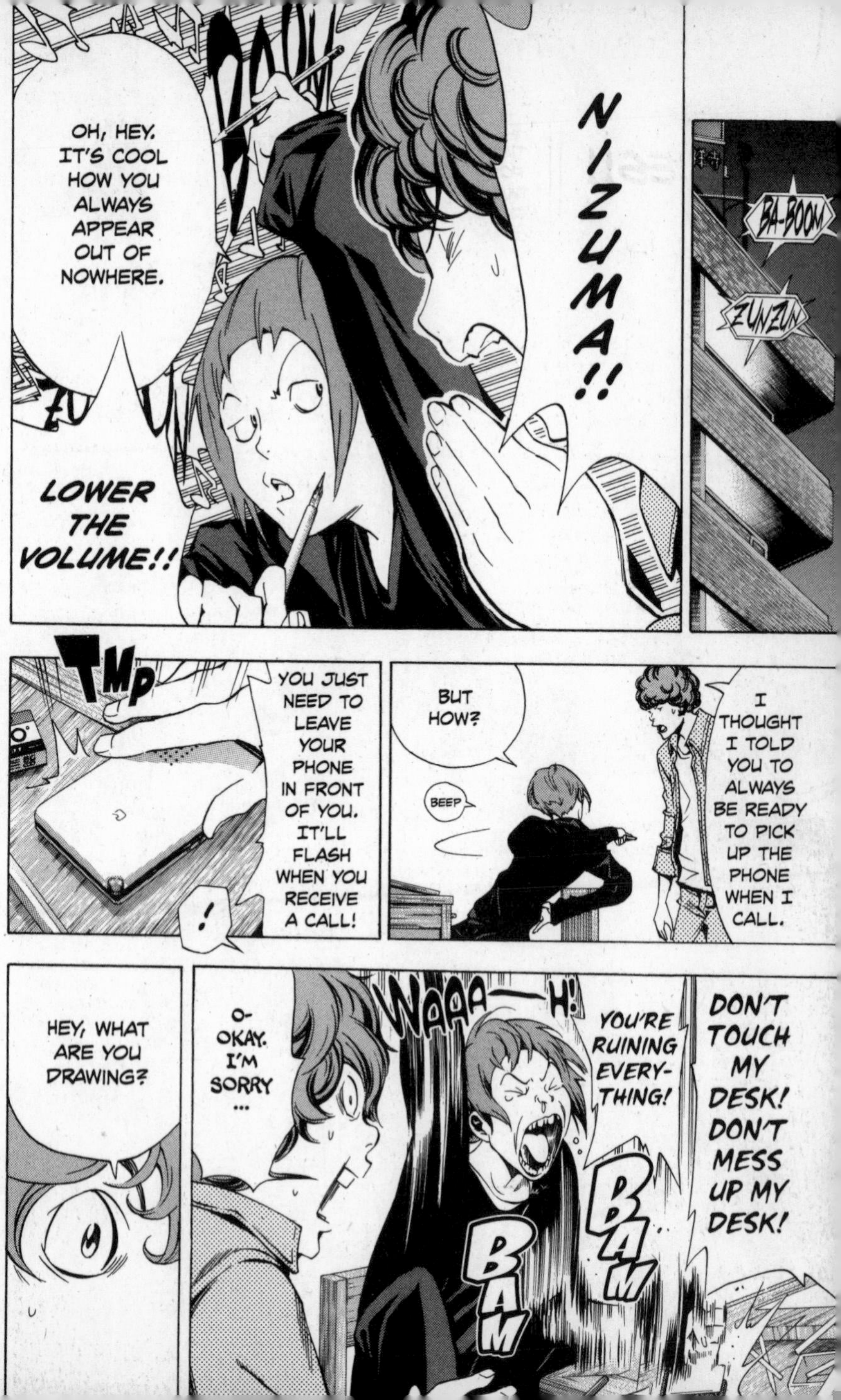
BA-BOOM
ZUNZUN
NIZUMA!!
OH, HEY. IT'S COOL HOW YOU ALWAYS APPEAR OUT OF NOWHERE.
LOWER THE VOLUME!!
I THOUGHT I TOLD YOU TO ALWAYS BE READY TO PICK UP THE PHONE WHEN I CALL.
BUT HOW?
BEEP
TMP
YOU JUST NEED TO LEAVE YOUR PHONE IN FRONT OF YOU. IT'LL FLASH WHEN YOU RECEIVE A CALL!
!
DON'T TOUCH MY DESK! DON'T MESS UP MY DESK!
YOU'RE RUINING EVERY-THING!
WAAA—H!
BAM
BAM
O-OKAY. I'M SORRY...
HEY, WHAT ARE YOU DRAWING?

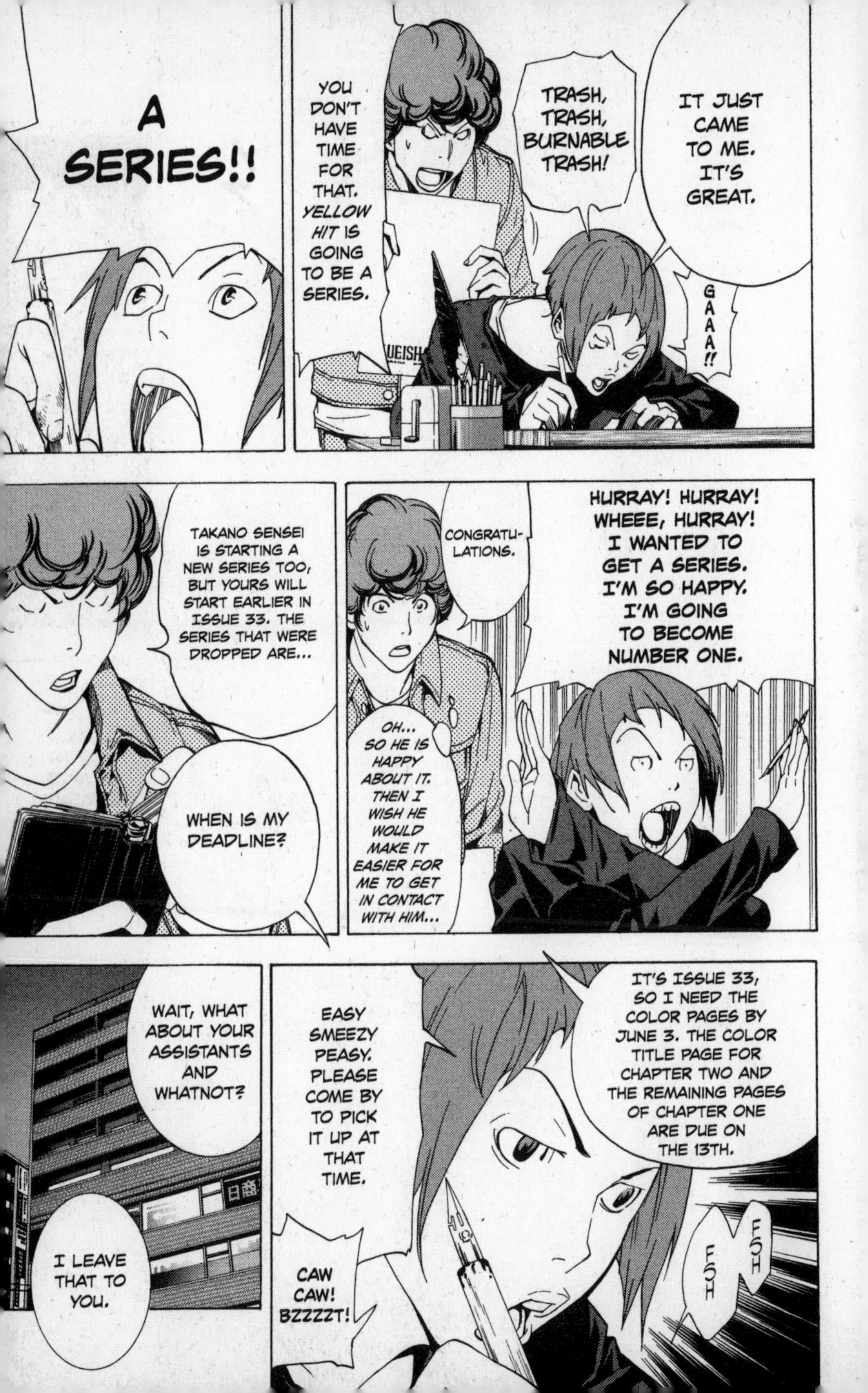
IT JUST CAME TO ME. IT'S GREAT.
TRASH, TRASH, BURNABLE TRASH!
YOU DON'T HAVE TIME FOR THAT. *YELLOW HIT* IS GOING TO BE A SERIES.
GAAAA!!
A SERIES!!
HURRAY! HURRAY! WHEEE, HURRAY! I WANTED TO GET A SERIES. I'M SO HAPPY. I'M GOING TO BECOME NUMBER ONE.
CONGRATULATIONS.
OH... SO HE IS HAPPY ABOUT IT. THEN I WISH HE WOULD MAKE IT EASIER FOR ME TO GET IN CONTACT WITH HIM...
TAKANO SENSEI IS STARTING A NEW SERIES TOO, BUT YOURS WILL START EARLIER IN ISSUE 33. THE SERIES THAT WERE DROPPED ARE...
WHEN IS MY DEADLINE?
IT'S ISSUE 33, SO I NEED THE COLOR PAGES BY JUNE 3. THE COLOR TITLE PAGE FOR CHAPTER TWO AND THE REMAINING PAGES OF CHAPTER ONE ARE DUE ON THE 13TH.
EASY SMEEZY PEASY. PLEASE COME BY TO PICK IT UP AT THAT TIME.
FSH
FSH
CAW CAW! BZZZZT!
WAIT, WHAT ABOUT YOUR ASSISTANTS AND WHATNOT?
I LEAVE THAT TO YOU.

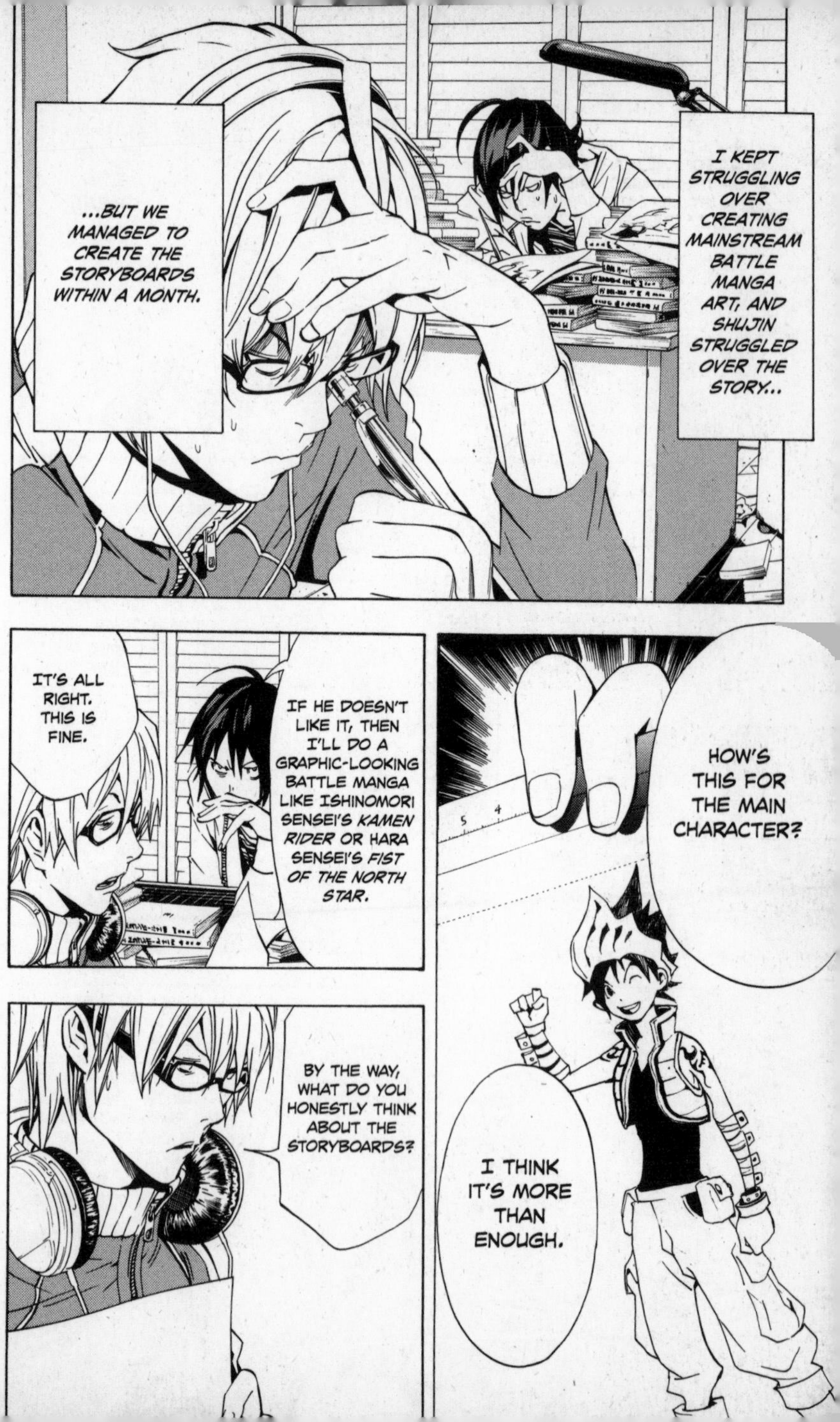
I KEPT STRUGGLING OVER CREATING MAINSTREAM BATTLE MANGA ART, AND SHUJIN STRUGGLED OVER THE STORY...
...BUT WE MANAGED TO CREATE THE STORYBOARDS WITHIN A MONTH.
HOW'S THIS FOR THE MAIN CHARACTER?
I THINK IT'S MORE THAN ENOUGH.
IF HE DOESN'T LIKE IT, THEN I'LL DO A GRAPHIC-LOOKING BATTLE MANGA LIKE ISHINOMORI SENSEI'S *KAMEN RIDER* OR HARA SENSEI'S *FIST OF THE NORTH STAR*.
IT'S ALL RIGHT. THIS IS FINE.
BY THE WAY, WHAT DO YOU HONESTLY THINK ABOUT THE STORYBOARDS?

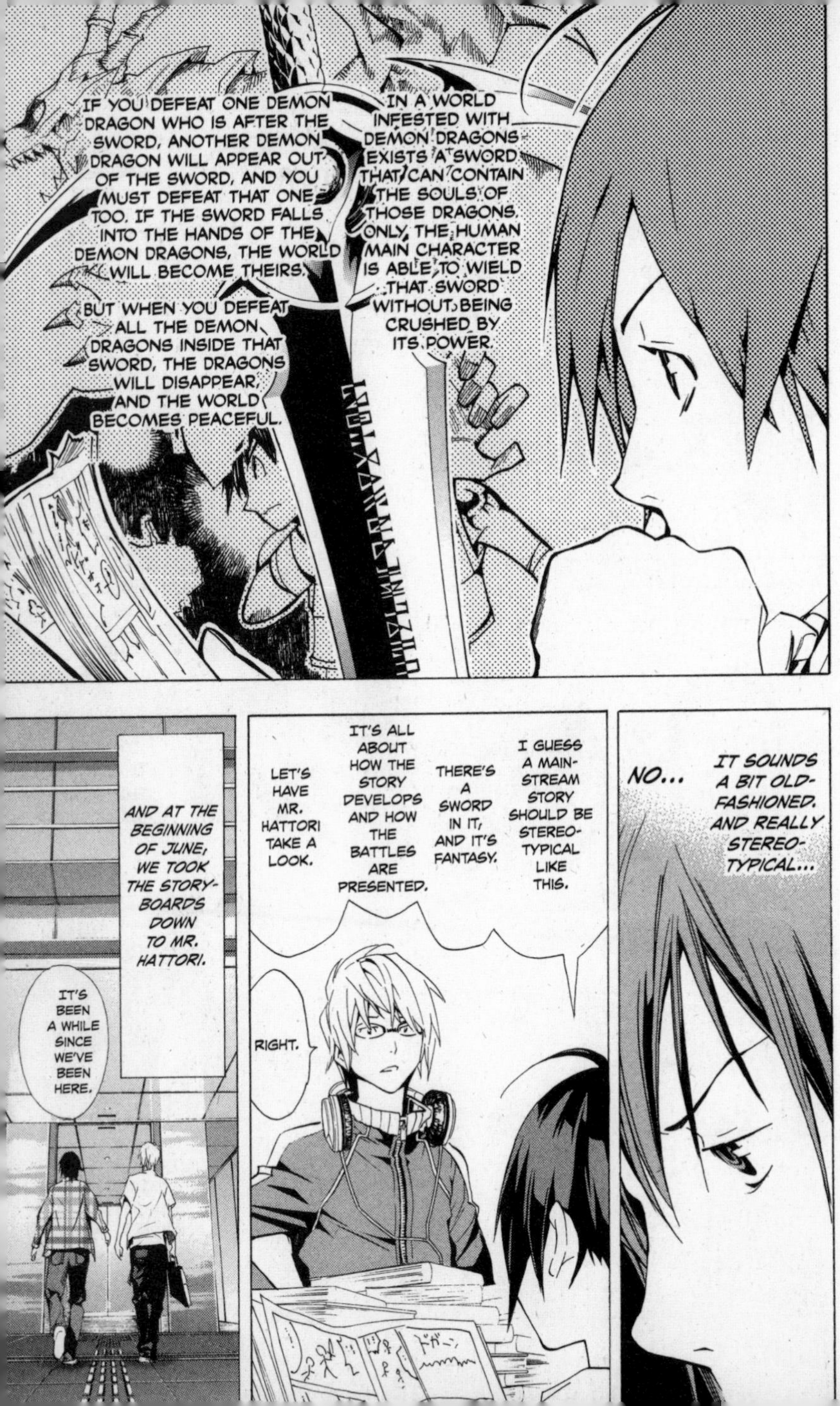
IN A WORLD INFESTED WITH DEMON DRAGONS EXISTS A SWORD THAT CAN CONTAIN THE SOULS OF THOSE DRAGONS. ONLY THE HUMAN MAIN CHARACTER IS ABLE TO WIELD THAT SWORD WITHOUT BEING CRUSHED BY ITS POWER.
IF YOU DEFEAT ONE DEMON DRAGON WHO IS AFTER THE SWORD, ANOTHER DEMON DRAGON WILL APPEAR OUT OF THE SWORD, AND YOU MUST DEFEAT THAT ONE TOO. IF THE SWORD FALLS INTO THE HANDS OF THE DEMON DRAGONS, THE WORLD WILL BECOME THEIRS.
BUT WHEN YOU DEFEAT ALL THE DEMON DRAGONS INSIDE THAT SWORD, THE DRAGONS WILL DISAPPEAR, AND THE WORLD BECOMES PEACEFUL.
IT SOUNDS A BIT OLD-FASHIONED. AND REALLY STEREO-TYPICAL...
NO...
I GUESS A MAIN-STREAM STORY SHOULD BE STEREO-TYPICAL LIKE THIS.
THERE'S A SWORD IN IT, AND IT'S FANTASY.
IT'S ALL ABOUT HOW THE STORY DEVELOPS AND HOW THE BATTLES ARE PRESENTED.
LET'S HAVE MR. HATTORI TAKE A LOOK.
RIGHT.
AND AT THE BEGINNING OF JUNE, WE TOOK THE STORY-BOARDS DOWN TO MR. HATTORI.
IT'S BEEN A WHILE SINCE WE'VE BEEN HERE.

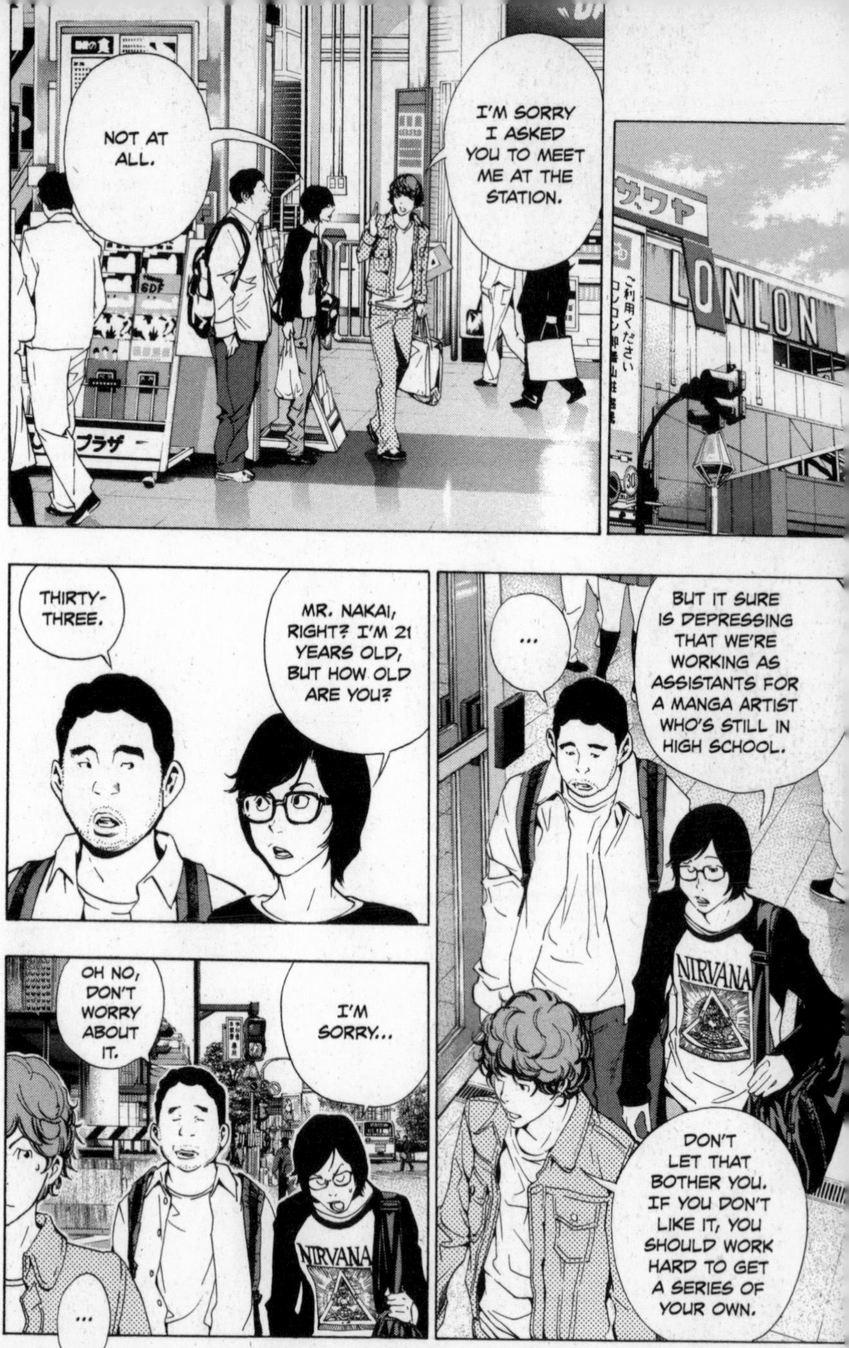
LONLON
I'M SORRY I ASKED YOU TO MEET ME AT THE STATION.
NOT AT ALL.
BUT IT SURE IS DEPRESSING THAT WE'RE WORKING AS ASSISTANTS FOR A MANGA ARTIST WHO'S STILL IN HIGH SCHOOL.
...
DON'T LET THAT BOTHER YOU. IF YOU DON'T LIKE IT, YOU SHOULD WORK HARD TO GET A SERIES OF YOUR OWN.
MR. NAKAI, RIGHT? I'M 21 YEARS OLD, BUT HOW OLD ARE YOU?
THIRTY-THREE.
I'M SORRY...
OH NO, DON'T WORRY ABOUT IT.
...

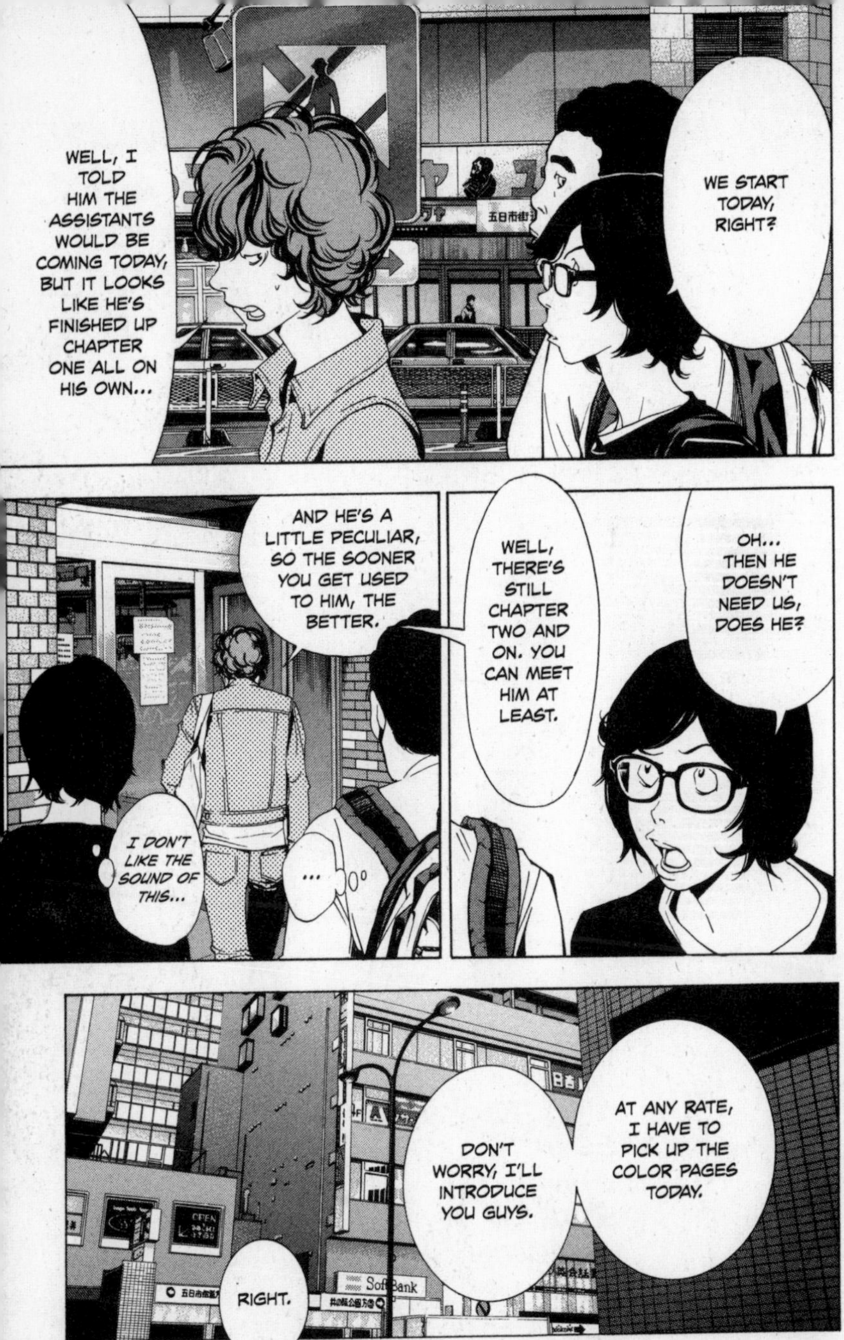
WE START TODAY, RIGHT?
WELL, I TOLD HIM THE ASSISTANTS WOULD BE COMING TODAY, BUT IT LOOKS LIKE HE'S FINISHED UP CHAPTER ONE ALL ON HIS OWN...
OH... THEN HE DOESN'T NEED US, DOES HE?
WELL, THERE'S STILL CHAPTER TWO AND ON. YOU CAN MEET HIM AT LEAST.
AND HE'S A LITTLE PECULIAR, SO THE SOONER YOU GET USED TO HIM, THE BETTER.
...
I DON'T LIKE THE SOUND OF THIS...
AT ANY RATE, I HAVE TO PICK UP THE COLOR PAGES TODAY.
DON'T WORRY, I'LL INTRODUCE YOU GUYS.
RIGHT.

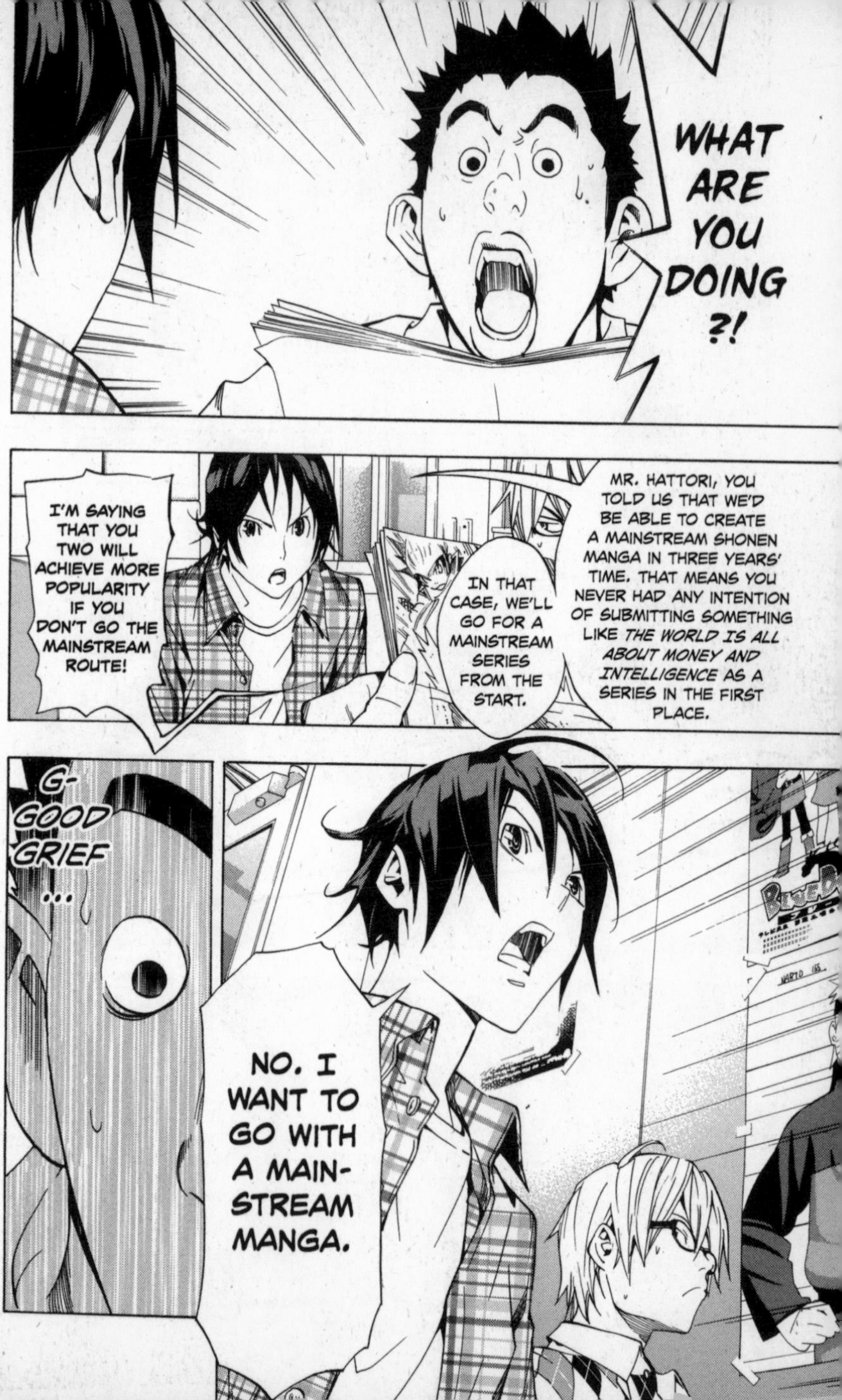
WHAT ARE YOU DOING?!
MR. HATTORI, YOU TOLD US THAT WE'D BE ABLE TO CREATE A MAINSTREAM SHONEN MANGA IN THREE YEARS' TIME. THAT MEANS YOU NEVER HAD ANY INTENTION OF SUBMITTING SOMETHING LIKE *THE WORLD IS ALL ABOUT MONEY AND INTELLIGENCE* AS A SERIES IN THE FIRST PLACE.
IN THAT CASE, WE'LL GO FOR A MAINSTREAM SERIES FROM THE START.
I'M SAYING THAT YOU TWO WILL ACHIEVE MORE POPULARITY IF YOU DON'T GO THE MAINSTREAM ROUTE!
NO. I WANT TO GO WITH A MAIN-STREAM MANGA.
G-GOOD GRIEF...

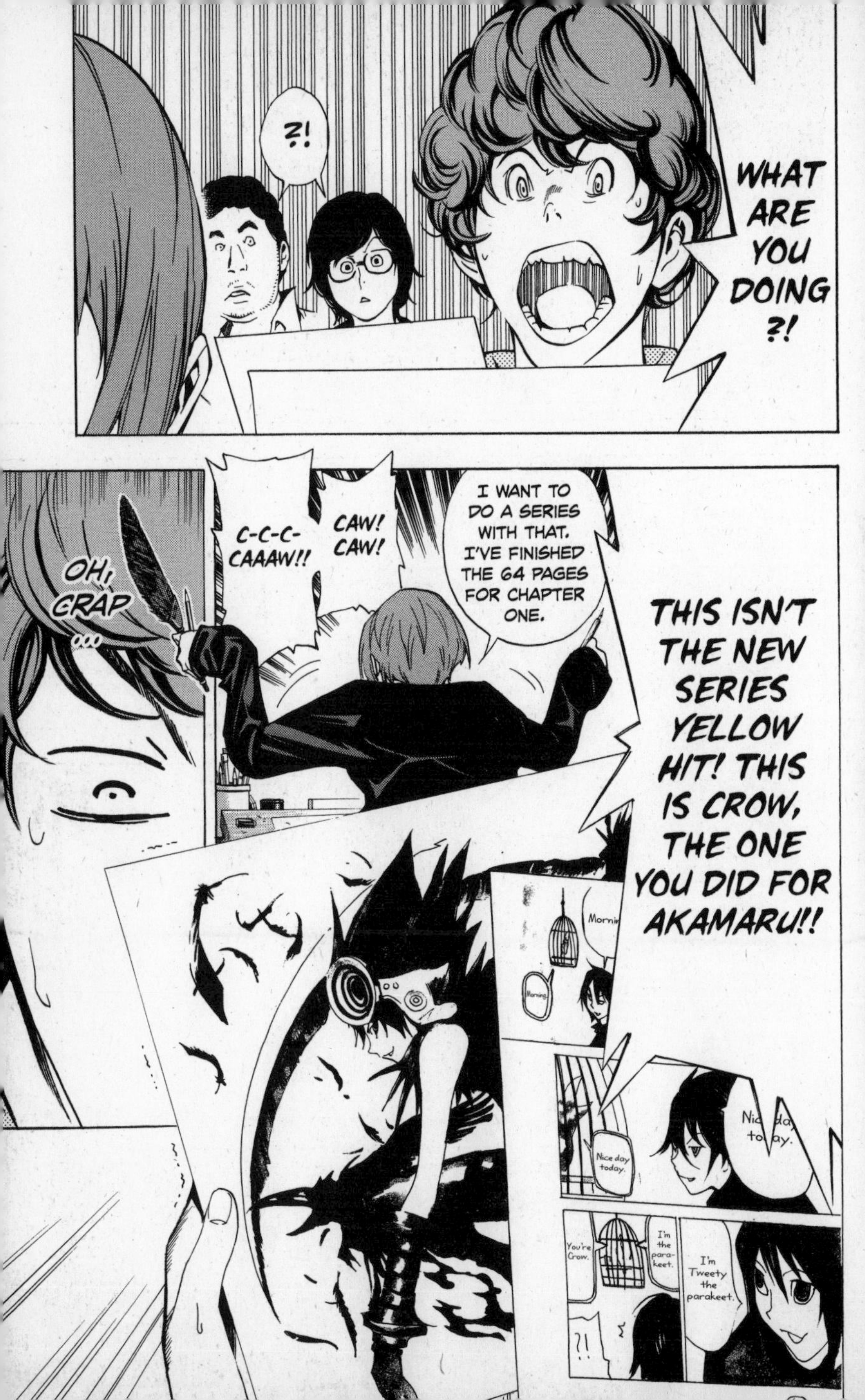
WHAT ARE YOU DOING?!
?!
THIS ISN'T THE NEW SERIES YELLOW HIT! THIS IS CROW, THE ONE YOU DID FOR AKAMARU!!
I WANT TO DO A SERIES WITH THAT. I'VE FINISHED THE 64 PAGES FOR CHAPTER ONE.
CAW! CAW!
C-C-C-CAAAW!!
OH, CRAP...
Morning.
Nice day today.
I'm Tweety the parakeet.
I'm the parakeet.
You're Crow.
?!

OHBA'S STORYBOARD

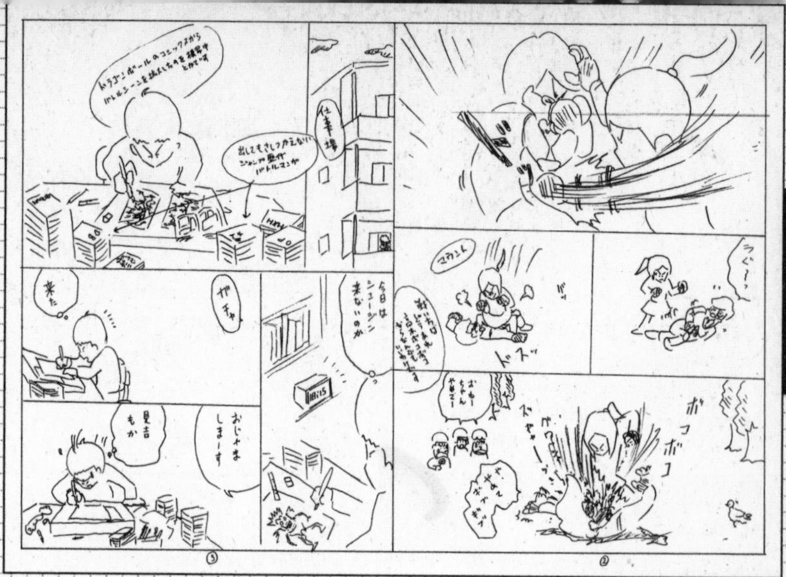
ドスッ
ボコ
ボコ
仕事場
今日は
シュージン
来ないのか
ガチャ
来た
おじゃま
しまーす
見吉
もか

OBATA'S STORYBOARD

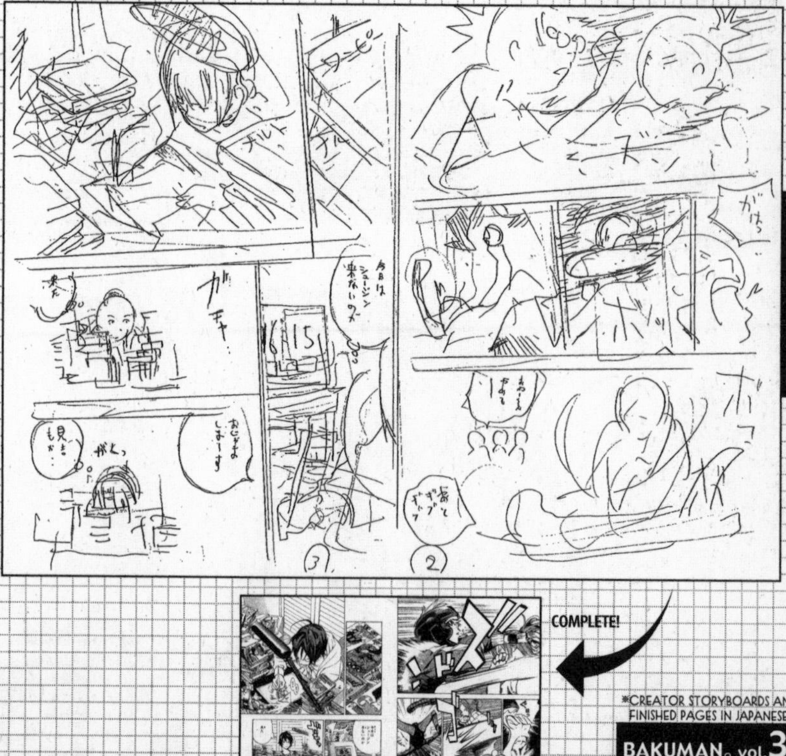
がはっ
ボコッ
今日は
シュージン
来ないのか
ガチャ…
おじゃま
しまーす
がくっ

COMPLETE!

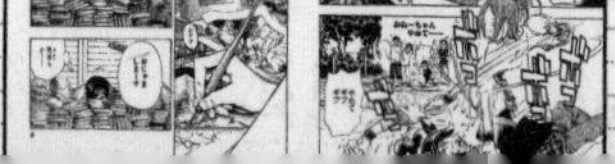

*CREATOR STORYBOARDS AND FINISHED PAGES IN JAPANESE

BAKUMAN。 vol.3

"Until the Final Draft Is Complete"

Chapter 17, pp. 8-9

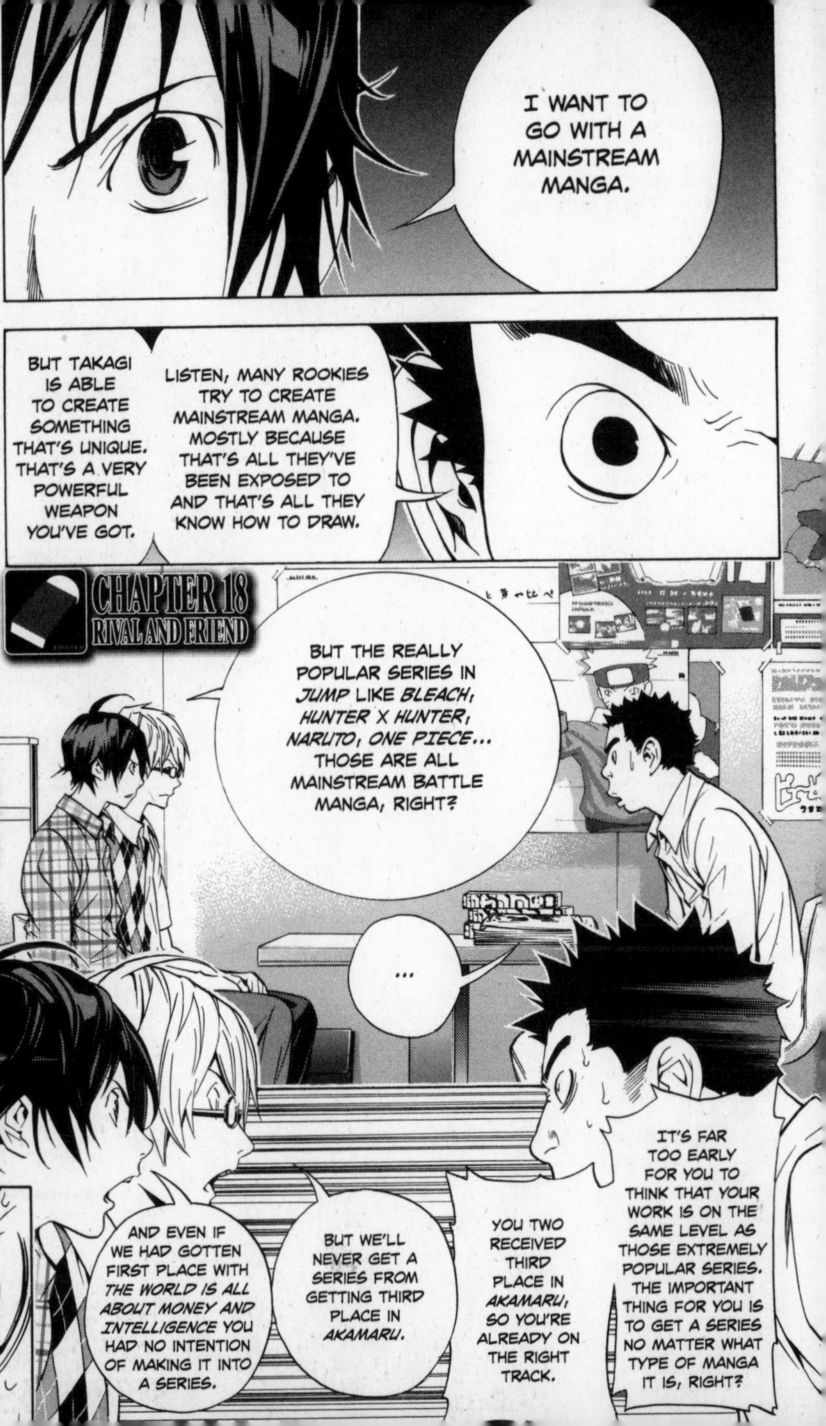
I WANT TO GO WITH A MAINSTREAM MANGA.
LISTEN, MANY ROOKIES TRY TO CREATE MAINSTREAM MANGA. MOSTLY BECAUSE THAT'S ALL THEY'VE BEEN EXPOSED TO AND THAT'S ALL THEY KNOW HOW TO DRAW.
BUT TAKAGI IS ABLE TO CREATE SOMETHING THAT'S UNIQUE. THAT'S A VERY POWERFUL WEAPON YOU'VE GOT.
CHAPTER 18
RIVAL AND FRIEND
BUT THE REALLY POPULAR SERIES IN *JUMP* LIKE *BLEACH*, *HUNTER X HUNTER*, *NARUTO*, *ONE PIECE*... THOSE ARE ALL MAINSTREAM BATTLE MANGA, RIGHT?
...
IT'S FAR TOO EARLY FOR YOU TO THINK THAT YOUR WORK IS ON THE SAME LEVEL AS THOSE EXTREMELY POPULAR SERIES. THE IMPORTANT THING FOR YOU IS TO GET A SERIES NO MATTER WHAT TYPE OF MANGA IT IS, RIGHT?
YOU TWO RECEIVED THIRD PLACE IN *AKAMARU*, SO YOU'RE ALREADY ON THE RIGHT TRACK.
BUT WE'LL NEVER GET A SERIES FROM GETTING THIRD PLACE IN *AKAMARU*.
AND EVEN IF WE HAD GOTTEN FIRST PLACE WITH *THE WORLD IS ALL ABOUT MONEY AND INTELLIGENCE* YOU HAD NO INTENTION OF MAKING IT INTO A SERIES.

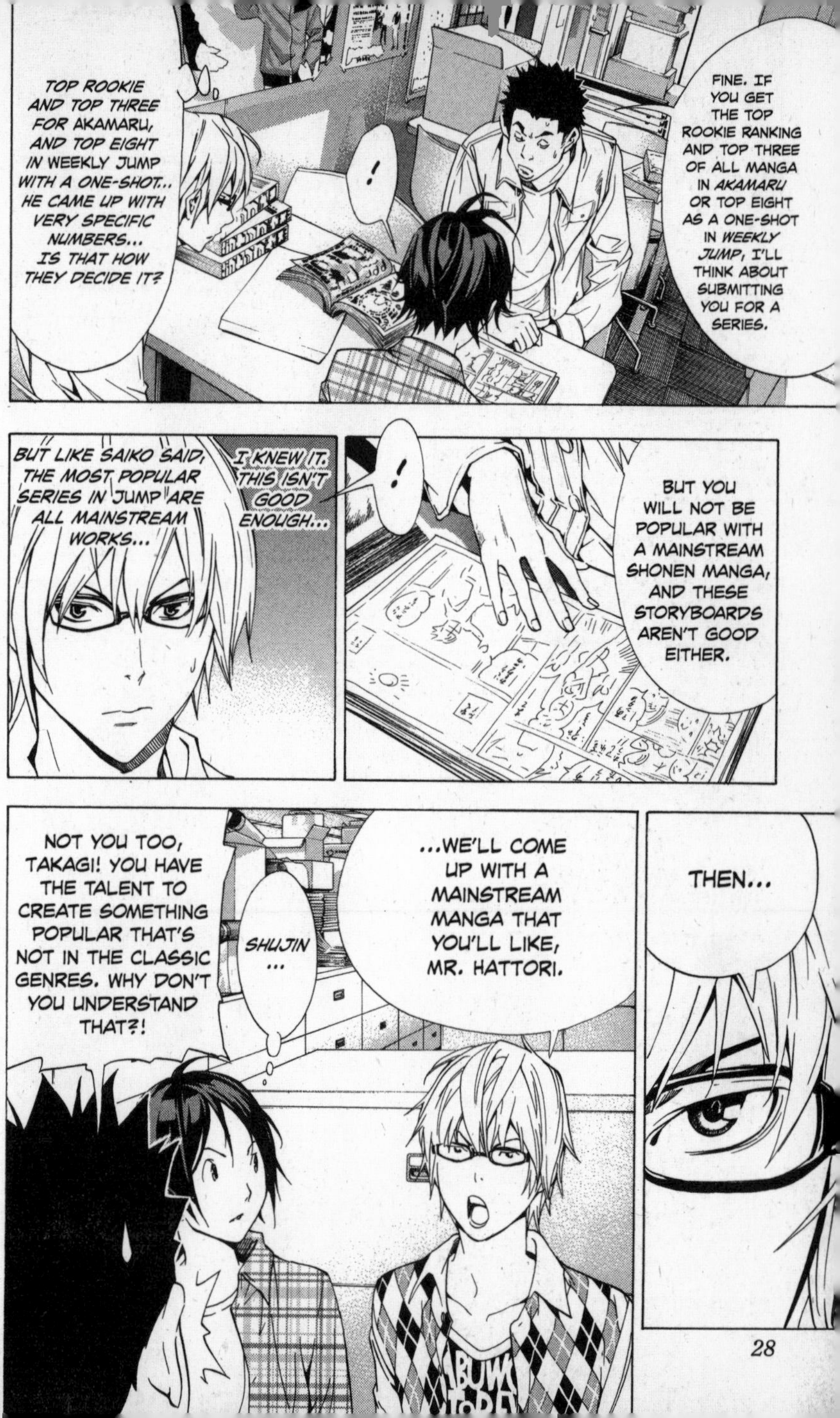
FINE. IF YOU GET THE TOP ROOKIE RANKING AND TOP THREE OF ALL MANGA IN *AKAMARU* OR TOP EIGHT AS A ONE-SHOT IN *WEEKLY JUMP*, I'LL THINK ABOUT SUBMITTING YOU FOR A SERIES.
!
TOP ROOKIE AND TOP THREE FOR AKAMARU, AND TOP EIGHT IN WEEKLY JUMP WITH A ONE-SHOT... HE CAME UP WITH VERY SPECIFIC NUMBERS... IS THAT HOW THEY DECIDE IT?
!
BUT YOU WILL NOT BE POPULAR WITH A MAINSTREAM SHONEN MANGA, AND THESE STORYBOARDS AREN'T GOOD EITHER.
I KNEW IT. THIS ISN'T GOOD ENOUGH...
BUT LIKE SAIKO SAID, THE MOST POPULAR SERIES IN JUMP ARE ALL MAINSTREAM WORKS...
THEN...
...WE'LL COME UP WITH A MAINSTREAM MANGA THAT YOU'LL LIKE, MR. HATTORI.
SHUJIN...
NOT YOU TOO, TAKAGI! YOU HAVE THE TALENT TO CREATE SOMETHING POPULAR THAT'S NOT IN THE CLASSIC GENRES. WHY DON'T YOU UNDERSTAND THAT?!

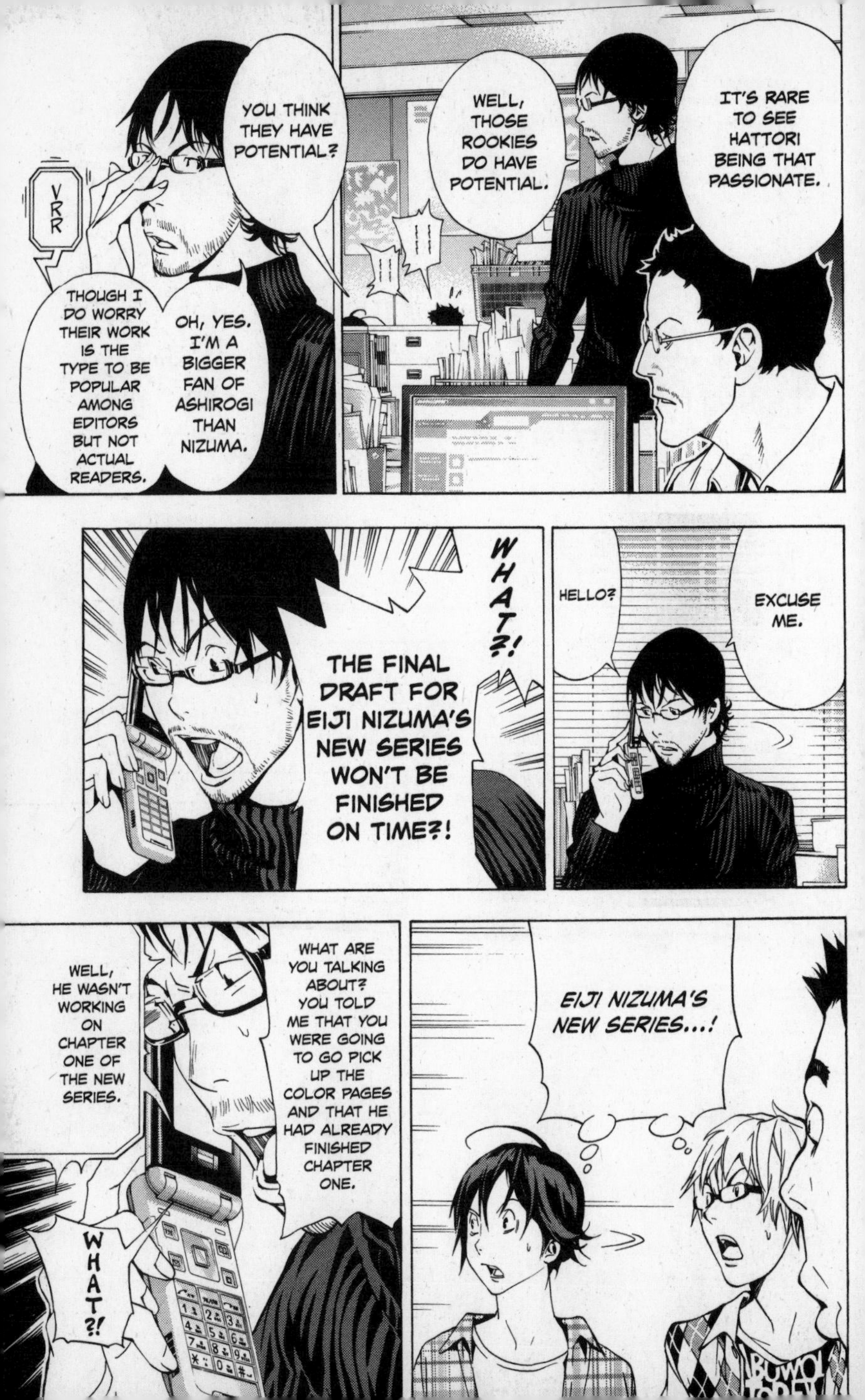
IT'S RARE TO SEE HATTORI BEING THAT PASSIONATE.
WELL, THOSE ROOKIES DO HAVE POTENTIAL.
YOU THINK THEY HAVE POTENTIAL?
VRR
OH, YES. I'M A BIGGER FAN OF ASHIROGI THAN NIZUMA.
THOUGH I DO WORRY THEIR WORK IS THE TYPE TO BE POPULAR AMONG EDITORS BUT NOT ACTUAL READERS.
EXCUSE ME.
HELLO?
WHAT?!
THE FINAL DRAFT FOR EIJI NIZUMA'S NEW SERIES WON'T BE FINISHED ON TIME?!
EIJI NIZUMA'S NEW SERIES...!
WHAT ARE YOU TALKING ABOUT? YOU TOLD ME THAT YOU WERE GOING TO GO PICK UP THE COLOR PAGES AND THAT HE HAD ALREADY FINISHED CHAPTER ONE.
WELL, HE WASN'T WORKING ON CHAPTER ONE OF THE NEW SERIES.
WHAT?!

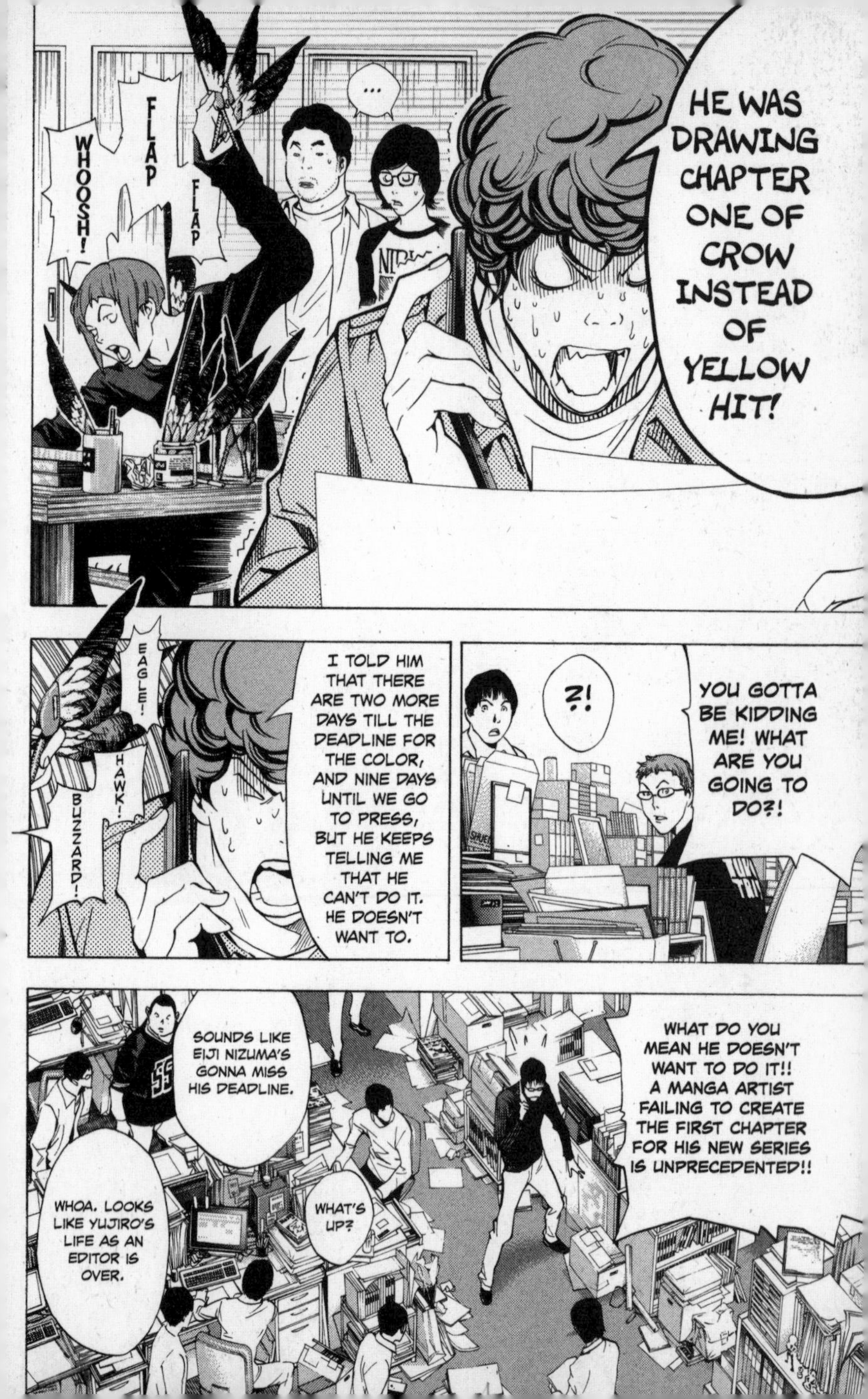
HE WAS DRAWING CHAPTER ONE OF CROW INSTEAD OF YELLOW HIT!
...
FLAP
FLAP
WHOOSH!
YOU GOTTA BE KIDDING ME! WHAT ARE YOU GOING TO DO?!
?!
I TOLD HIM THAT THERE ARE TWO MORE DAYS TILL THE DEADLINE FOR THE COLOR, AND NINE DAYS UNTIL WE GO TO PRESS, BUT HE KEEPS TELLING ME THAT HE CAN'T DO IT. HE DOESN'T WANT TO.
EAGLE!
HAWK!
BUZZARD!
WHAT DO YOU MEAN HE DOESN'T WANT TO DO IT!! A MANGA ARTIST FAILING TO CREATE THE FIRST CHAPTER FOR HIS NEW SERIES IS UNPRECEDENTED!!
SOUNDS LIKE EIJI NIZUMA'S GONNA MISS HIS DEADLINE.
WHAT'S UP?
WHOA. LOOKS LIKE YUJIRO'S LIFE AS AN EDITOR IS OVER.

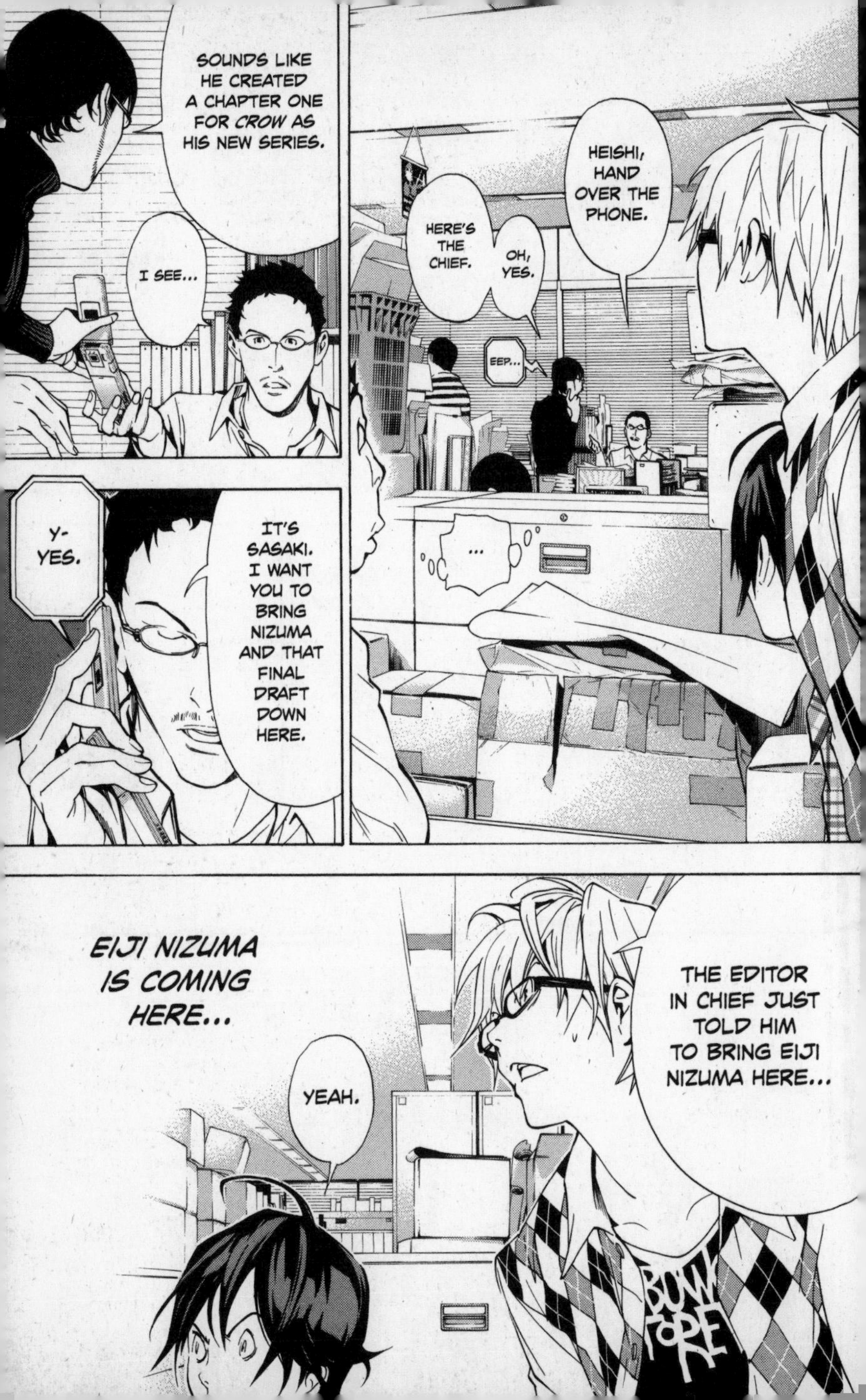
HEISHI, HAND OVER THE PHONE.
OH, YES.
HERE'S THE CHIEF.
EEP...
...
SOUNDS LIKE HE CREATED A CHAPTER ONE FOR *CROW* AS HIS NEW SERIES.
I SEE...
IT'S SASAKI. I WANT YOU TO BRING NIZUMA AND THAT FINAL DRAFT DOWN HERE.
Y-YES.
THE EDITOR IN CHIEF JUST TOLD HIM TO BRING EIJI NIZUMA HERE...
YEAH.
EIJI NIZUMA IS COMING HERE...

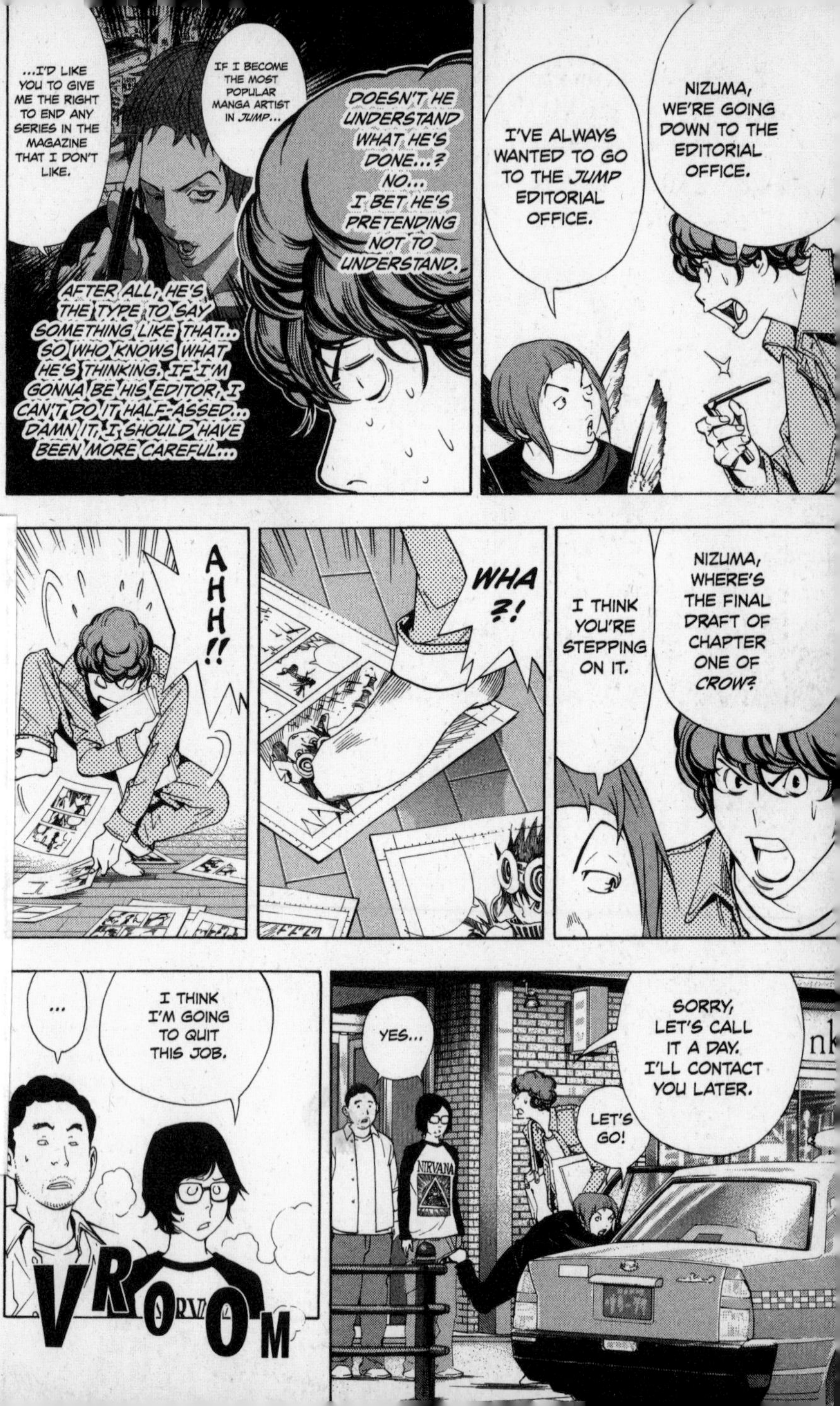
NIZUMA, WE'RE GOING DOWN TO THE EDITORIAL OFFICE.
I'VE ALWAYS WANTED TO GO TO THE *JUMP* EDITORIAL OFFICE.
IF I BECOME THE MOST POPULAR MANGA ARTIST IN *JUMP*...
...I'D LIKE YOU TO GIVE ME THE RIGHT TO END ANY SERIES IN THE MAGAZINE THAT I DON'T LIKE.
DOESN'T HE UNDERSTAND WHAT HE'S DONE...? NO... I BET HE'S PRETENDING NOT TO UNDERSTAND.
AFTER ALL, HE'S THE TYPE TO SAY SOMETHING LIKE THAT... SO WHO KNOWS WHAT HE'S THINKING. IF I'M GONNA BE HIS EDITOR, I CAN'T DO IT HALF-ASSED... DAMN IT, I SHOULD HAVE BEEN MORE CAREFUL...
NIZUMA, WHERE'S THE FINAL DRAFT OF CHAPTER ONE OF *CROW*?
I THINK YOU'RE STEPPING ON IT.
WHA?!
AHH!!
SORRY, LET'S CALL IT A DAY. I'LL CONTACT YOU LATER.
LET'S GO!
YES...
I THINK I'M GOING TO QUIT THIS JOB.
...
VROOM

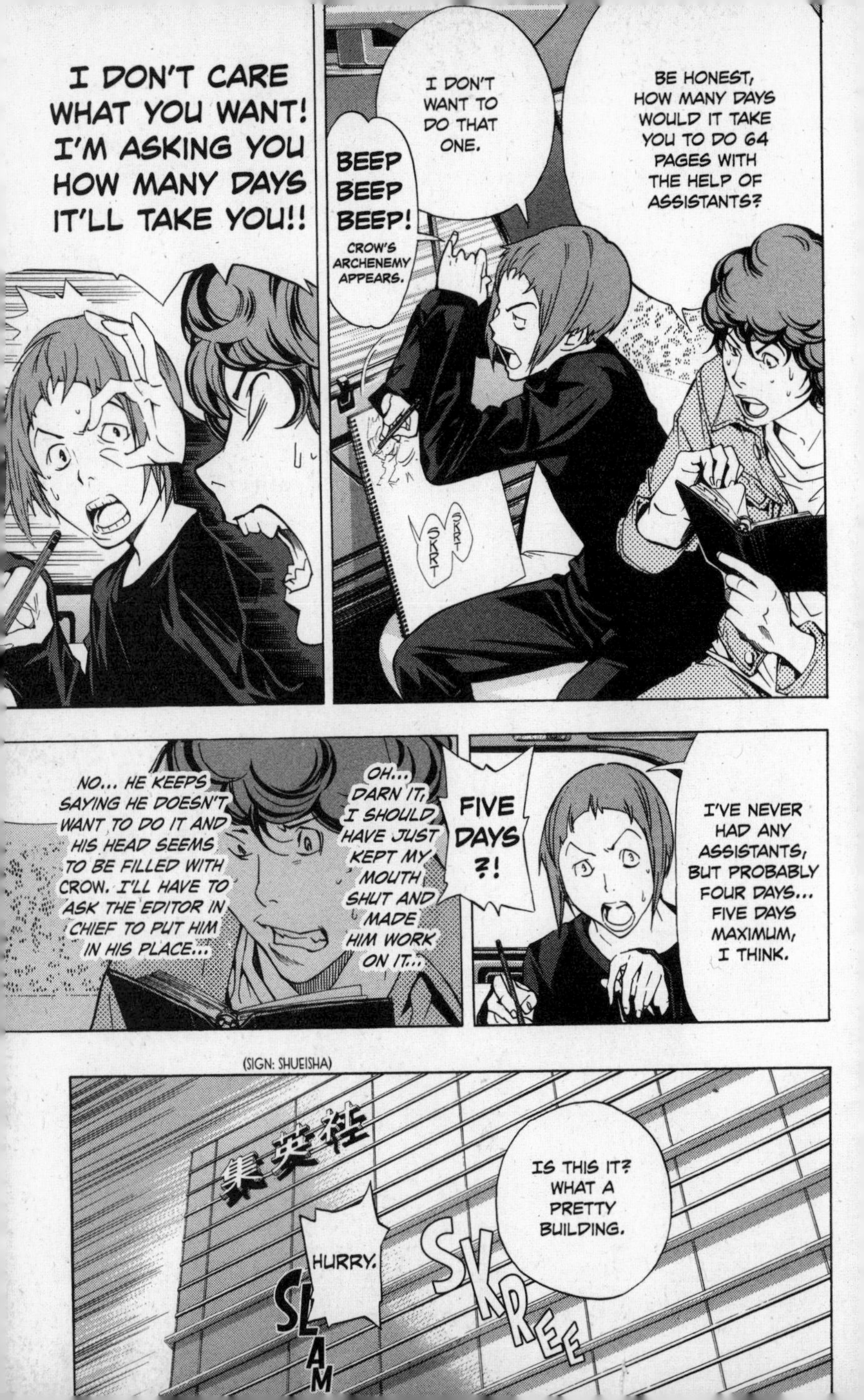
BE HONEST, HOW MANY DAYS WOULD IT TAKE YOU TO DO 64 PAGES WITH THE HELP OF ASSISTANTS?
I DON'T WANT TO DO THAT ONE.
BEEP BEEP BEEP!
CROW'S ARCHENEMY APPEARS.
SKRT
SKRT
I DON'T CARE WHAT YOU WANT! I'M ASKING YOU HOW MANY DAYS IT'LL TAKE YOU!!
I'VE NEVER HAD ANY ASSISTANTS, BUT PROBABLY FOUR DAYS... FIVE DAYS MAXIMUM, I THINK.
FIVE DAYS?!
OH... DARN IT, I SHOULD HAVE JUST KEPT MY MOUTH SHUT AND MADE HIM WORK ON IT...
NO... HE KEEPS SAYING HE DOESN'T WANT TO DO IT AND HIS HEAD SEEMS TO BE FILLED WITH CROW. I'LL HAVE TO ASK THE EDITOR IN CHIEF TO PUT HIM IN HIS PLACE...
(SIGN: SHUEISHA)
集英社
IS THIS IT? WHAT A PRETTY BUILDING.
SKREE
HURRY.
SLAM

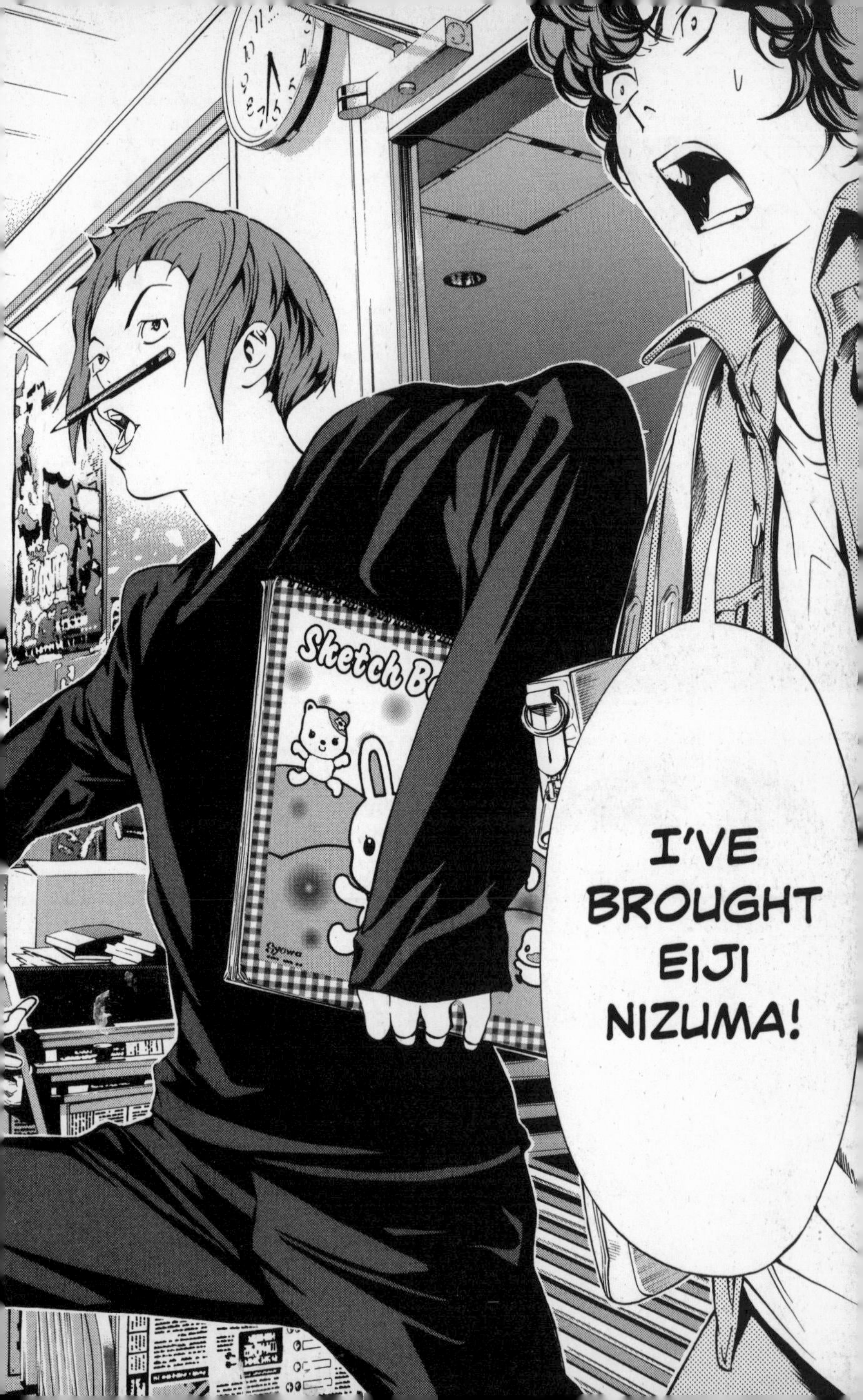
I'VE BROUGHT EIJI NIZUMA!
Sketch Bo

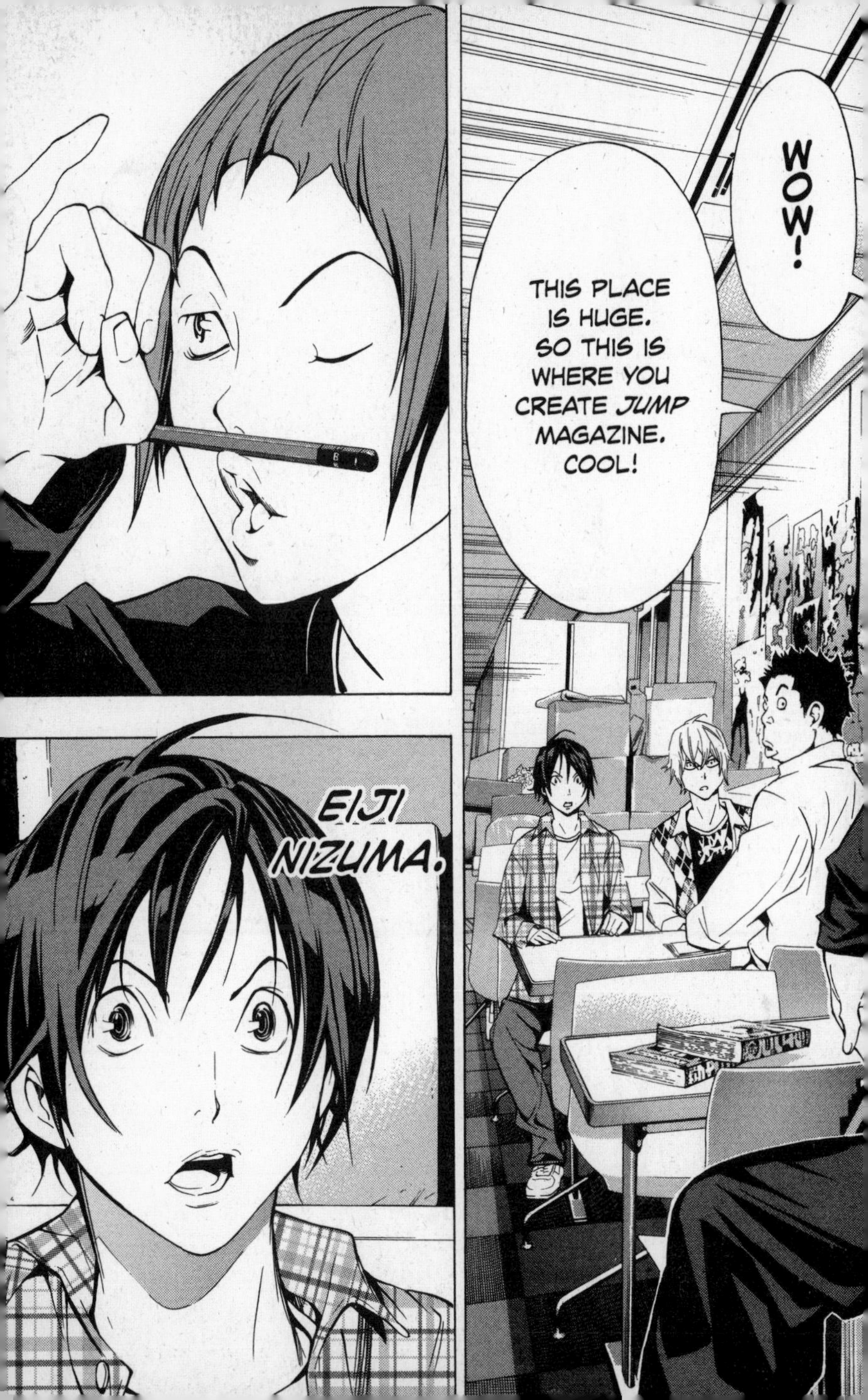
WOW!
THIS PLACE IS HUGE. SO THIS IS WHERE YOU CREATE *JUMP* MAGAZINE. COOL!
EIJI NIZUMA.

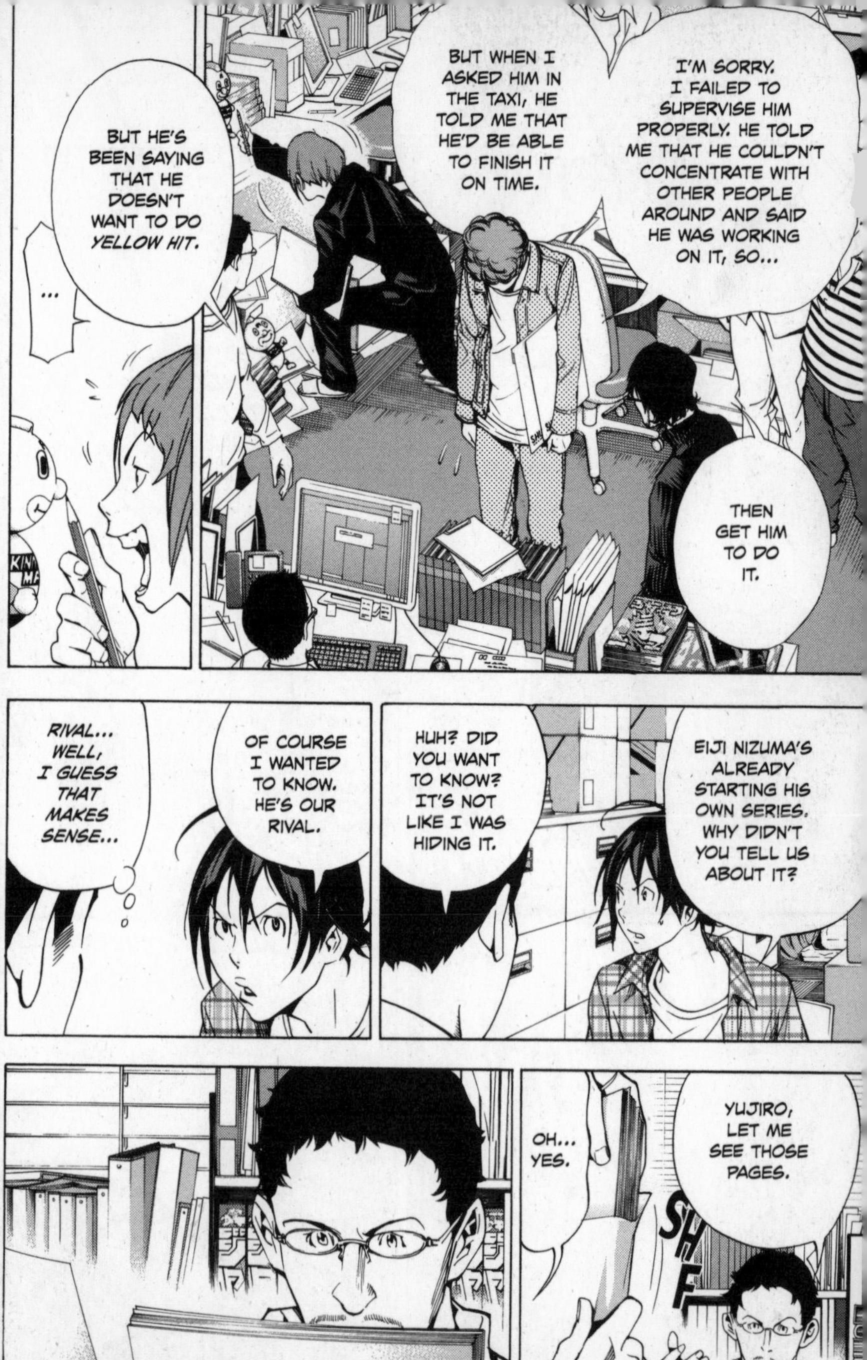
I'M SORRY. I FAILED TO SUPERVISE HIM PROPERLY. HE TOLD ME THAT HE COULDN'T CONCENTRATE WITH OTHER PEOPLE AROUND AND SAID HE WAS WORKING ON IT, SO...
BUT WHEN I ASKED HIM IN THE TAXI, HE TOLD ME THAT HE'D BE ABLE TO FINISH IT ON TIME.
THEN GET HIM TO DO IT.
BUT HE'S BEEN SAYING THAT HE DOESN'T WANT TO DO *YELLOW HIT*.
...
EIJI NIZUMA'S ALREADY STARTING HIS OWN SERIES. WHY DIDN'T YOU TELL US ABOUT IT?
HUH? DID YOU WANT TO KNOW? IT'S NOT LIKE I WAS HIDING IT.
OF COURSE I WANTED TO KNOW. HE'S OUR RIVAL.
RIVAL... WELL, I GUESS THAT MAKES SENSE...
YUJIRO, LET ME SEE THOSE PAGES.
SHF
OH... YES.

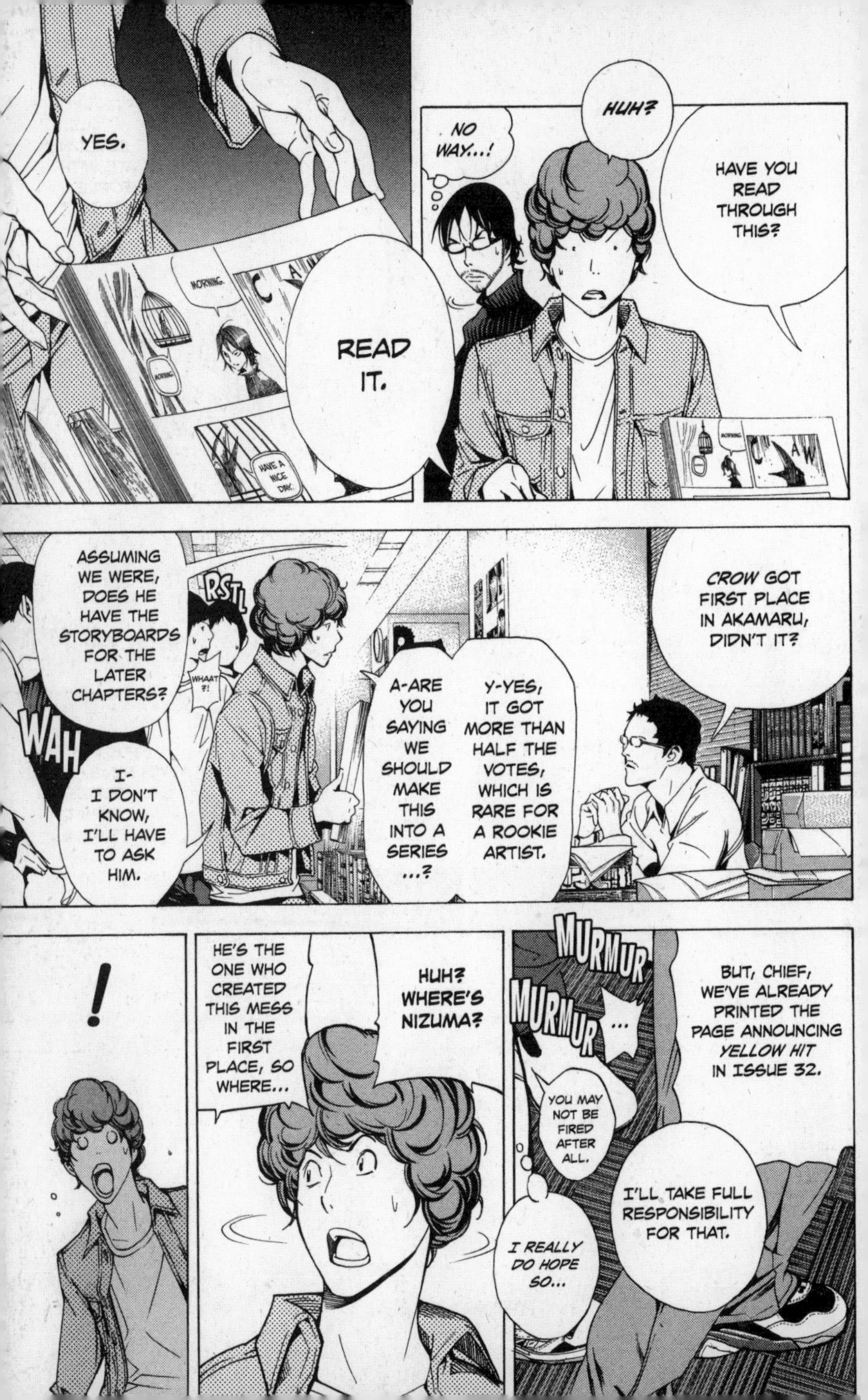
HUH?
HAVE YOU READ THROUGH THIS?
NO WAY...!
READ IT.
YES.
MORNING.
HAVE A NICE DAY.
CROW GOT FIRST PLACE IN AKAMARU, DIDN'T IT?
Y-YES, IT GOT MORE THAN HALF THE VOTES, WHICH IS RARE FOR A ROOKIE ARTIST.
A-ARE YOU SAYING WE SHOULD MAKE THIS INTO A SERIES ...?
ASSUMING WE WERE, DOES HE HAVE THE STORYBOARDS FOR THE LATER CHAPTERS?
RSTL
WHAAT?!
WAH
I- I DON'T KNOW, I'LL HAVE TO ASK HIM.
BUT, CHIEF, WE'VE ALREADY PRINTED THE PAGE ANNOUNCING *YELLOW HIT* IN ISSUE 32.
MURMUR
MURMUR
...
I'LL TAKE FULL RESPONSIBILITY FOR THAT.
YOU MAY NOT BE FIRED AFTER ALL.
I REALLY DO HOPE SO...
HUH? WHERE'S NIZUMA?
HE'S THE ONE WHO CREATED THIS MESS IN THE FIRST PLACE, SO WHERE...
!

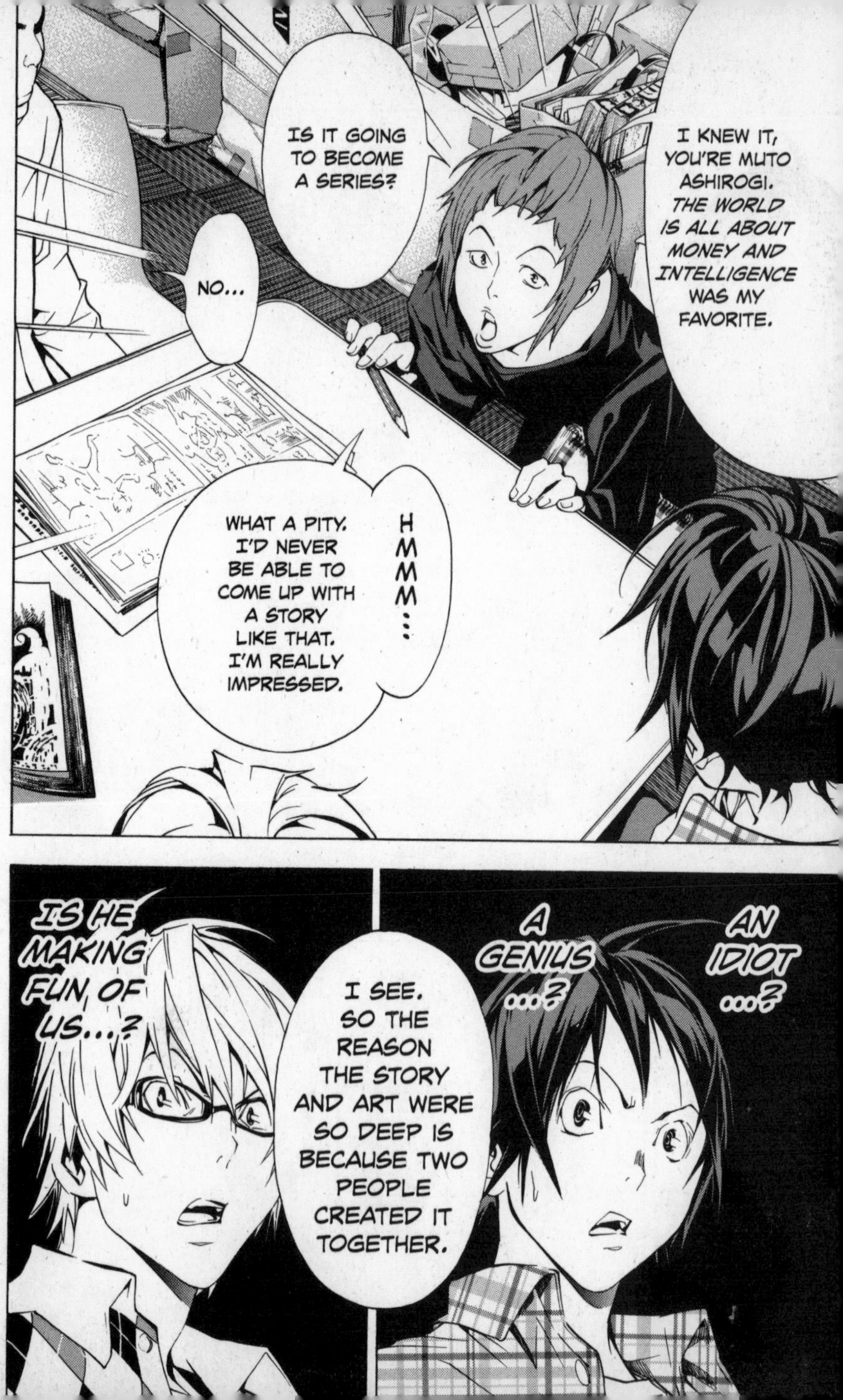
I KNEW IT, YOU'RE MUTO ASHIROGI. *THE WORLD IS ALL ABOUT MONEY AND INTELLIGENCE* WAS MY FAVORITE.
IS IT GOING TO BECOME A SERIES?
NO...
HMMM...
WHAT A PITY. I'D NEVER BE ABLE TO COME UP WITH A STORY LIKE THAT. I'M REALLY IMPRESSED.
AN IDIOT ...?
A GENIUS ...?
I SEE. SO THE REASON THE STORY AND ART WERE SO DEEP IS BECAUSE TWO PEOPLE CREATED IT TOGETHER.
IS HE MAKING FUN OF US...?

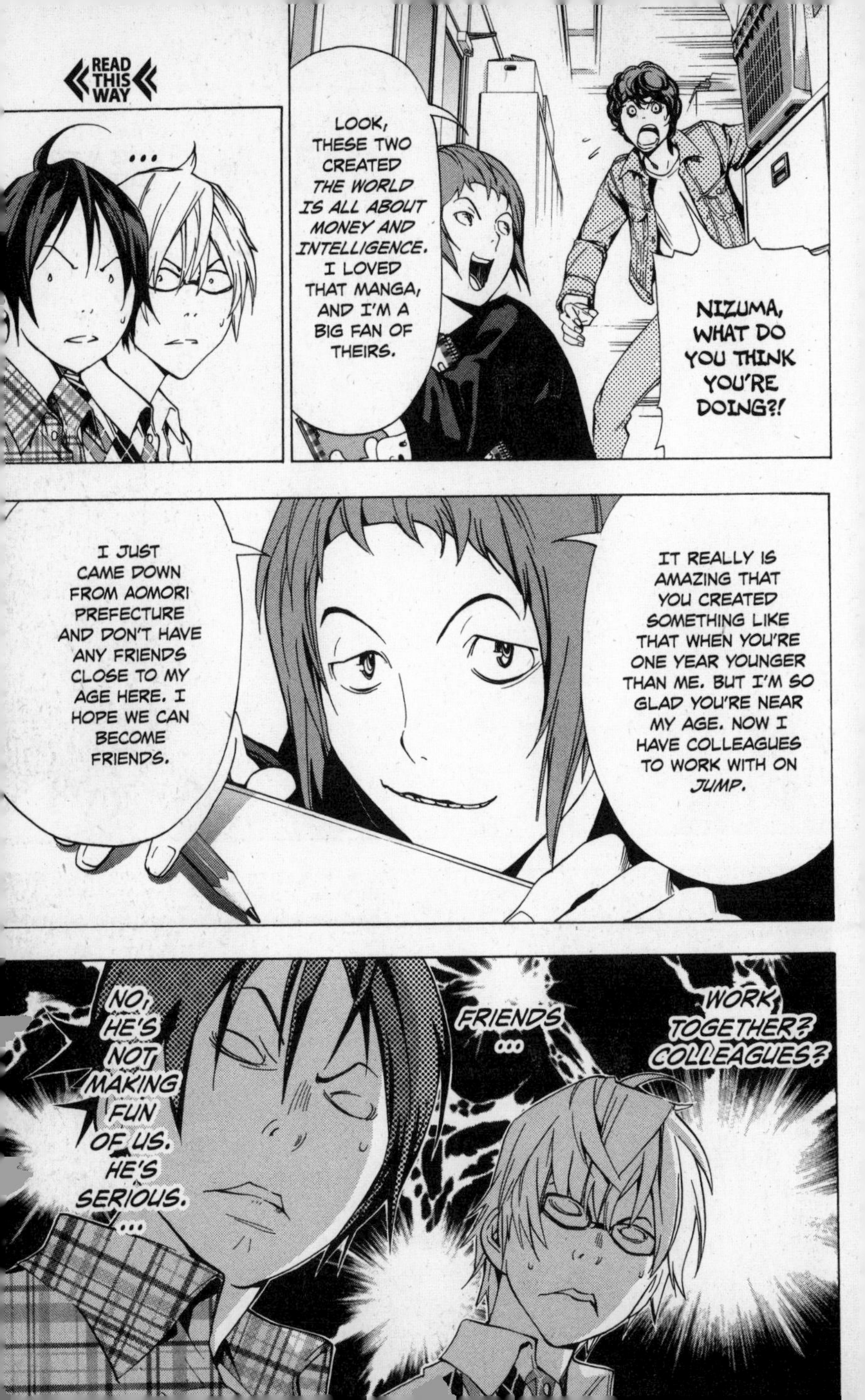
READ THIS WAY
LOOK, THESE TWO CREATED *THE WORLD IS ALL ABOUT MONEY AND INTELLIGENCE.* I LOVED THAT MANGA, AND I'M A BIG FAN OF THEIRS.
NIZUMA, WHAT DO YOU THINK YOU'RE DOING?!
...
IT REALLY IS AMAZING THAT YOU CREATED SOMETHING LIKE THAT WHEN YOU'RE ONE YEAR YOUNGER THAN ME. BUT I'M SO GLAD YOU'RE NEAR MY AGE. NOW I HAVE COLLEAGUES TO WORK WITH ON *JUMP*.
I JUST CAME DOWN FROM AOMORI PREFECTURE AND DON'T HAVE ANY FRIENDS CLOSE TO MY AGE HERE. I HOPE WE CAN BECOME FRIENDS.
WORK TOGETHER? COLLEAGUES?
FRIENDS...
NO, HE'S NOT MAKING FUN OF US. HE'S SERIOUS.
...

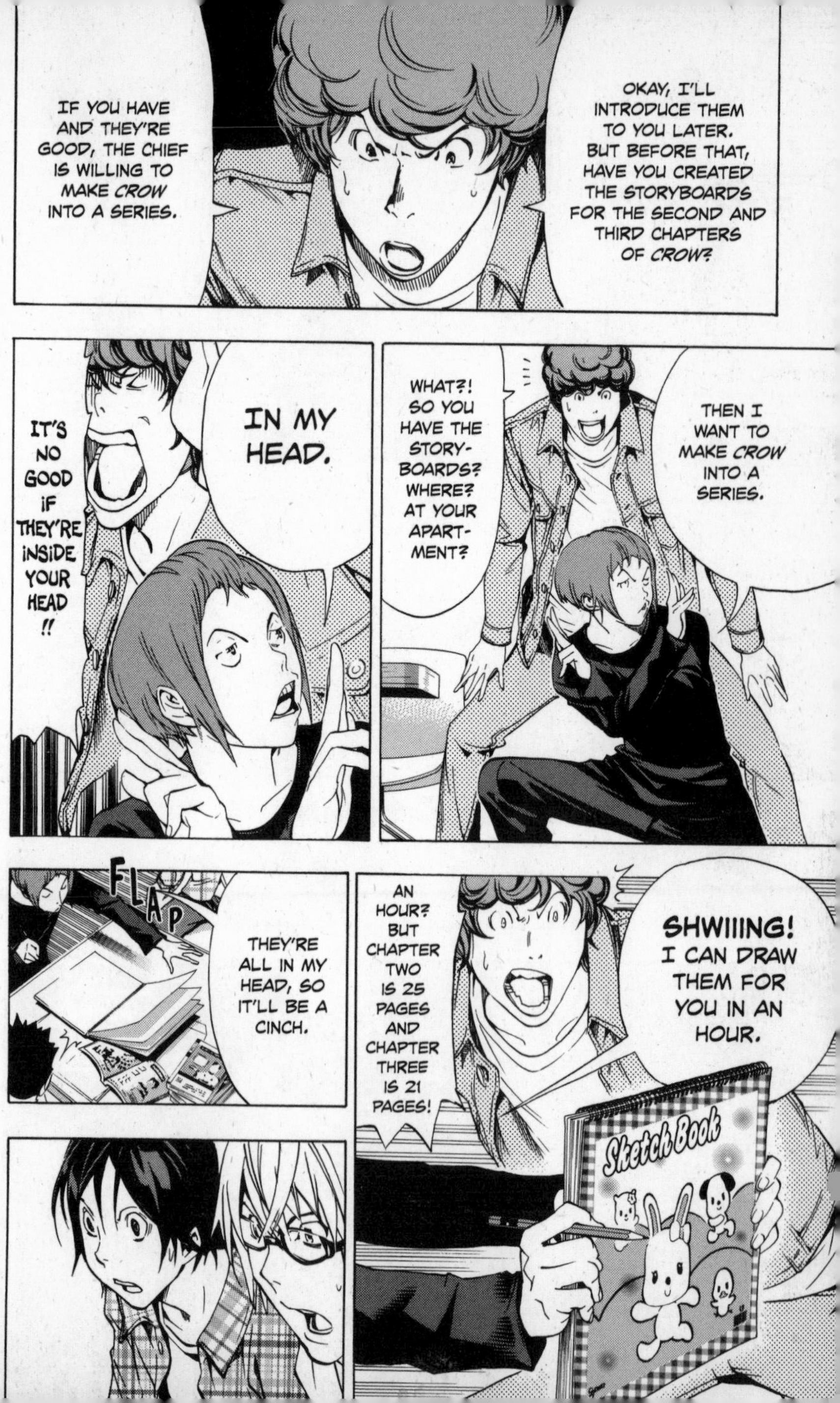
OKAY, I'LL INTRODUCE THEM TO YOU LATER. BUT BEFORE THAT, HAVE YOU CREATED THE STORYBOARDS FOR THE SECOND AND THIRD CHAPTERS OF *CROW*?
IF YOU HAVE AND THEY'RE GOOD, THE CHIEF IS WILLING TO MAKE *CROW* INTO A SERIES.
THEN I WANT TO MAKE *CROW* INTO A SERIES.
WHAT?! SO YOU HAVE THE STORY-BOARDS? WHERE? AT YOUR APART-MENT?
IN MY HEAD.
IT'S NO GOOD IF THEY'RE INSIDE YOUR HEAD!!
SHWIIING! I CAN DRAW THEM FOR YOU IN AN HOUR.
AN HOUR? BUT CHAPTER TWO IS 25 PAGES AND CHAPTER THREE IS 21 PAGES!
FLAP
THEY'RE ALL IN MY HEAD, SO IT'LL BE A CINCH.
Sketch Book

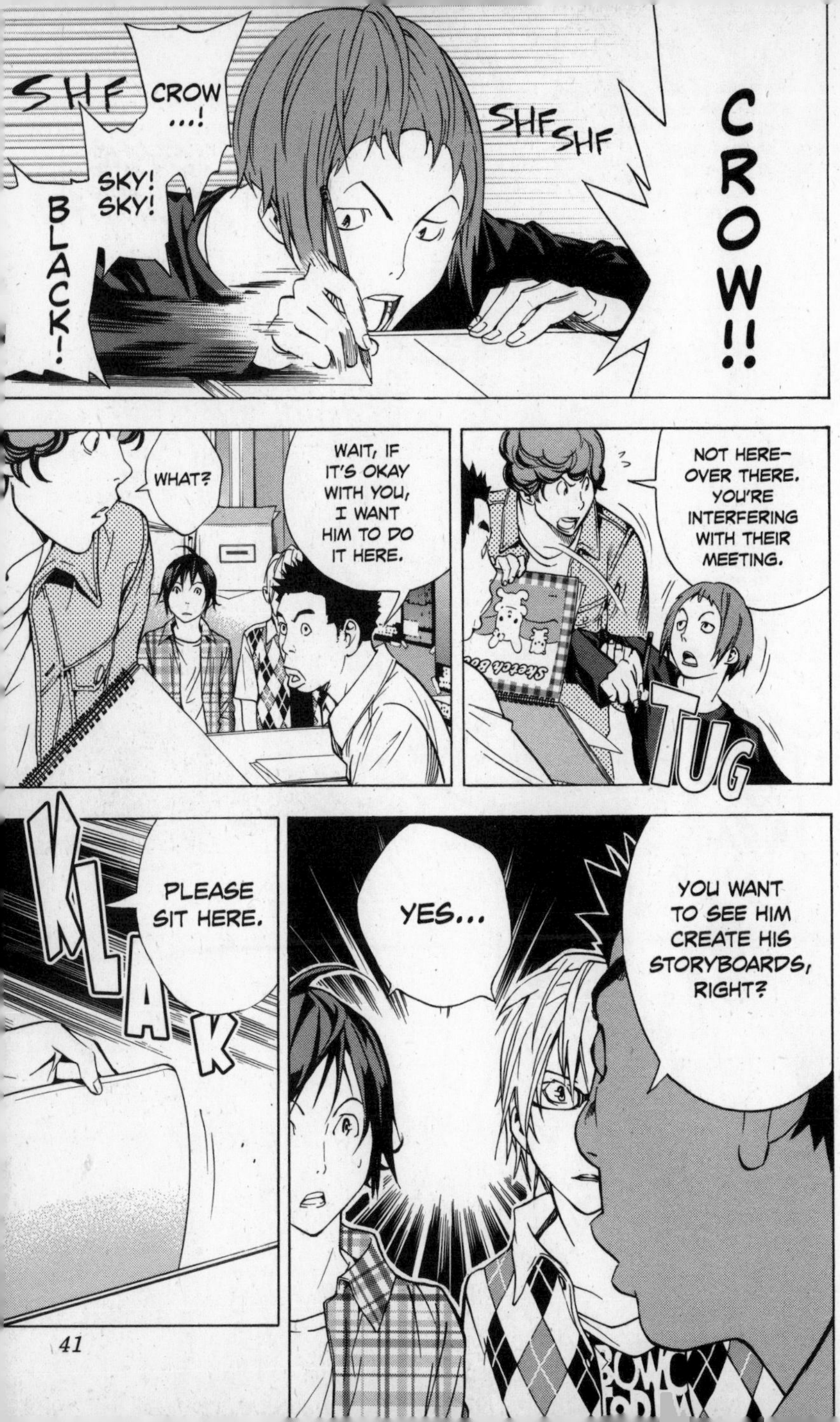

CROW!!
SHF SHF
CROW ...!
SHF
SKY! SKY!
BLACK!
NOT HERE— OVER THERE. YOU'RE INTERFERING WITH THEIR MEETING.
TUG
WAIT, IF IT'S OKAY WITH YOU, I WANT HIM TO DO IT HERE.
WHAT?
YOU WANT TO SEE HIM CREATE HIS STORYBOARDS, RIGHT?
YES...
PLEASE SIT HERE.
KLAK

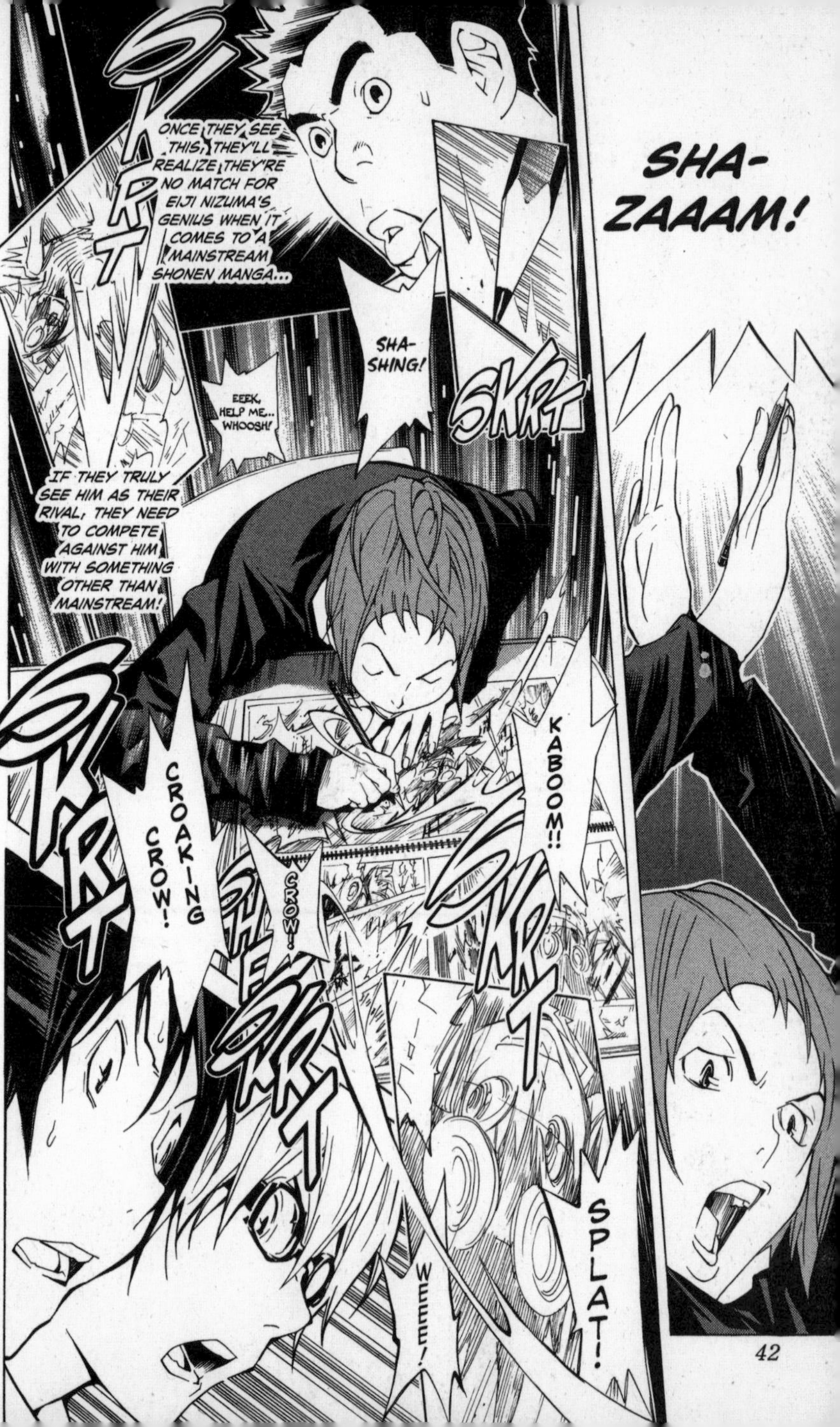
SHA-ZAAAM!
SKRT
ONCE THEY SEE THIS, THEY'LL REALIZE THEY'RE NO MATCH FOR EIJI NIZUMA'S GENIUS WHEN IT COMES TO A MAINSTREAM SHONEN MANGA...
SHA-SHING!
SKRT
EEEK, HELP ME... WHOOSH!
IF THEY TRULY SEE HIM AS THEIR RIVAL, THEY NEED TO COMPETE AGAINST HIM WITH SOMETHING OTHER THAN MAINSTREAM!
KABOOM!!
SKRT
CROAKING CROW!
SKRT
CROW!
SKRT
SPLAT!
WEEE!

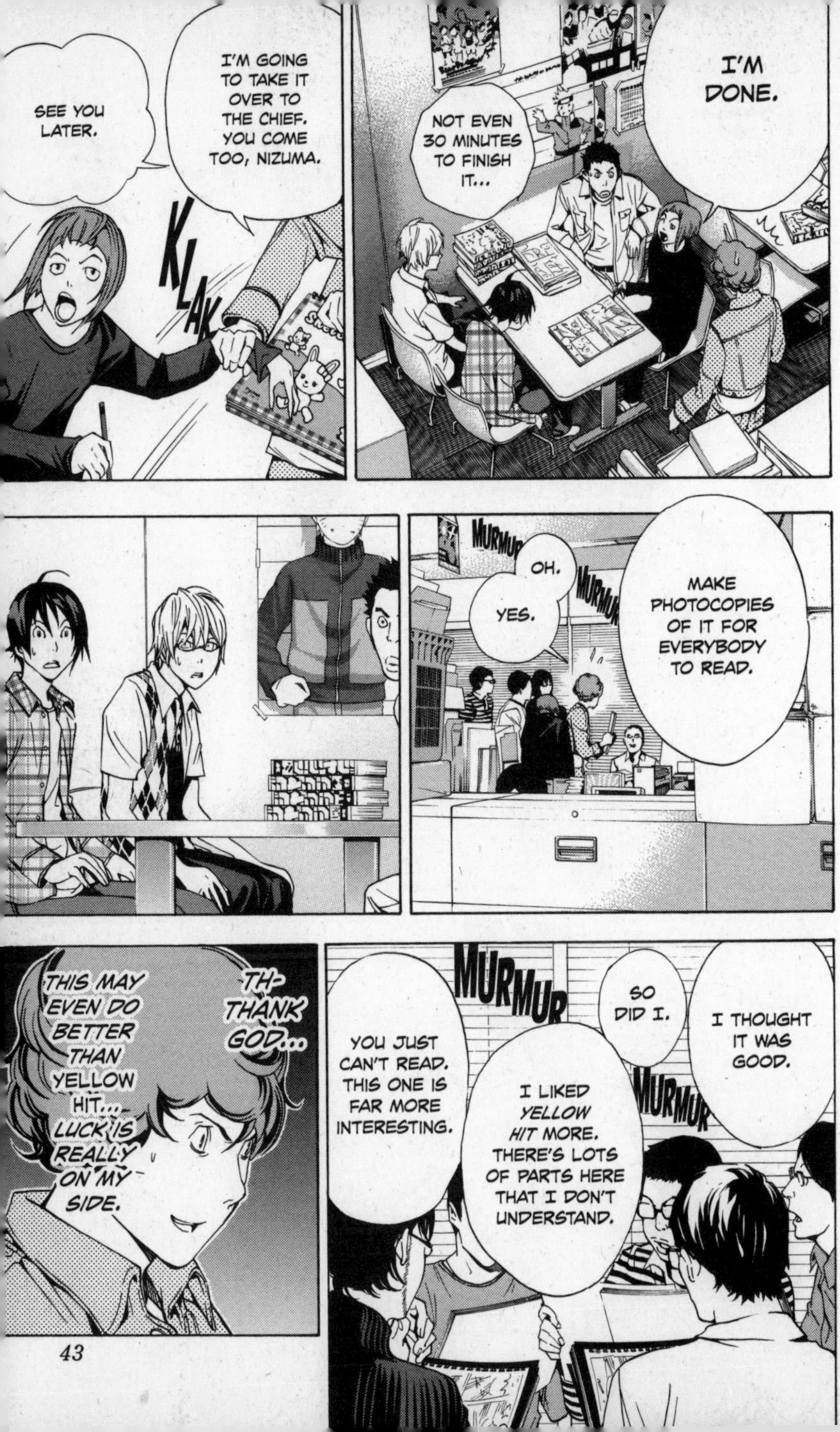

I'M DONE.
NOT EVEN 30 MINUTES TO FINISH IT...
I'M GOING TO TAKE IT OVER TO THE CHIEF. YOU COME TOO, NIZUMA.
SEE YOU LATER.
KLAK
MAKE PHOTOCOPIES OF IT FOR EVERYBODY TO READ.
MURMUR
OH.
YES.
MURMUR
I THOUGHT IT WAS GOOD.
SO DID I.
MURMUR
MURMUR
I LIKED *YELLOW HIT* MORE. THERE'S LOTS OF PARTS HERE THAT I DON'T UNDERSTAND.
YOU JUST CAN'T READ. THIS ONE IS FAR MORE INTERESTING.
TH-THANK GOD...
THIS MAY EVEN DO BETTER THAN YELLOW HIT... LUCK IS REALLY ON MY SIDE.

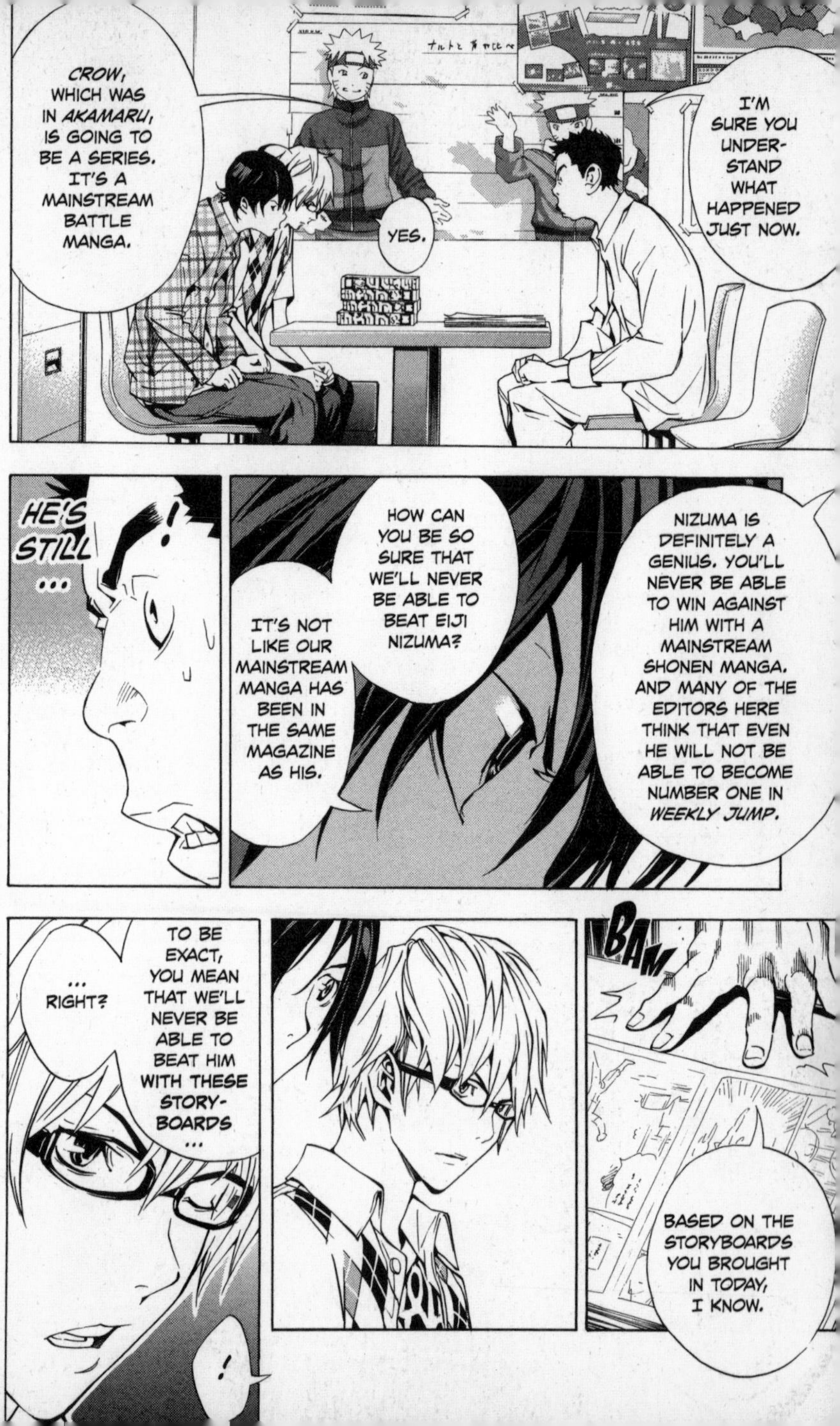
I'M SURE YOU UNDERSTAND WHAT HAPPENED JUST NOW.
CROW, WHICH WAS IN AKAMARU, IS GOING TO BE A SERIES. IT'S A MAINSTREAM BATTLE MANGA.
YES.
NIZUMA IS DEFINITELY A GENIUS. YOU'LL NEVER BE ABLE TO WIN AGAINST HIM WITH A MAINSTREAM SHONEN MANGA. AND MANY OF THE EDITORS HERE THINK THAT EVEN HE WILL NOT BE ABLE TO BECOME NUMBER ONE IN WEEKLY JUMP.
HOW CAN YOU BE SO SURE THAT WE'LL NEVER BE ABLE TO BEAT EIJI NIZUMA?
IT'S NOT LIKE OUR MAINSTREAM MANGA HAS BEEN IN THE SAME MAGAZINE AS HIS.
HE'S STILL...
BAM
BASED ON THE STORYBOARDS YOU BROUGHT IN TODAY, I KNOW.
TO BE EXACT, YOU MEAN THAT WE'LL NEVER BE ABLE TO BEAT HIM WITH THESE STORYBOARDS...
... RIGHT?
!

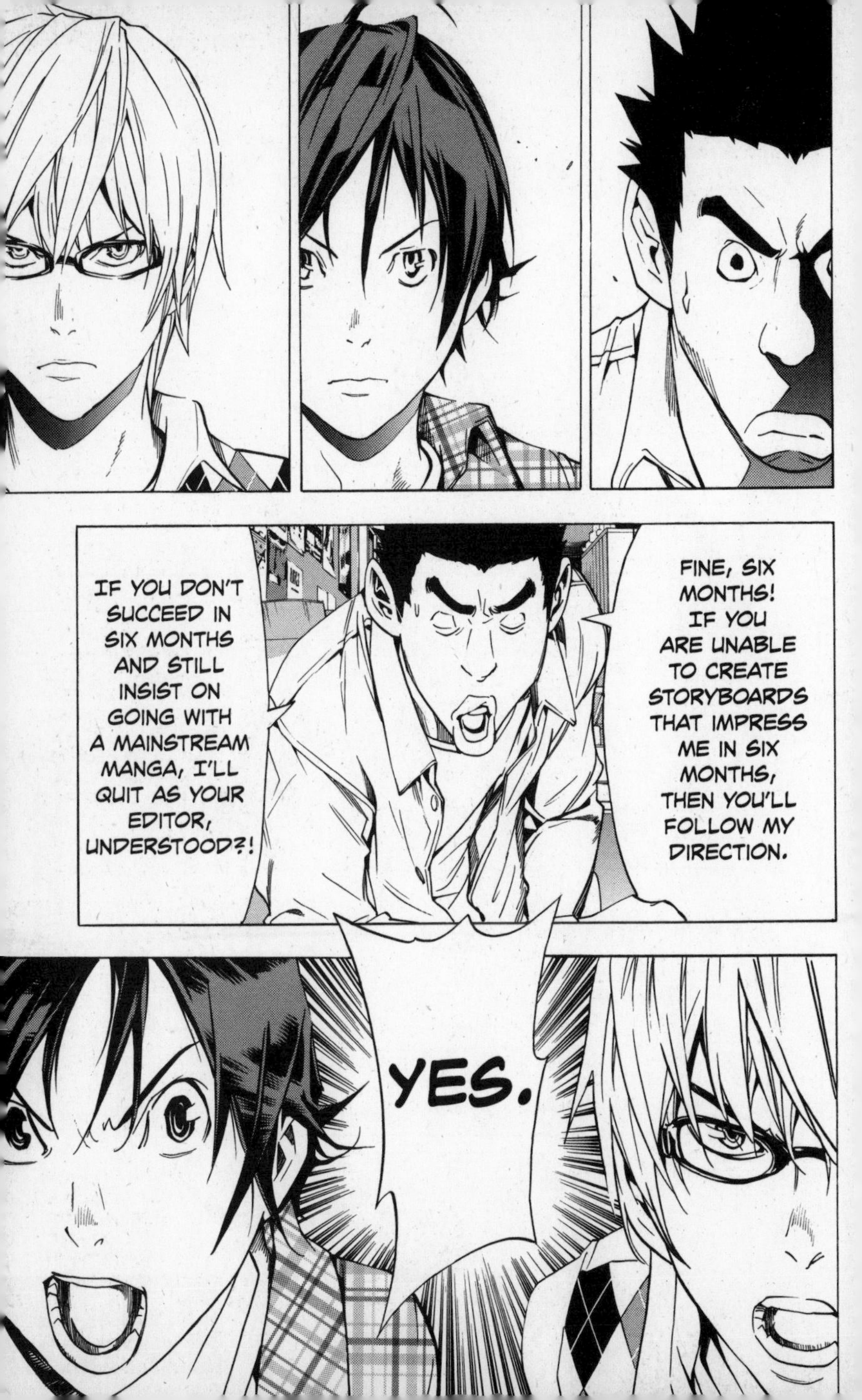
FINE, SIX MONTHS! IF YOU ARE UNABLE TO CREATE STORYBOARDS THAT IMPRESS ME IN SIX MONTHS, THEN YOU'LL FOLLOW MY DIRECTION.
IF YOU DON'T SUCCEED IN SIX MONTHS AND STILL INSIST ON GOING WITH A MAINSTREAM MANGA, I'LL QUIT AS YOUR EDITOR, UNDERSTOOD?!
YES.

OHBA'S STORYBOARD

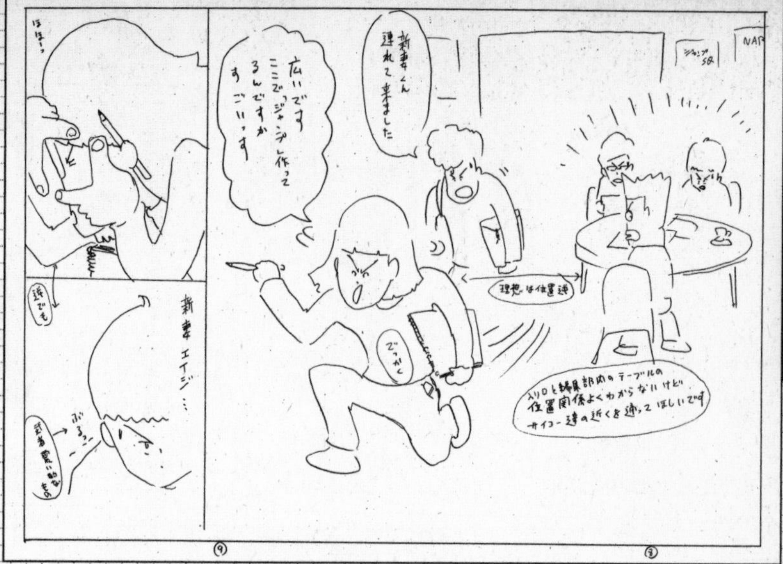

新妻くん連れて来ました
広いです ここでジャンプ作ってるんですか すごいっす
でっかく
入り口と編集部内のテーブルの位置関係よくわからないけど サイコー達の近くを通ってほしいです
ほほーっ
新妻 エイジ…
ぶるっ

OBATA'S STORYBOARD

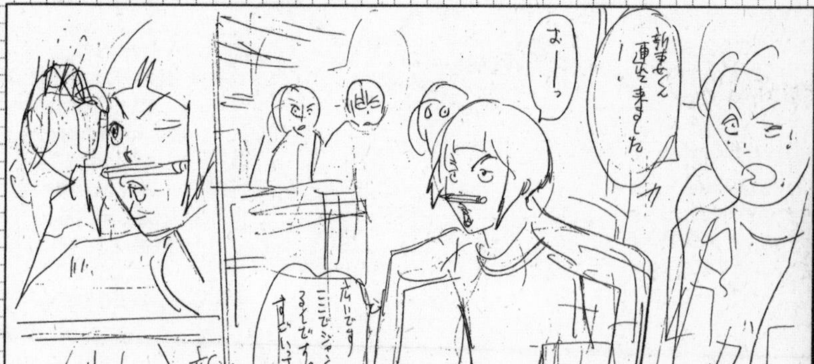

おーっ
新妻くん連れて来ました
広いです ここでジャンプ作ってるんですか すごいっす
新妻エイジ

COMPLETE!

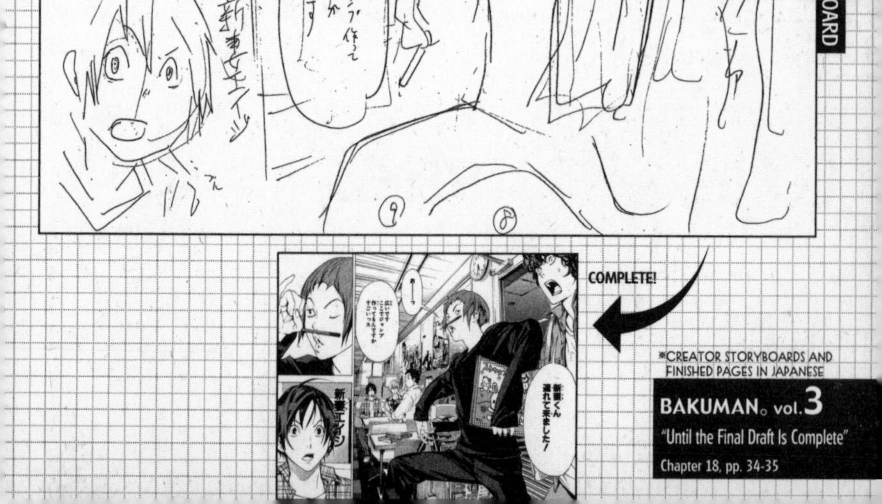

おーっ
新妻くん 連れて来ました!
新妻エイジ

*CREATOR STORYBOARDS AND FINISHED PAGES IN JAPANESE

BAKUMAN。 vol.3

"Until the Final Draft Is Complete"

Chapter 18, pp. 34-35

CHAPTER 19
DEBUT AND IMPATIENCE

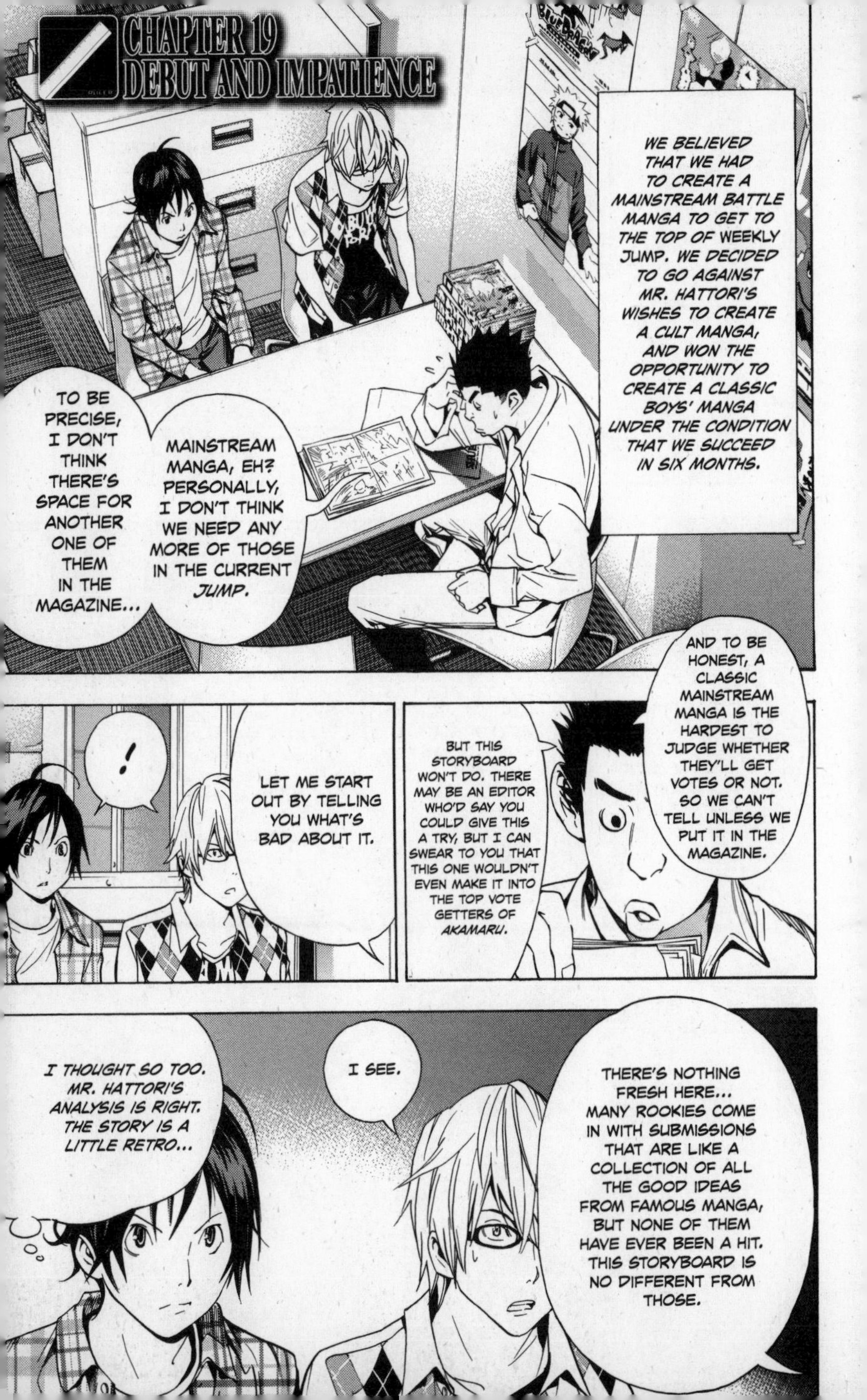
WE BELIEVED THAT WE HAD TO CREATE A MAINSTREAM BATTLE MANGA TO GET TO THE TOP OF WEEKLY JUMP. WE DECIDED TO GO AGAINST MR. HATTORI'S WISHES TO CREATE A CULT MANGA, AND WON THE OPPORTUNITY TO CREATE A CLASSIC BOYS' MANGA UNDER THE CONDITION THAT WE SUCCEED IN SIX MONTHS.
MAINSTREAM MANGA, EH? PERSONALLY, I DON'T THINK WE NEED ANY MORE OF THOSE IN THE CURRENT *JUMP*.
TO BE PRECISE, I DON'T THINK THERE'S SPACE FOR ANOTHER ONE OF THEM IN THE MAGAZINE...
AND TO BE HONEST, A CLASSIC MAINSTREAM MANGA IS THE HARDEST TO JUDGE WHETHER THEY'LL GET VOTES OR NOT. SO WE CAN'T TELL UNLESS WE PUT IT IN THE MAGAZINE.
BUT THIS STORYBOARD WON'T DO. THERE MAY BE AN EDITOR WHO'D SAY YOU COULD GIVE THIS A TRY, BUT I CAN SWEAR TO YOU THAT THIS ONE WOULDN'T EVEN MAKE IT INTO THE TOP VOTE GETTERS OF *AKAMARU*.
LET ME START OUT BY TELLING YOU WHAT'S BAD ABOUT IT.
!
THERE'S NOTHING FRESH HERE... MANY ROOKIES COME IN WITH SUBMISSIONS THAT ARE LIKE A COLLECTION OF ALL THE GOOD IDEAS FROM FAMOUS MANGA, BUT NONE OF THEM HAVE EVER BEEN A HIT. THIS STORYBOARD IS NO DIFFERENT FROM THOSE.
I SEE.
I THOUGHT SO TOO. MR. HATTORI'S ANALYSIS IS RIGHT. THE STORY IS A LITTLE RETRO...

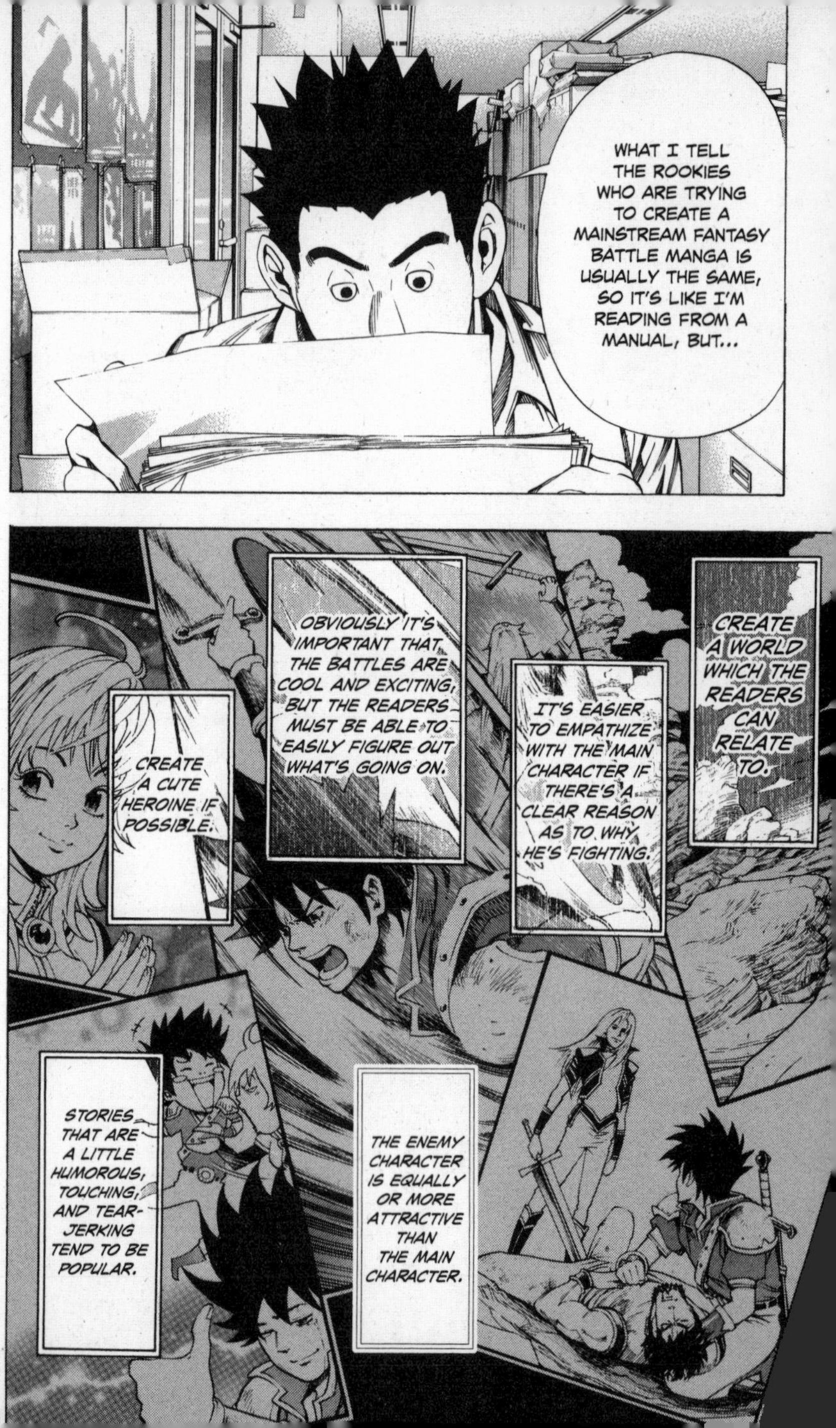
WHAT I TELL THE ROOKIES WHO ARE TRYING TO CREATE A MAINSTREAM FANTASY BATTLE MANGA IS USUALLY THE SAME, SO IT'S LIKE I'M READING FROM A MANUAL, BUT...
CREATE A WORLD WHICH THE READERS CAN RELATE TO.
IT'S EASIER TO EMPATHIZE WITH THE MAIN CHARACTER IF THERE'S A CLEAR REASON AS TO WHY HE'S FIGHTING.
OBVIOUSLY IT'S IMPORTANT THAT THE BATTLES ARE COOL AND EXCITING, BUT THE READERS MUST BE ABLE TO EASILY FIGURE OUT WHAT'S GOING ON.
CREATE A CUTE HEROINE IF POSSIBLE.
THE ENEMY CHARACTER IS EQUALLY OR MORE ATTRACTIVE THAN THE MAIN CHARACTER.
STORIES THAT ARE A LITTLE HUMOROUS, TOUCHING, AND TEAR-JERKING TEND TO BE POPULAR.

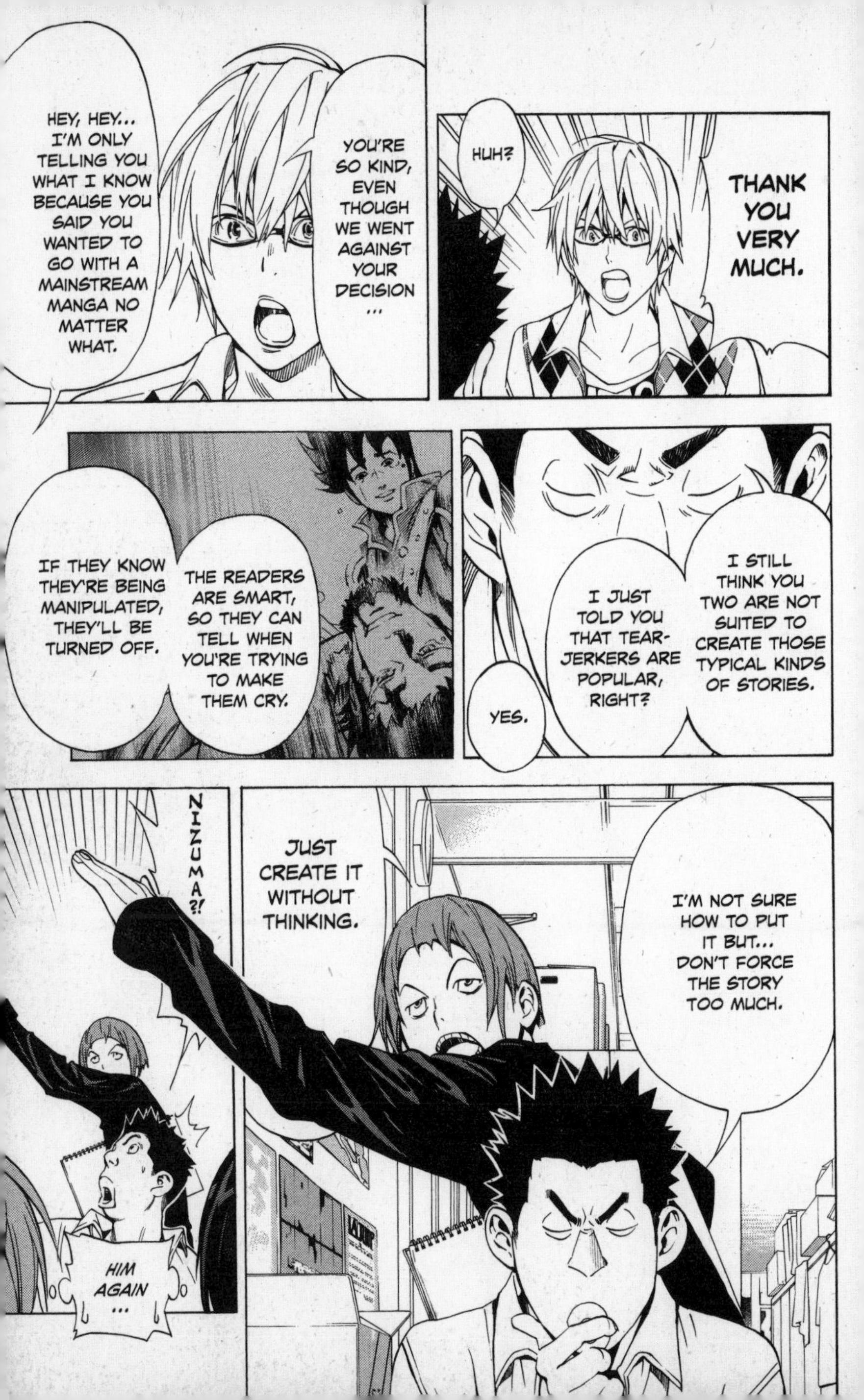
THANK YOU VERY MUCH.
HUH?
YOU'RE SO KIND, EVEN THOUGH WE WENT AGAINST YOUR DECISION...
HEY, HEY... I'M ONLY TELLING YOU WHAT I KNOW BECAUSE YOU SAID YOU WANTED TO GO WITH A MAINSTREAM MANGA NO MATTER WHAT.
I STILL THINK YOU TWO ARE NOT SUITED TO CREATE THOSE TYPICAL KINDS OF STORIES.
I JUST TOLD YOU THAT TEAR-JERKERS ARE POPULAR, RIGHT?
YES.
THE READERS ARE SMART, SO THEY CAN TELL WHEN YOU'RE TRYING TO MAKE THEM CRY.
IF THEY KNOW THEY'RE BEING MANIPULATED, THEY'LL BE TURNED OFF.
I'M NOT SURE HOW TO PUT IT BUT... DON'T FORCE THE STORY TOO MUCH.
JUST CREATE IT WITHOUT THINKING.
NIZUMA?!
HIM AGAIN...

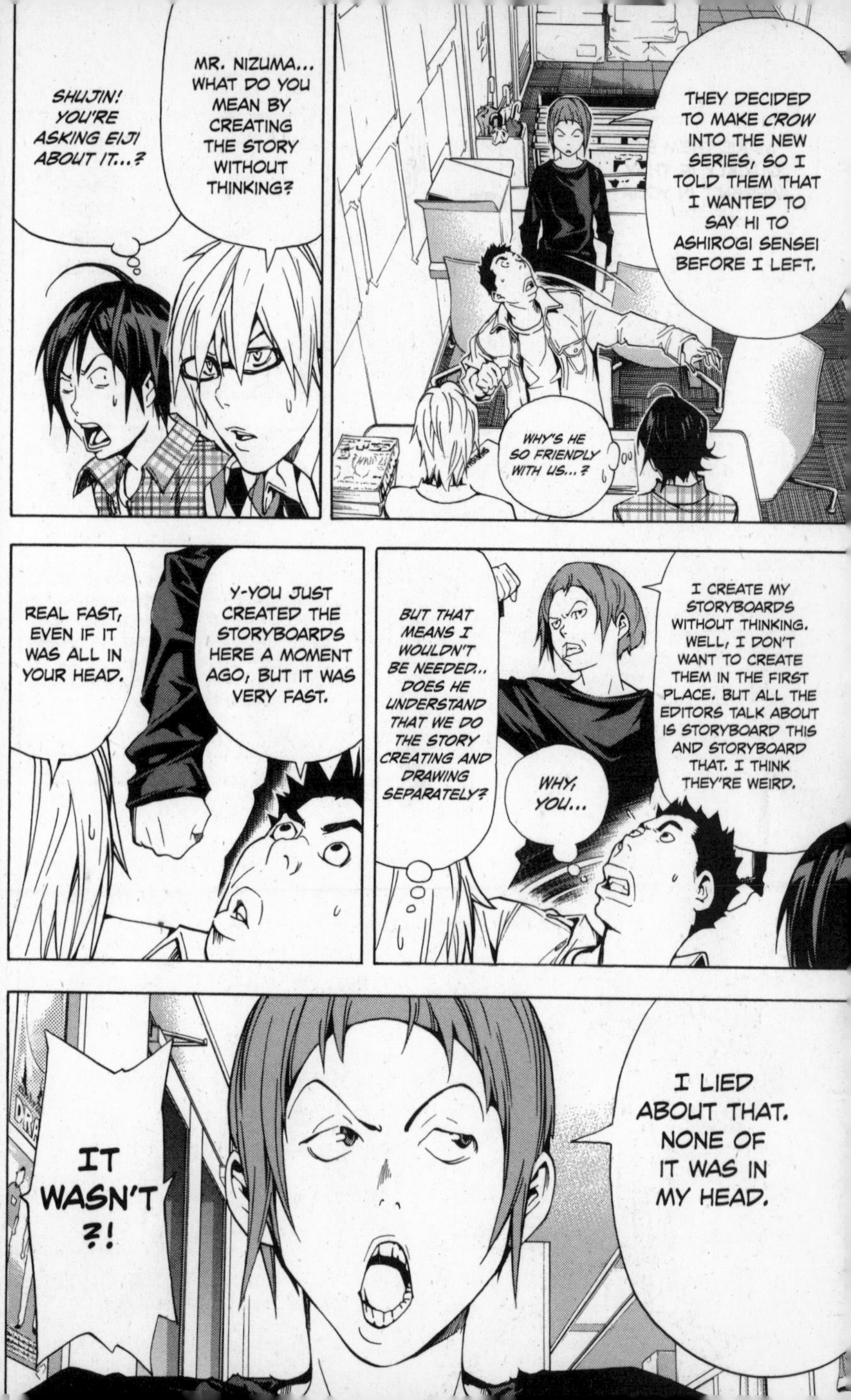
THEY DECIDED TO MAKE CROW INTO THE NEW SERIES, SO I TOLD THEM THAT I WANTED TO SAY HI TO ASHIROGI SENSEI BEFORE I LEFT.
WHY'S HE SO FRIENDLY WITH US...?
MR. NIZUMA... WHAT DO YOU MEAN BY CREATING THE STORY WITHOUT THINKING?
SHUJIN! YOU'RE ASKING EIJI ABOUT IT...?
I CREATE MY STORYBOARDS WITHOUT THINKING. WELL, I DON'T WANT TO CREATE THEM IN THE FIRST PLACE. BUT ALL THE EDITORS TALK ABOUT IS STORYBOARD THIS AND STORYBOARD THAT. I THINK THEY'RE WEIRD.
WHY, YOU...
BUT THAT MEANS I WOULDN'T BE NEEDED... DOES HE UNDERSTAND THAT WE DO THE STORY CREATING AND DRAWING SEPARATELY?
Y-YOU JUST CREATED THE STORYBOARDS HERE A MOMENT AGO, BUT IT WAS VERY FAST.
REAL FAST, EVEN IF IT WAS ALL IN YOUR HEAD.
I LIED ABOUT THAT. NONE OF IT WAS IN MY HEAD.
IT WASN'T ?!

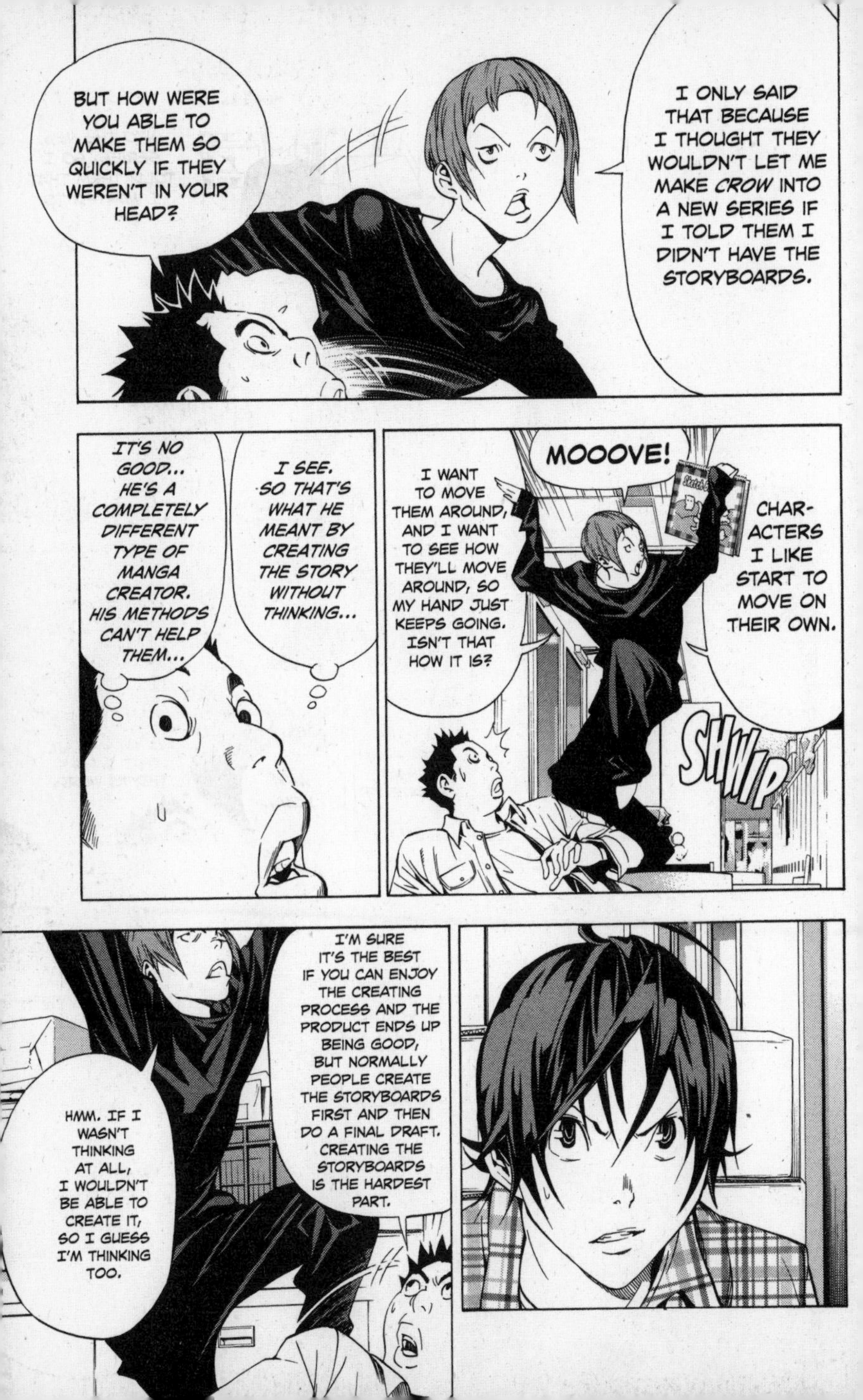
I ONLY SAID THAT BECAUSE I THOUGHT THEY WOULDN'T LET ME MAKE *CROW* INTO A NEW SERIES IF I TOLD THEM I DIDN'T HAVE THE STORYBOARDS.
BUT HOW WERE YOU ABLE TO MAKE THEM SO QUICKLY IF THEY WEREN'T IN YOUR HEAD?
CHAR-ACTERS I LIKE START TO MOVE ON THEIR OWN.
MOOOVE!
I WANT TO MOVE THEM AROUND, AND I WANT TO SEE HOW THEY'LL MOVE AROUND, SO MY HAND JUST KEEPS GOING. ISN'T THAT HOW IT IS?
SHWIP
I SEE. SO THAT'S WHAT HE MEANT BY CREATING THE STORY WITHOUT THINKING...
IT'S NO GOOD... HE'S A COMPLETELY DIFFERENT TYPE OF MANGA CREATOR. HIS METHODS CAN'T HELP THEM...
I'M SURE IT'S THE BEST IF YOU CAN ENJOY THE CREATING PROCESS AND THE PRODUCT ENDS UP BEING GOOD, BUT NORMALLY PEOPLE CREATE THE STORYBOARDS FIRST AND THEN DO A FINAL DRAFT. CREATING THE STORYBOARDS IS THE HARDEST PART.
HMM. IF I WASN'T THINKING AT ALL, I WOULDN'T BE ABLE TO CREATE IT, SO I GUESS I'M THINKING TOO.

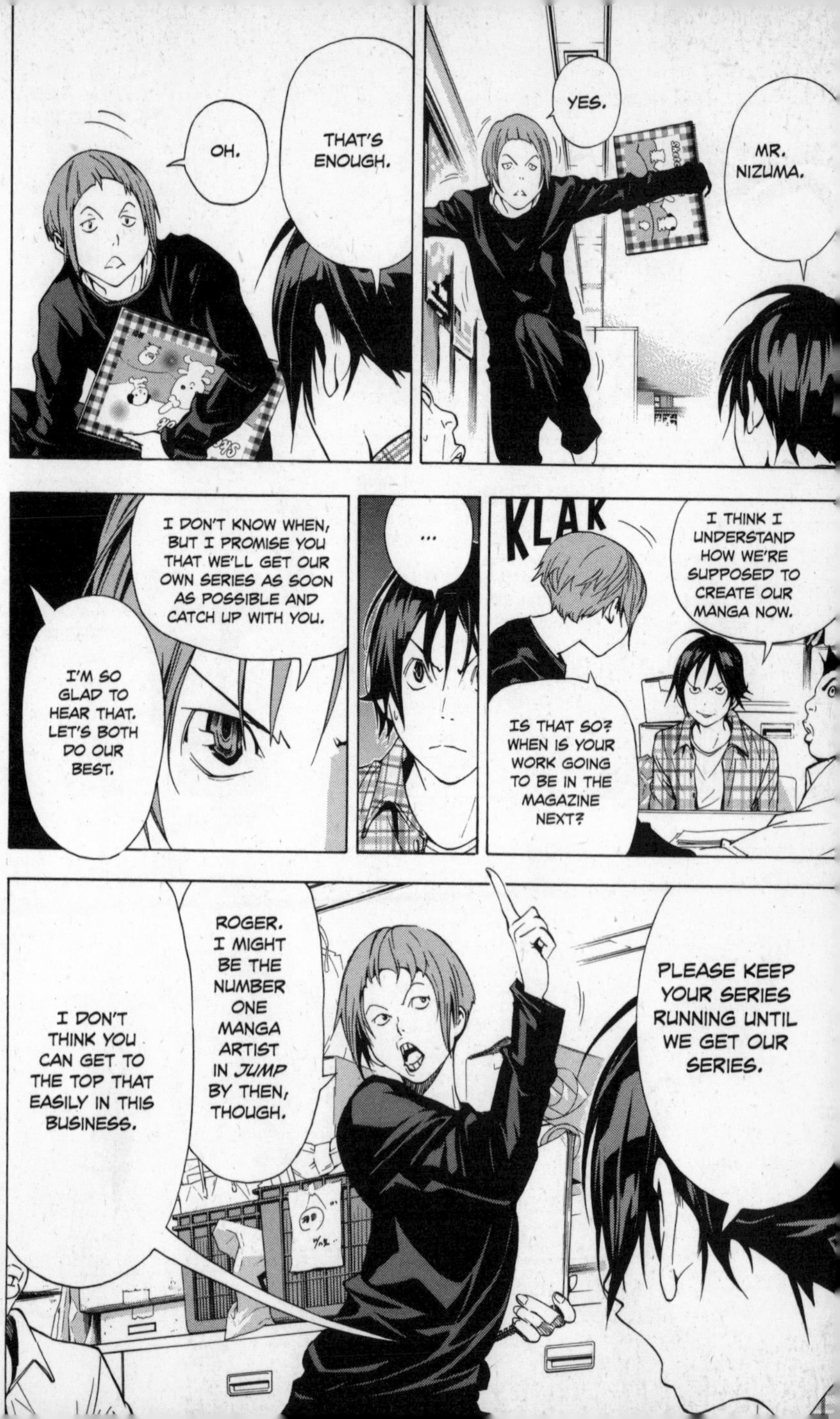
MR. NIZUMA.
YES.
THAT'S ENOUGH.
OH.
I THINK I UNDERSTAND HOW WE'RE SUPPOSED TO CREATE OUR MANGA NOW.
KLAK
IS THAT SO? WHEN IS YOUR WORK GOING TO BE IN THE MAGAZINE NEXT?
...
I DON'T KNOW WHEN, BUT I PROMISE YOU THAT WE'LL GET OUR OWN SERIES AS SOON AS POSSIBLE AND CATCH UP WITH YOU.
I'M SO GLAD TO HEAR THAT. LET'S BOTH DO OUR BEST.
PLEASE KEEP YOUR SERIES RUNNING UNTIL WE GET OUR SERIES.
ROGER. I MIGHT BE THE NUMBER ONE MANGA ARTIST IN *JUMP* BY THEN, THOUGH.
I DON'T THINK YOU CAN GET TO THE TOP THAT EASILY IN THIS BUSINESS.

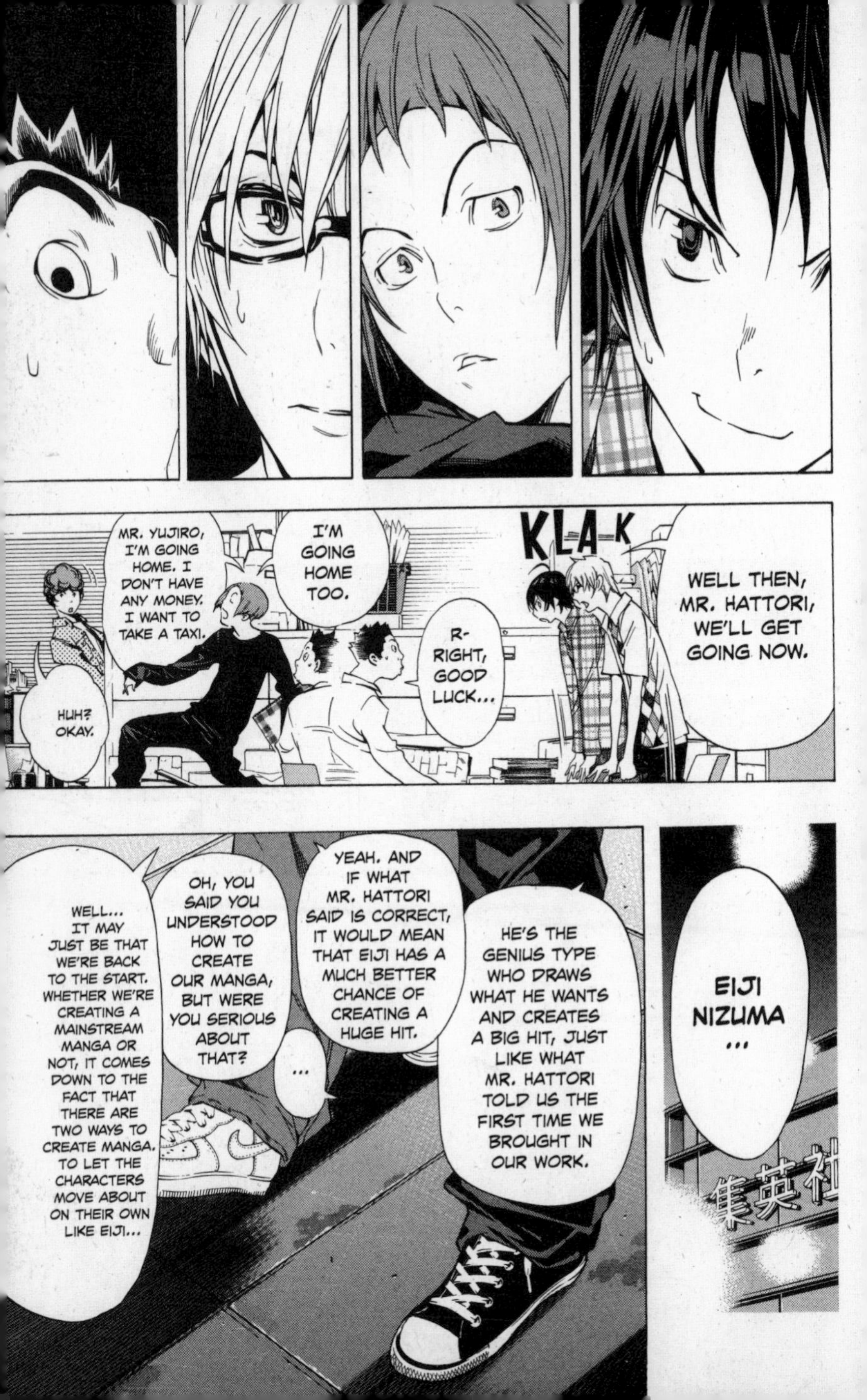

WELL THEN, MR. HATTORI, WE'LL GET GOING NOW.
KLA-K
R-RIGHT, GOOD LUCK...
I'M GOING HOME TOO.
MR. YUJIRO, I'M GOING HOME. I DON'T HAVE ANY MONEY. I WANT TO TAKE A TAXI.
HUH? OKAY.
EIJI NIZUMA ...
HE'S THE GENIUS TYPE WHO DRAWS WHAT HE WANTS AND CREATES A BIG HIT, JUST LIKE WHAT MR. HATTORI TOLD US THE FIRST TIME WE BROUGHT IN OUR WORK.
YEAH. AND IF WHAT MR. HATTORI SAID IS CORRECT, IT WOULD MEAN THAT EIJI HAS A MUCH BETTER CHANCE OF CREATING A HUGE HIT.
...
OH, YOU SAID YOU UNDERSTOOD HOW TO CREATE OUR MANGA, BUT WERE YOU SERIOUS ABOUT THAT?
WELL... IT MAY JUST BE THAT WE'RE BACK TO THE START. WHETHER WE'RE CREATING A MAINSTREAM MANGA OR NOT, IT COMES DOWN TO THE FACT THAT THERE ARE TWO WAYS TO CREATE MANGA. TO LET THE CHARACTERS MOVE ABOUT ON THEIR OWN LIKE EIJI...
集英社

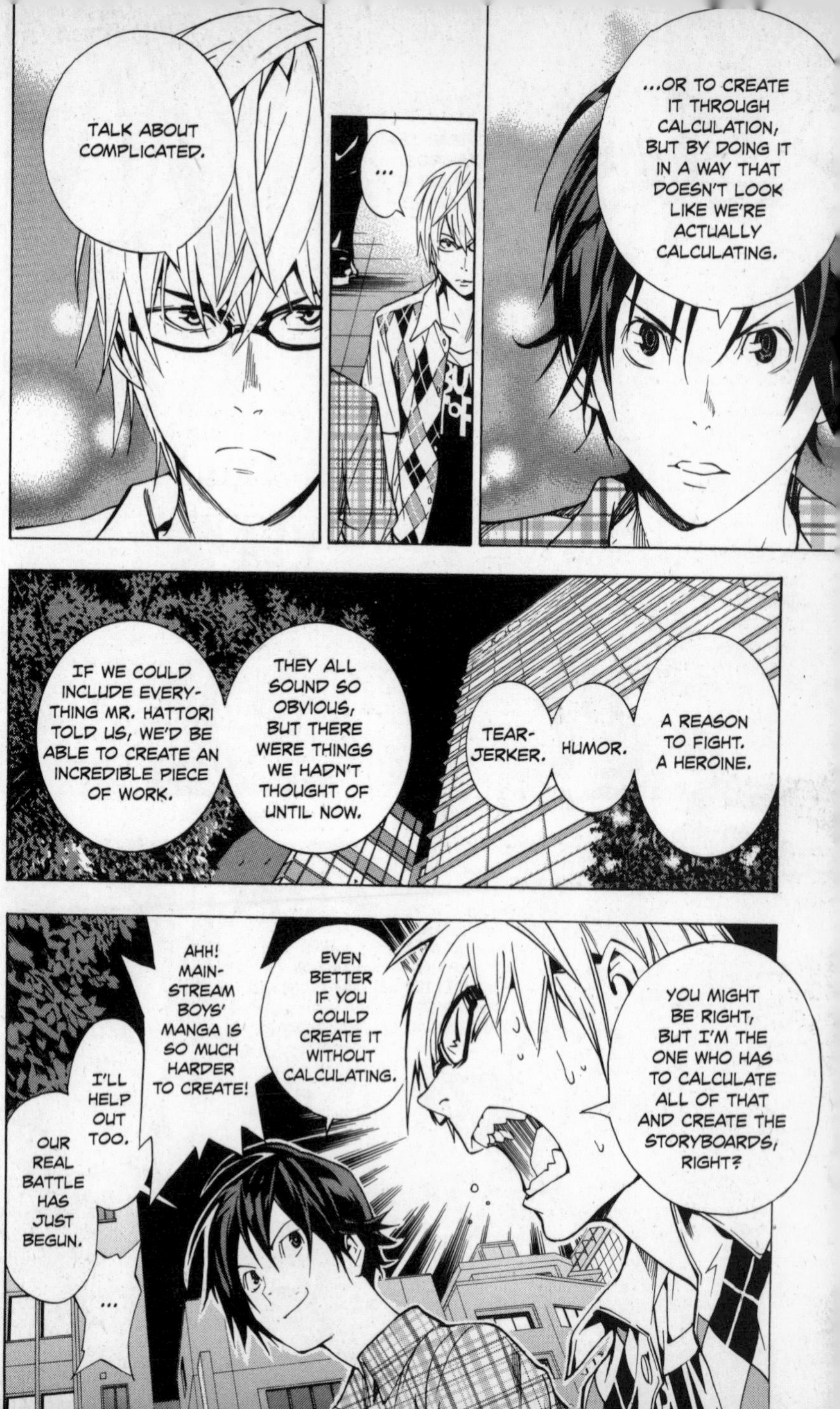
...OR TO CREATE IT THROUGH CALCULATION, BUT BY DOING IT IN A WAY THAT DOESN'T LOOK LIKE WE'RE ACTUALLY CALCULATING.
...
TALK ABOUT COMPLICATED.
A REASON TO FIGHT. A HEROINE.
HUMOR.
TEAR-JERKER.
THEY ALL SOUND SO OBVIOUS, BUT THERE WERE THINGS WE HADN'T THOUGHT OF UNTIL NOW.
IF WE COULD INCLUDE EVERY-THING MR. HATTORI TOLD US, WE'D BE ABLE TO CREATE AN INCREDIBLE PIECE OF WORK.
YOU MIGHT BE RIGHT, BUT I'M THE ONE WHO HAS TO CALCULATE ALL OF THAT AND CREATE THE STORYBOARDS, RIGHT?
EVEN BETTER IF YOU COULD CREATE IT WITHOUT CALCULATING.
AHH! MAIN-STREAM BOYS' MANGA IS SO MUCH HARDER TO CREATE!
I'LL HELP OUT TOO.
OUR REAL BATTLE HAS JUST BEGUN.
...

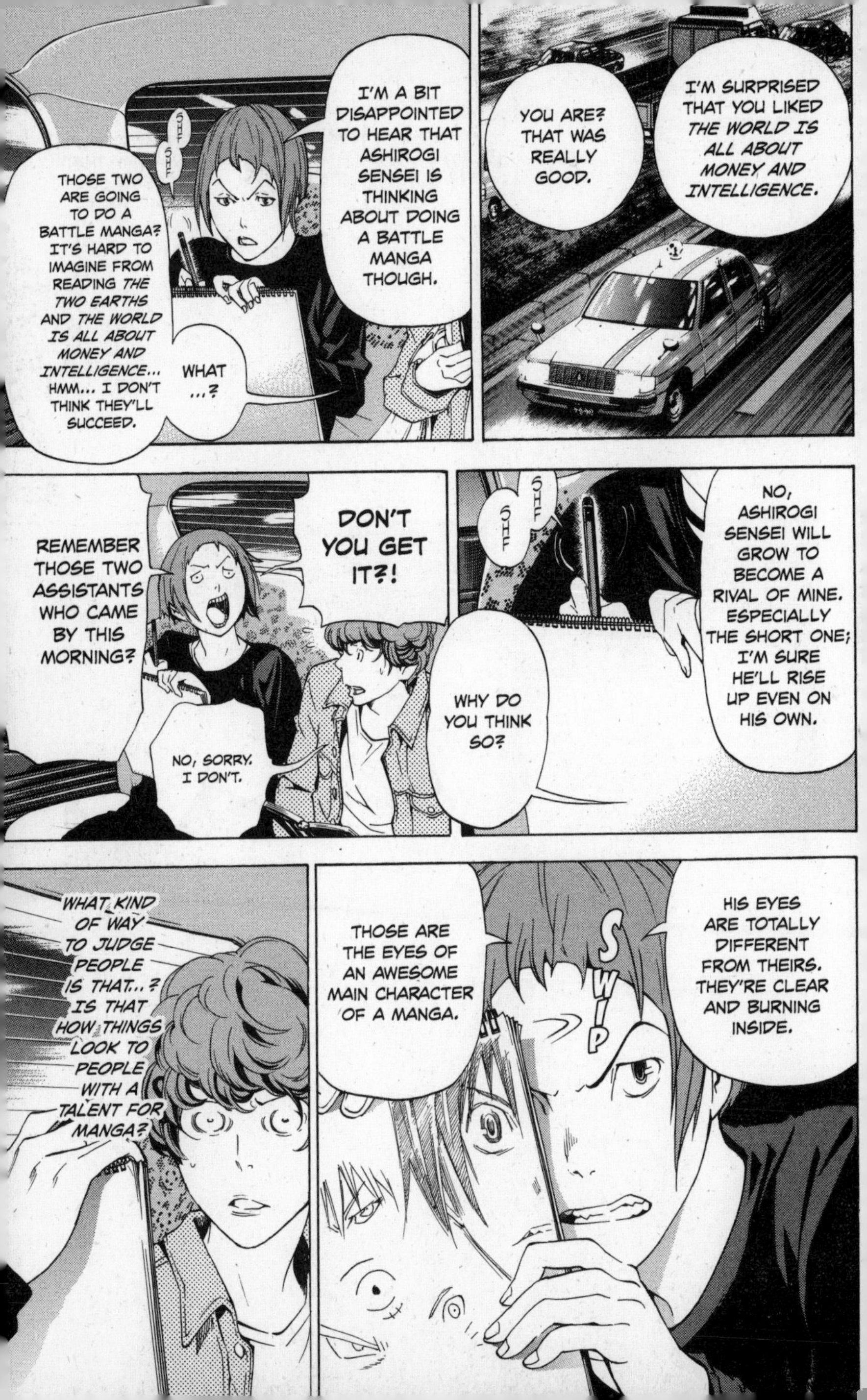
I'M SURPRISED THAT YOU LIKED *THE WORLD IS ALL ABOUT MONEY AND INTELLIGENCE.*
YOU ARE? THAT WAS REALLY GOOD.
I'M A BIT DISAPPOINTED TO HEAR THAT ASHIROGI SENSEI IS THINKING ABOUT DOING A BATTLE MANGA THOUGH.
SHF SHF
THOSE TWO ARE GOING TO DO A BATTLE MANGA? IT'S HARD TO IMAGINE FROM READING *THE TWO EARTHS* AND *THE WORLD IS ALL ABOUT MONEY AND INTELLIGENCE*... HMM... I DON'T THINK THEY'LL SUCCEED.
WHAT ...?
NO, ASHIROGI SENSEI WILL GROW TO BECOME A RIVAL OF MINE. ESPECIALLY THE SHORT ONE; I'M SURE HE'LL RISE UP EVEN ON HIS OWN.
SHF SHF
WHY DO YOU THINK SO?
DON'T YOU GET IT?!
REMEMBER THOSE TWO ASSISTANTS WHO CAME BY THIS MORNING?
NO, SORRY. I DON'T.
HIS EYES ARE TOTALLY DIFFERENT FROM THEIRS. THEY'RE CLEAR AND BURNING INSIDE.
SWIP
THOSE ARE THE EYES OF AN AWESOME MAIN CHARACTER OF A MANGA.
WHAT KIND OF WAY TO JUDGE PEOPLE IS THAT...? IS THAT HOW THINGS LOOK TO PEOPLE WITH A TALENT FOR MANGA?

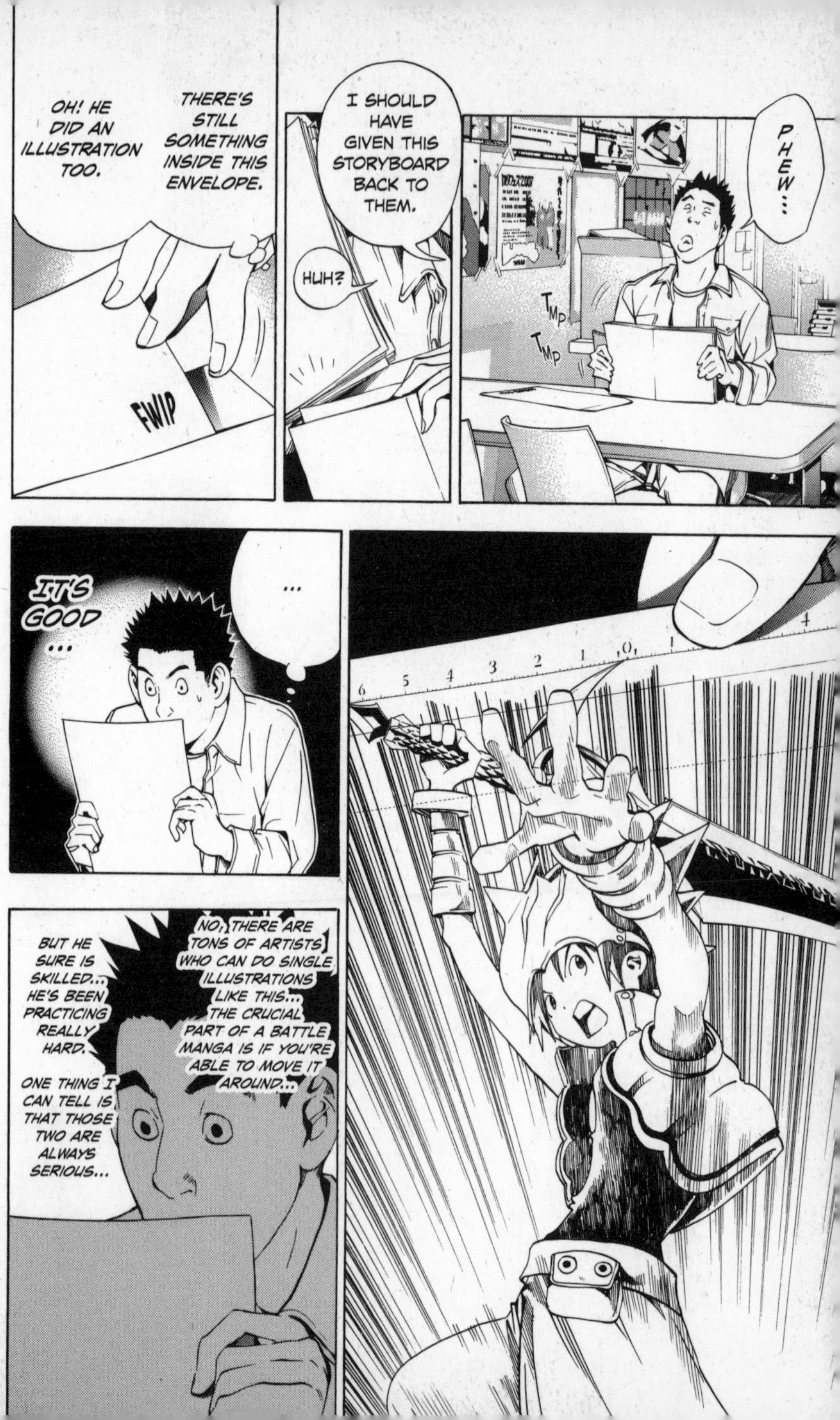
PHEW...
TMP
TMP
I SHOULD HAVE GIVEN THIS STORYBOARD BACK TO THEM.
HUH?
THERE'S STILL SOMETHING INSIDE THIS ENVELOPE.
OH! HE DID AN ILLUSTRATION TOO.
FWIP
...
IT'S GOOD ...
NO, THERE ARE TONS OF ARTISTS WHO CAN DO SINGLE ILLUSTRATIONS LIKE THIS... THE CRUCIAL PART OF A BATTLE MANGA IS IF YOU'RE ABLE TO MOVE IT AROUND...
BUT HE SURE IS SKILLED... HE'S BEEN PRACTICING REALLY HARD.
ONE THING I CAN TELL IS THAT THOSE TWO ARE ALWAYS SERIOUS...

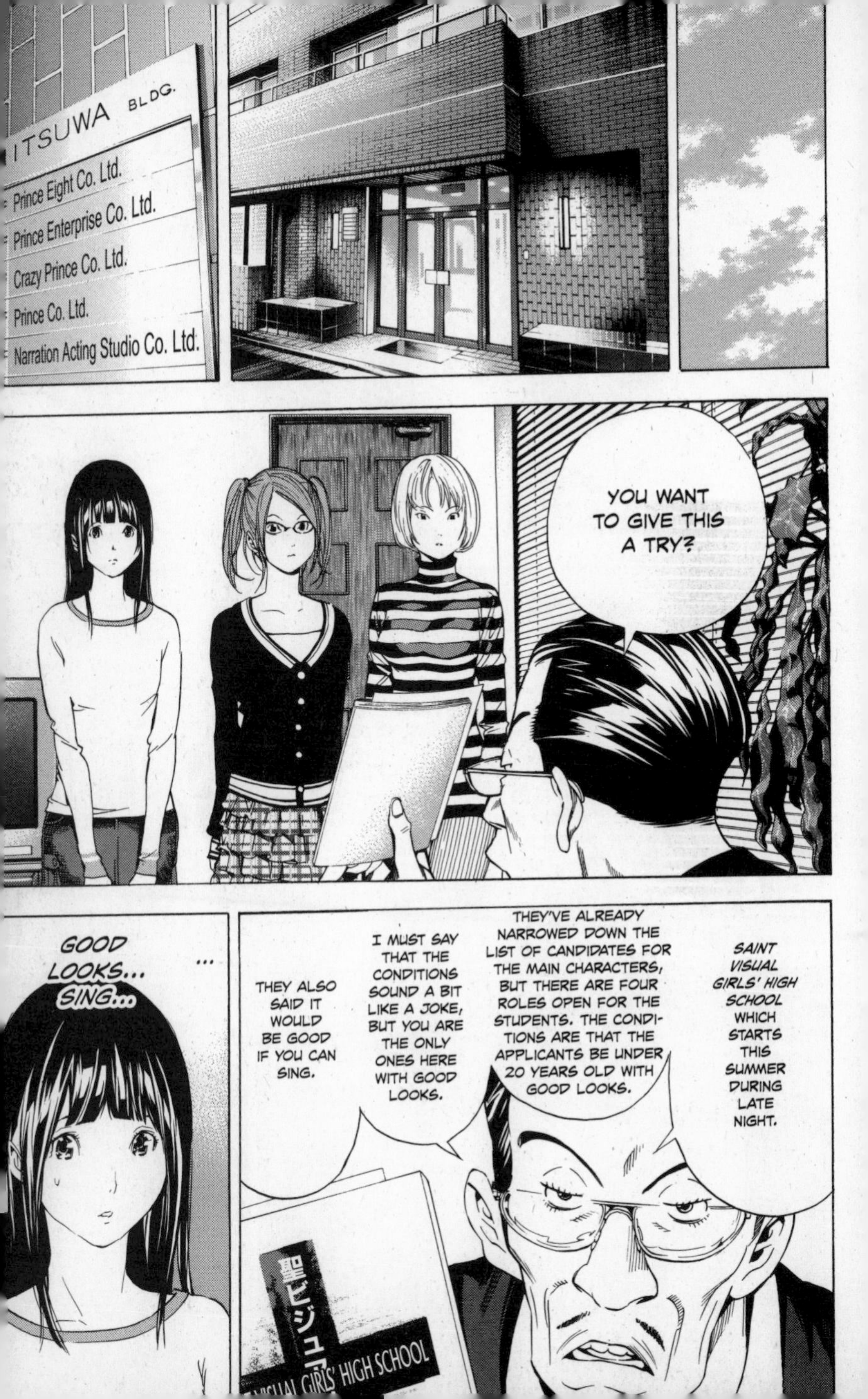
ITSUWA BLDG.
Prince Eight Co. Ltd.
Prince Enterprise Co. Ltd.
Crazy Prince Co. Ltd.
Prince Co. Ltd.
Narration Acting Studio Co. Ltd.
YOU WANT TO GIVE THIS A TRY?
SAINT VISUAL GIRLS' HIGH SCHOOL WHICH STARTS THIS SUMMER DURING LATE NIGHT.
THEY'VE ALREADY NARROWED DOWN THE LIST OF CANDIDATES FOR THE MAIN CHARACTERS, BUT THERE ARE FOUR ROLES OPEN FOR THE STUDENTS. THE CONDITIONS ARE THAT THE APPLICANTS BE UNDER 20 YEARS OLD WITH GOOD LOOKS.
I MUST SAY THAT THE CONDITIONS SOUND A BIT LIKE A JOKE, BUT YOU ARE THE ONLY ONES HERE WITH GOOD LOOKS.
THEY ALSO SAID IT WOULD BE GOOD IF YOU CAN SING.
聖ビジュア
VISUAL GIRLS' HIGH SCHOOL
...
GOOD LOOKS... SING...

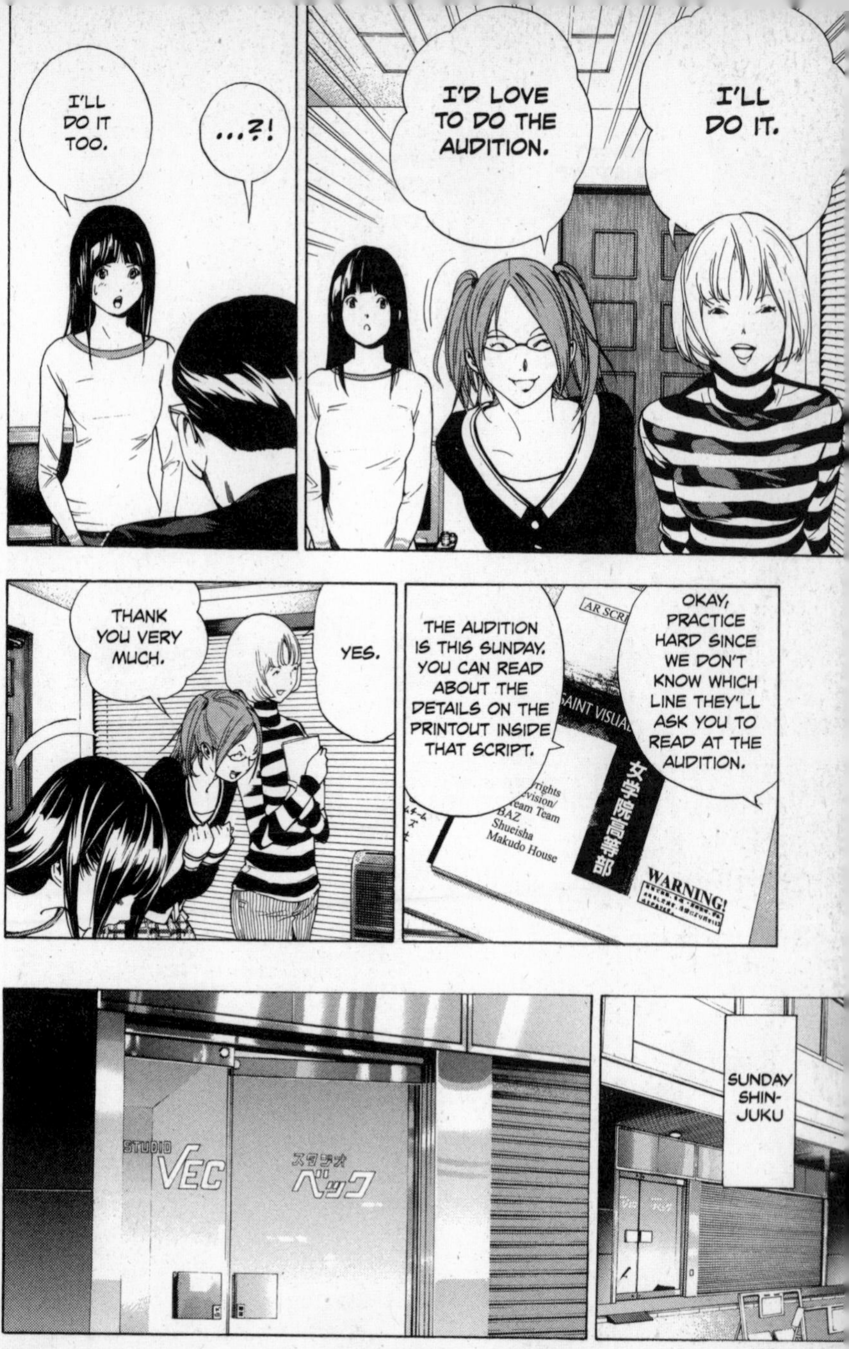
I'LL DO IT.
I'D LOVE TO DO THE AUDITION.
...?!
I'LL DO IT TOO.
OKAY, PRACTICE HARD SINCE WE DON'T KNOW WHICH LINE THEY'LL ASK YOU TO READ AT THE AUDITION.
THE AUDITION IS THIS SUNDAY. YOU CAN READ ABOUT THE DETAILS ON THE PRINTOUT INSIDE THAT SCRIPT.
女学院高等部
Shueisha
Makudo House
WARNING!
YES.
THANK YOU VERY MUCH.
SUNDAY SHIN-JUKU
STUDIO VEC
スタジオ ベック

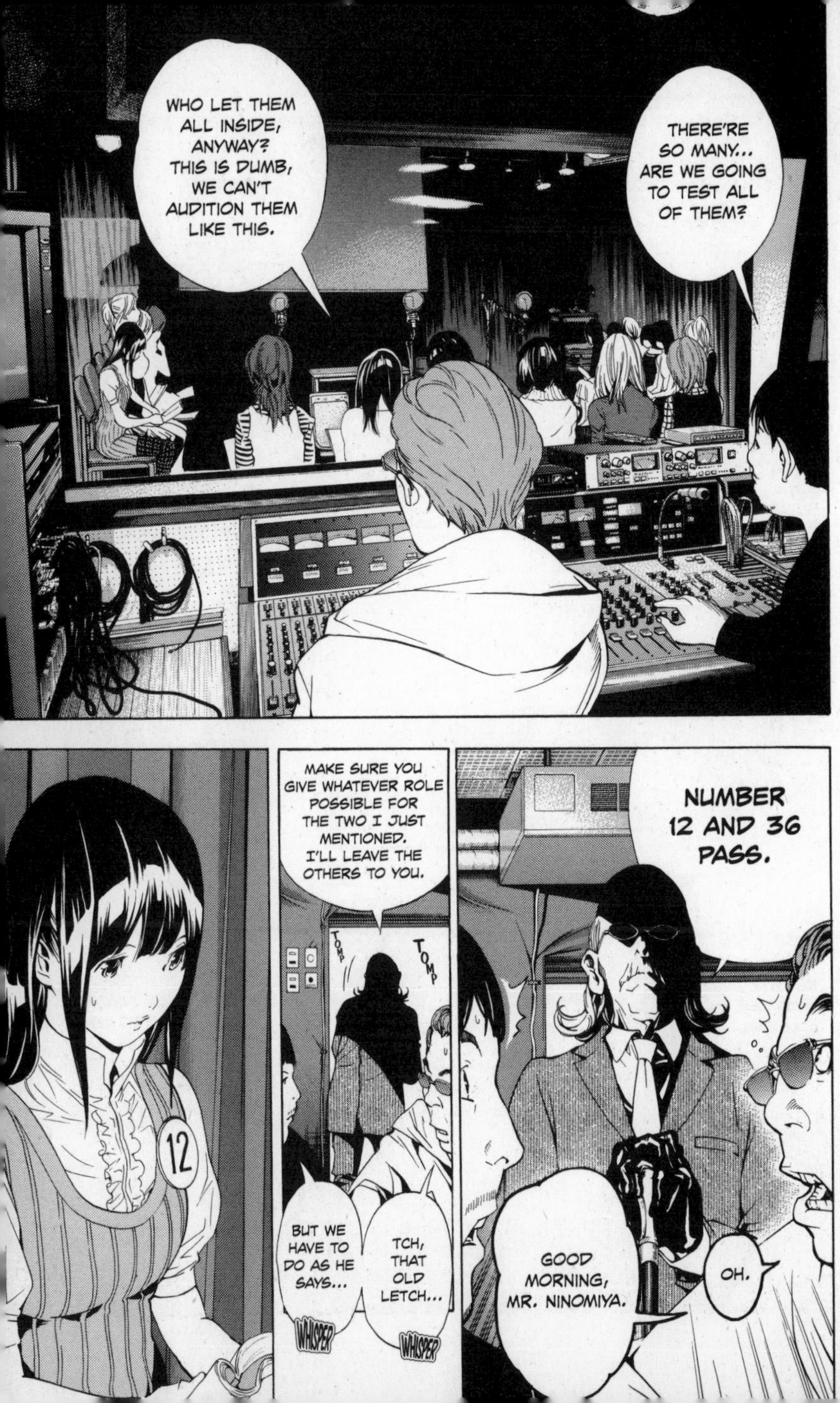
THERE'RE SO MANY... ARE WE GOING TO TEST ALL OF THEM?
WHO LET THEM ALL INSIDE, ANYWAY? THIS IS DUMB, WE CAN'T AUDITION THEM LIKE THIS.
NUMBER 12 AND 36 PASS.
OH.
GOOD MORNING, MR. NINOMIYA.
MAKE SURE YOU GIVE WHATEVER ROLE POSSIBLE FOR THE TWO I JUST MENTIONED. I'LL LEAVE THE OTHERS TO YOU.
TOMP
TOMP
TCH, THAT OLD LETCH...
WHISPER
BUT WE HAVE TO DO AS HE SAYS...
WHISPER
12

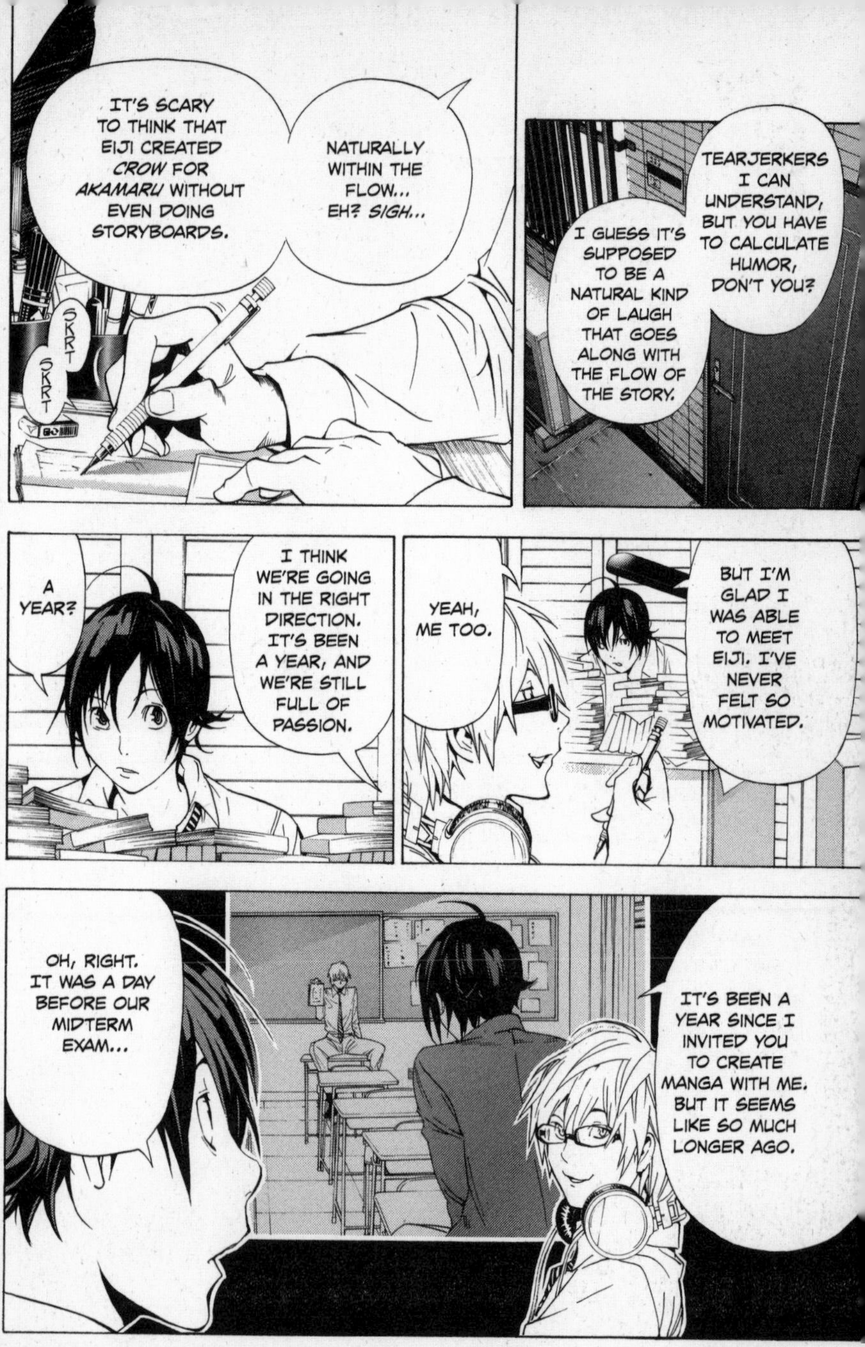
TEARJERKERS I CAN UNDERSTAND, BUT YOU HAVE TO CALCULATE HUMOR, DON'T YOU?
I GUESS IT'S SUPPOSED TO BE A NATURAL KIND OF LAUGH THAT GOES ALONG WITH THE FLOW OF THE STORY.
IT'S SCARY TO THINK THAT EIJI CREATED *CROW* FOR *AKAMARU* WITHOUT EVEN DOING STORYBOARDS.
NATURALLY WITHIN THE FLOW... EH? *SIGH...*
SKRT
SKRT
BUT I'M GLAD I WAS ABLE TO MEET EIJI. I'VE NEVER FELT SO MOTIVATED.
YEAH, ME TOO.
I THINK WE'RE GOING IN THE RIGHT DIRECTION. IT'S BEEN A YEAR, AND WE'RE STILL FULL OF PASSION.
A YEAR?
IT'S BEEN A YEAR SINCE I INVITED YOU TO CREATE MANGA WITH ME. BUT IT SEEMS LIKE SO MUCH LONGER AGO.
OH, RIGHT. IT WAS A DAY BEFORE OUR MIDTERM EXAM...

READ THIS WAY

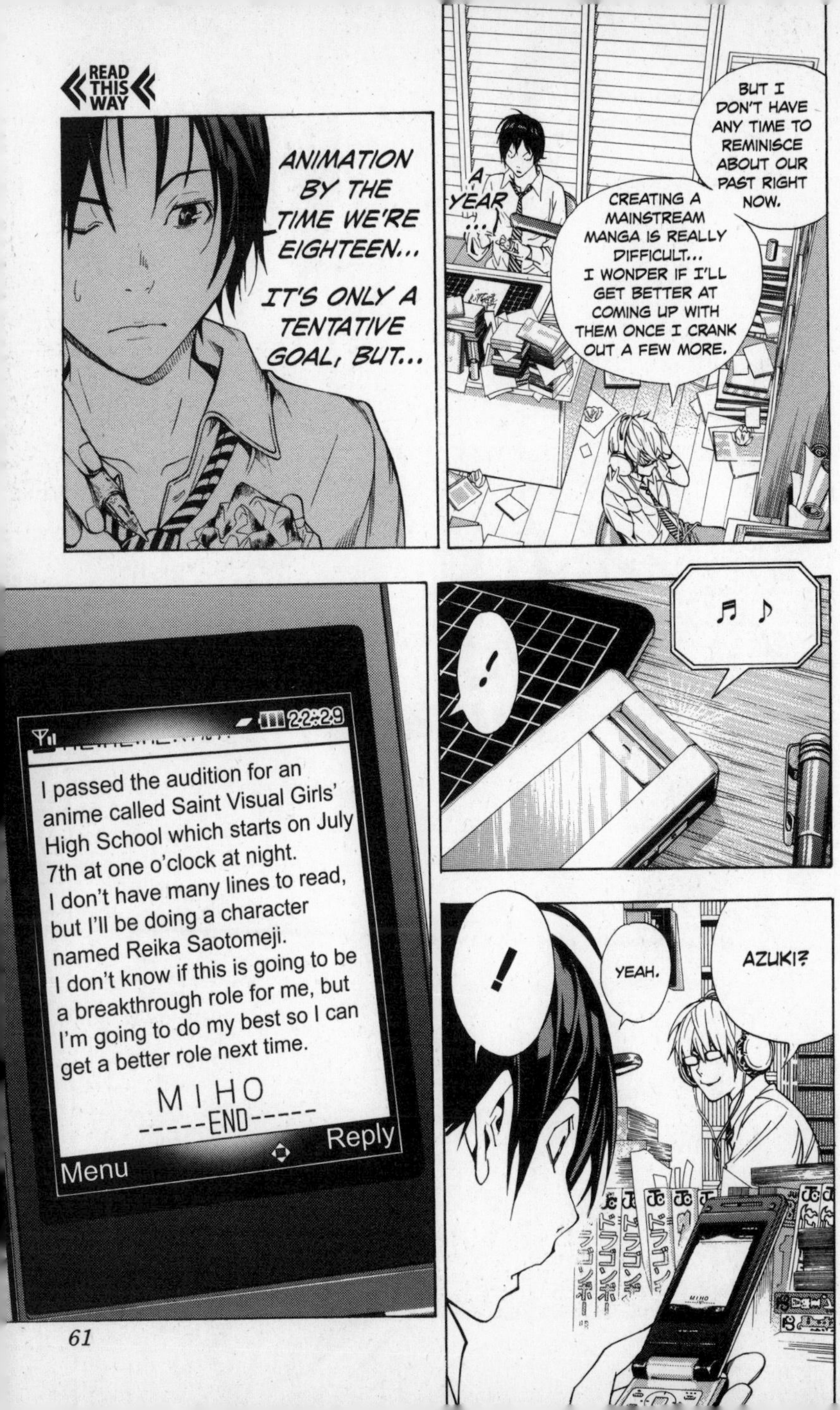
BUT I DON'T HAVE ANY TIME TO REMINISCE ABOUT OUR PAST RIGHT NOW.
CREATING A MAINSTREAM MANGA IS REALLY DIFFICULT... I WONDER IF I'LL GET BETTER AT COMING UP WITH THEM ONCE I CRANK OUT A FEW MORE.
A YEAR ...
ANIMATION BY THE TIME WE'RE EIGHTEEN...
IT'S ONLY A TENTATIVE GOAL, BUT...
♬ ♪
!
AZUKI?
YEAH.
!
22:29
I passed the audition for an anime called Saint Visual Girls' High School which starts on July 7th at one o'clock at night. I don't have many lines to read, but I'll be doing a character named Reika Saotomeji. I don't know if this is going to be a breakthrough role for me, but I'm going to do my best so I can get a better role next time.
MIHO
-----END-----
Reply
Menu

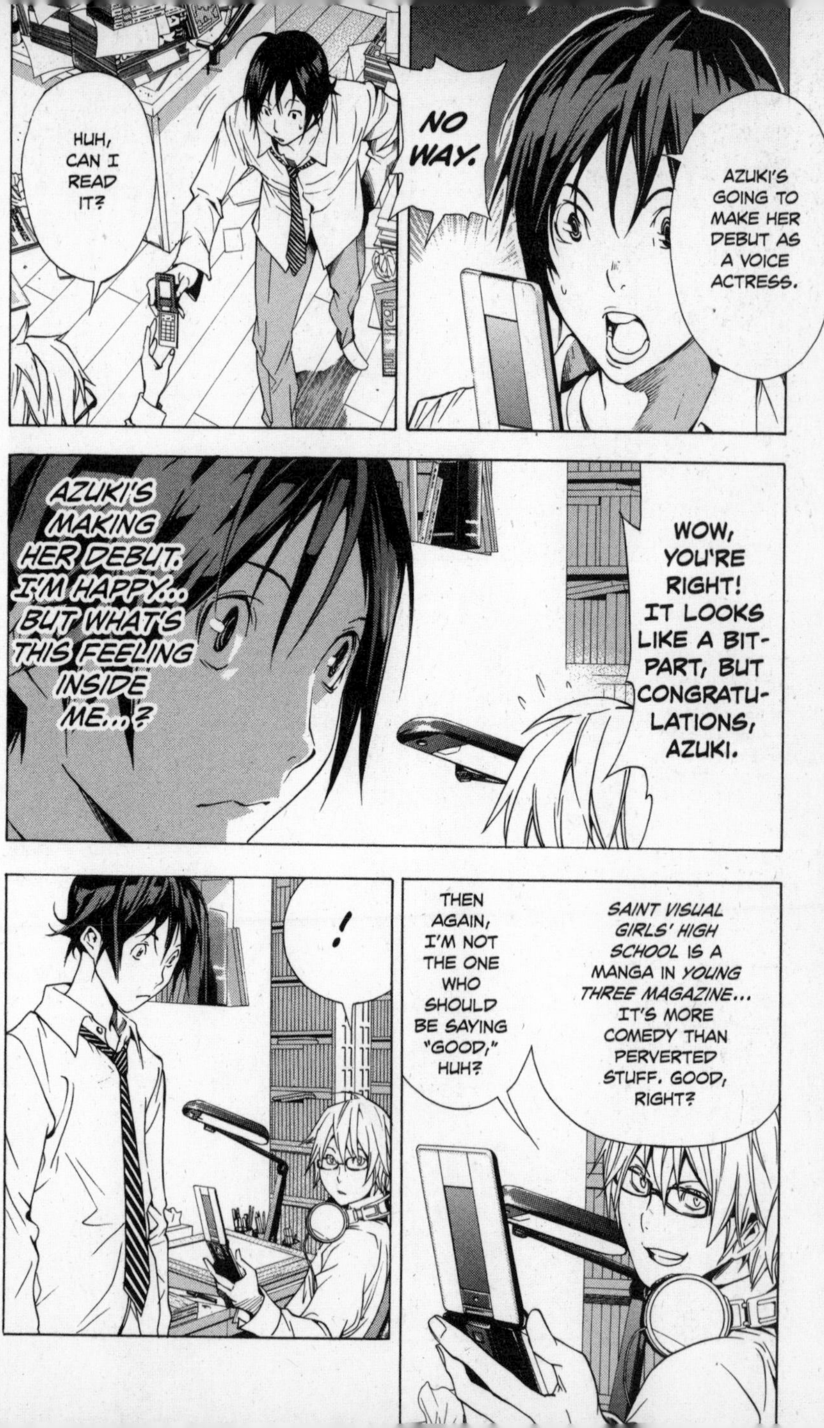
AZUKI'S GOING TO MAKE HER DEBUT AS A VOICE ACTRESS.
NO WAY.
HUH, CAN I READ IT?
WOW, YOU'RE RIGHT! IT LOOKS LIKE A BIT-PART, BUT CONGRATULATIONS, AZUKI.
AZUKI'S MAKING HER DEBUT. I'M HAPPY... BUT WHAT'S THIS FEELING INSIDE ME...?
SAINT VISUAL GIRLS' HIGH SCHOOL IS A MANGA IN *YOUNG THREE MAGAZINE*... IT'S MORE COMEDY THAN PERVERTED STUFF. GOOD, RIGHT?
THEN AGAIN, I'M NOT THE ONE WHO SHOULD BE SAYING "GOOD," HUH?
!

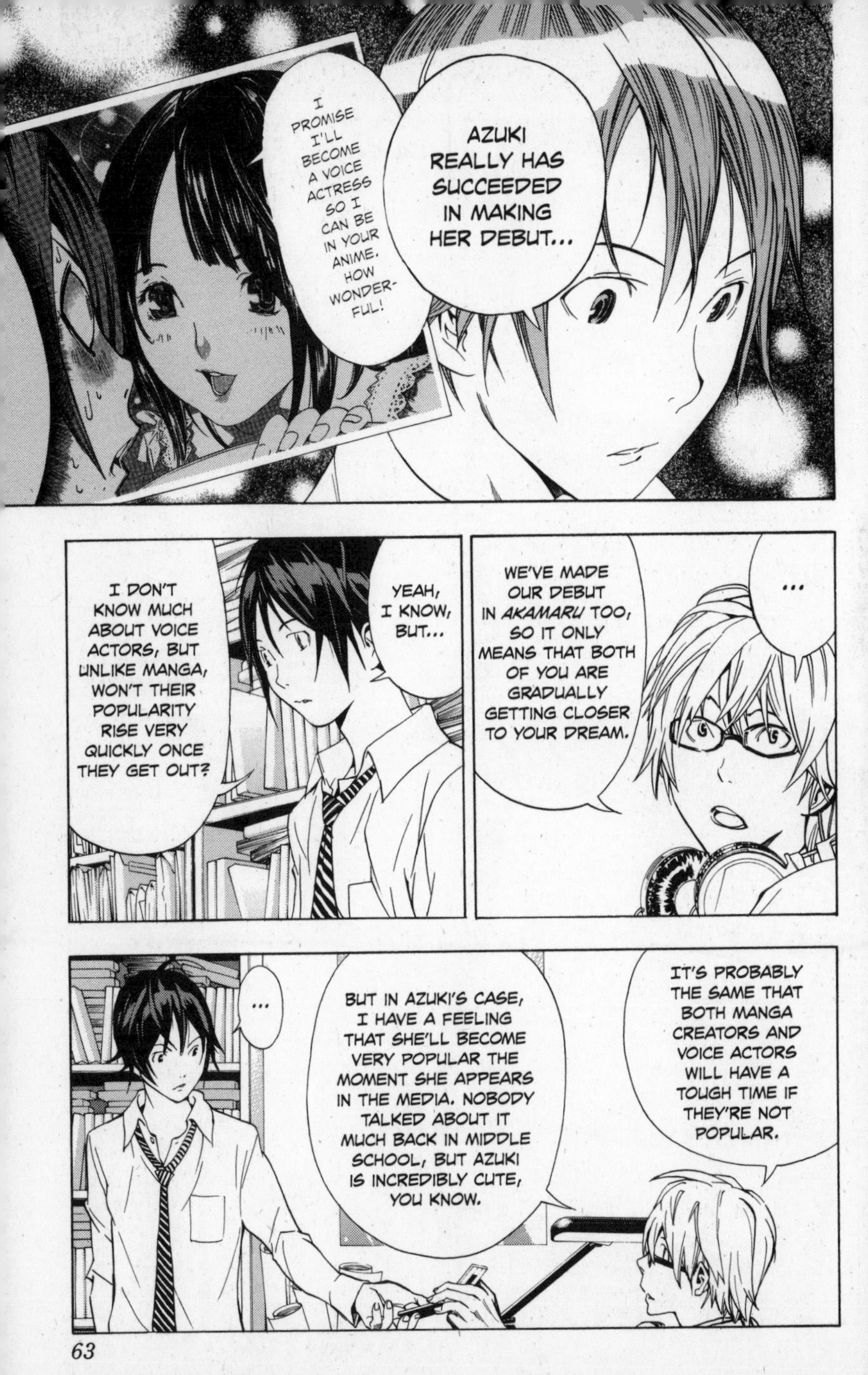
AZUKI REALLY HAS SUCCEEDED IN MAKING HER DEBUT...
I PROMISE I'LL BECOME A VOICE ACTRESS SO I CAN BE IN YOUR ANIME. HOW WONDERFUL!
...
WE'VE MADE OUR DEBUT IN *AKAMARU* TOO, SO IT ONLY MEANS THAT BOTH OF YOU ARE GRADUALLY GETTING CLOSER TO YOUR DREAM.
YEAH, I KNOW, BUT...
I DON'T KNOW MUCH ABOUT VOICE ACTORS, BUT UNLIKE MANGA, WON'T THEIR POPULARITY RISE VERY QUICKLY ONCE THEY GET OUT?
IT'S PROBABLY THE SAME THAT BOTH MANGA CREATORS AND VOICE ACTORS WILL HAVE A TOUGH TIME IF THEY'RE NOT POPULAR.
BUT IN AZUKI'S CASE, I HAVE A FEELING THAT SHE'LL BECOME VERY POPULAR THE MOMENT SHE APPEARS IN THE MEDIA. NOBODY TALKED ABOUT IT MUCH BACK IN MIDDLE SCHOOL, BUT AZUKI IS INCREDIBLY CUTE, YOU KNOW.
...

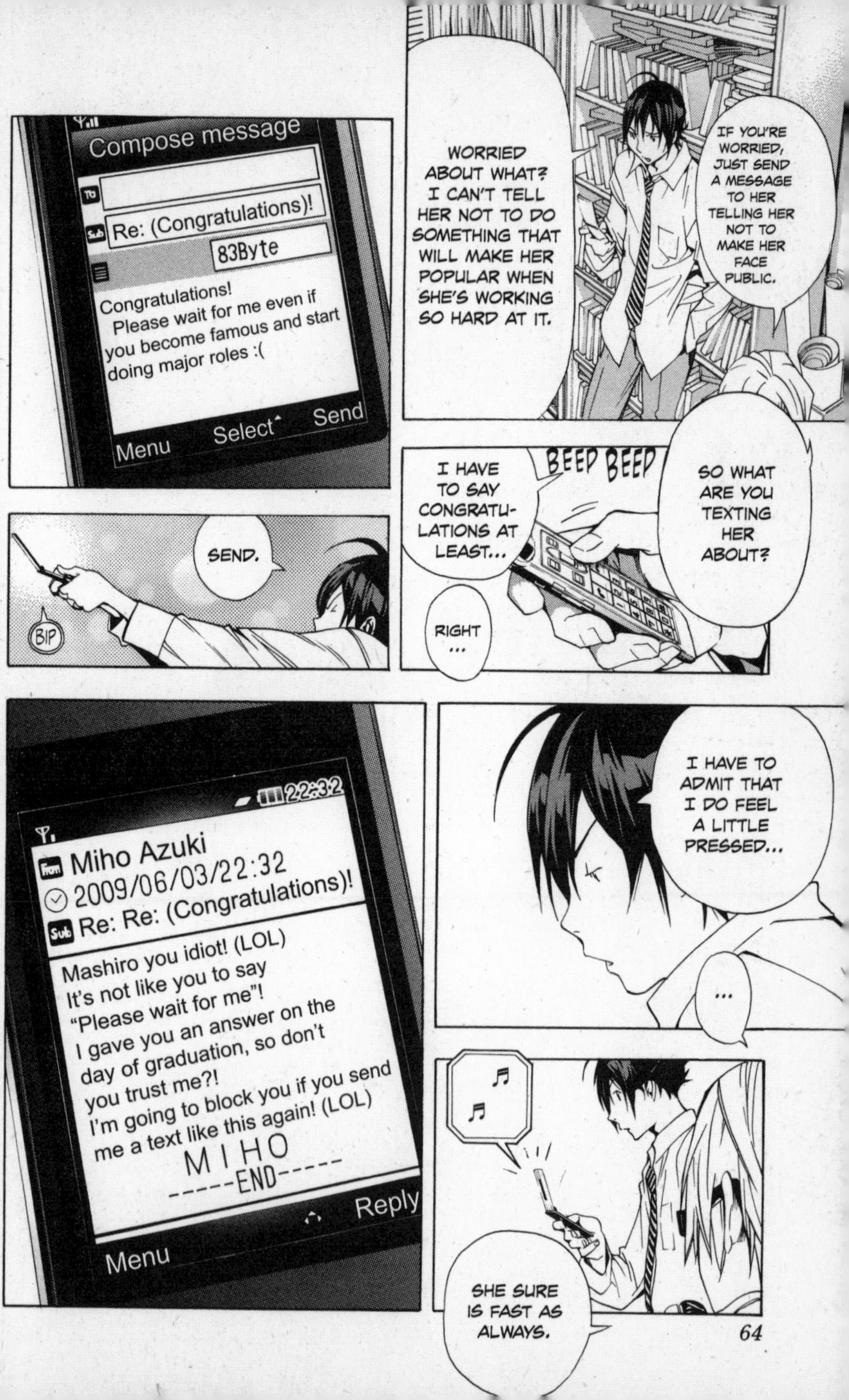
IF YOU'RE WORRIED, JUST SEND A MESSAGE TO HER TELLING HER NOT TO MAKE HER FACE PUBLIC.
WORRIED ABOUT WHAT? I CAN'T TELL HER NOT TO DO SOMETHING THAT WILL MAKE HER POPULAR WHEN SHE'S WORKING SO HARD AT IT.
SO WHAT ARE YOU TEXTING HER ABOUT?
BEEP BEEP
I HAVE TO SAY CONGRATU-LATIONS AT LEAST...
RIGHT...
Compose message
To
Sub Re: (Congratulations)!
83Byte
Congratulations!
Please wait for me even if you become famous and start doing major roles :(
Menu
Select
Send
SEND.
BIP
I HAVE TO ADMIT THAT I DO FEEL A LITTLE PRESSED...
...
SHE SURE IS FAST AS ALWAYS.
22:32
From Miho Azuki
2009/06/03/22:32
Sub Re: Re: (Congratulations)!
Mashiro you idiot! (LOL)
It's not like you to say
"Please wait for me"!
I gave you an answer on the
day of graduation, so don't
you trust me?!
I'm going to block you if you send
me a text like this again! (LOL)
MIHO
-----END-----
Reply
Menu

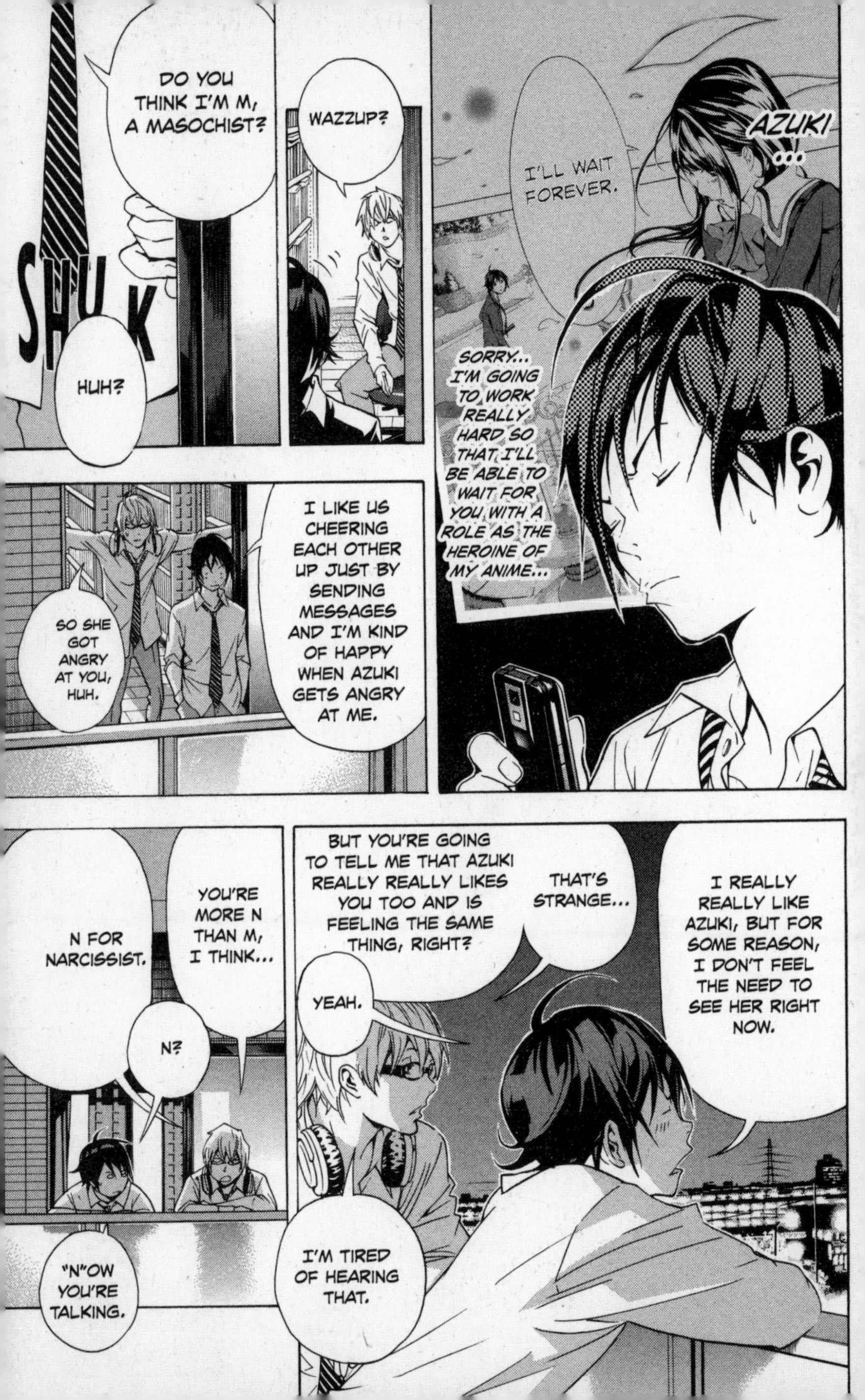
AZUKI...
I'LL WAIT FOREVER.
SORRY... I'M GOING TO WORK REALLY HARD SO THAT I'LL BE ABLE TO WAIT FOR YOU WITH A ROLE AS THE HEROINE OF MY ANIME...
WAZZUP?
DO YOU THINK I'M M, A MASOCHIST?
SHUK
HUH?
I LIKE US CHEERING EACH OTHER UP JUST BY SENDING MESSAGES AND I'M KIND OF HAPPY WHEN AZUKI GETS ANGRY AT ME.
SO SHE GOT ANGRY AT YOU, HUH.
I REALLY REALLY LIKE AZUKI, BUT FOR SOME REASON, I DON'T FEEL THE NEED TO SEE HER RIGHT NOW.
THAT'S STRANGE...
BUT YOU'RE GOING TO TELL ME THAT AZUKI REALLY REALLY LIKES YOU TOO AND IS FEELING THE SAME THING, RIGHT?
YEAH.
I'M TIRED OF HEARING THAT.
YOU'RE MORE N THAN M, I THINK...
N FOR NARCISSIST.
N?
"N"OW YOU'RE TALKING.

OHBA'S STORYBOARD

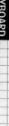

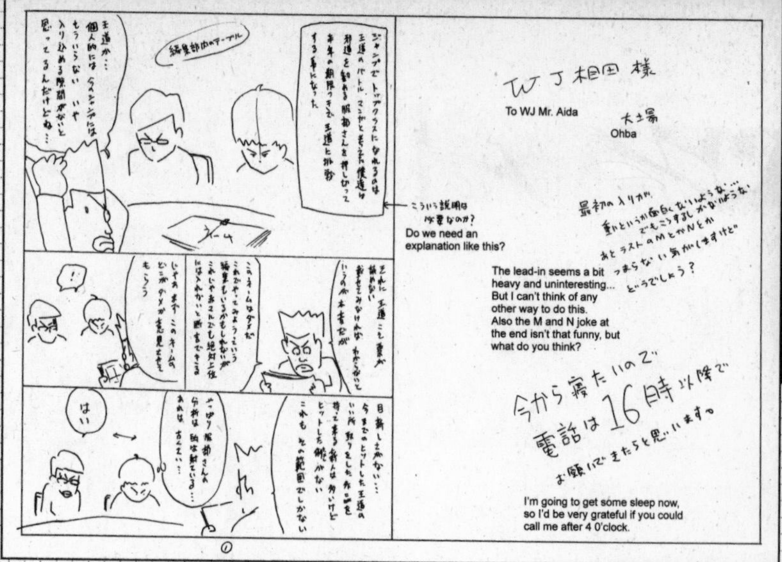
WJ 相田 様
To WJ Mr. Aida
大場
Ohba
こういう説明は必要なのか?
Do we need an explanation like this?
最初の入りが重たいし面白くないような…でもこうするしかないような あとラストのMとかNとかつまらない気がしますけど どうでしょう?
The lead-in seems a bit heavy and uninteresting... But I can't think of any other way to do this. Also the M and N joke at the end isn't that funny, but what do you think?
今から寝たいので 電話は16時以降で お願いできたらと思います。
I'm going to get some sleep now, so I'd be very grateful if you could call me after 4 0'clock.

OBATA'S STORYBOARD

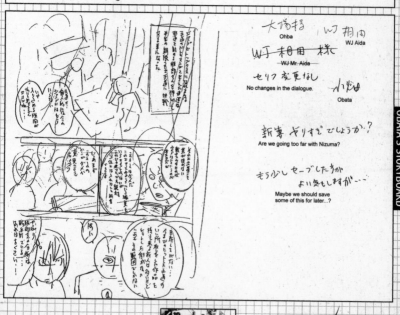

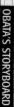

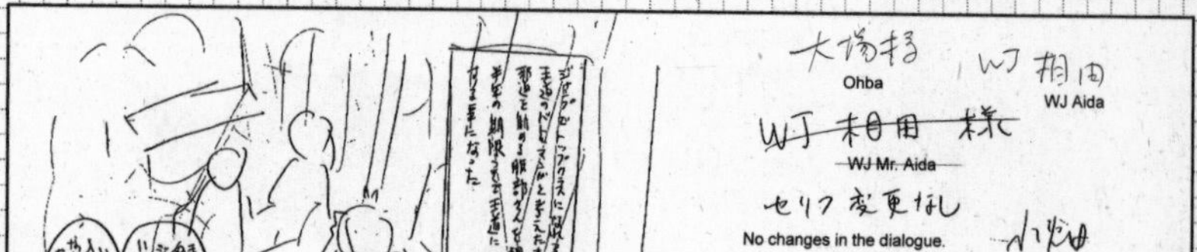
大場様
Ohba
WJ 相田
WJ Aida
~~WJ 相田 様~~
~~WJ Mr. Aida~~
セリフ変更なし
No changes in the dialogue.
小畑
Obata
新妻やりすぎでしょうか?
Are we going too far with Nizuma?
もう少しセーブした方がよい気もしますが…
Maybe we should save some of this for later...?

COMPLETE!

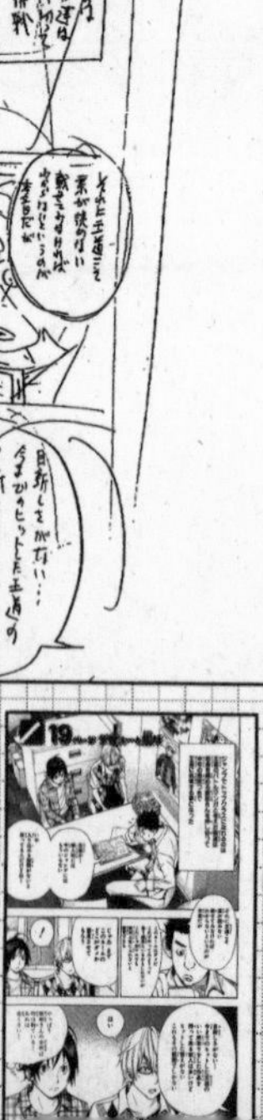

BAKUMAN。 vol.3
"Until the Final Draft Is Complete"
Chapter 19, pp. 47

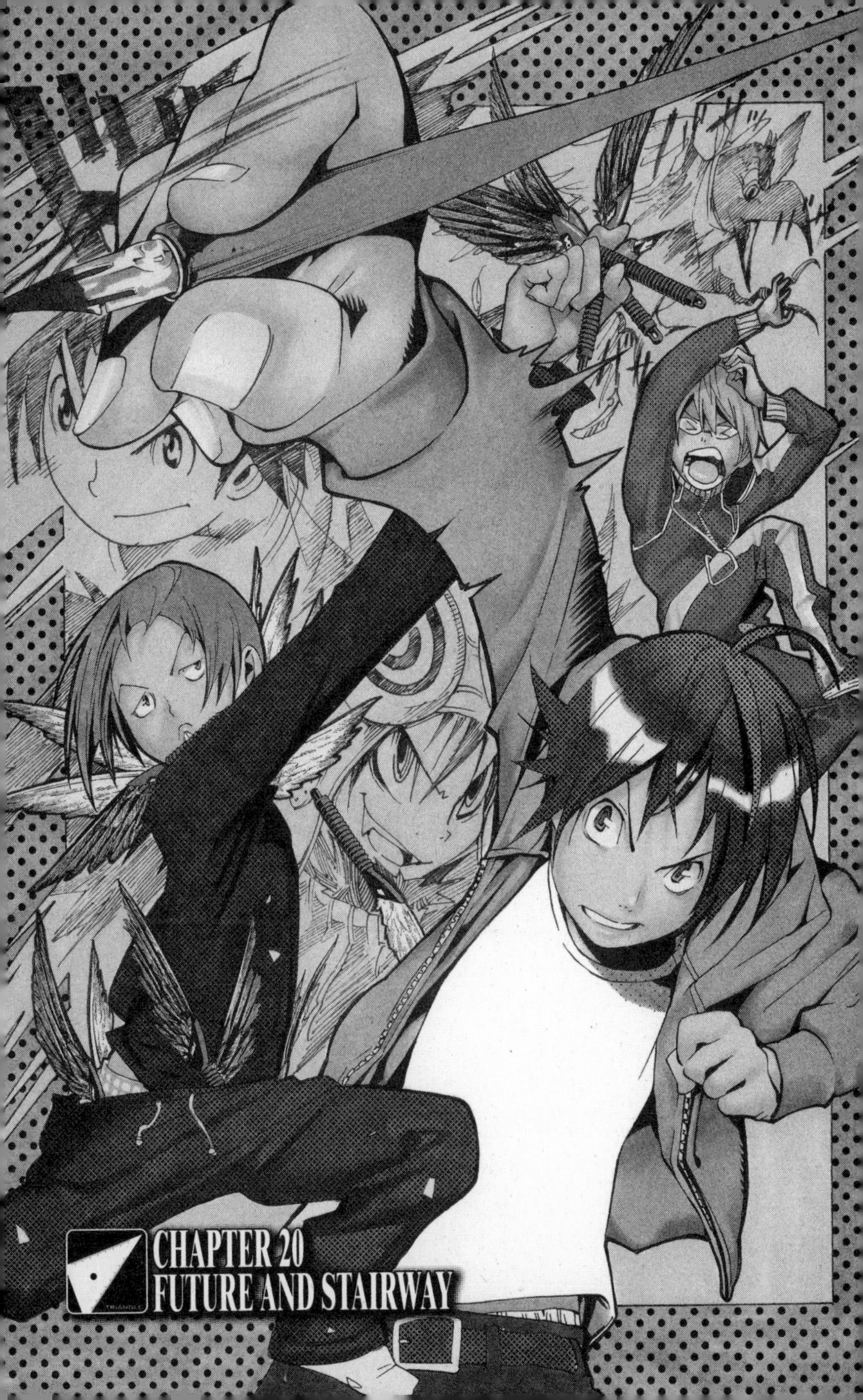

CHAPTER 20
FUTURE AND STAIRWAY

BAKUMAN。

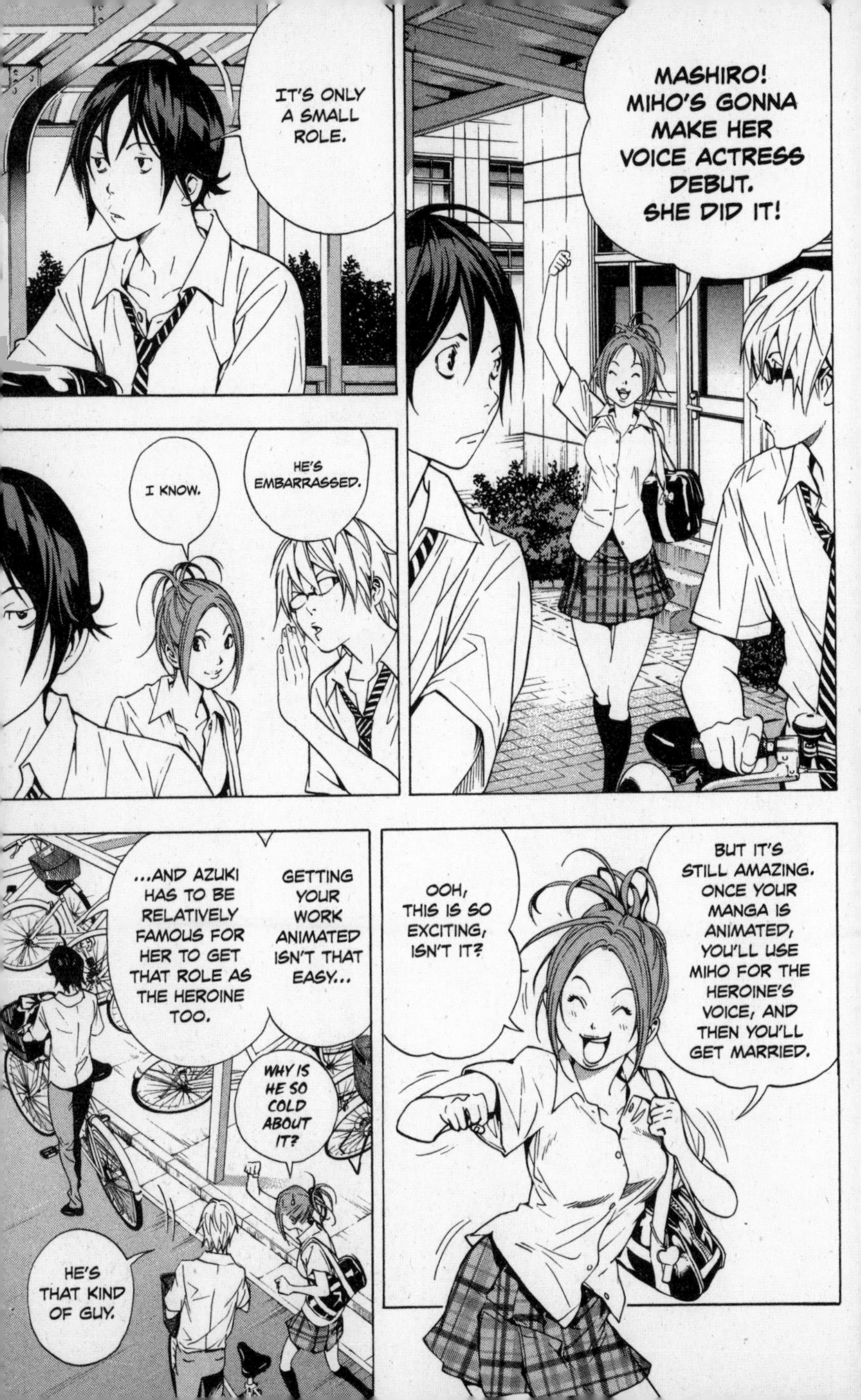
MASHIRO! MIHO'S GONNA MAKE HER VOICE ACTRESS DEBUT. SHE DID IT!
IT'S ONLY A SMALL ROLE.
HE'S EMBARRASSED.
I KNOW.
BUT IT'S STILL AMAZING. ONCE YOUR MANGA IS ANIMATED, YOU'LL USE MIHO FOR THE HEROINE'S VOICE, AND THEN YOU'LL GET MARRIED.
OOH, THIS IS SO EXCITING, ISN'T IT?
GETTING YOUR WORK ANIMATED ISN'T THAT EASY...
...AND AZUKI HAS TO BE RELATIVELY FAMOUS FOR HER TO GET THAT ROLE AS THE HEROINE TOO.
WHY IS HE SO COLD ABOUT IT?
HE'S THAT KIND OF GUY.

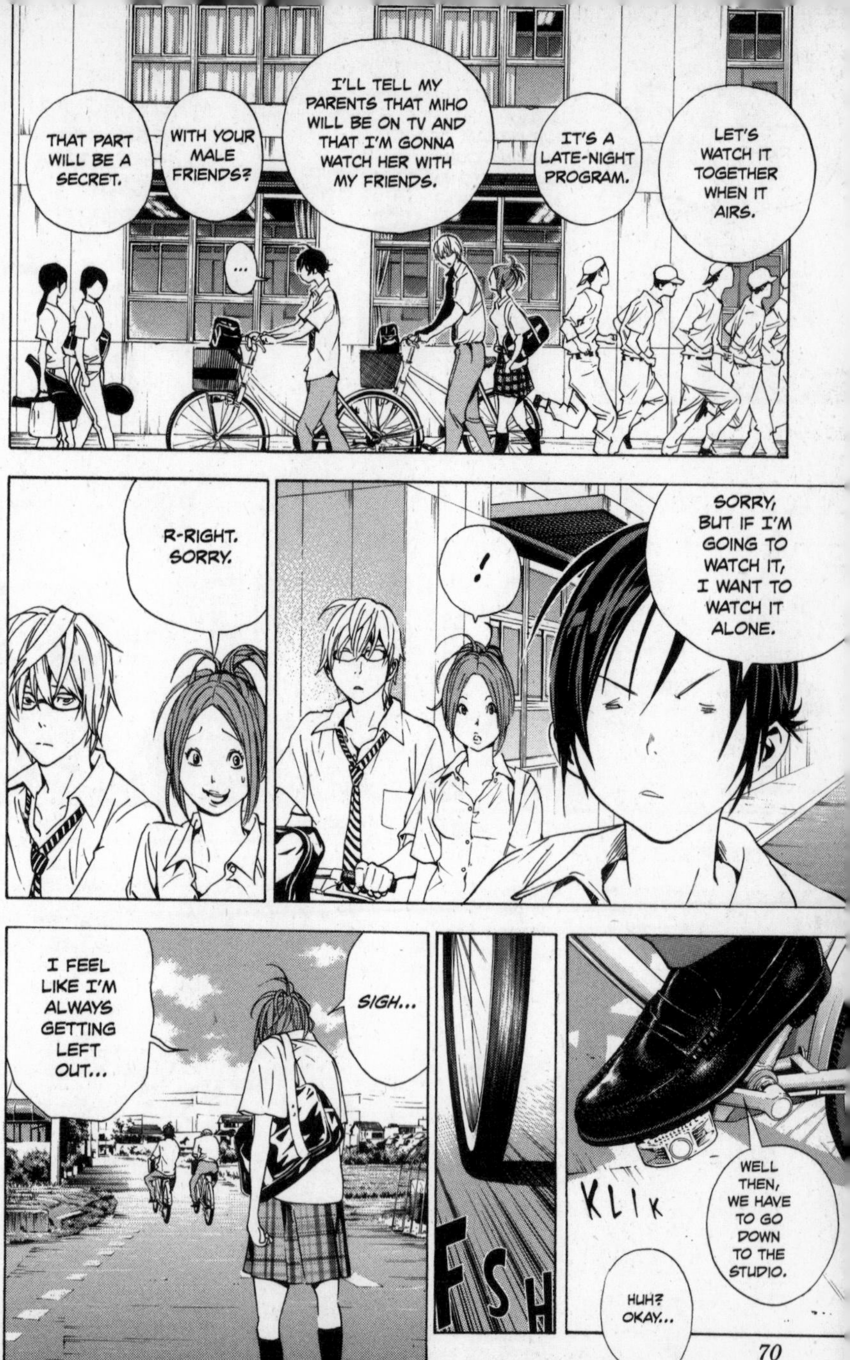
LET'S WATCH IT TOGETHER WHEN IT AIRS.
IT'S A LATE-NIGHT PROGRAM.
I'LL TELL MY PARENTS THAT MIHO WILL BE ON TV AND THAT I'M GONNA WATCH HER WITH MY FRIENDS.
WITH YOUR MALE FRIENDS?
THAT PART WILL BE A SECRET.
...
SORRY, BUT IF I'M GOING TO WATCH IT, I WANT TO WATCH IT ALONE.
!
R-RIGHT. SORRY.
KLIK
WELL THEN, WE HAVE TO GO DOWN TO THE STUDIO.
HUH? OKAY...
FSH
SIGH...
I FEEL LIKE I'M ALWAYS GETTING LEFT OUT...

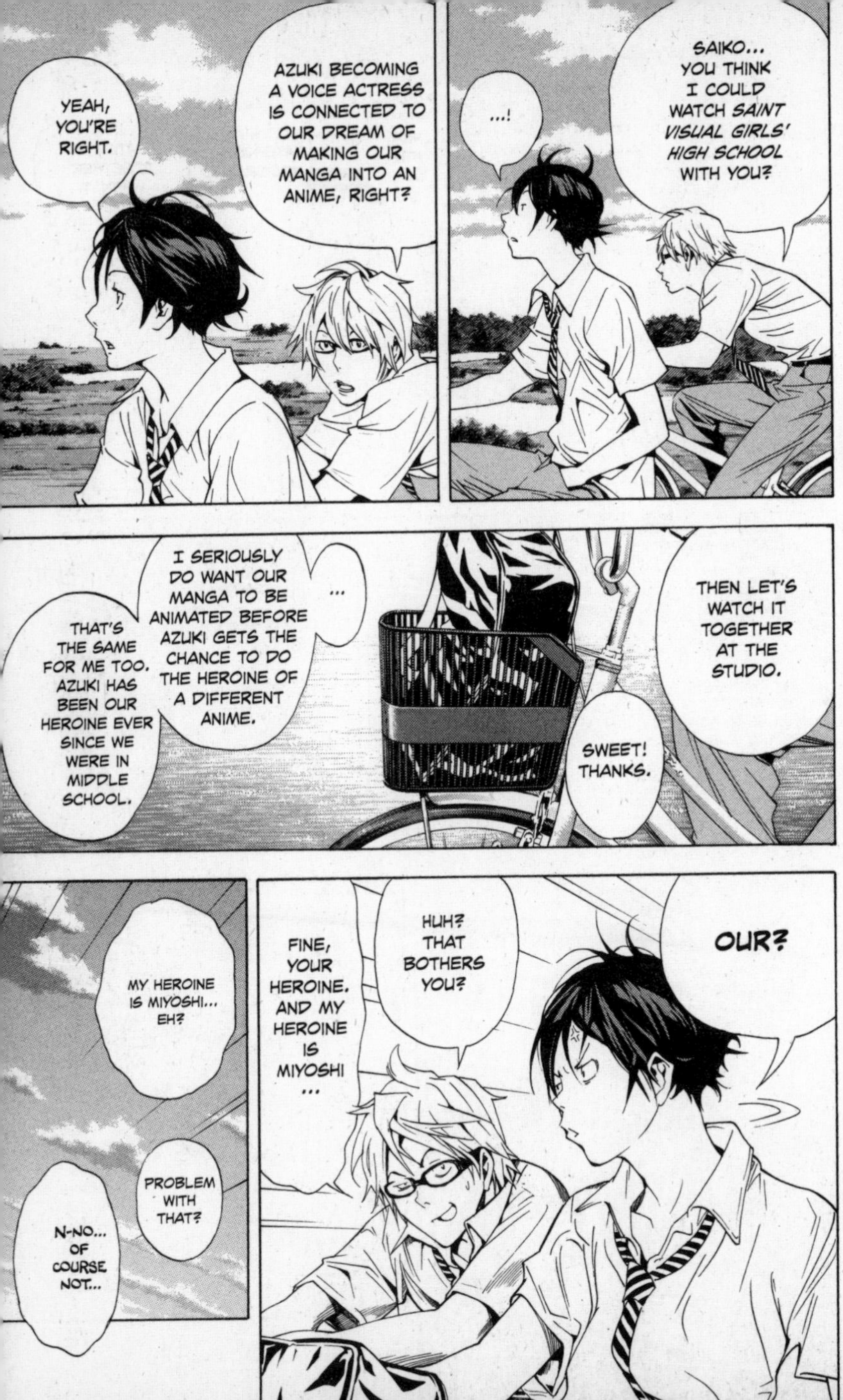
SAIKO... YOU THINK I COULD WATCH *SAINT VISUAL GIRLS' HIGH SCHOOL* WITH YOU?
...!
AZUKI BECOMING A VOICE ACTRESS IS CONNECTED TO OUR DREAM OF MAKING OUR MANGA INTO AN ANIME, RIGHT?
YEAH, YOU'RE RIGHT.
THEN LET'S WATCH IT TOGETHER AT THE STUDIO.
SWEET! THANKS.
...
I SERIOUSLY DO WANT OUR MANGA TO BE ANIMATED BEFORE AZUKI GETS THE CHANCE TO DO THE HEROINE OF A DIFFERENT ANIME.
THAT'S THE SAME FOR ME TOO. AZUKI HAS BEEN OUR HEROINE EVER SINCE WE WERE IN MIDDLE SCHOOL.
OUR?
HUH? THAT BOTHERS YOU?
FINE, YOUR HEROINE. AND MY HEROINE IS MIYOSHI...
MY HEROINE IS MIYOSHI... EH?
PROBLEM WITH THAT?
N-NO... OF COURSE NOT...

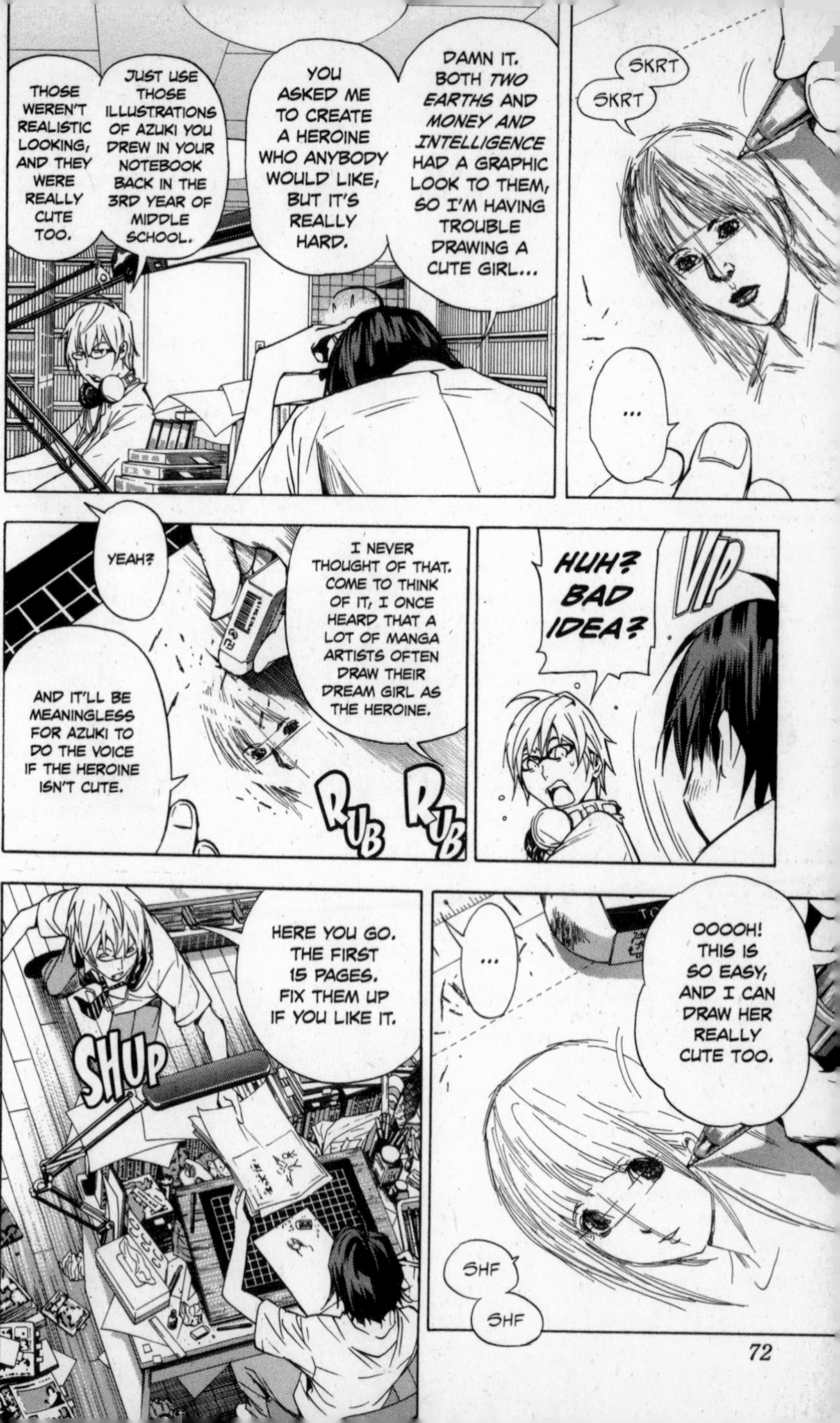
SKRT
SKRT
...
DAMN IT. BOTH *TWO EARTHS* AND *MONEY AND INTELLIGENCE* HAD A GRAPHIC LOOK TO THEM, SO I'M HAVING TROUBLE DRAWING A CUTE GIRL...
YOU ASKED ME TO CREATE A HEROINE WHO ANYBODY WOULD LIKE, BUT IT'S REALLY HARD.
JUST USE THOSE ILLUSTRATIONS OF AZUKI YOU DREW IN YOUR NOTEBOOK BACK IN THE 3RD YEAR OF MIDDLE SCHOOL.
THOSE WEREN'T REALISTIC LOOKING, AND THEY WERE REALLY CUTE TOO.
HUH? BAD IDEA?
I NEVER THOUGHT OF THAT. COME TO THINK OF IT, I ONCE HEARD THAT A LOT OF MANGA ARTISTS OFTEN DRAW THEIR DREAM GIRL AS THE HEROINE.
YEAH?
AND IT'LL BE MEANINGLESS FOR AZUKI TO DO THE VOICE IF THE HEROINE ISN'T CUTE.
RUB
RUB
OOOOH! THIS IS SO EASY, AND I CAN DRAW HER REALLY CUTE TOO.
...
SHF
SHF
HERE YOU GO. THE FIRST 15 PAGES. FIX THEM UP IF YOU LIKE IT.
SHUP

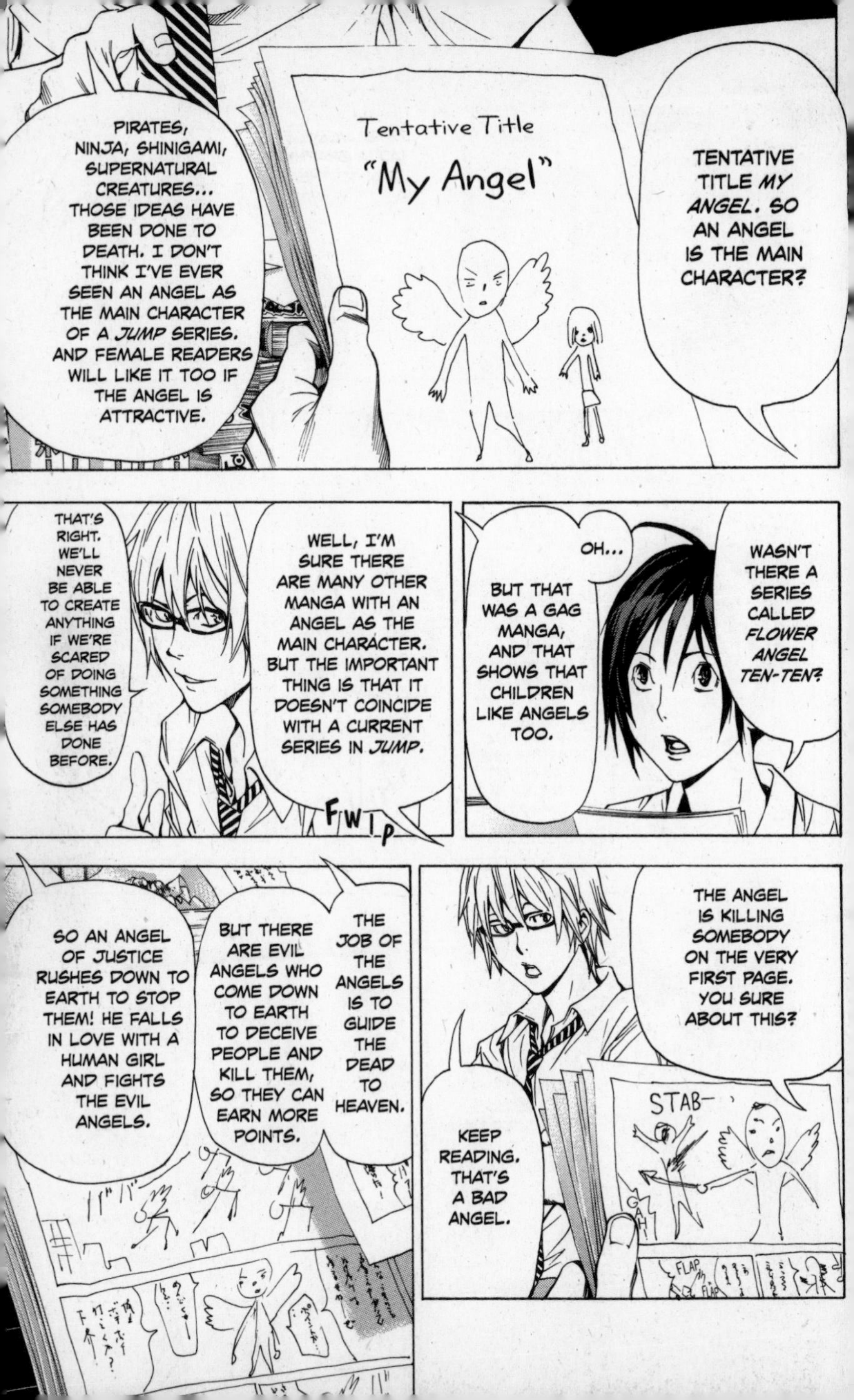
TENTATIVE TITLE MY ANGEL. SO AN ANGEL IS THE MAIN CHARACTER?
Tentative Title "My Angel"
PIRATES, NINJA, SHINIGAMI, SUPERNATURAL CREATURES... THOSE IDEAS HAVE BEEN DONE TO DEATH. I DON'T THINK I'VE EVER SEEN AN ANGEL AS THE MAIN CHARACTER OF A JUMP SERIES. AND FEMALE READERS WILL LIKE IT TOO IF THE ANGEL IS ATTRACTIVE.
WASN'T THERE A SERIES CALLED FLOWER ANGEL TEN-TEN?
OH...
BUT THAT WAS A GAG MANGA, AND THAT SHOWS THAT CHILDREN LIKE ANGELS TOO.
WELL, I'M SURE THERE ARE MANY OTHER MANGA WITH AN ANGEL AS THE MAIN CHARACTER. BUT THE IMPORTANT THING IS THAT IT DOESN'T COINCIDE WITH A CURRENT SERIES IN JUMP.
FWIP
THAT'S RIGHT. WE'LL NEVER BE ABLE TO CREATE ANYTHING IF WE'RE SCARED OF DOING SOMETHING SOMEBODY ELSE HAS DONE BEFORE.
THE ANGEL IS KILLING SOMEBODY ON THE VERY FIRST PAGE. YOU SURE ABOUT THIS?
STAB-
GAH!
FLAP FLAP
KEEP READING. THAT'S A BAD ANGEL.
THE JOB OF THE ANGELS IS TO GUIDE THE DEAD TO HEAVEN.
BUT THERE ARE EVIL ANGELS WHO COME DOWN TO EARTH TO DECEIVE PEOPLE AND KILL THEM, SO THEY CAN EARN MORE POINTS.
SO AN ANGEL OF JUSTICE RUSHES DOWN TO EARTH TO STOP THEM! HE FALLS IN LOVE WITH A HUMAN GIRL AND FIGHTS THE EVIL ANGELS.

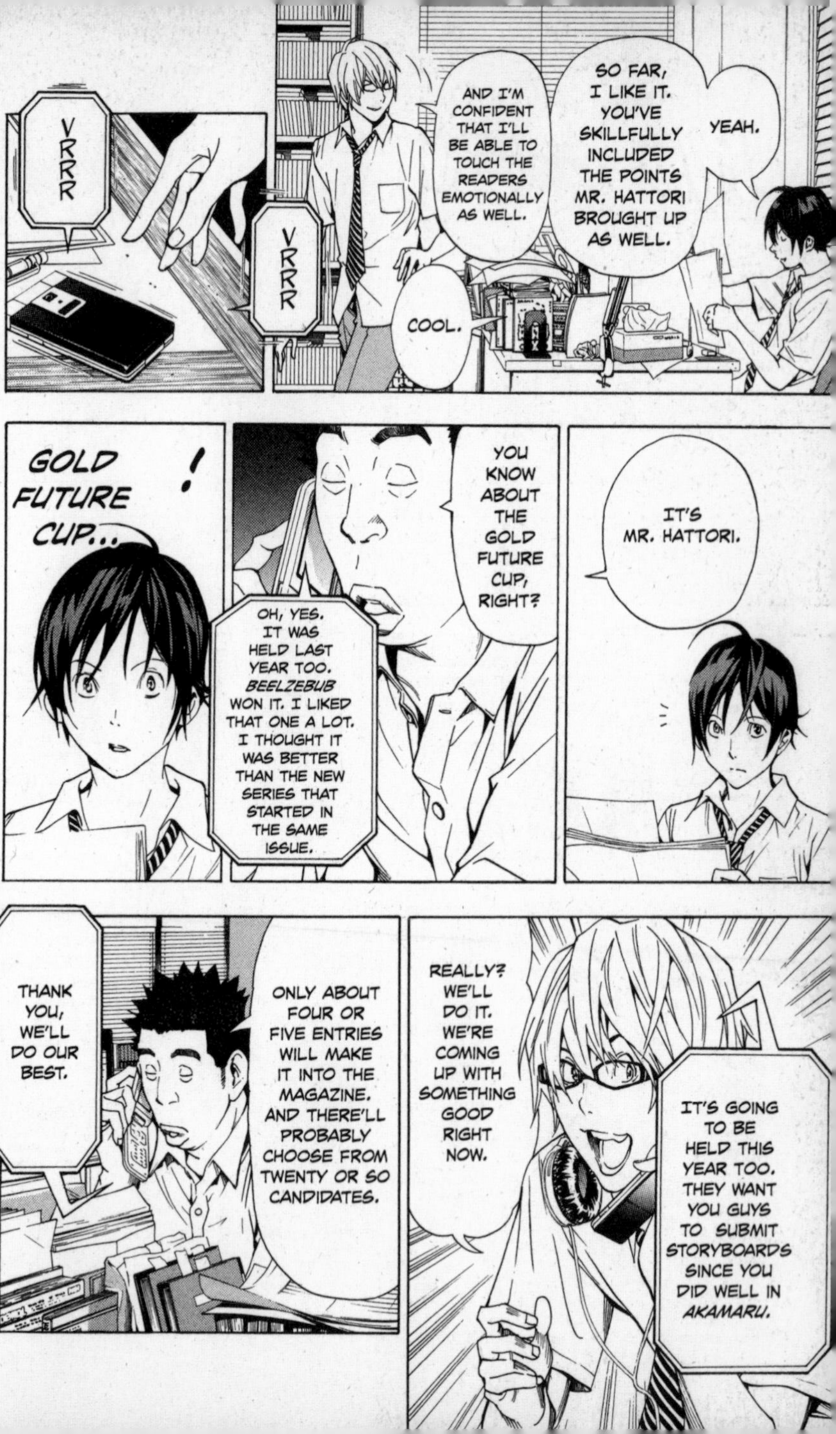

YEAH.
SO FAR, I LIKE IT. YOU'VE SKILLFULLY INCLUDED THE POINTS MR. HATTORI BROUGHT UP AS WELL.
AND I'M CONFIDENT THAT I'LL BE ABLE TO TOUCH THE READERS EMOTIONALLY AS WELL.
COOL.
VRRR
VRRR
IT'S MR. HATTORI.
YOU KNOW ABOUT THE GOLD FUTURE CUP, RIGHT?
OH, YES. IT WAS HELD LAST YEAR TOO. *BEELZEBUB* WON IT. I LIKED THAT ONE A LOT. I THOUGHT IT WAS BETTER THAN THE NEW SERIES THAT STARTED IN THE SAME ISSUE.
GOLD FUTURE CUP...
!
IT'S GOING TO BE HELD THIS YEAR TOO. THEY WANT YOU GUYS TO SUBMIT STORYBOARDS SINCE YOU DID WELL IN *AKAMARU*.
REALLY? WE'LL DO IT. WE'RE COMING UP WITH SOMETHING GOOD RIGHT NOW.
ONLY ABOUT FOUR OR FIVE ENTRIES WILL MAKE IT INTO THE MAGAZINE. AND THERE'LL PROBABLY CHOOSE FROM TWENTY OR SO CANDIDATES.
THANK YOU, WE'LL DO OUR BEST.

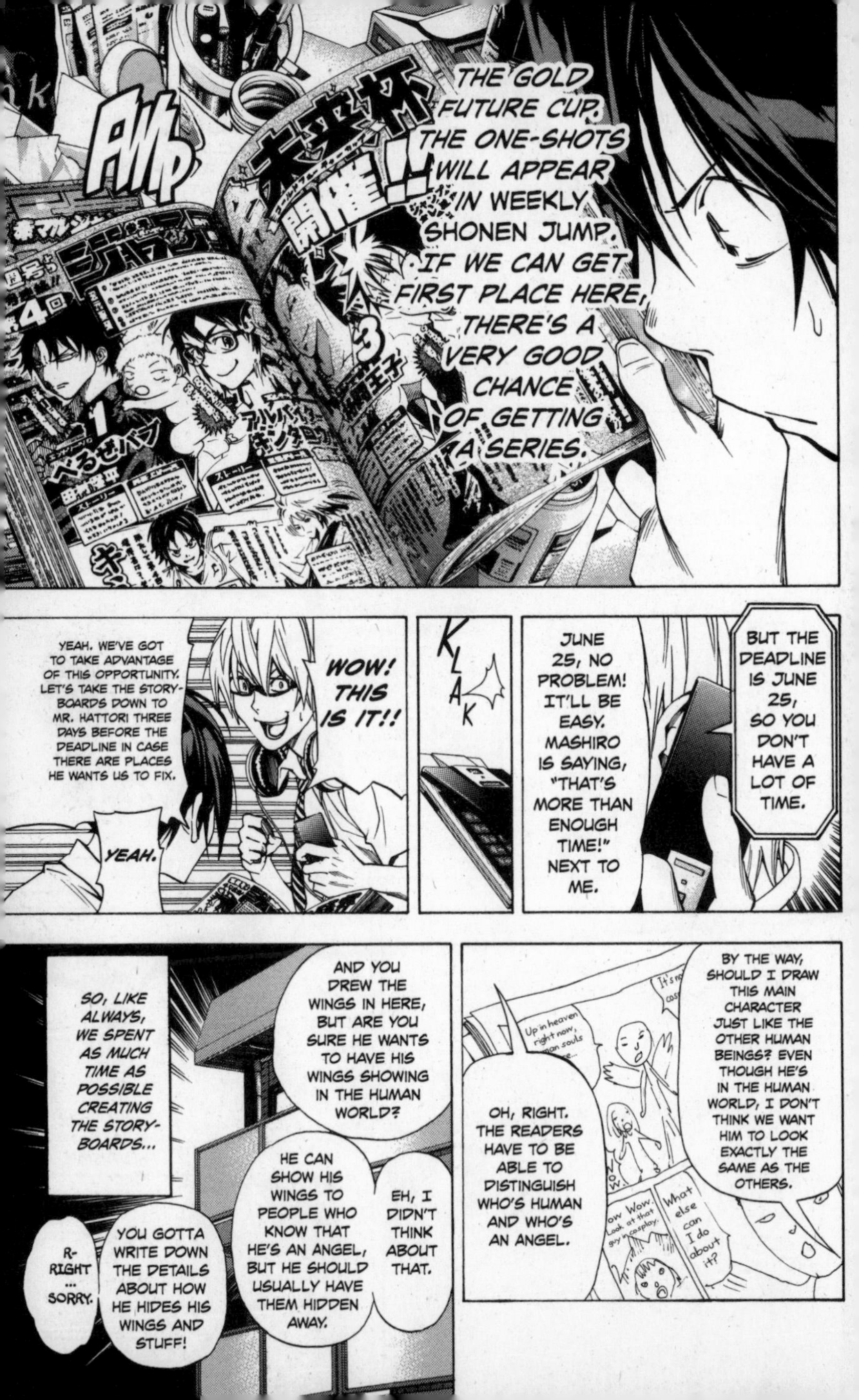
PWMP
THE GOLD FUTURE CUP. THE ONE-SHOTS WILL APPEAR IN WEEKLY SHONEN JUMP. IF WE CAN GET FIRST PLACE HERE, THERE'S A VERY GOOD CHANCE OF GETTING A SERIES.
BUT THE DEADLINE IS JUNE 25, SO YOU DON'T HAVE A LOT OF TIME.
JUNE 25, NO PROBLEM! IT'LL BE EASY. MASHIRO IS SAYING, "THAT'S MORE THAN ENOUGH TIME!" NEXT TO ME.
KLAK
WOW! THIS IS IT!!
YEAH. WE'VE GOT TO TAKE ADVANTAGE OF THIS OPPORTUNITY. LET'S TAKE THE STORY-BOARDS DOWN TO MR. HATTORI THREE DAYS BEFORE THE DEADLINE IN CASE THERE ARE PLACES HE WANTS US TO FIX.
YEAH.
BY THE WAY, SHOULD I DRAW THIS MAIN CHARACTER JUST LIKE THE OTHER HUMAN BEINGS? EVEN THOUGH HE'S IN THE HUMAN WORLD, I DON'T THINK WE WANT HIM TO LOOK EXACTLY THE SAME AS THE OTHERS.
Wow Wow. Look at that guy in cosplay.
What else can I do about it?
OH, RIGHT. THE READERS HAVE TO BE ABLE TO DISTINGUISH WHO'S HUMAN AND WHO'S AN ANGEL.
AND YOU DREW THE WINGS IN HERE, BUT ARE YOU SURE HE WANTS TO HAVE HIS WINGS SHOWING IN THE HUMAN WORLD?
SO, LIKE ALWAYS, WE SPENT AS MUCH TIME AS POSSIBLE CREATING THE STORY-BOARDS...
EH, I DIDN'T THINK ABOUT THAT.
HE CAN SHOW HIS WINGS TO PEOPLE WHO KNOW THAT HE'S AN ANGEL, BUT HE SHOULD USUALLY HAVE THEM HIDDEN AWAY.
YOU GOTTA WRITE DOWN THE DETAILS ABOUT HOW HE HIDES HIS WINGS AND STUFF!
R-RIGHT... SORRY.

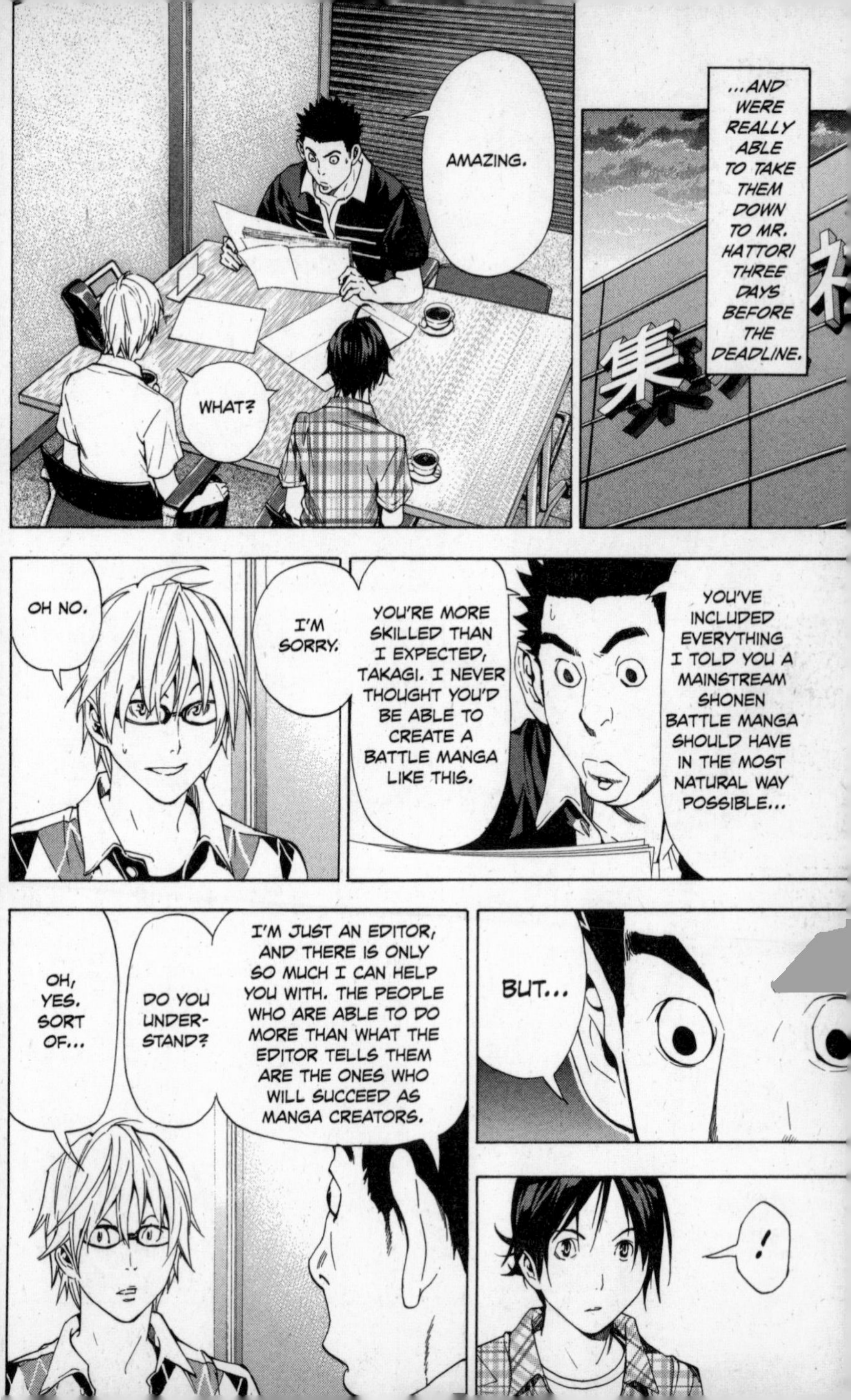
...AND WERE REALLY ABLE TO TAKE THEM DOWN TO MR. HATTORI THREE DAYS BEFORE THE DEADLINE.
AMAZING.
WHAT?
YOU'VE INCLUDED EVERYTHING I TOLD YOU A MAINSTREAM SHONEN BATTLE MANGA SHOULD HAVE IN THE MOST NATURAL WAY POSSIBLE...
YOU'RE MORE SKILLED THAN I EXPECTED, TAKAGI. I NEVER THOUGHT YOU'D BE ABLE TO CREATE A BATTLE MANGA LIKE THIS.
I'M SORRY.
OH NO.
BUT...
!
I'M JUST AN EDITOR, AND THERE IS ONLY SO MUCH I CAN HELP YOU WITH. THE PEOPLE WHO ARE ABLE TO DO MORE THAN WHAT THE EDITOR TELLS THEM ARE THE ONES WHO WILL SUCCEED AS MANGA CREATORS.
DO YOU UNDER-STAND?
OH, YES. SORT OF...

READ THIS WAY

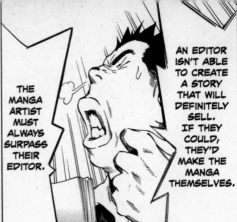

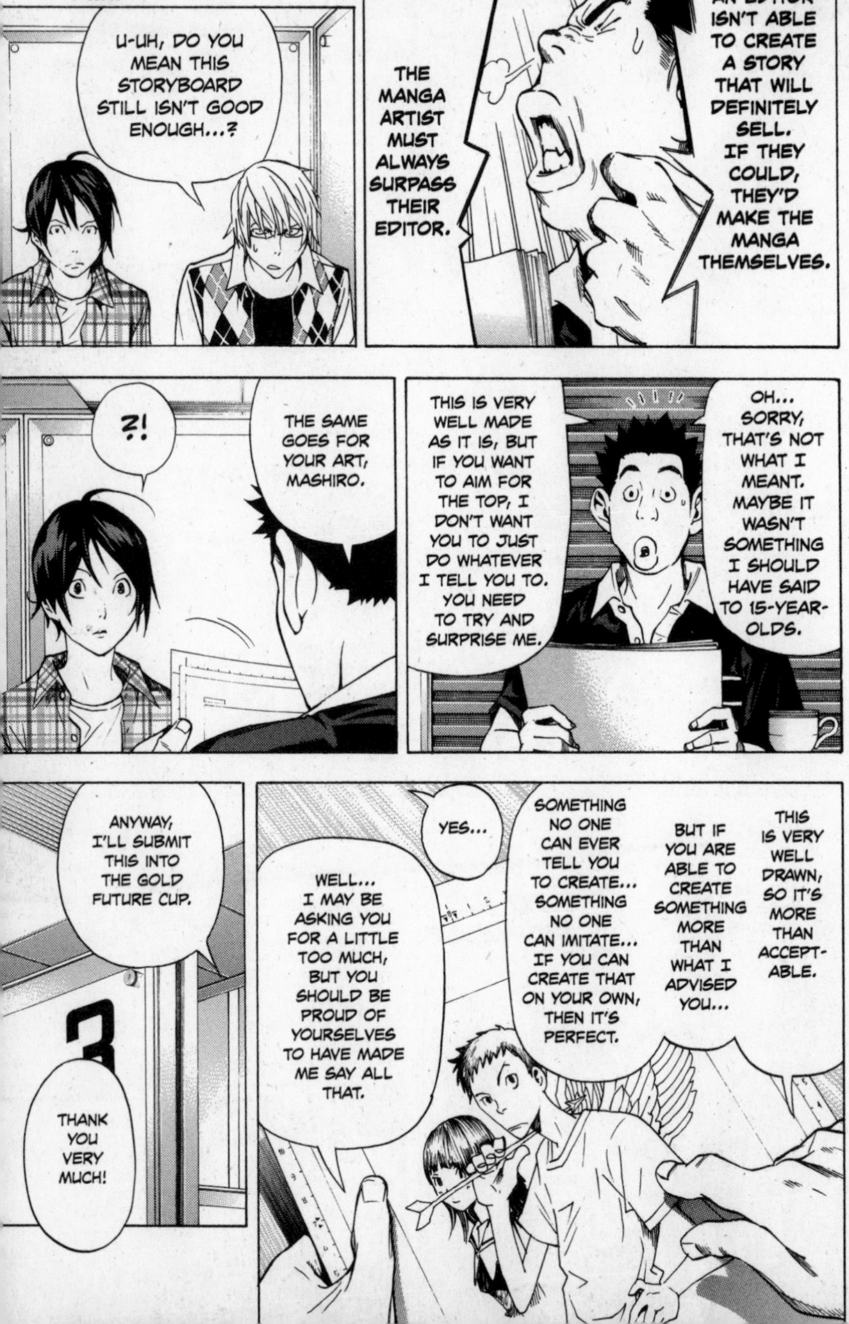
AN EDITOR ISN'T ABLE TO CREATE A STORY THAT WILL DEFINITELY SELL. IF THEY COULD, THEY'D MAKE THE MANGA THEMSELVES.
THE MANGA ARTIST MUST ALWAYS SURPASS THEIR EDITOR.
U-UH, DO YOU MEAN THIS STORYBOARD STILL ISN'T GOOD ENOUGH...?
OH... SORRY, THAT'S NOT WHAT I MEANT. MAYBE IT WASN'T SOMETHING I SHOULD HAVE SAID TO 15-YEAR-OLDS.
THIS IS VERY WELL MADE AS IT IS, BUT IF YOU WANT TO AIM FOR THE TOP, I DON'T WANT YOU TO JUST DO WHATEVER I TELL YOU TO. YOU NEED TO TRY AND SURPRISE ME.
THE SAME GOES FOR YOUR ART, MASHIRO.
?!
THIS IS VERY WELL DRAWN, SO IT'S MORE THAN ACCEPT-ABLE.
BUT IF YOU ARE ABLE TO CREATE SOMETHING MORE THAN WHAT I ADVISED YOU...
SOMETHING NO ONE CAN EVER TELL YOU TO CREATE... SOMETHING NO ONE CAN IMITATE... IF YOU CAN CREATE THAT ON YOUR OWN, THEN IT'S PERFECT.
YES...
WELL... I MAY BE ASKING YOU FOR A LITTLE TOO MUCH, BUT YOU SHOULD BE PROUD OF YOURSELVES TO HAVE MADE ME SAY ALL THAT.
ANYWAY, I'LL SUBMIT THIS INTO THE GOLD FUTURE CUP.
THANK YOU VERY MUCH!

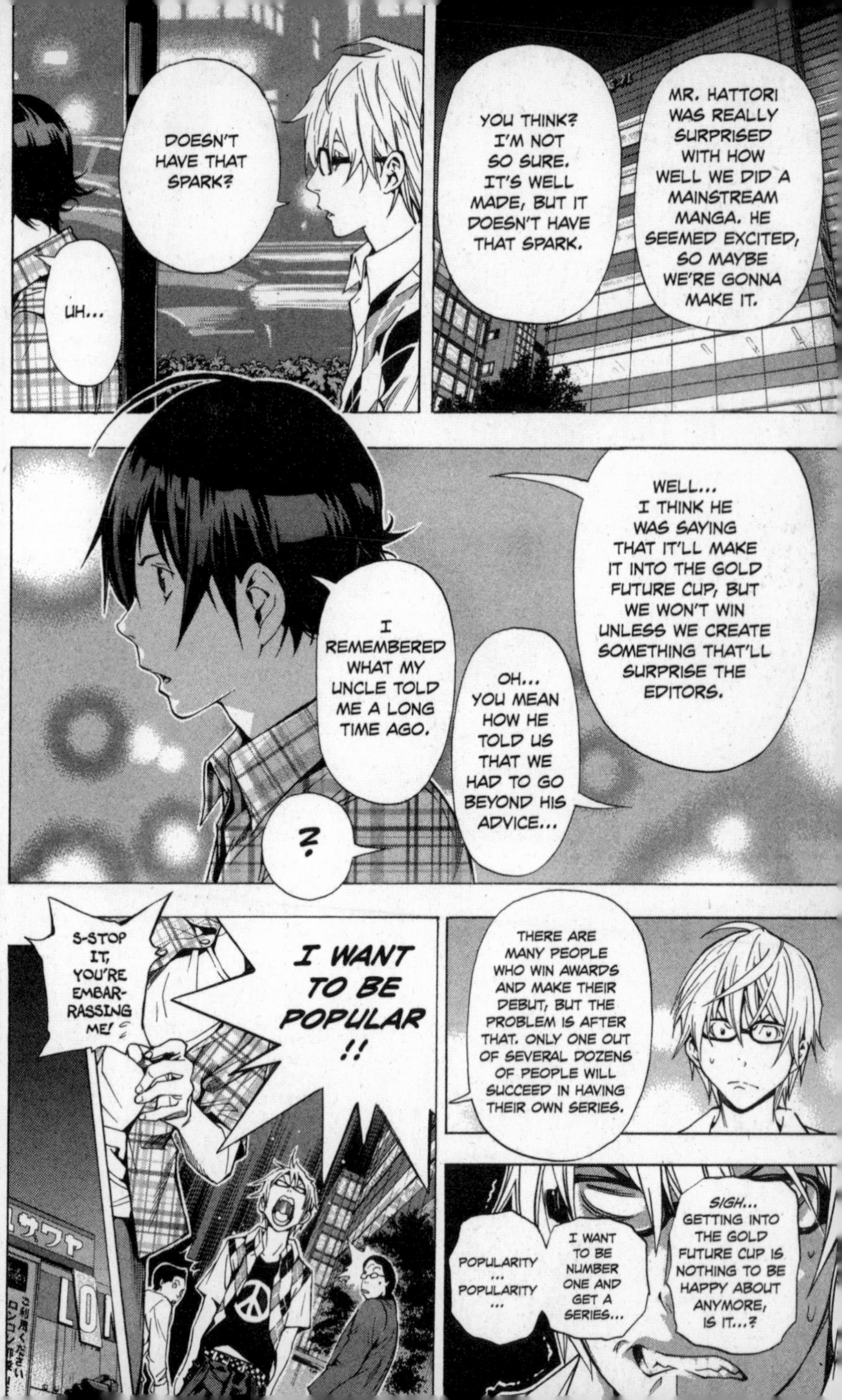
MR. HATTORI WAS REALLY SURPRISED WITH HOW WELL WE DID A MAINSTREAM MANGA. HE SEEMED EXCITED, SO MAYBE WE'RE GONNA MAKE IT.
YOU THINK? I'M NOT SO SURE. IT'S WELL MADE, BUT IT DOESN'T HAVE THAT SPARK.
DOESN'T HAVE THAT SPARK?
UH...
WELL... I THINK HE WAS SAYING THAT IT'LL MAKE IT INTO THE GOLD FUTURE CUP, BUT WE WON'T WIN UNLESS WE CREATE SOMETHING THAT'LL SURPRISE THE EDITORS.
OH... YOU MEAN HOW HE TOLD US THAT WE HAD TO GO BEYOND HIS ADVICE...
I REMEMBERED WHAT MY UNCLE TOLD ME A LONG TIME AGO.
?
THERE ARE MANY PEOPLE WHO WIN AWARDS AND MAKE THEIR DEBUT, BUT THE PROBLEM IS AFTER THAT. ONLY ONE OUT OF SEVERAL DOZENS OF PEOPLE WILL SUCCEED IN HAVING THEIR OWN SERIES.
SIGH... GETTING INTO THE GOLD FUTURE CUP IS NOTHING TO BE HAPPY ABOUT ANYMORE, IS IT...?
I WANT TO BE NUMBER ONE AND GET A SERIES...
POPULARITY... POPULARITY...
I WANT TO BE POPULAR!!
S-STOP IT, YOU'RE EMBARRASSING ME!

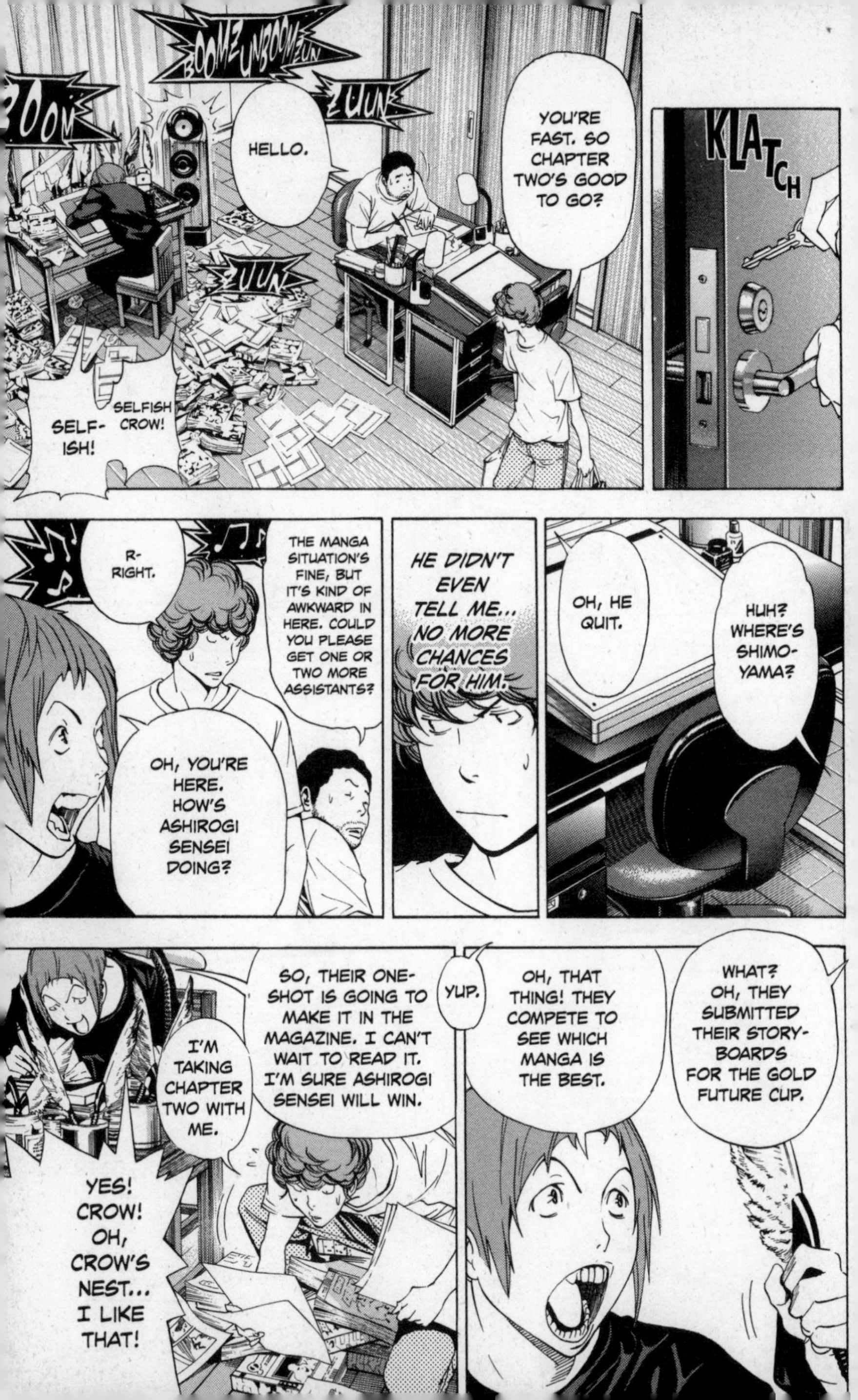
KLATCH
YOU'RE FAST. SO CHAPTER TWO'S GOOD TO GO?
ZUUN
HELLO.
BOOMZUNBOOMZUN
ZOOM
ZUUN
SELFISH CROW!
SELF-ISH!
HUH? WHERE'S SHIMO-YAMA?
OH, HE QUIT.
HE DIDN'T EVEN TELL ME... NO MORE CHANCES FOR HIM.
THE MANGA SITUATION'S FINE, BUT IT'S KIND OF AWKWARD IN HERE. COULD YOU PLEASE GET ONE OR TWO MORE ASSISTANTS?
R-RIGHT.
OH, YOU'RE HERE. HOW'S ASHIROGI SENSEI DOING?
WHAT? OH, THEY SUBMITTED THEIR STORY-BOARDS FOR THE GOLD FUTURE CUP.
OH, THAT THING! THEY COMPETE TO SEE WHICH MANGA IS THE BEST.
YUP.
SO, THEIR ONE-SHOT IS GOING TO MAKE IT IN THE MAGAZINE. I CAN'T WAIT TO READ IT. I'M SURE ASHIROGI SENSEI WILL WIN.
I'M TAKING CHAPTER TWO WITH ME.
YES! CROW! OH, CROW'S NEST... I LIKE THAT!

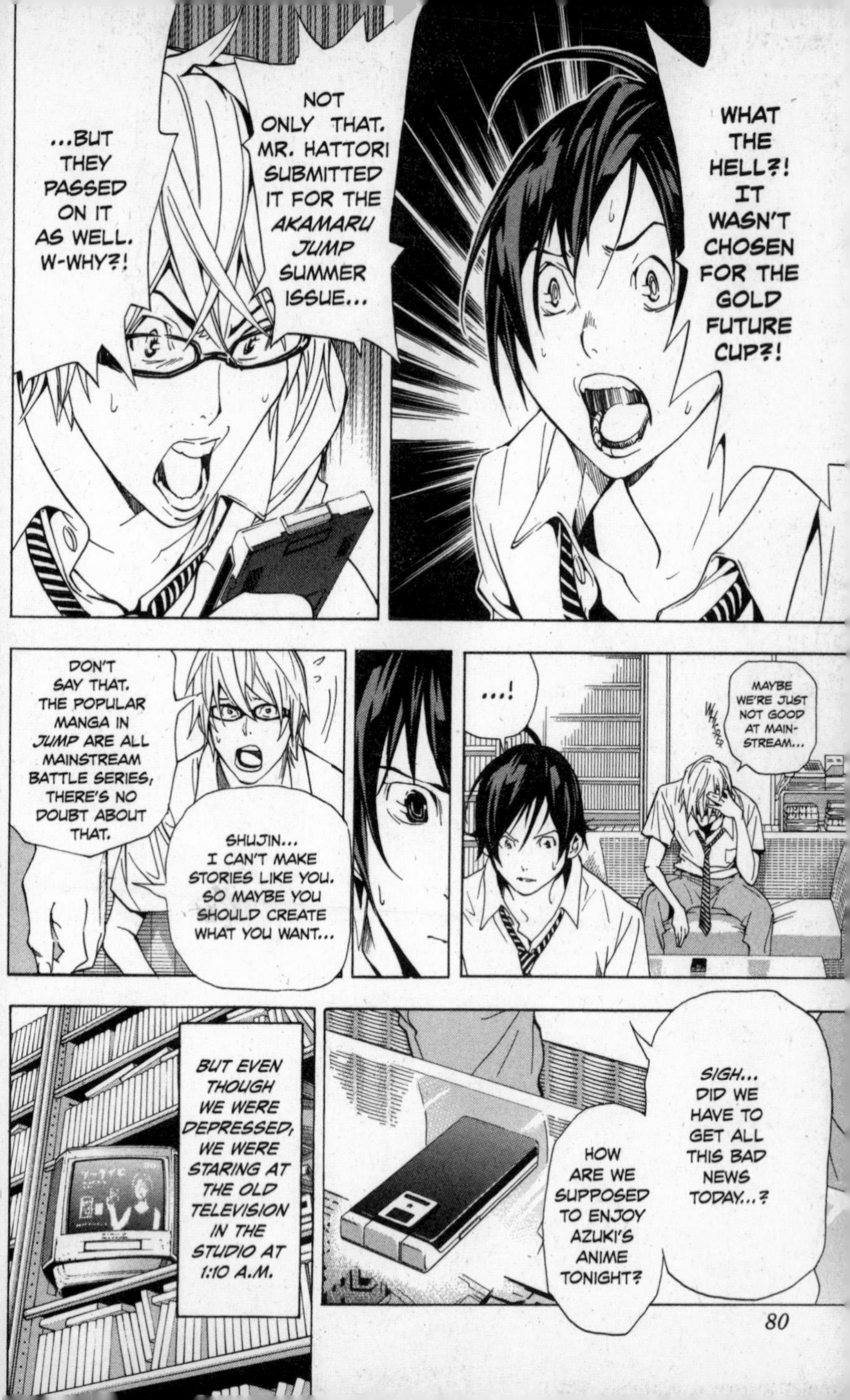
WHAT THE HELL?! IT WASN'T CHOSEN FOR THE GOLD FUTURE CUP?!
NOT ONLY THAT. MR. HATTORI SUBMITTED IT FOR THE AKAMARU JUMP SUMMER ISSUE...
...BUT THEY PASSED ON IT AS WELL. W-WHY?!
MAYBE WE'RE JUST NOT GOOD AT MAIN-STREAM...
WHISPER
...!
SHUJIN... I CAN'T MAKE STORIES LIKE YOU. SO MAYBE YOU SHOULD CREATE WHAT YOU WANT...
DON'T SAY THAT. THE POPULAR MANGA IN JUMP ARE ALL MAINSTREAM BATTLE SERIES, THERE'S NO DOUBT ABOUT THAT.
SIGH... DID WE HAVE TO GET ALL THIS BAD NEWS TODAY...?
HOW ARE WE SUPPOSED TO ENJOY AZUKI'S ANIME TONIGHT?
BUT EVEN THOUGH WE WERE DEPRESSED, WE WERE STARING AT THE OLD TELEVISION IN THE STUDIO AT 1:10 A.M.

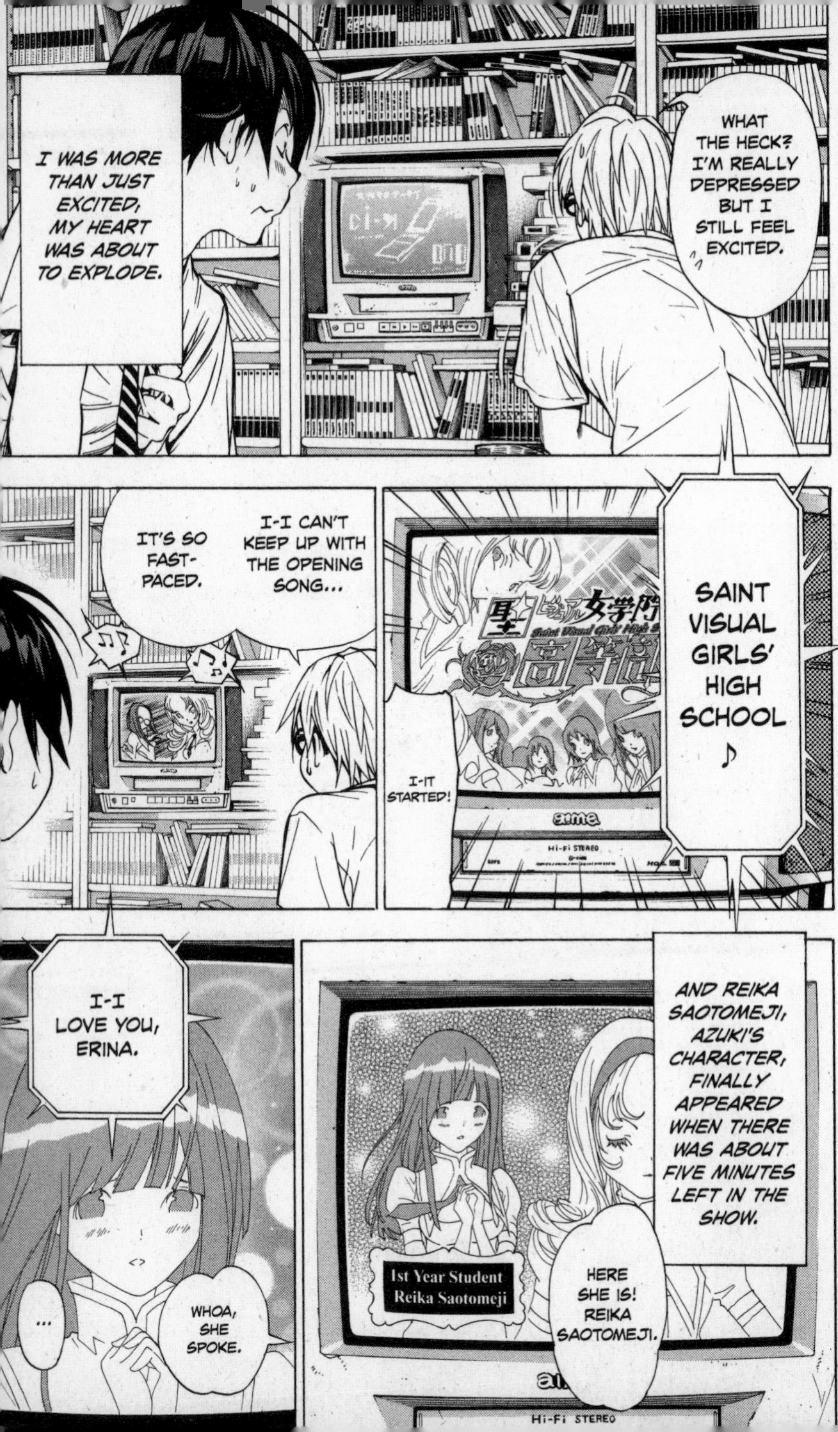

WHAT THE HECK? I'M REALLY DEPRESSED BUT I STILL FEEL EXCITED.
I WAS MORE THAN JUST EXCITED, MY HEART WAS ABOUT TO EXPLODE.
SAINT VISUAL GIRLS' HIGH SCHOOL ♪
I-IT STARTED!
I-I CAN'T KEEP UP WITH THE OPENING SONG...
IT'S SO FAST-PACED.
AND REIKA SAOTOMEJI, AZUKI'S CHARACTER, FINALLY APPEARED WHEN THERE WAS ABOUT FIVE MINUTES LEFT IN THE SHOW.
1st Year Student Reika Saotomeji
HERE SHE IS! REIKA SAOTOMEJI.
I-I LOVE YOU, ERINA.
WHOA, SHE SPOKE.
...

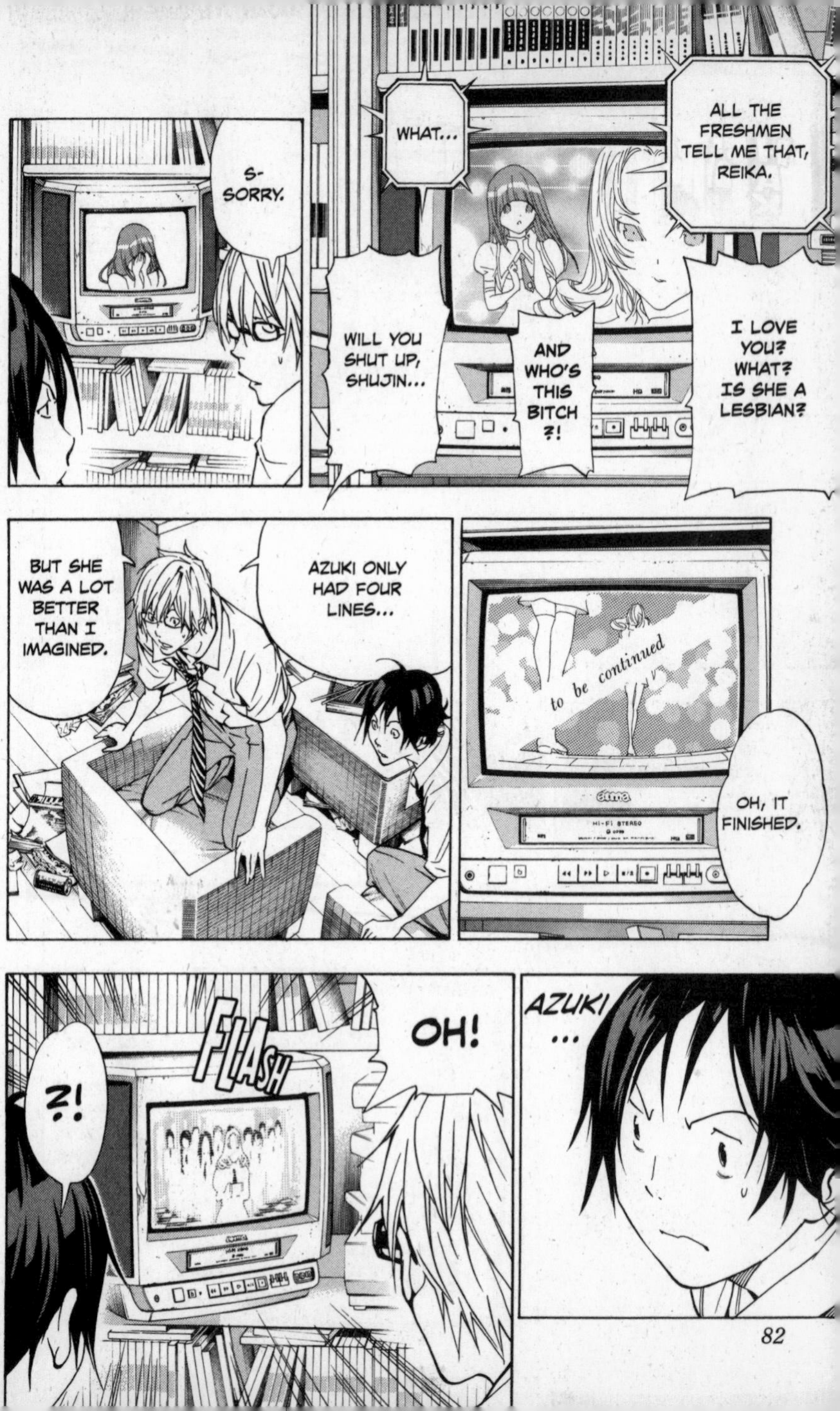

ALL THE FRESHMEN TELL ME THAT, REIKA.
WHAT...
I LOVE YOU? WHAT? IS SHE A LESBIAN?
AND WHO'S THIS BITCH ?!
WILL YOU SHUT UP, SHUJIN...
S-SORRY.
to be continued
OH, IT FINISHED.
AZUKI ONLY HAD FOUR LINES...
BUT SHE WAS A LOT BETTER THAN I IMAGINED.
AZUKI ...
OH!
FLASH
?!

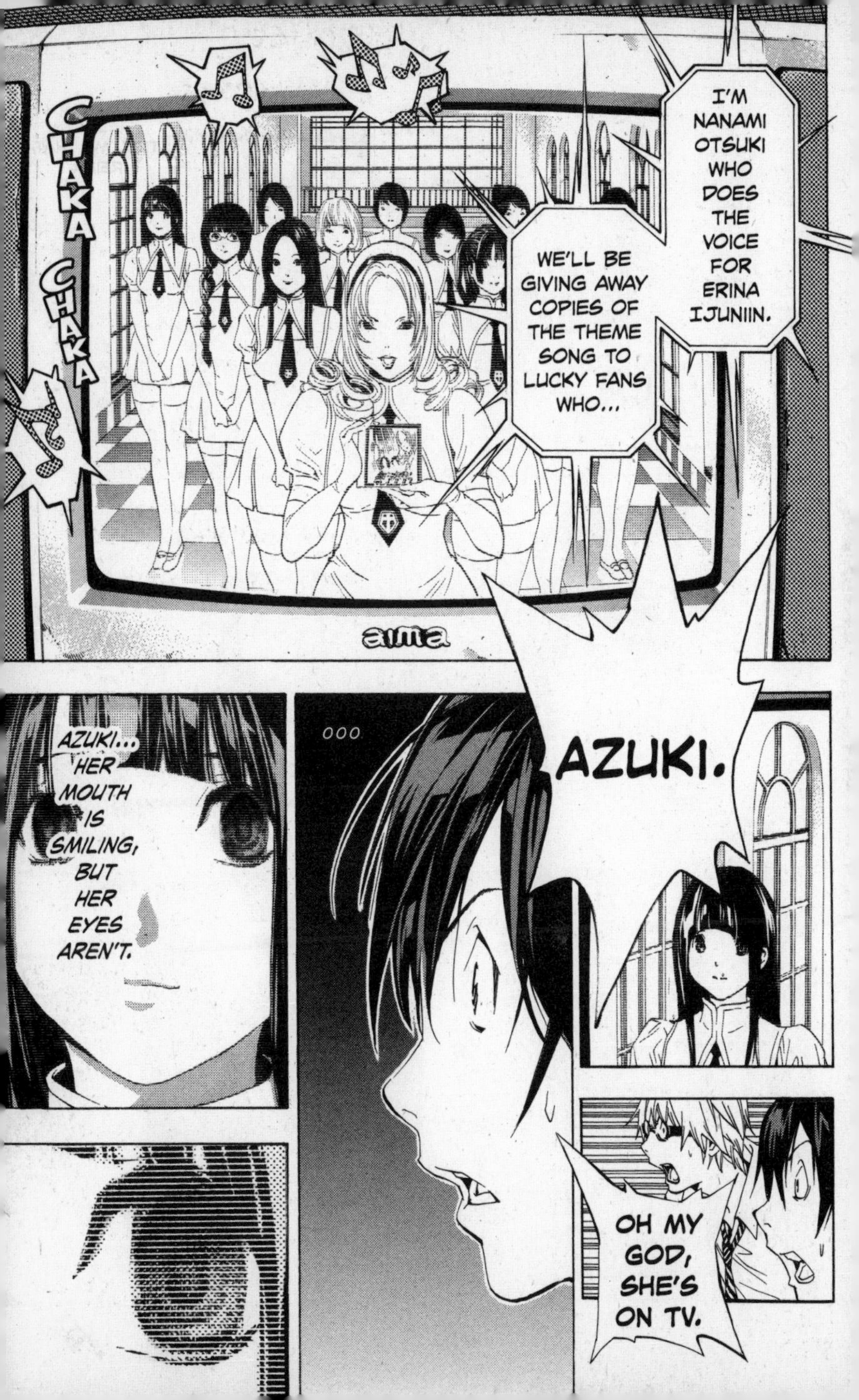
I'M NANAMI OTSUKI WHO DOES THE VOICE FOR ERINA IJUNIIN.
WE'LL BE GIVING AWAY COPIES OF THE THEME SONG TO LUCKY FANS WHO...
CHAKA CHAKA
aima
AZUKI.
ooo.
AZUKI... HER MOUTH IS SMILING, BUT HER EYES AREN'T.
OH MY GOD, SHE'S ON TV.

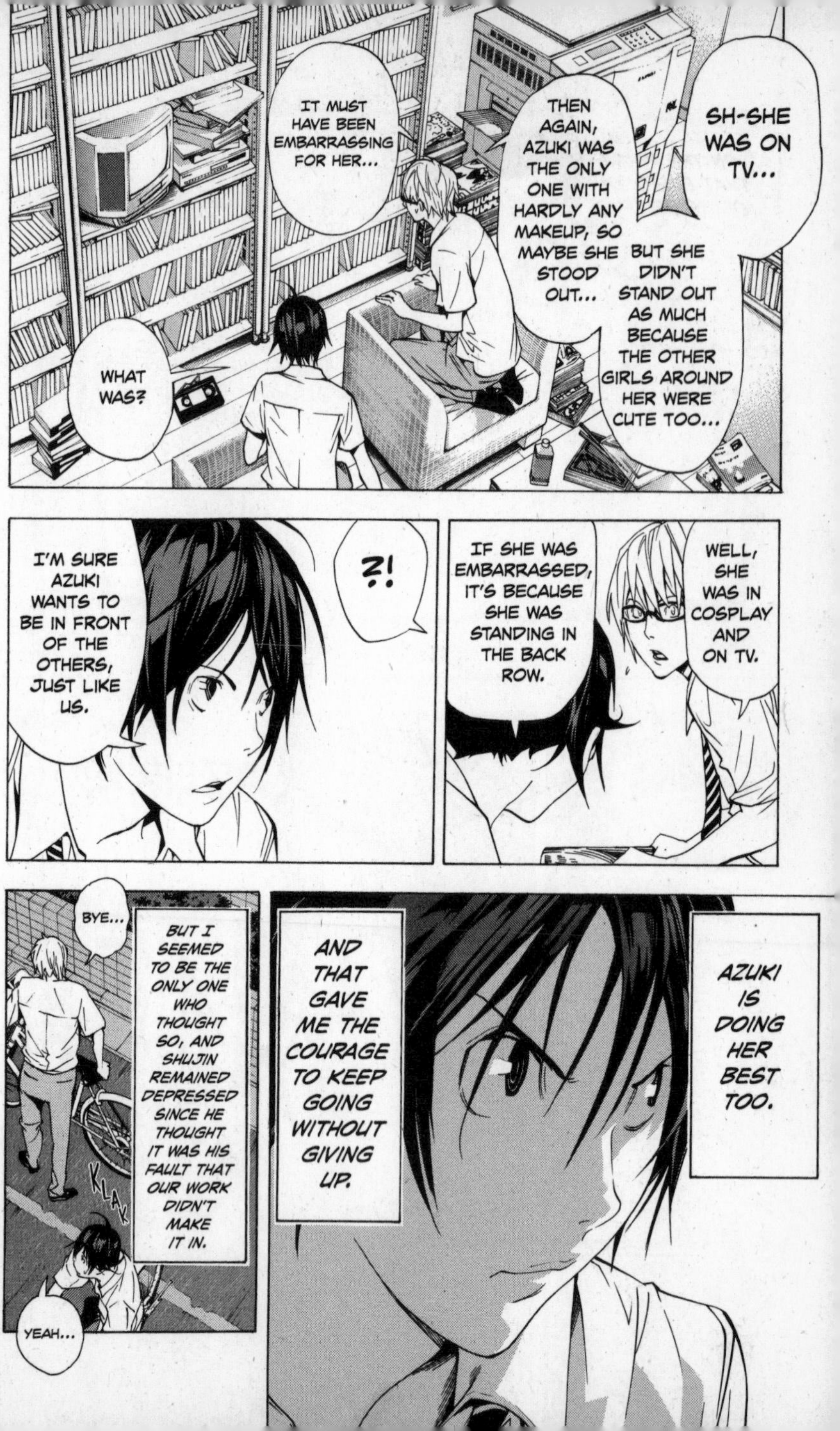
SH-SHE WAS ON TV...
THEN AGAIN, AZUKI WAS THE ONLY ONE WITH HARDLY ANY MAKEUP, SO MAYBE SHE STOOD OUT...
BUT SHE DIDN'T STAND OUT AS MUCH BECAUSE THE OTHER GIRLS AROUND HER WERE CUTE TOO...
IT MUST HAVE BEEN EMBARRASSING FOR HER...
WHAT WAS?
WELL, SHE WAS IN COSPLAY AND ON TV.
IF SHE WAS EMBARRASSED, IT'S BECAUSE SHE WAS STANDING IN THE BACK ROW.
?!
I'M SURE AZUKI WANTS TO BE IN FRONT OF THE OTHERS, JUST LIKE US.
AZUKI IS DOING HER BEST TOO.
AND THAT GAVE ME THE COURAGE TO KEEP GOING WITHOUT GIVING UP.
BYE...
BUT I SEEMED TO BE THE ONLY ONE WHO THOUGHT SO, AND SHUJIN REMAINED DEPRESSED SINCE HE THOUGHT IT WAS HIS FAULT THAT OUR WORK DIDN'T MAKE IT IN.
KLAK
YEAH...

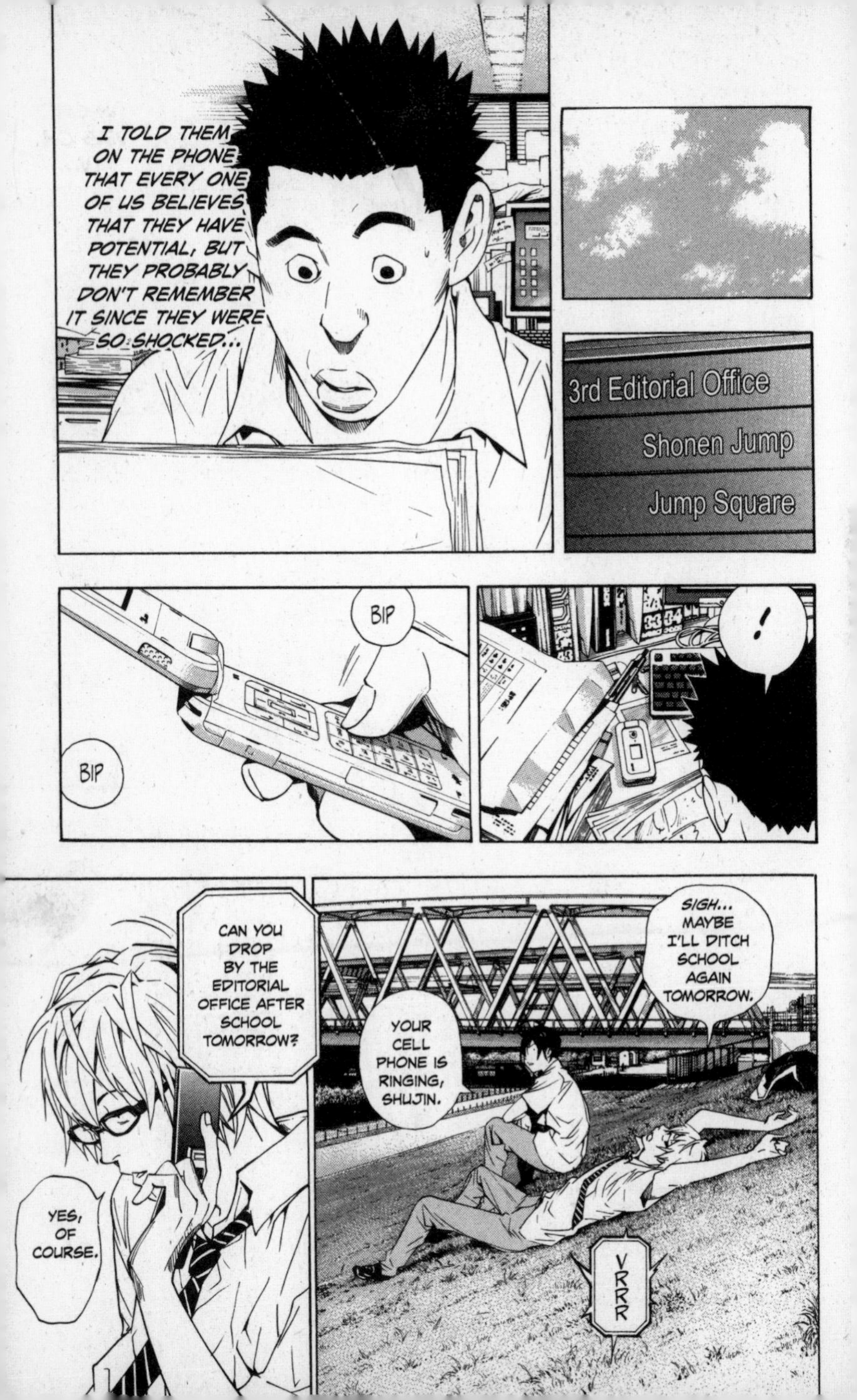
3rd Editorial Office
Shonen Jump
Jump Square
I TOLD THEM ON THE PHONE THAT EVERY ONE OF US BELIEVES THAT THEY HAVE POTENTIAL, BUT THEY PROBABLY DON'T REMEMBER IT SINCE THEY WERE SO SHOCKED...
!
BIP
BIP
SIGH... MAYBE I'LL DITCH SCHOOL AGAIN TOMORROW.
YOUR CELL PHONE IS RINGING, SHUJIN.
VRRR
CAN YOU DROP BY THE EDITORIAL OFFICE AFTER SCHOOL TOMORROW?
YES, OF COURSE.

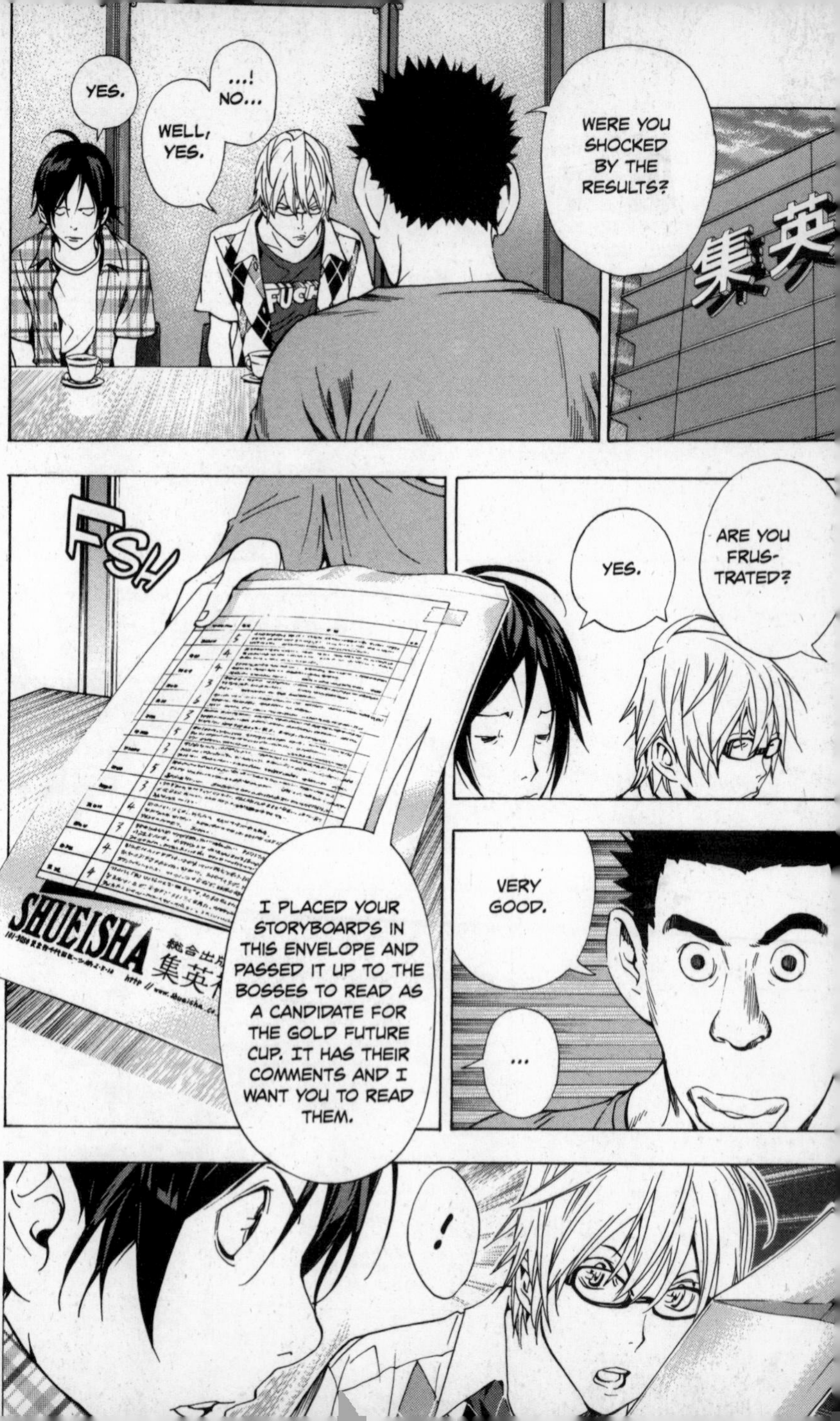
集英
WERE YOU SHOCKED BY THE RESULTS?
...! NO... WELL, YES.
YES.
ARE YOU FRUS-TRATED?
YES.
VERY GOOD.
...
FSH
SHUEISHA
I PLACED YOUR STORYBOARDS IN THIS ENVELOPE AND PASSED IT UP TO THE BOSSES TO READ AS A CANDIDATE FOR THE GOLD FUTURE CUP. IT HAS THEIR COMMENTS AND I WANT YOU TO READ THEM.
!

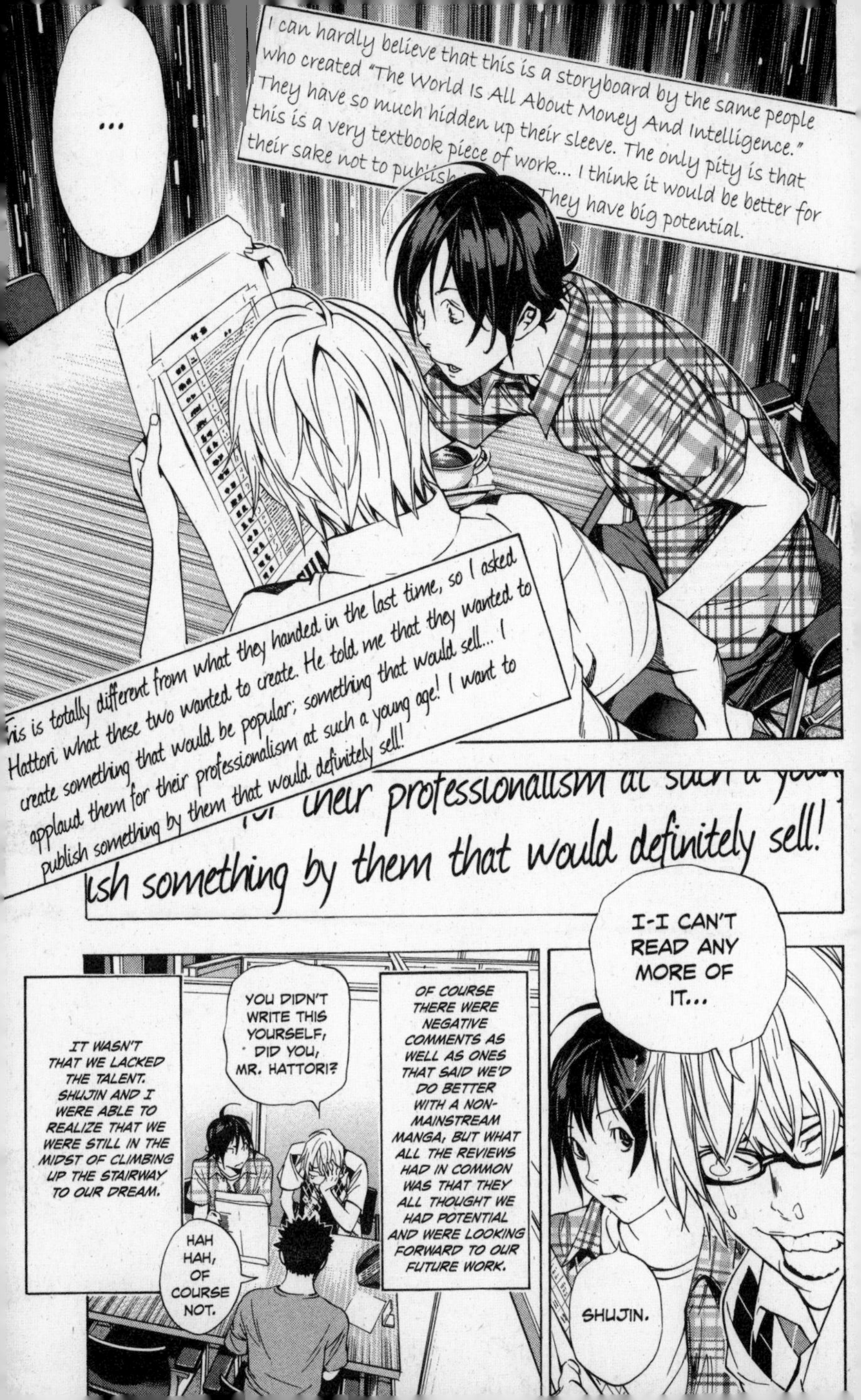
I can hardly believe that this is a storyboard by the same people who created "The World Is All About Money And Intelligence." They have so much hidden up their sleeve. The only pity is that this is a very textbook piece of work... I think it would be better for their sake not to publish They have big potential.
...
This is totally different from what they handed in the last time, so I asked Hattori what these two wanted to create. He told me that they wanted to create something that would be popular; something that would sell... I applaud them for their professionalism at such a young age! I want to publish something by them that would definitely sell!
their professionalism at such a
ish something by them that would definitely sell!
I-I CAN'T READ ANY MORE OF IT...
SHUJIN.
OF COURSE THERE WERE NEGATIVE COMMENTS AS WELL AS ONES THAT SAID WE'D DO BETTER WITH A NON-MAINSTREAM MANGA, BUT WHAT ALL THE REVIEWS HAD IN COMMON WAS THAT THEY ALL THOUGHT WE HAD POTENTIAL AND WERE LOOKING FORWARD TO OUR FUTURE WORK.
YOU DIDN'T WRITE THIS YOURSELF, DID YOU, MR. HATTORI?
HAH HAH, OF COURSE NOT.
IT WASN'T THAT WE LACKED THE TALENT. SHUJIN AND I WERE ABLE TO REALIZE THAT WE WERE STILL IN THE MIDST OF CLIMBING UP THE STAIRWAY TO OUR DREAM.

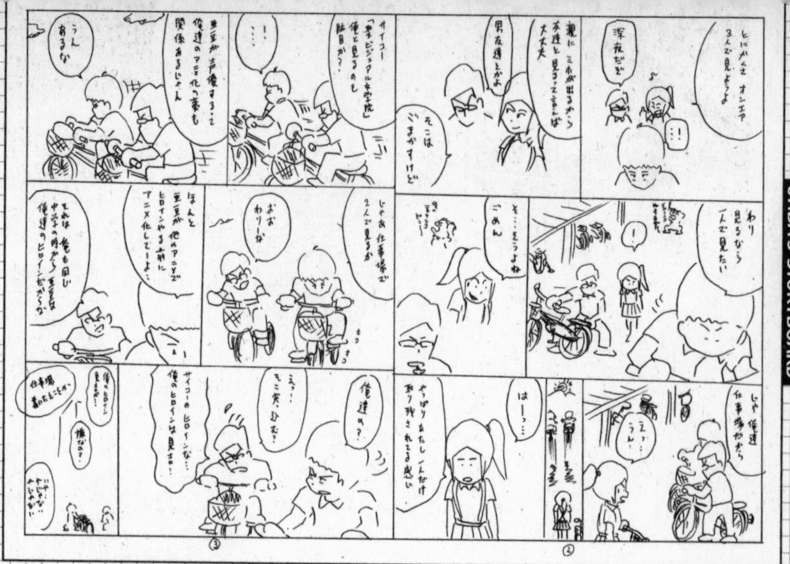
深夜だぞ
親にミホが出るから友達と見るって言えば大丈夫
男友達とかよ
そこはごまかすけど
サイコー「聖ビジュアル女学院」俺と見るのも駄目か?
…!
亜豆が声優するって俺達のアニメ化の夢も関係あるじゃん
うん あるな
わり 見るなら1人で見たい
!
そ…そうよね
ごめん
じゃあ仕事場で2人で見るか
おお わりーな
ほんと亜豆が他のアニメでヒロインやる前にアニメ化してーよ…
それは俺も同じ 中学の時から亜豆は俺達のヒロインだからな
えっ…うん
はーっ…
やっぱりあたし一人だけ取り残されてる感じ
俺達の?
サイコーのヒロインな…俺のヒロインは見吉…
様なの?

OHBA'S STORYBOARD

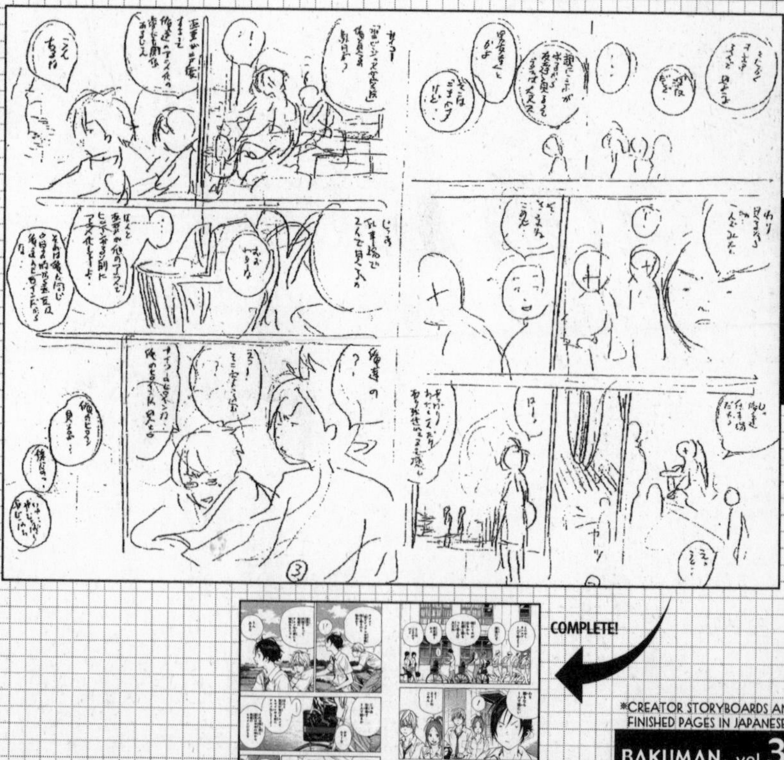

OBATA'S STORYBOARD

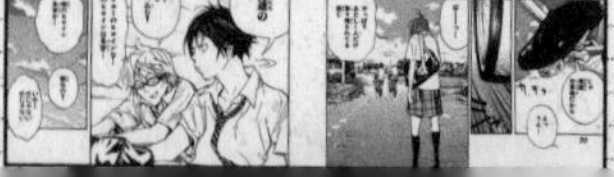

COMPLETE!

※CREATOR STORYBOARDS AND FINISHED PAGES IN JAPANESE

BAKUMAN。vol.3

"Until the Final Draft Is Complete"

Chapter 20, pp. 70-71

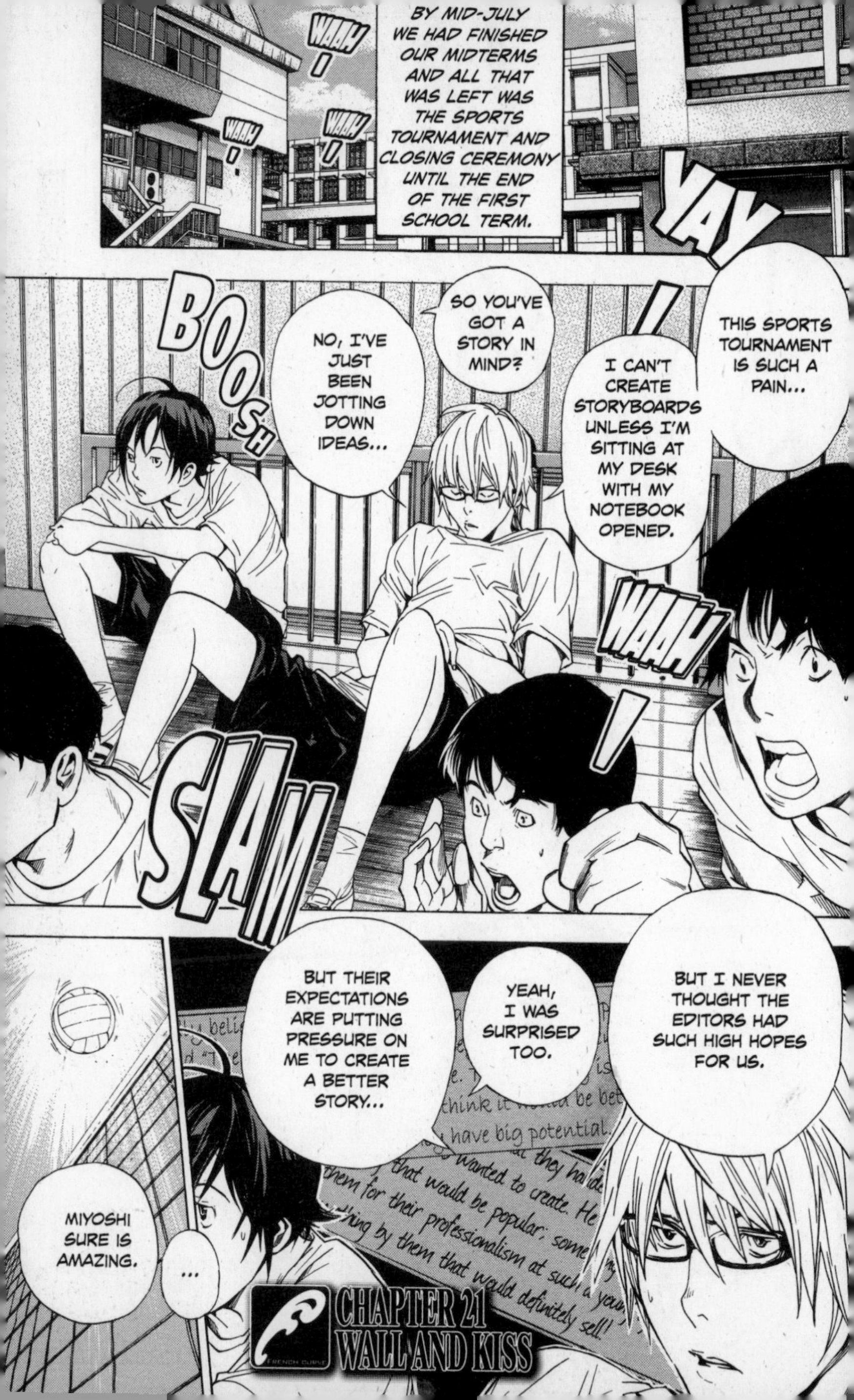
BY MID-JULY WE HAD FINISHED OUR MIDTERMS AND ALL THAT WAS LEFT WAS THE SPORTS TOURNAMENT AND CLOSING CEREMONY UNTIL THE END OF THE FIRST SCHOOL TERM.
YAY!
WAAH!
WAAH!
WAAH!
THIS SPORTS TOURNAMENT IS SUCH A PAIN...
I CAN'T CREATE STORYBOARDS UNLESS I'M SITTING AT MY DESK WITH MY NOTEBOOK OPENED.
SO YOU'VE GOT A STORY IN MIND?
NO, I'VE JUST BEEN JOTTING DOWN IDEAS...
BOOSH
WAAH!
SLAM
BUT I NEVER THOUGHT THE EDITORS HAD SUCH HIGH HOPES FOR US.
YEAH, I WAS SURPRISED TOO.
BUT THEIR EXPECTATIONS ARE PUTTING PRESSURE ON ME TO CREATE A BETTER STORY...
...
MIYOSHI SURE IS AMAZING.
CHAPTER 21
WALL AND KISS

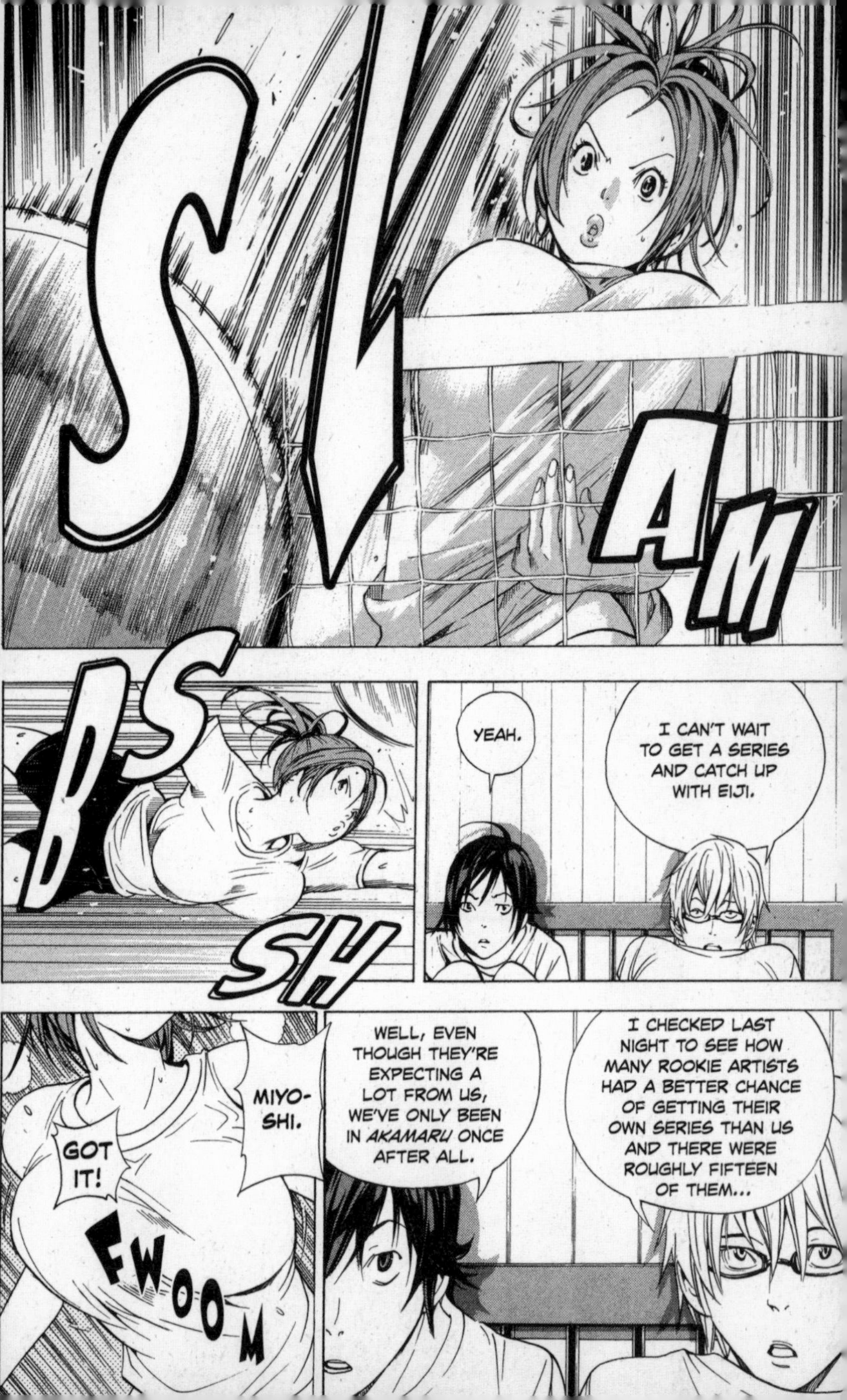
SLAM
I CAN'T WAIT TO GET A SERIES AND CATCH UP WITH EIJI.
YEAH.
BSSH
I CHECKED LAST NIGHT TO SEE HOW MANY ROOKIE ARTISTS HAD A BETTER CHANCE OF GETTING THEIR OWN SERIES THAN US AND THERE WERE ROUGHLY FIFTEEN OF THEM...
WELL, EVEN THOUGH THEY'RE EXPECTING A LOT FROM US, WE'VE ONLY BEEN IN *AKAMARU* ONCE AFTER ALL.
MIYO-SHI.
GOT IT!
FWOOM

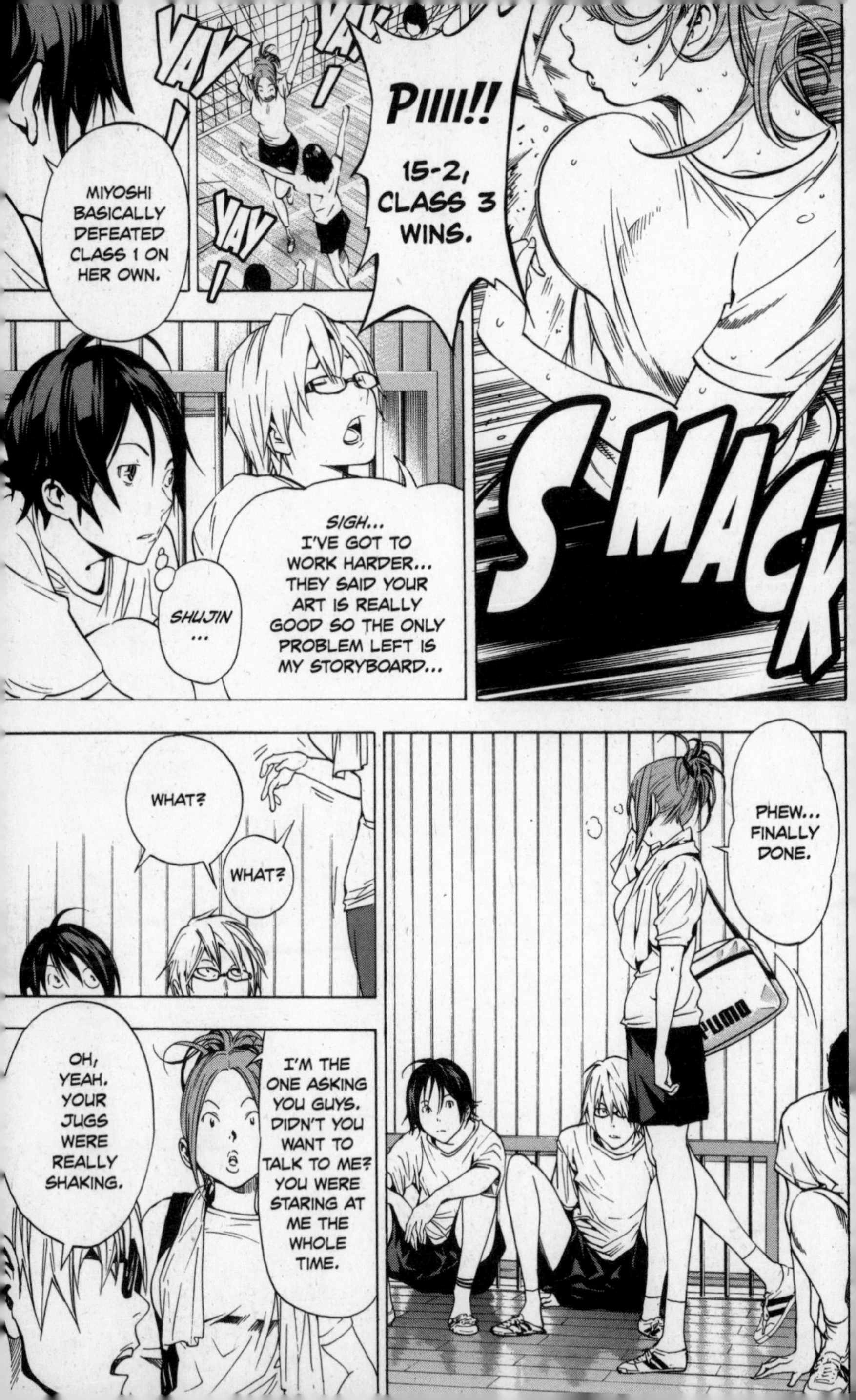
S-MACK
YAY
YAY
YAY
PIIII!!
15-2, CLASS 3 WINS.
MIYOSHI BASICALLY DEFEATED CLASS 1 ON HER OWN.
SIGH... I'VE GOT TO WORK HARDER... THEY SAID YOUR ART IS REALLY GOOD SO THE ONLY PROBLEM LEFT IS MY STORYBOARD...
SHUJIN...
PHEW... FINALLY DONE.
PUMA
WHAT?
WHAT?
I'M THE ONE ASKING YOU GUYS. DIDN'T YOU WANT TO TALK TO ME? YOU WERE STARING AT ME THE WHOLE TIME.
OH, YEAH. YOUR JUGS WERE REALLY SHAKING.

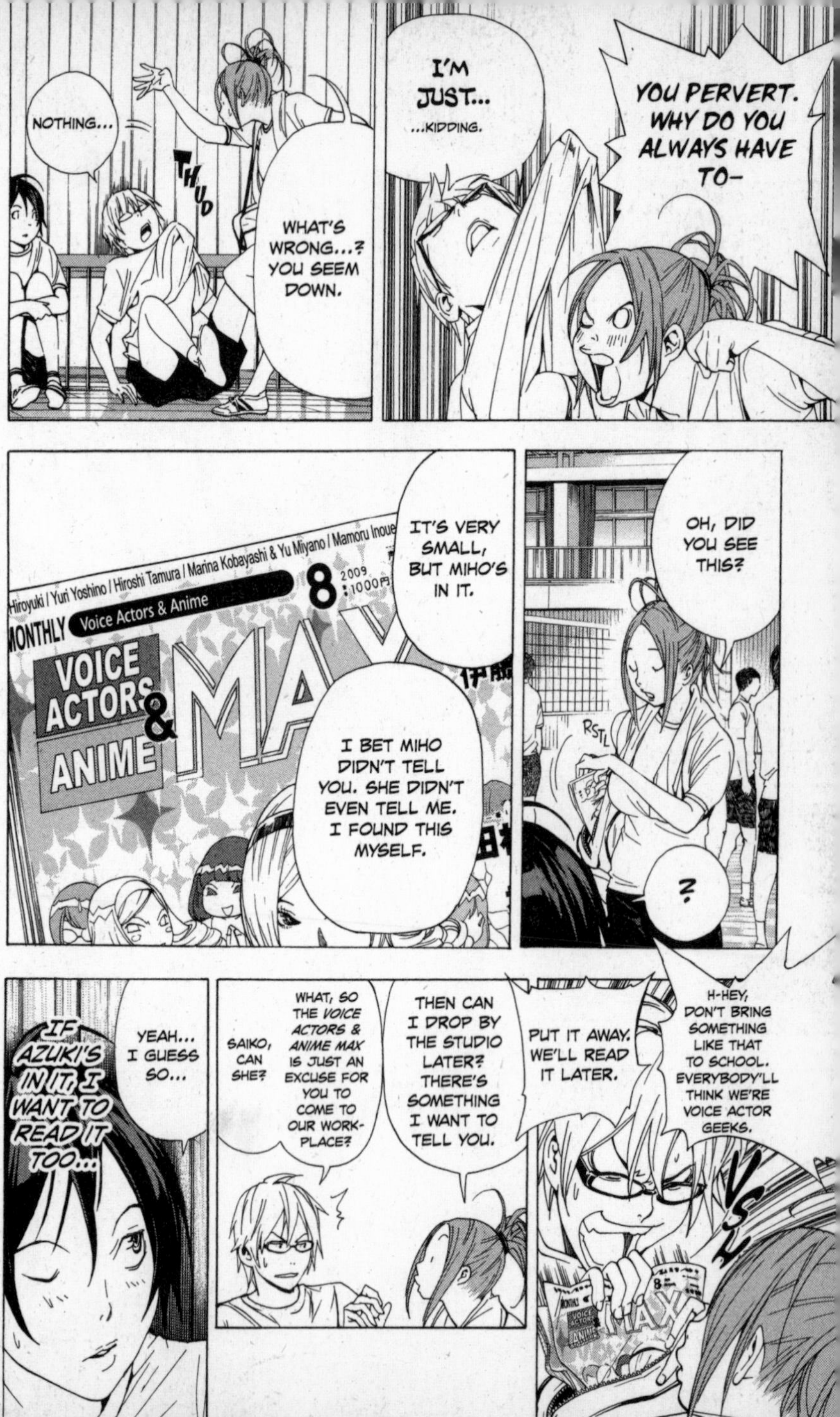
YOU PERVERT. WHY DO YOU ALWAYS HAVE TO–
I'M JUST...
...KIDDING.
WHAT'S WRONG...? YOU SEEM DOWN.
NOTHING...
THUD
OH, DID YOU SEE THIS?
RSTL
?
Hiroyuki / Yuri Yoshino / Hiroshi Tamura / Marina Kobayashi & Yu Miyano / Mamoru Inoue
8 2009 1000円
MONTHLY Voice Actors & Anime
VOICE ACTORS & ANIME MAX
IT'S VERY SMALL, BUT MIHO'S IN IT.
I BET MIHO DIDN'T TELL YOU. SHE DIDN'T EVEN TELL ME. I FOUND THIS MYSELF.
H-HEY, DON'T BRING SOMETHING LIKE THAT TO SCHOOL. EVERYBODY'LL THINK WE'RE VOICE ACTOR GEEKS.
PUT IT AWAY. WE'LL READ IT LATER.
THEN CAN I DROP BY THE STUDIO LATER? THERE'S SOMETHING I WANT TO TELL YOU.
WHAT, SO THE *VOICE ACTORS & ANIME MAX* IS JUST AN EXCUSE FOR YOU TO COME TO OUR WORKPLACE?
SAIKO, CAN SHE?
YEAH... I GUESS SO...
IF AZUKI'S IN IT, I WANT TO READ IT TOO...

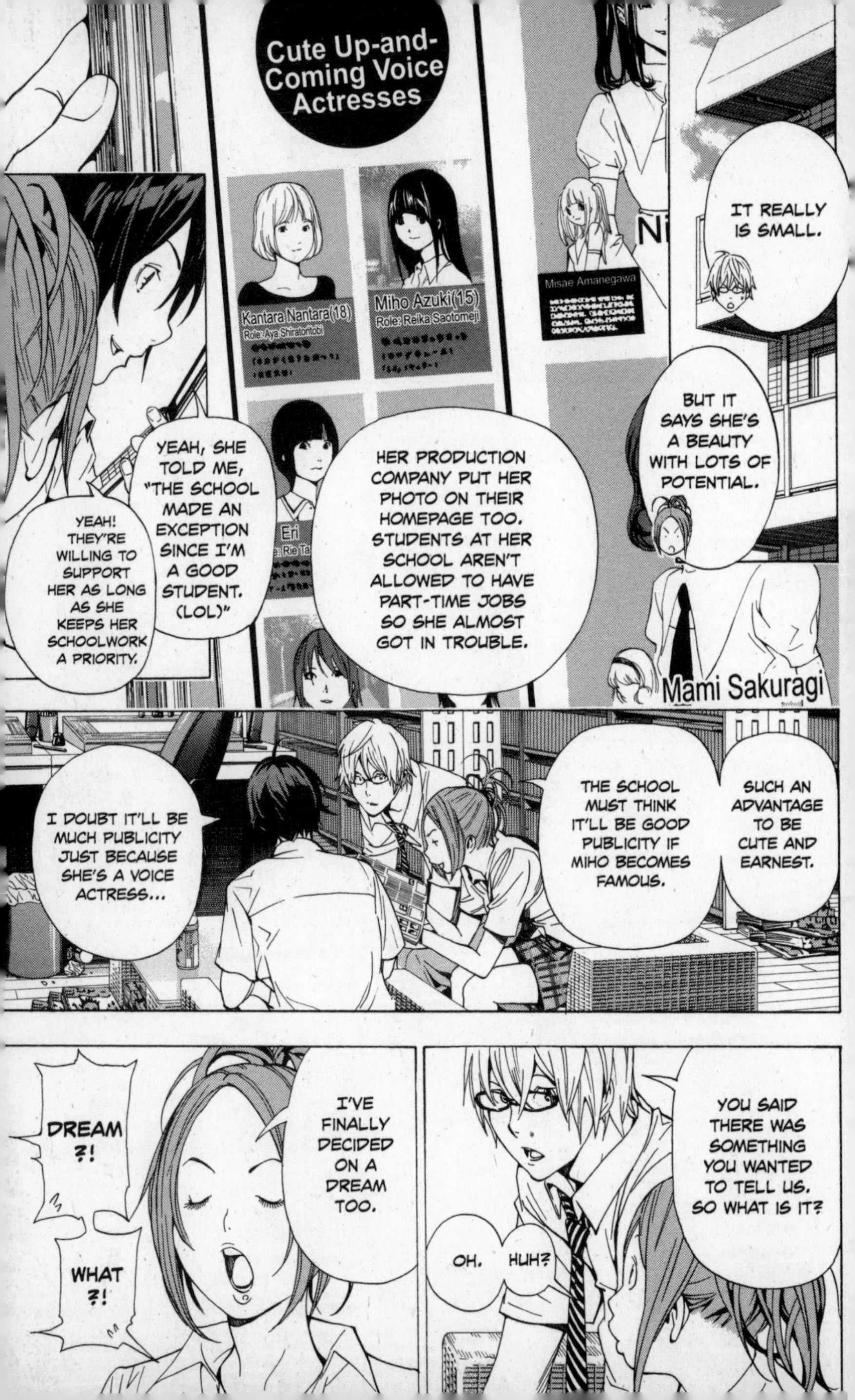
IT REALLY IS SMALL.
BUT IT SAYS SHE'S A BEAUTY WITH LOTS OF POTENTIAL.
Mami Sakuragi
Cute Up-and-Coming Voice Actresses
Misae Amanegawa
Miho Azuki (15)
Role: Reika Saotomeji
Kantara Nantara (18)
Role: Aya Shiratoritobi
Eri
HER PRODUCTION COMPANY PUT HER PHOTO ON THEIR HOMEPAGE TOO. STUDENTS AT HER SCHOOL AREN'T ALLOWED TO HAVE PART-TIME JOBS SO SHE ALMOST GOT IN TROUBLE.
YEAH, SHE TOLD ME, "THE SCHOOL MADE AN EXCEPTION SINCE I'M A GOOD STUDENT. (LOL)"
YEAH! THEY'RE WILLING TO SUPPORT HER AS LONG AS SHE KEEPS HER SCHOOLWORK A PRIORITY.
SUCH AN ADVANTAGE TO BE CUTE AND EARNEST.
THE SCHOOL MUST THINK IT'LL BE GOOD PUBLICITY IF MIHO BECOMES FAMOUS.
I DOUBT IT'LL BE MUCH PUBLICITY JUST BECAUSE SHE'S A VOICE ACTRESS...
YOU SAID THERE WAS SOMETHING YOU WANTED TO TELL US. SO WHAT IS IT?
HUH?
OH.
I'VE FINALLY DECIDED ON A DREAM TOO.
DREAM?!
WHAT?!

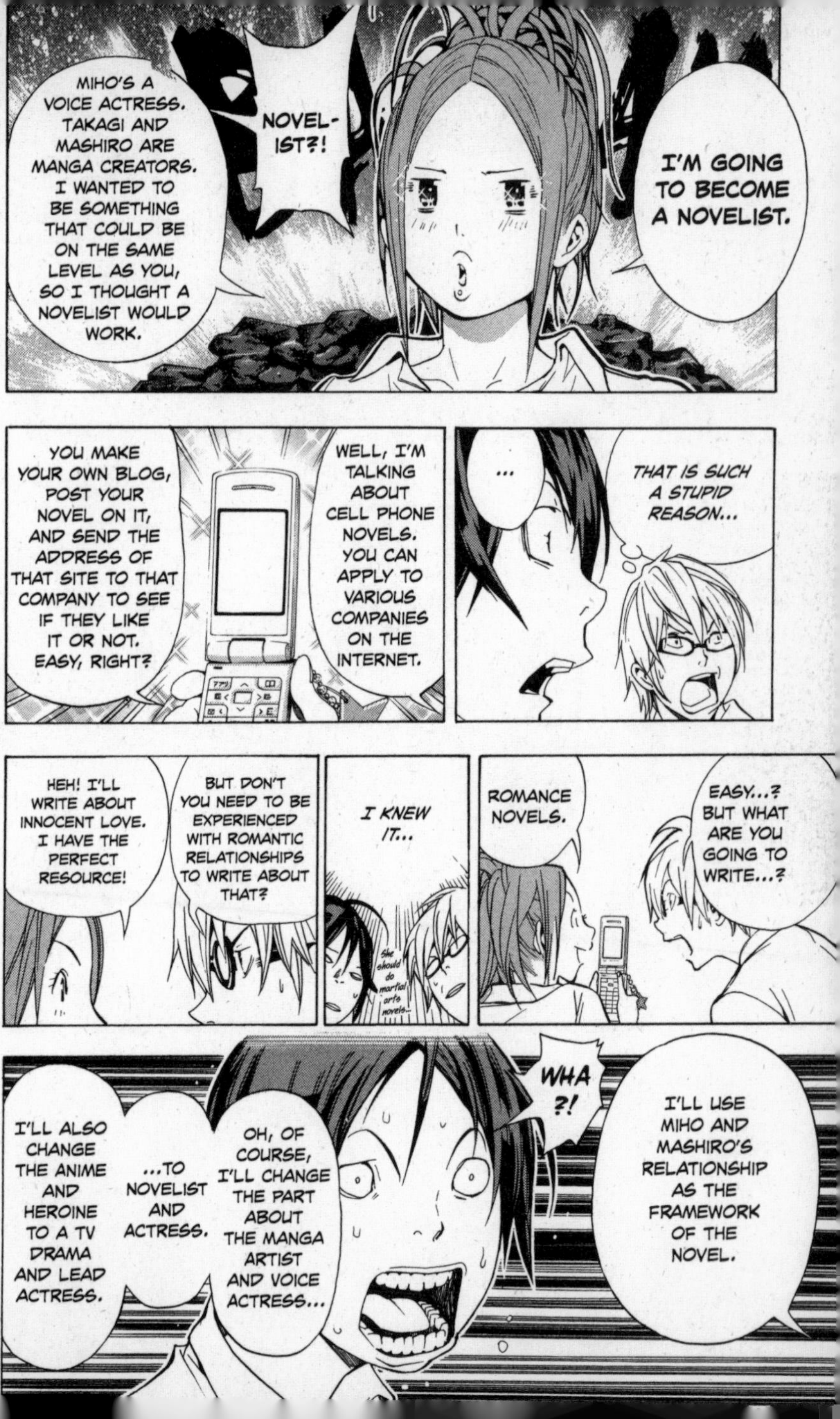
I'M GOING TO BECOME A NOVELIST.
NOVEL-IST?!
MIHO'S A VOICE ACTRESS. TAKAGI AND MASHIRO ARE MANGA CREATORS. I WANTED TO BE SOMETHING THAT COULD BE ON THE SAME LEVEL AS YOU, SO I THOUGHT A NOVELIST WOULD WORK.
THAT IS SUCH A STUPID REASON...
...
WELL, I'M TALKING ABOUT CELL PHONE NOVELS. YOU CAN APPLY TO VARIOUS COMPANIES ON THE INTERNET.
YOU MAKE YOUR OWN BLOG, POST YOUR NOVEL ON IT, AND SEND THE ADDRESS OF THAT SITE TO THAT COMPANY TO SEE IF THEY LIKE IT OR NOT. EASY, RIGHT?
EASY...? BUT WHAT ARE YOU GOING TO WRITE...?
ROMANCE NOVELS.
I KNEW IT...
She should do martial arts novels...
BUT DON'T YOU NEED TO BE EXPERIENCED WITH ROMANTIC RELATIONSHIPS TO WRITE ABOUT THAT?
HEH! I'LL WRITE ABOUT INNOCENT LOVE. I HAVE THE PERFECT RESOURCE!
I'LL USE MIHO AND MASHIRO'S RELATIONSHIP AS THE FRAMEWORK OF THE NOVEL.
WHA?!
OH, OF COURSE, I'LL CHANGE THE PART ABOUT THE MANGA ARTIST AND VOICE ACTRESS...
...TO NOVELIST AND ACTRESS.
I'LL ALSO CHANGE THE ANIME AND HEROINE TO A TV DRAMA AND LEAD ACTRESS.

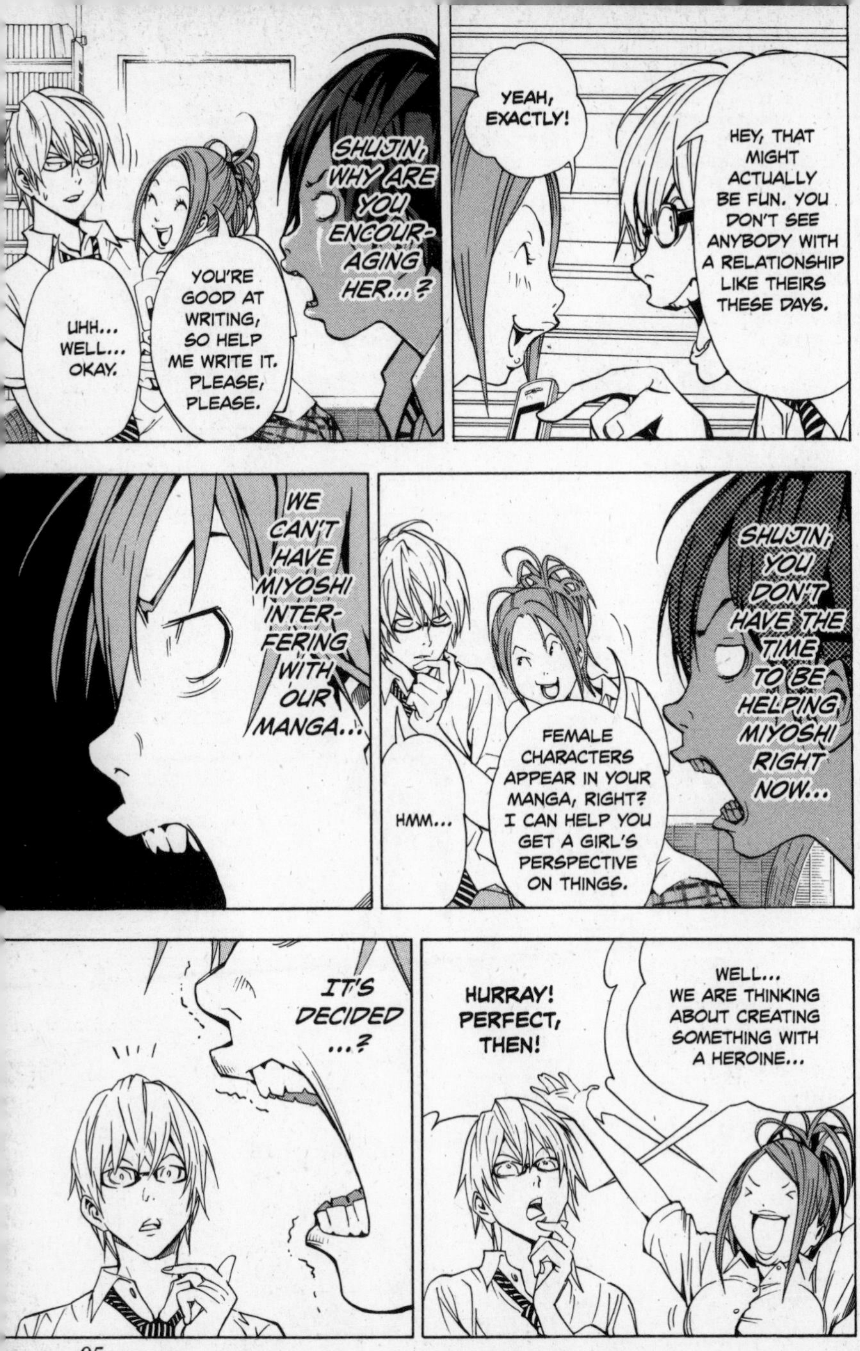
HEY, THAT MIGHT ACTUALLY BE FUN. YOU DON'T SEE ANYBODY WITH A RELATIONSHIP LIKE THEIRS THESE DAYS.
YEAH, EXACTLY!
SHUJIN, WHY ARE YOU ENCOUR-AGING HER...?
YOU'RE GOOD AT WRITING, SO HELP ME WRITE IT. PLEASE, PLEASE.
UHH... WELL... OKAY.
SHUJIN, YOU DON'T HAVE THE TIME TO BE HELPING MIYOSHI RIGHT NOW...
FEMALE CHARACTERS APPEAR IN YOUR MANGA, RIGHT? I CAN HELP YOU GET A GIRL'S PERSPECTIVE ON THINGS.
HMM...
WE CAN'T HAVE MIYOSHI INTER-FERING WITH OUR MANGA...
WELL... WE ARE THINKING ABOUT CREATING SOMETHING WITH A HEROINE...
HURRAY! PERFECT, THEN!
IT'S DECIDED...?

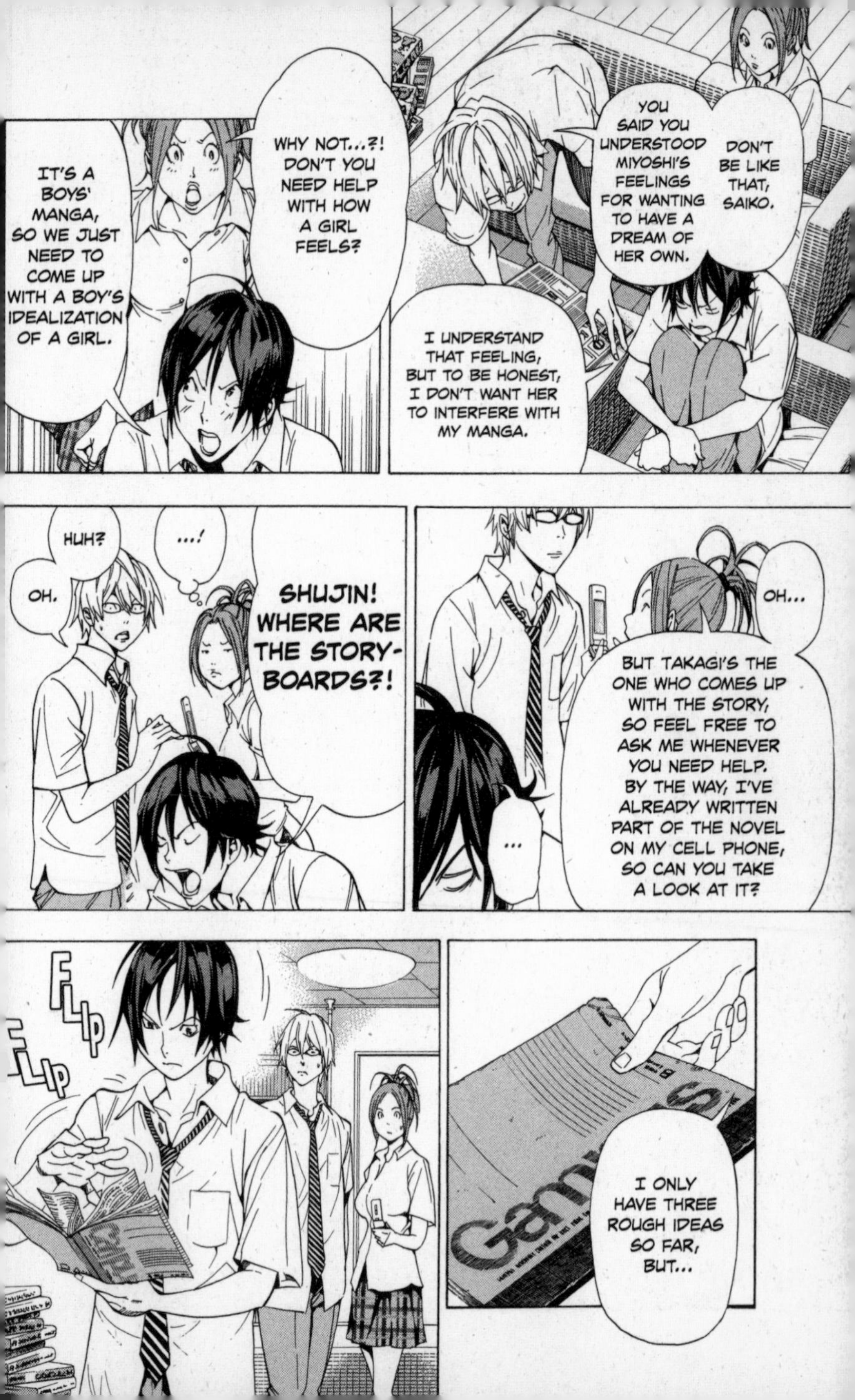
DON'T BE LIKE THAT, SAIKO.
YOU SAID YOU UNDERSTOOD MIYOSHI'S FEELINGS FOR WANTING TO HAVE A DREAM OF HER OWN.
I UNDERSTAND THAT FEELING, BUT TO BE HONEST, I DON'T WANT HER TO INTERFERE WITH MY MANGA.
WHY NOT...?! DON'T YOU NEED HELP WITH HOW A GIRL FEELS?
IT'S A BOYS' MANGA, SO WE JUST NEED TO COME UP WITH A BOY'S IDEALIZATION OF A GIRL.
OH...
BUT TAKAGI'S THE ONE WHO COMES UP WITH THE STORY, SO FEEL FREE TO ASK ME WHENEVER YOU NEED HELP. BY THE WAY, I'VE ALREADY WRITTEN PART OF THE NOVEL ON MY CELL PHONE, SO CAN YOU TAKE A LOOK AT IT?
...
SHUJIN! WHERE ARE THE STORY-BOARDS?!
...!
HUH?
OH.
I ONLY HAVE THREE ROUGH IDEAS SO FAR, BUT...
FLIP
FLIP

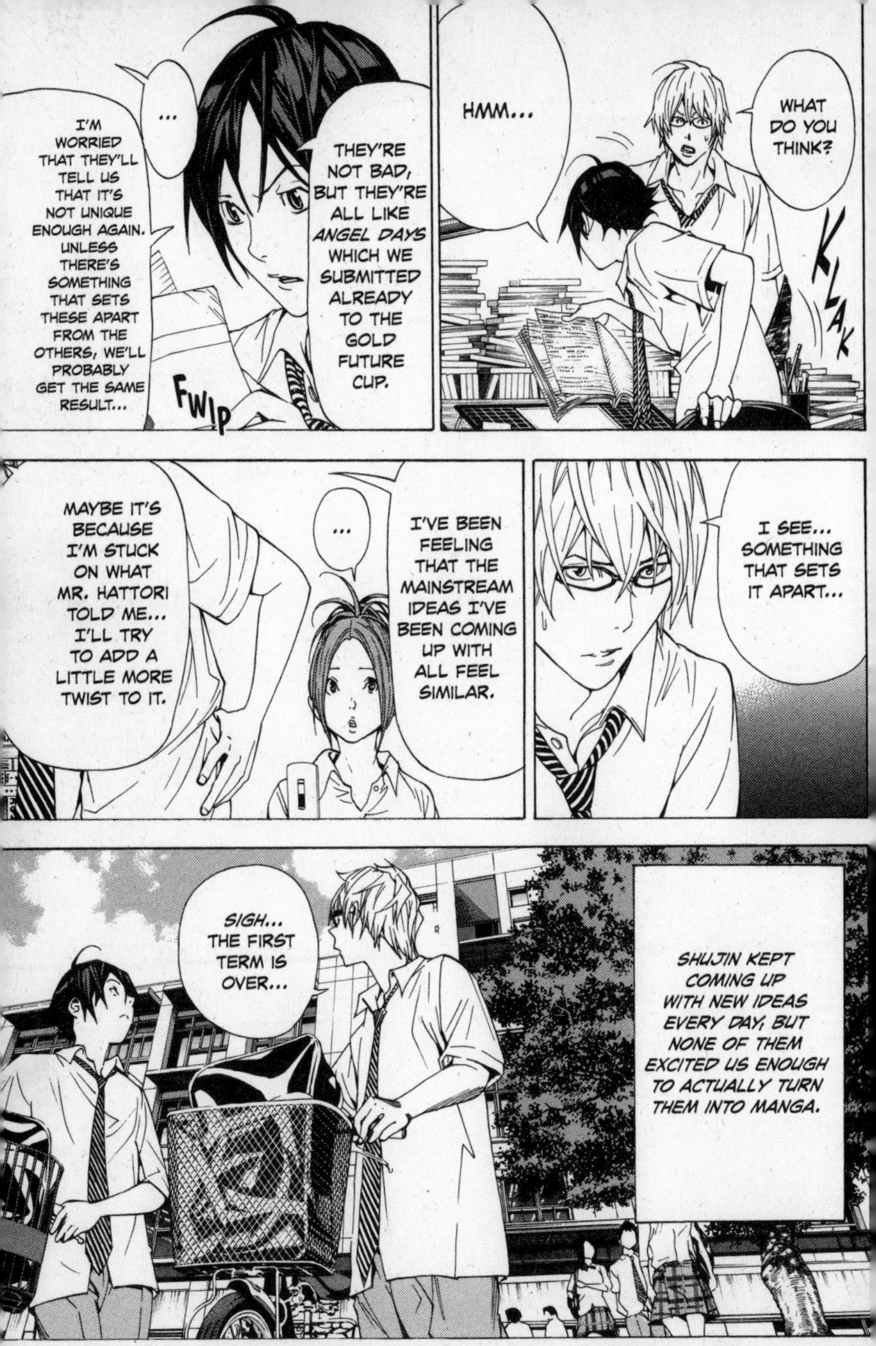
WHAT DO YOU THINK?
KLAK
HMM...
...
THEY'RE NOT BAD, BUT THEY'RE ALL LIKE *ANGEL DAYS* WHICH WE SUBMITTED ALREADY TO THE GOLD FUTURE CUP.
I'M WORRIED THAT THEY'LL TELL US THAT IT'S NOT UNIQUE ENOUGH AGAIN. UNLESS THERE'S SOMETHING THAT SETS THESE APART FROM THE OTHERS, WE'LL PROBABLY GET THE SAME RESULT...
FWIP
I SEE... SOMETHING THAT SETS IT APART...
I'VE BEEN FEELING THAT THE MAINSTREAM IDEAS I'VE BEEN COMING UP WITH ALL FEEL SIMILAR.
...
MAYBE IT'S BECAUSE I'M STUCK ON WHAT MR. HATTORI TOLD ME... I'LL TRY TO ADD A LITTLE MORE TWIST TO IT.
SHUJIN KEPT COMING UP WITH NEW IDEAS EVERY DAY, BUT NONE OF THEM EXCITED US ENOUGH TO ACTUALLY TURN THEM INTO MANGA.
SIGH... THE FIRST TERM IS OVER...

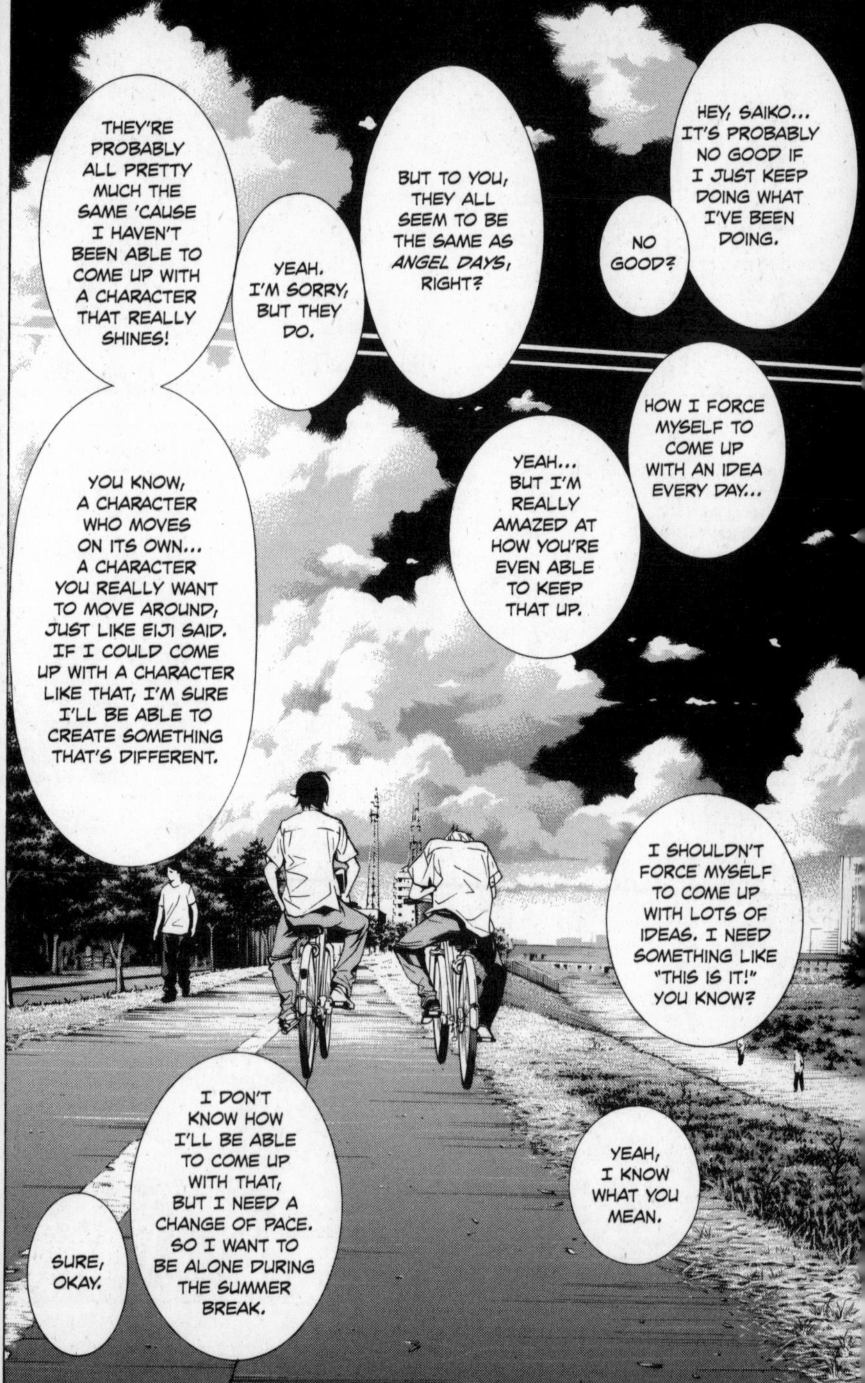
HEY, SAIKO... IT'S PROBABLY NO GOOD IF I JUST KEEP DOING WHAT I'VE BEEN DOING.
NO GOOD?
HOW I FORCE MYSELF TO COME UP WITH AN IDEA EVERY DAY...
YEAH... BUT I'M REALLY AMAZED AT HOW YOU'RE EVEN ABLE TO KEEP THAT UP.
BUT TO YOU, THEY ALL SEEM TO BE THE SAME AS *ANGEL DAYS*, RIGHT?
YEAH. I'M SORRY, BUT THEY DO.
THEY'RE PROBABLY ALL PRETTY MUCH THE SAME 'CAUSE I HAVEN'T BEEN ABLE TO COME UP WITH A CHARACTER THAT REALLY SHINES!
YOU KNOW, A CHARACTER WHO MOVES ON ITS OWN... A CHARACTER YOU REALLY WANT TO MOVE AROUND, JUST LIKE EIJI SAID. IF I COULD COME UP WITH A CHARACTER LIKE THAT, I'M SURE I'LL BE ABLE TO CREATE SOMETHING THAT'S DIFFERENT.
I SHOULDN'T FORCE MYSELF TO COME UP WITH LOTS OF IDEAS. I NEED SOMETHING LIKE "THIS IS IT!" YOU KNOW?
YEAH, I KNOW WHAT YOU MEAN.
I DON'T KNOW HOW I'LL BE ABLE TO COME UP WITH THAT, BUT I NEED A CHANGE OF PACE. SO I WANT TO BE ALONE DURING THE SUMMER BREAK.
SURE, OKAY.

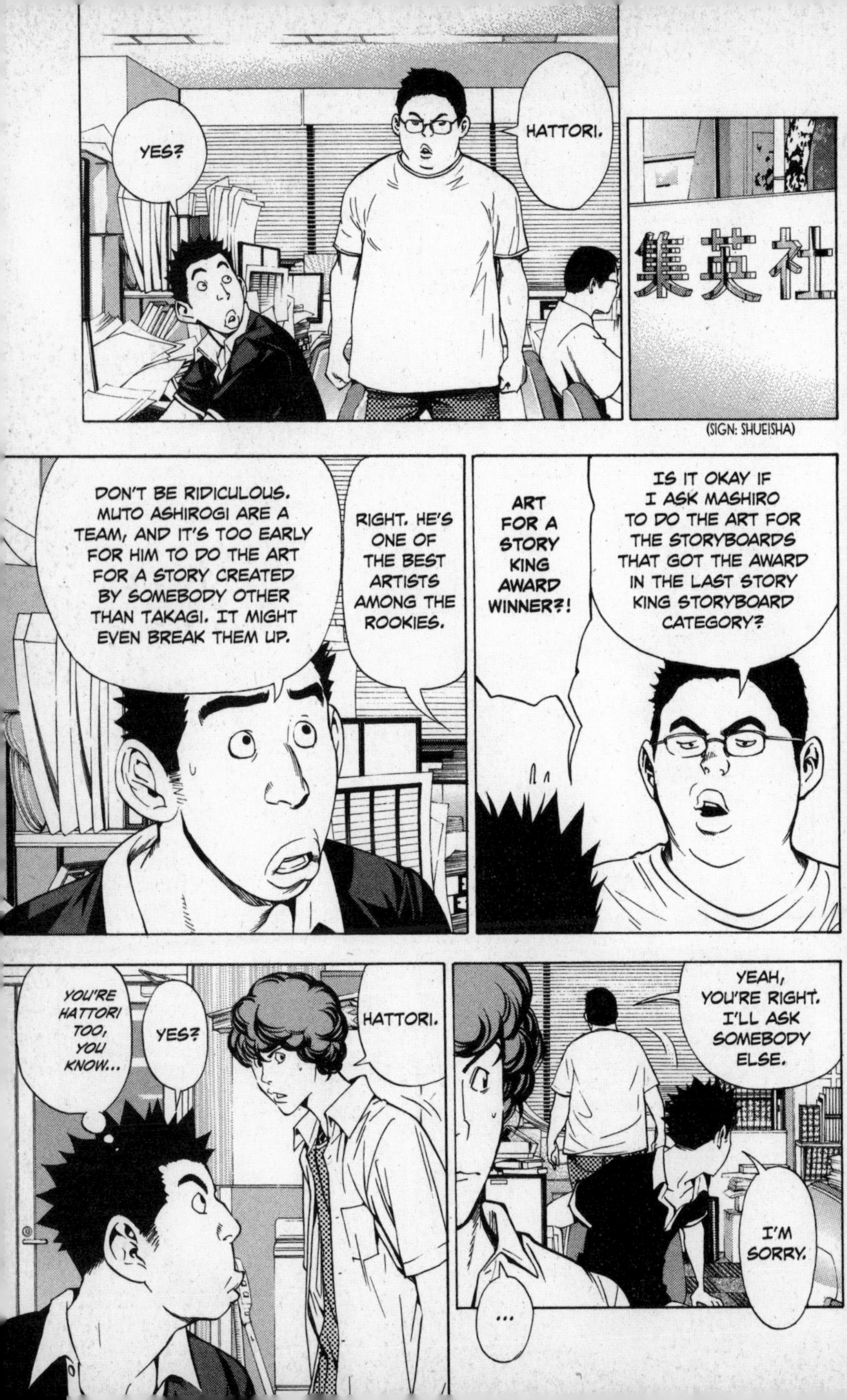
集英社
(SIGN: SHUEISHA)
HATTORI.
YES?
IS IT OKAY IF I ASK MASHIRO TO DO THE ART FOR THE STORYBOARDS THAT GOT THE AWARD IN THE LAST STORY KING STORYBOARD CATEGORY?
ART FOR A STORY KING AWARD WINNER?!
RIGHT. HE'S ONE OF THE BEST ARTISTS AMONG THE ROOKIES.
DON'T BE RIDICULOUS. MUTO ASHIROGI ARE A TEAM, AND IT'S TOO EARLY FOR HIM TO DO THE ART FOR A STORY CREATED BY SOMEBODY OTHER THAN TAKAGI. IT MIGHT EVEN BREAK THEM UP.
YEAH, YOU'RE RIGHT. I'LL ASK SOMEBODY ELSE.
I'M SORRY.
...
HATTORI.
YES?
YOU'RE HATTORI TOO, YOU KNOW...

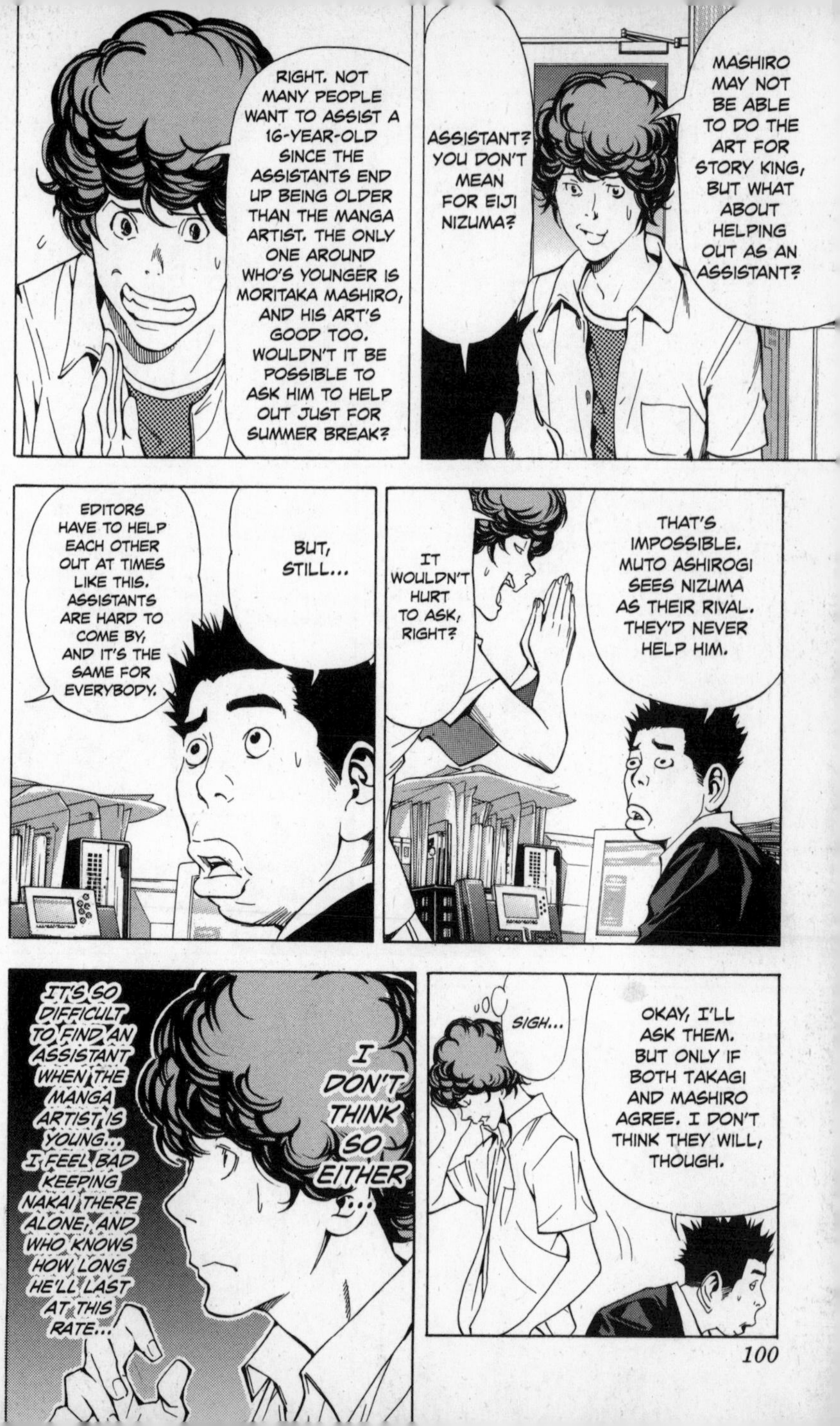
MASHIRO MAY NOT BE ABLE TO DO THE ART FOR STORY KING, BUT WHAT ABOUT HELPING OUT AS AN ASSISTANT?
ASSISTANT? YOU DON'T MEAN FOR EIJI NIZUMA?
RIGHT. NOT MANY PEOPLE WANT TO ASSIST A 16-YEAR-OLD SINCE THE ASSISTANTS END UP BEING OLDER THAN THE MANGA ARTIST. THE ONLY ONE AROUND WHO'S YOUNGER IS MORITAKA MASHIRO, AND HIS ART'S GOOD TOO. WOULDN'T IT BE POSSIBLE TO ASK HIM TO HELP OUT JUST FOR SUMMER BREAK?
THAT'S IMPOSSIBLE. MUTO ASHIROGI SEES NIZUMA AS THEIR RIVAL. THEY'D NEVER HELP HIM.
IT WOULDN'T HURT TO ASK, RIGHT?
BUT, STILL...
EDITORS HAVE TO HELP EACH OTHER OUT AT TIMES LIKE THIS. ASSISTANTS ARE HARD TO COME BY, AND IT'S THE SAME FOR EVERYBODY.
OKAY, I'LL ASK THEM. BUT ONLY IF BOTH TAKAGI AND MASHIRO AGREE. I DON'T THINK THEY WILL, THOUGH.
SIGH...
I DON'T THINK SO EITHER...
IT'S SO DIFFICULT TO FIND AN ASSISTANT WHEN THE MANGA ARTIST IS YOUNG... I FEEL BAD KEEPING NAKAI THERE ALONE, AND WHO KNOWS HOW LONG HE'LL LAST AT THIS RATE...

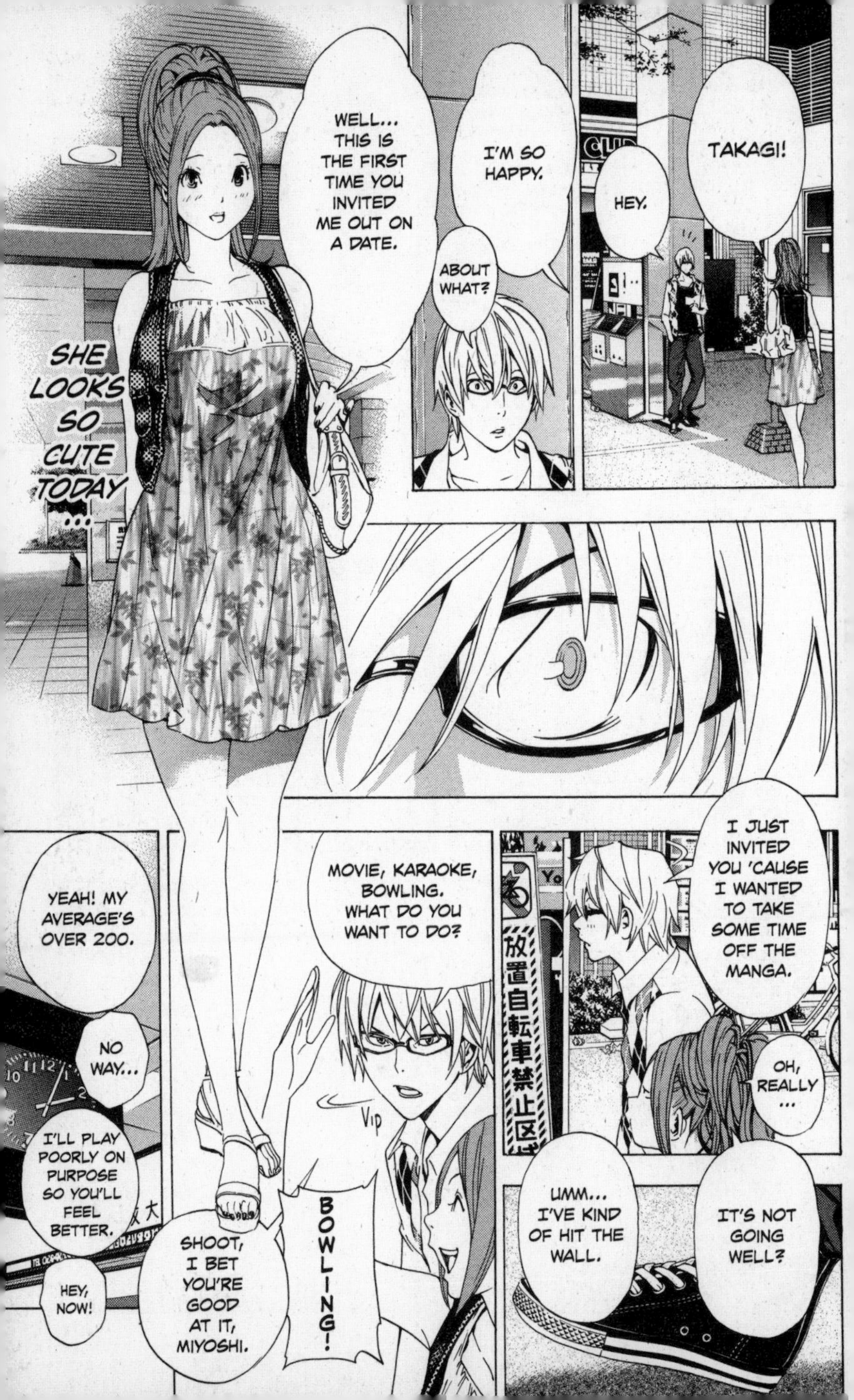

TAKAGI!
HEY.
I'M SO HAPPY.
ABOUT WHAT?
WELL... THIS IS THE FIRST TIME YOU INVITED ME OUT ON A DATE.
SHE LOOKS SO CUTE TODAY...
I JUST INVITED YOU 'CAUSE I WANTED TO TAKE SOME TIME OFF THE MANGA.
放置自転車禁止区
OH, REALLY...
IT'S NOT GOING WELL?
UMM... I'VE KIND OF HIT THE WALL.
MOVIE, KARAOKE, BOWLING. WHAT DO YOU WANT TO DO?
Vip
BOWLING!
SHOOT, I BET YOU'RE GOOD AT IT, MIYOSHI.
YEAH! MY AVERAGE'S OVER 200.
NO WAY...
I'LL PLAY POORLY ON PURPOSE SO YOU'LL FEEL BETTER.
HEY, NOW!

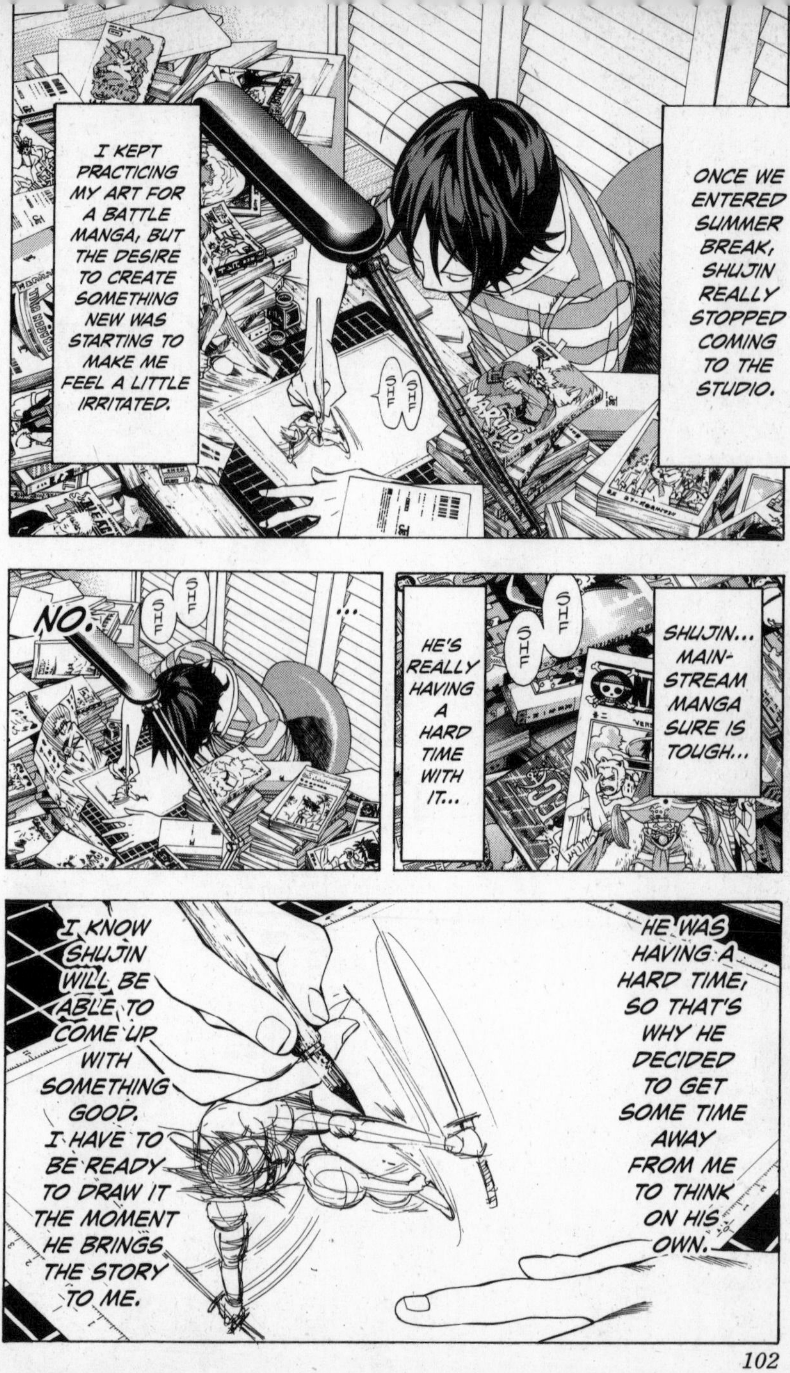

ONCE WE ENTERED SUMMER BREAK, SHUJIN REALLY STOPPED COMING TO THE STUDIO.
I KEPT PRACTICING MY ART FOR A BATTLE MANGA, BUT THE DESIRE TO CREATE SOMETHING NEW WAS STARTING TO MAKE ME FEEL A LITTLE IRRITATED.
SHF SHF
SHUJIN... MAIN-STREAM MANGA SURE IS TOUGH...
SHF SHF
HE'S REALLY HAVING A HARD TIME WITH IT...
...
SHF SHF
NO.
HE WAS HAVING A HARD TIME, SO THAT'S WHY HE DECIDED TO GET SOME TIME AWAY FROM ME TO THINK ON HIS OWN.
I KNOW SHUJIN WILL BE ABLE TO COME UP WITH SOMETHING GOOD. I HAVE TO BE READY TO DRAW IT THE MOMENT HE BRINGS THE STORY TO ME.

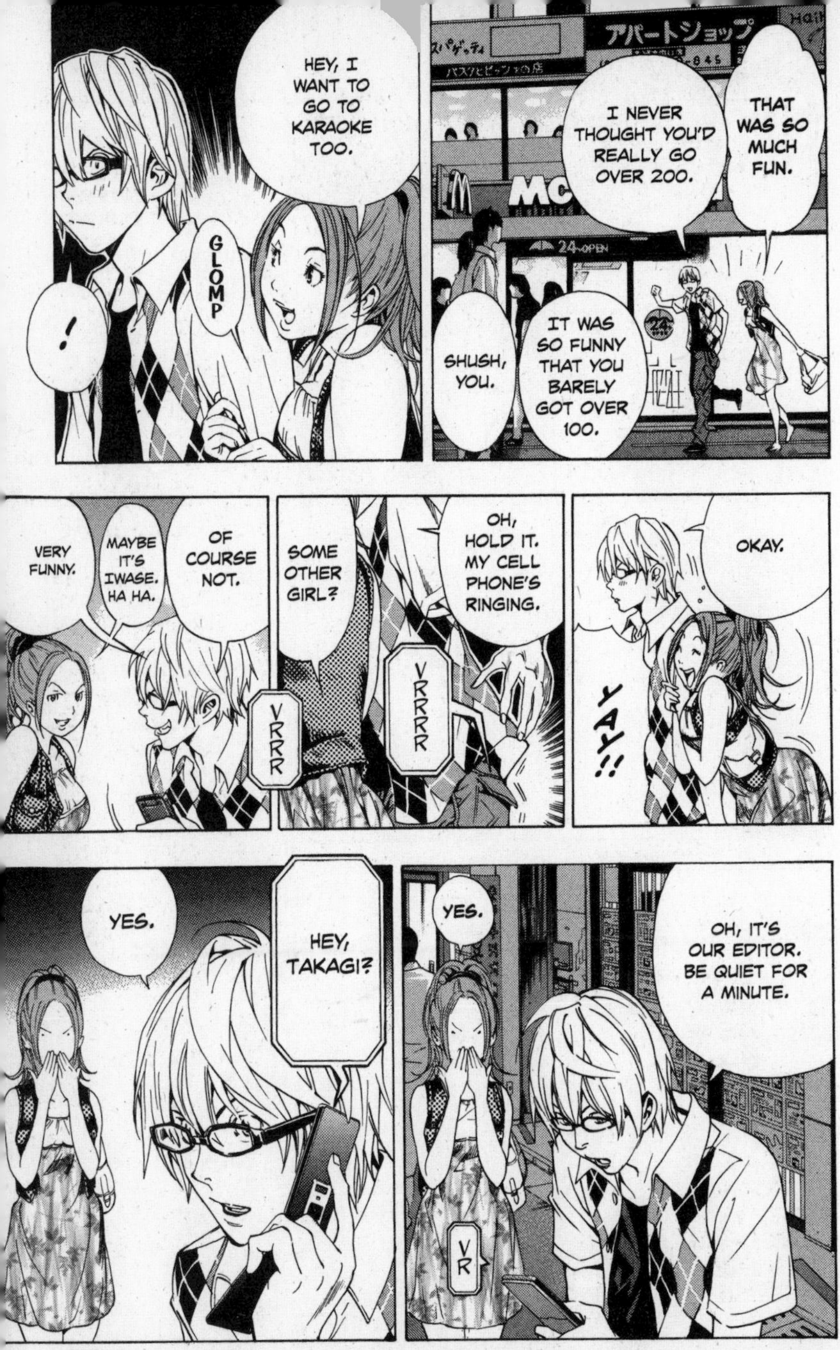
アパートショップ
THAT WAS SO MUCH FUN.
I NEVER THOUGHT YOU'D REALLY GO OVER 200.
IT WAS SO FUNNY THAT YOU BARELY GOT OVER 100.
SHUSH, YOU.
HEY, I WANT TO GO TO KARAOKE TOO.
GLOMP
!
OKAY.
YAY!!
OH, HOLD IT. MY CELL PHONE'S RINGING.
VRRRR
SOME OTHER GIRL?
VRRR
OF COURSE NOT.
MAYBE IT'S IWASE. HA HA.
VERY FUNNY.
OH, IT'S OUR EDITOR. BE QUIET FOR A MINUTE.
YES.
VR
HEY, TAKAGI?
YES.

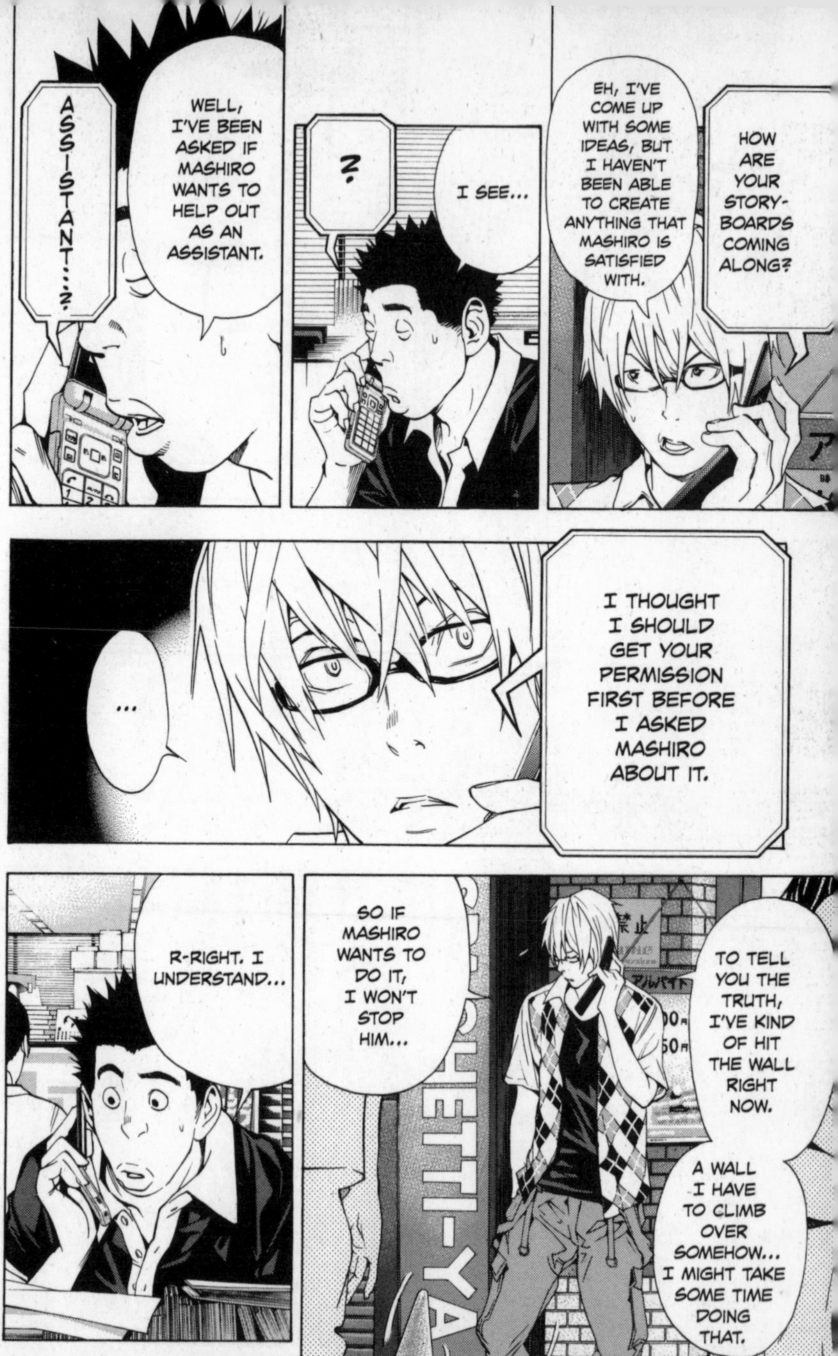
HOW ARE YOUR STORY-BOARDS COMING ALONG?
EH, I'VE COME UP WITH SOME IDEAS, BUT I HAVEN'T BEEN ABLE TO CREATE ANYTHING THAT MASHIRO IS SATISFIED WITH.
I SEE...
?
WELL, I'VE BEEN ASKED IF MASHIRO WANTS TO HELP OUT AS AN ASSISTANT.
ASSISTANT...?
I THOUGHT I SHOULD GET YOUR PERMISSION FIRST BEFORE I ASKED MASHIRO ABOUT IT.
...
TO TELL YOU THE TRUTH, I'VE KIND OF HIT THE WALL RIGHT NOW.
A WALL I HAVE TO CLIMB OVER SOMEHOW... I MIGHT TAKE SOME TIME DOING THAT.
SO IF MASHIRO WANTS TO DO IT, I WON'T STOP HIM...
R-RIGHT. I UNDERSTAND...

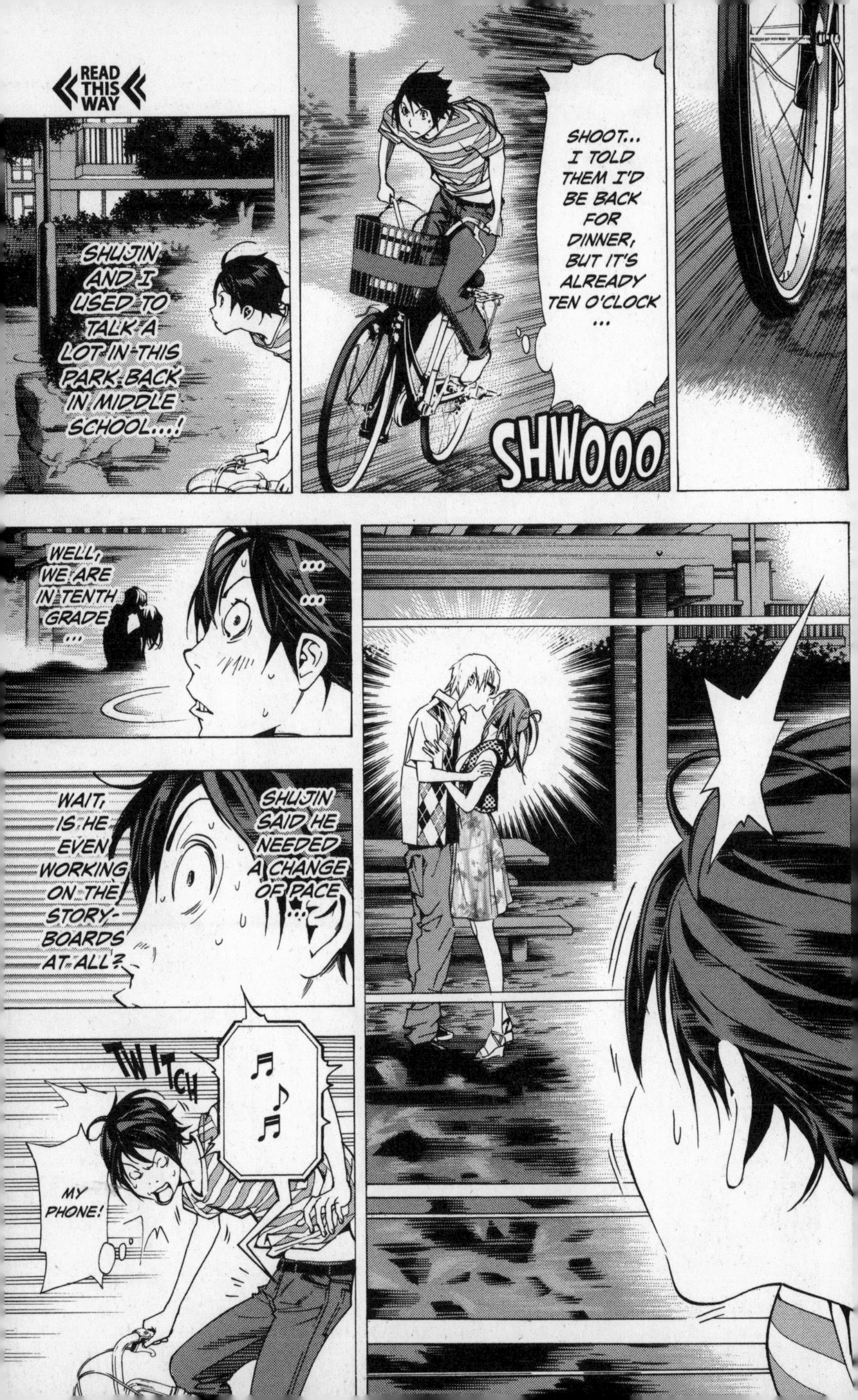
READ THIS WAY
SHOOT... I TOLD THEM I'D BE BACK FOR DINNER, BUT IT'S ALREADY TEN O'CLOCK...
SHWOOO
SHUJIN AND I USED TO TALK A LOT IN THIS PARK BACK IN MIDDLE SCHOOL...!
...
...
WELL, WE ARE IN TENTH GRADE...
SHUJIN SAID HE NEEDED A CHANGE OF PACE...
WAIT, IS HE EVEN WORKING ON THE STORY-BOARDS AT ALL?
♫ ♪ ♫
TWITCH
MY PHONE!

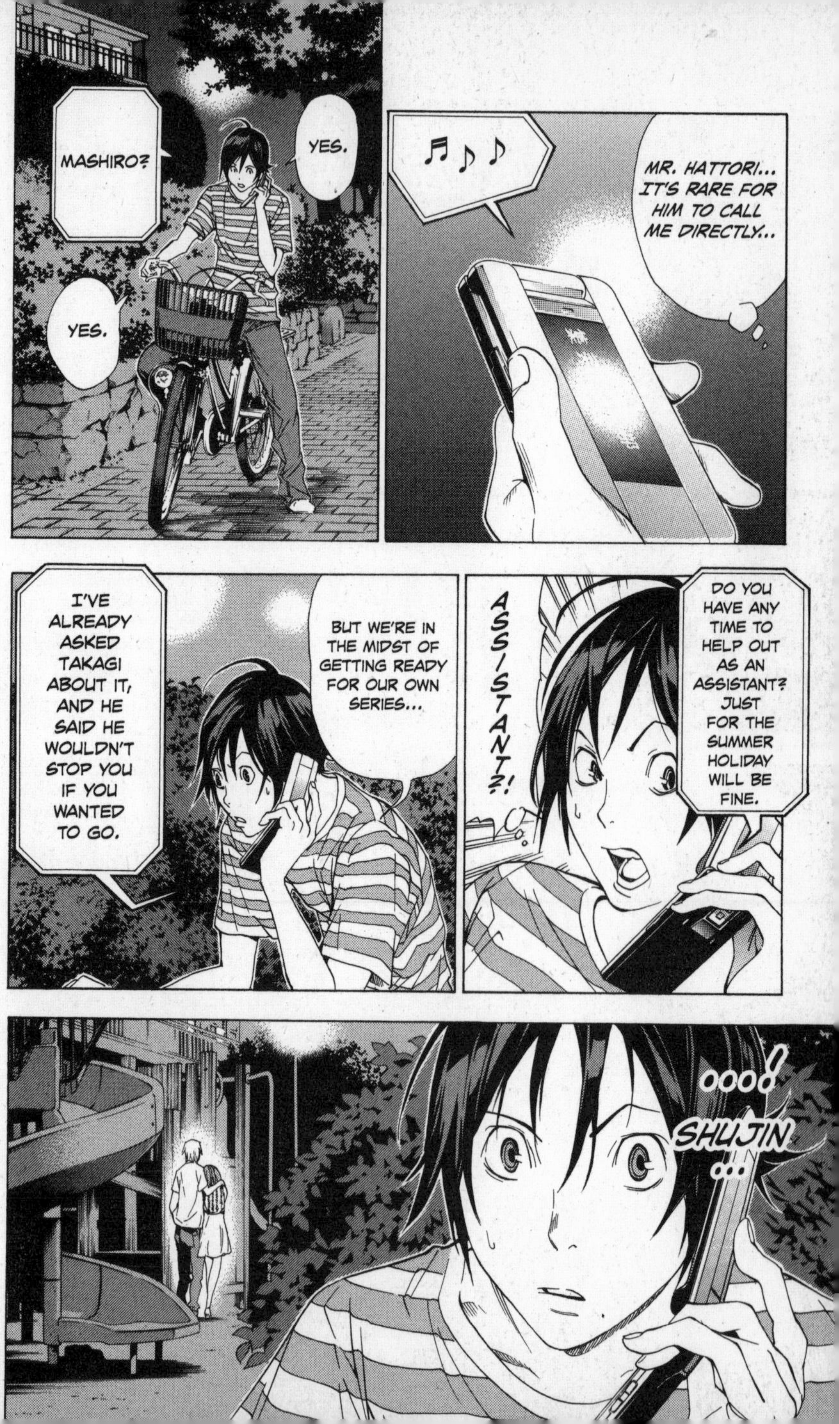
♬ ♪ ♪
MR. HATTORI... IT'S RARE FOR HIM TO CALL ME DIRECTLY...
YES.
MASHIRO?
YES.
DO YOU HAVE ANY TIME TO HELP OUT AS AN ASSISTANT? JUST FOR THE SUMMER HOLIDAY WILL BE FINE.
ASSISTANT?!
BUT WE'RE IN THE MIDST OF GETTING READY FOR OUR OWN SERIES...
I'VE ALREADY ASKED TAKAGI ABOUT IT, AND HE SAID HE WOULDN'T STOP YOU IF YOU WANTED TO GO.
OOO!
SHUJIN...

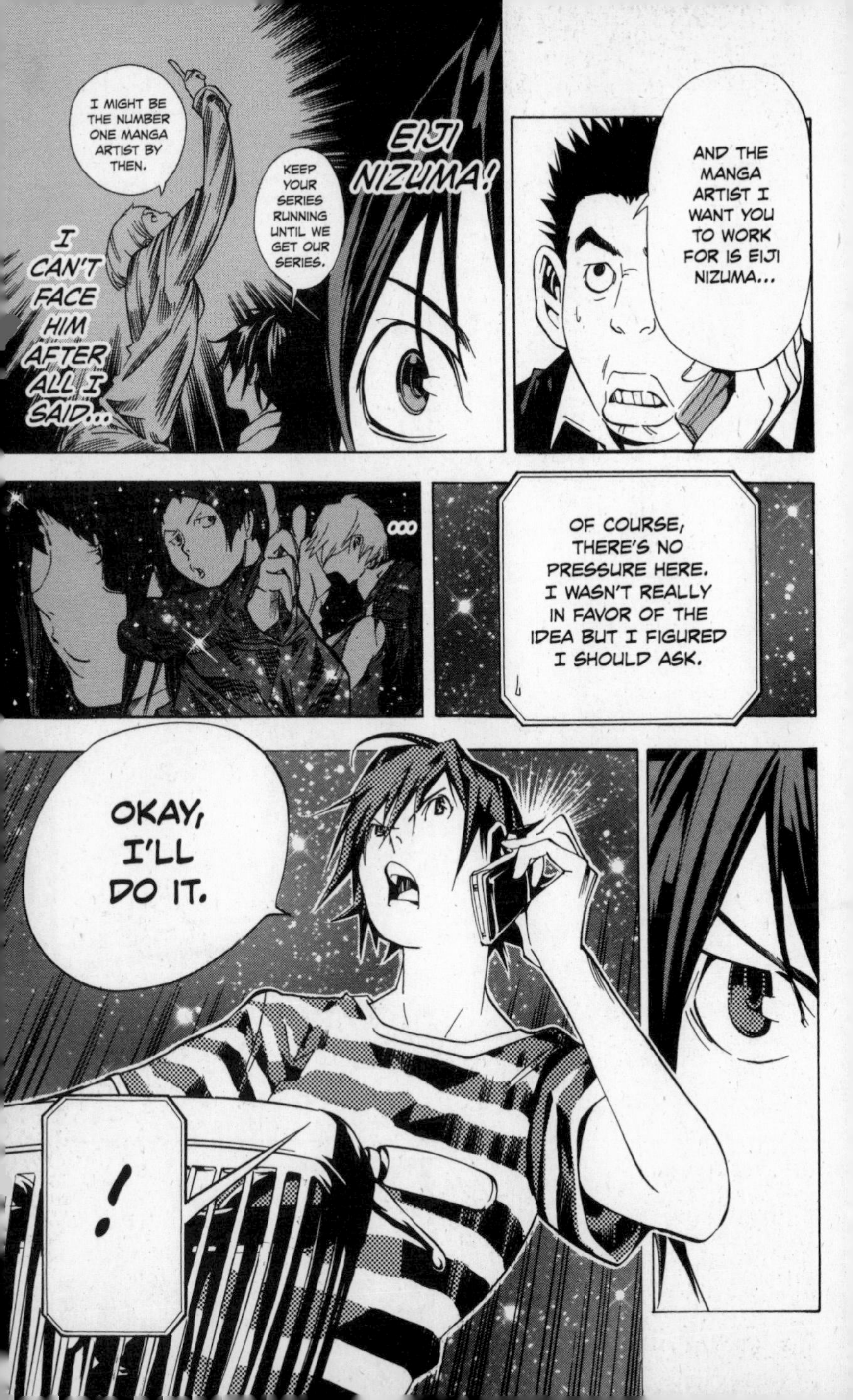
AND THE MANGA ARTIST I WANT YOU TO WORK FOR IS EIJI NIZUMA...
EIJI NIZUMA!
KEEP YOUR SERIES RUNNING UNTIL WE GET OUR SERIES.
I MIGHT BE THE NUMBER ONE MANGA ARTIST BY THEN.
I CAN'T FACE HIM AFTER ALL I SAID...
OF COURSE, THERE'S NO PRESSURE HERE. I WASN'T REALLY IN FAVOR OF THE IDEA BUT I FIGURED I SHOULD ASK.
...
OKAY, I'LL DO IT.
!

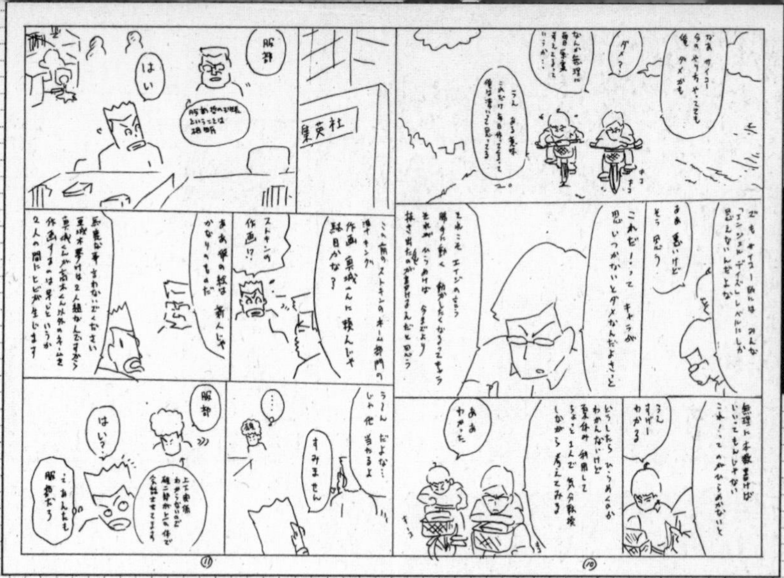
ダメ？
集英社
服部
はい
服部
はい？

OHBA'S STORYBOARD

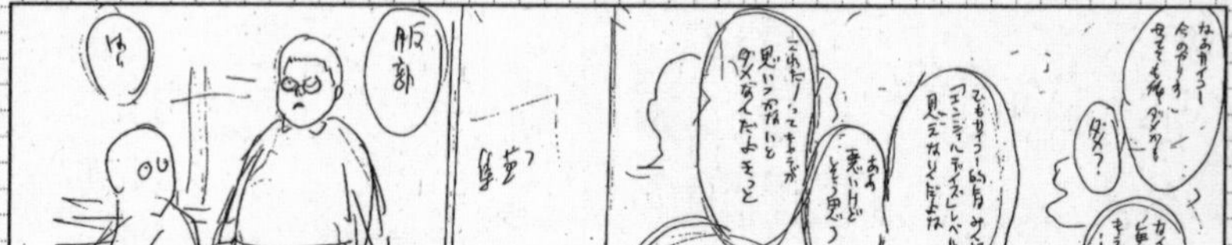
服部

OBATA'S STORYBOARD

COMPLETE!

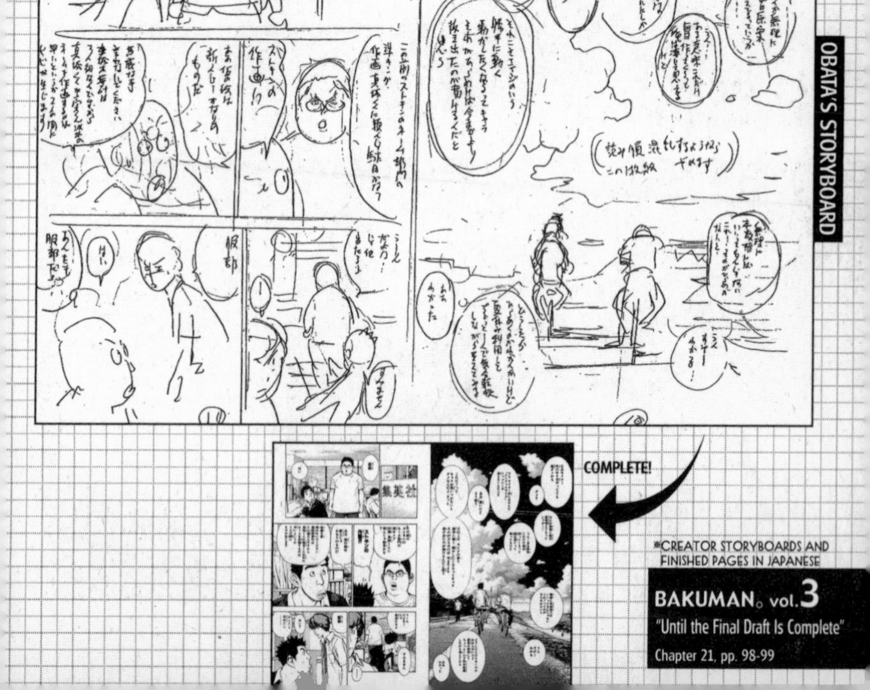

*CREATOR STORYBOARDS AND FINISHED PAGES IN JAPANESE

BAKUMAN。 vol.3
"Until the Final Draft Is Complete"
Chapter 21, pp. 98-99

CHAPTER 22
IN THE WAY AND YOUTH

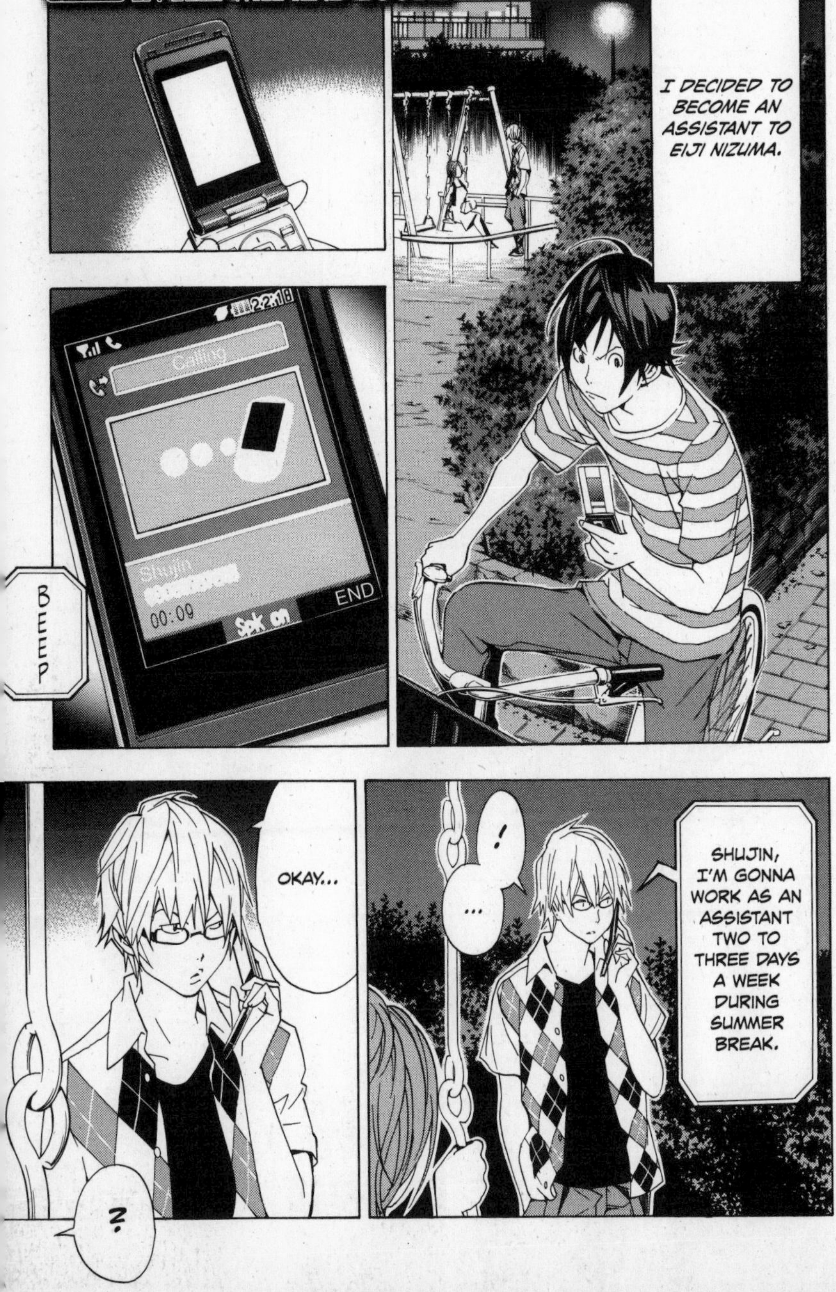
I DECIDED TO BECOME AN ASSISTANT TO EIJI NIZUMA.
Calling
Shujin
00:09
END
Spk on
BEEP
SHUJIN, I'M GONNA WORK AS AN ASSISTANT TWO TO THREE DAYS A WEEK DURING SUMMER BREAK.
!
...
OKAY...
?

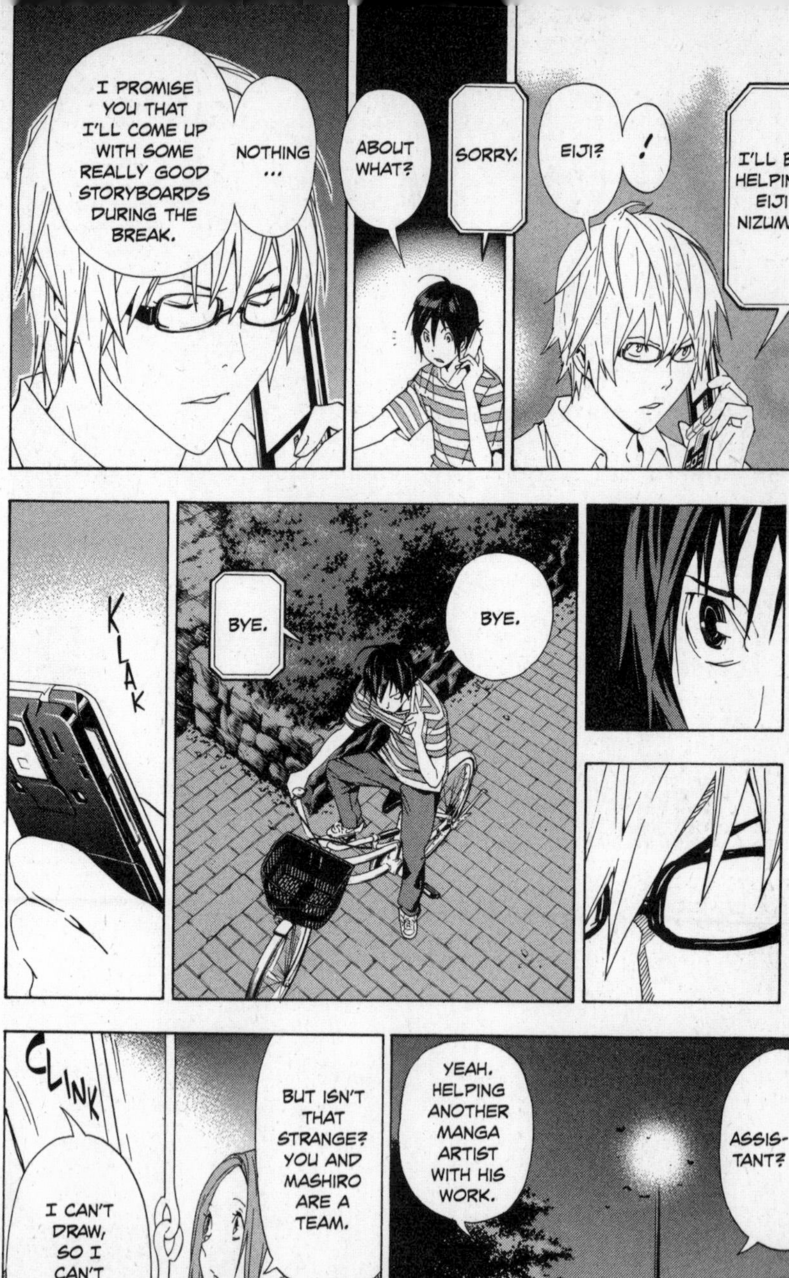

I'LL BE HELPING EIJI NIZUMA.
!
EIJI?
SORRY.
ABOUT WHAT?
NOTHING...
I PROMISE YOU THAT I'LL COME UP WITH SOME REALLY GOOD STORYBOARDS DURING THE BREAK.
BYE.
BYE.
KLAK
ASSIS-TANT?
YEAH. HELPING ANOTHER MANGA ARTIST WITH HIS WORK.
BUT ISN'T THAT STRANGE? YOU AND MASHIRO ARE A TEAM.
CLINK
I CAN'T DRAW, SO I CAN'T GO WITH HIM.

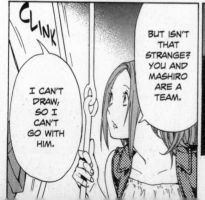

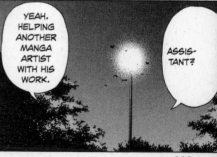

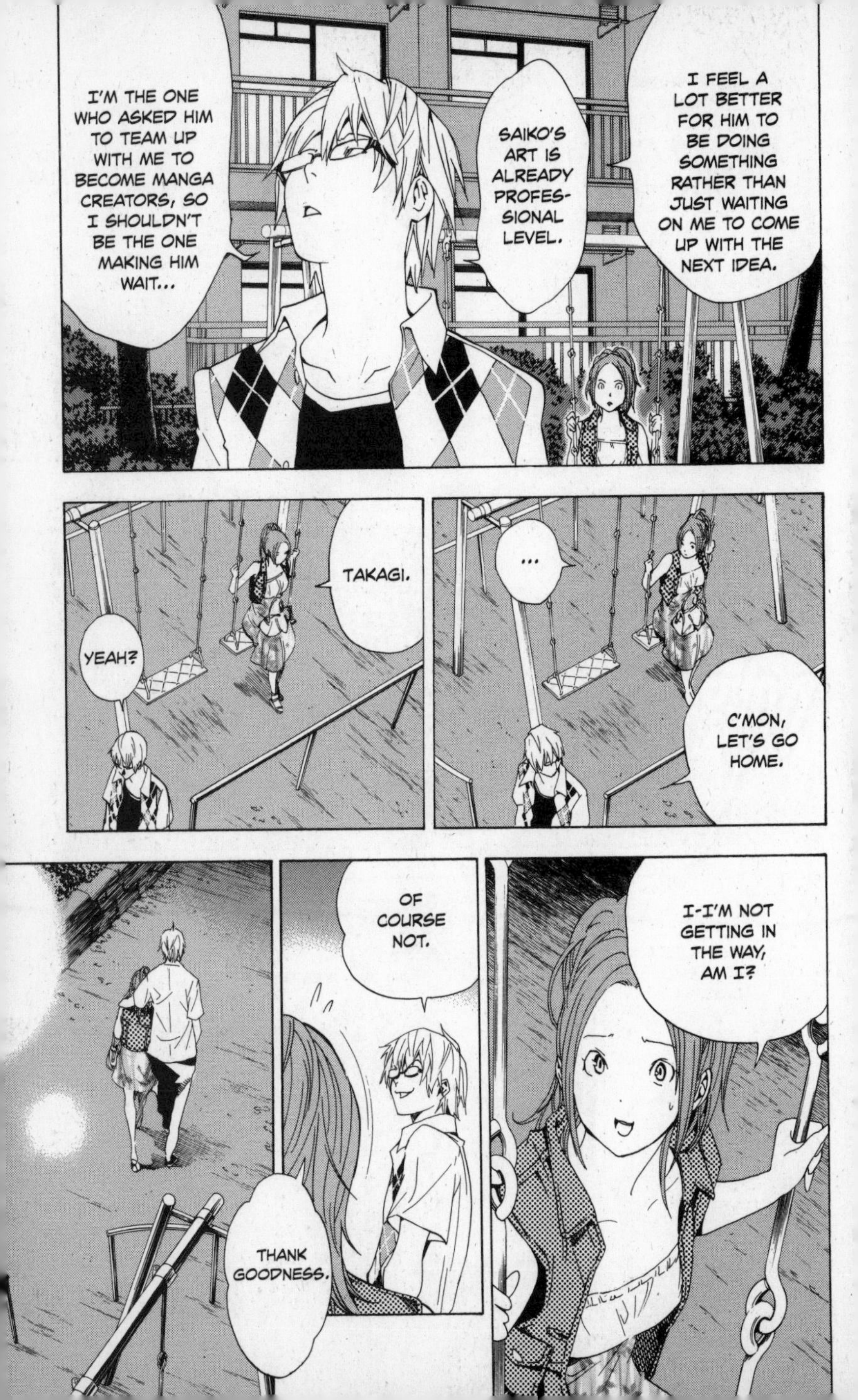
I FEEL A LOT BETTER FOR HIM TO BE DOING SOMETHING RATHER THAN JUST WAITING ON ME TO COME UP WITH THE NEXT IDEA.
SAIKO'S ART IS ALREADY PROFES-SIONAL LEVEL.
I'M THE ONE WHO ASKED HIM TO TEAM UP WITH ME TO BECOME MANGA CREATORS, SO I SHOULDN'T BE THE ONE MAKING HIM WAIT...
...
C'MON, LET'S GO HOME.
TAKAGI.
YEAH?
I-I'M NOT GETTING IN THE WAY, AM I?
OF COURSE NOT.
THANK GOODNESS.

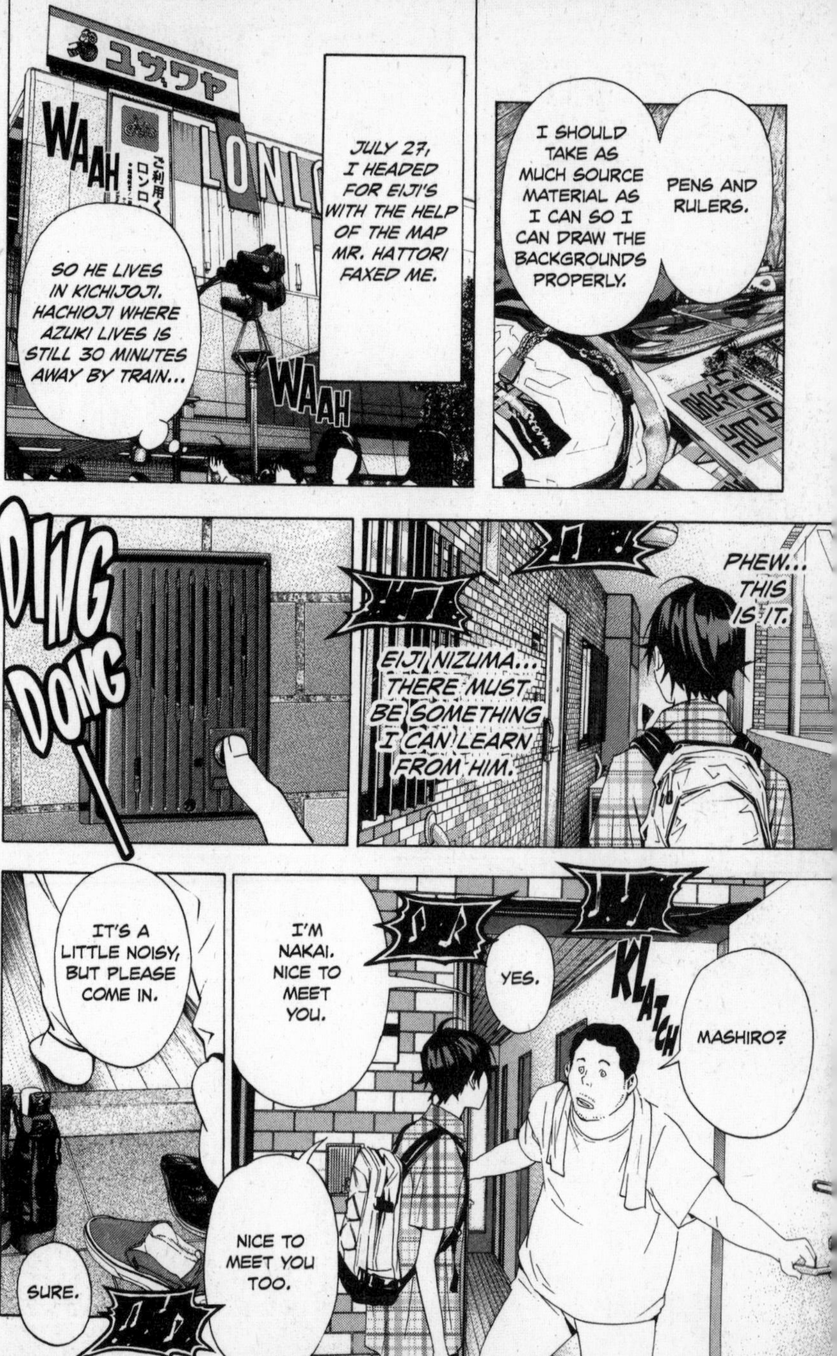
PENS AND RULERS.
I SHOULD TAKE AS MUCH SOURCE MATERIAL AS I CAN SO I CAN DRAW THE BACKGROUNDS PROPERLY.
JULY 27, I HEADED FOR EIJI'S WITH THE HELP OF THE MAP MR. HATTORI FAXED ME.
ユザワヤ
WAAH
SO HE LIVES IN KICHIJOJI. HACHIOJI WHERE AZUKI LIVES IS STILL 30 MINUTES AWAY BY TRAIN...
WAAH
PHEW... THIS IS IT.
EIJI NIZUMA... THERE MUST BE SOMETHING I CAN LEARN FROM HIM.
DING DONG
MASHIRO?
KLATCH
YES.
I'M NAKAI. NICE TO MEET YOU.
NICE TO MEET YOU TOO.
IT'S A LITTLE NOISY, BUT PLEASE COME IN.
SURE.

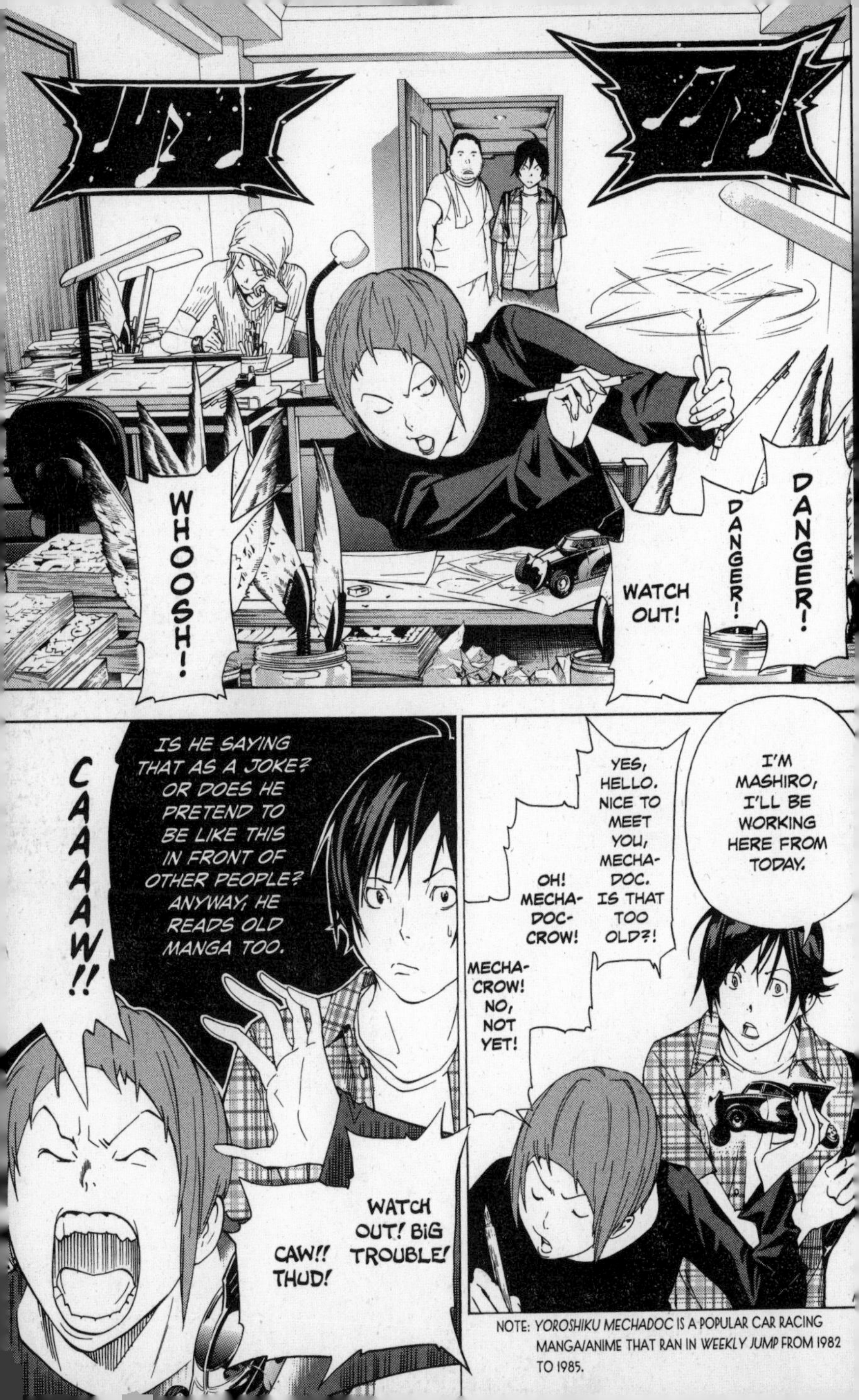
DANGER!
DANGER!
WATCH OUT!
WHOOSH!
I'M MASHIRO, I'LL BE WORKING HERE FROM TODAY.
YES, HELLO. NICE TO MEET YOU, MECHA-DOC. IS THAT TOO OLD?!
OH! MECHA-DOC-CROW!
MECHA-CROW! NO, NOT YET!
IS HE SAYING THAT AS A JOKE? OR DOES HE PRETEND TO BE LIKE THIS IN FRONT OF OTHER PEOPLE? ANYWAY, HE READS OLD MANGA TOO.
CAAAAAW!!
WATCH OUT! BIG TROUBLE!
CAW!! THUD!

NOTE: *YOROSHIKU MECHADOC* IS A POPULAR CAR RACING MANGA/ANIME THAT RAN IN *WEEKLY JUMP* FROM 1982 TO 1985.

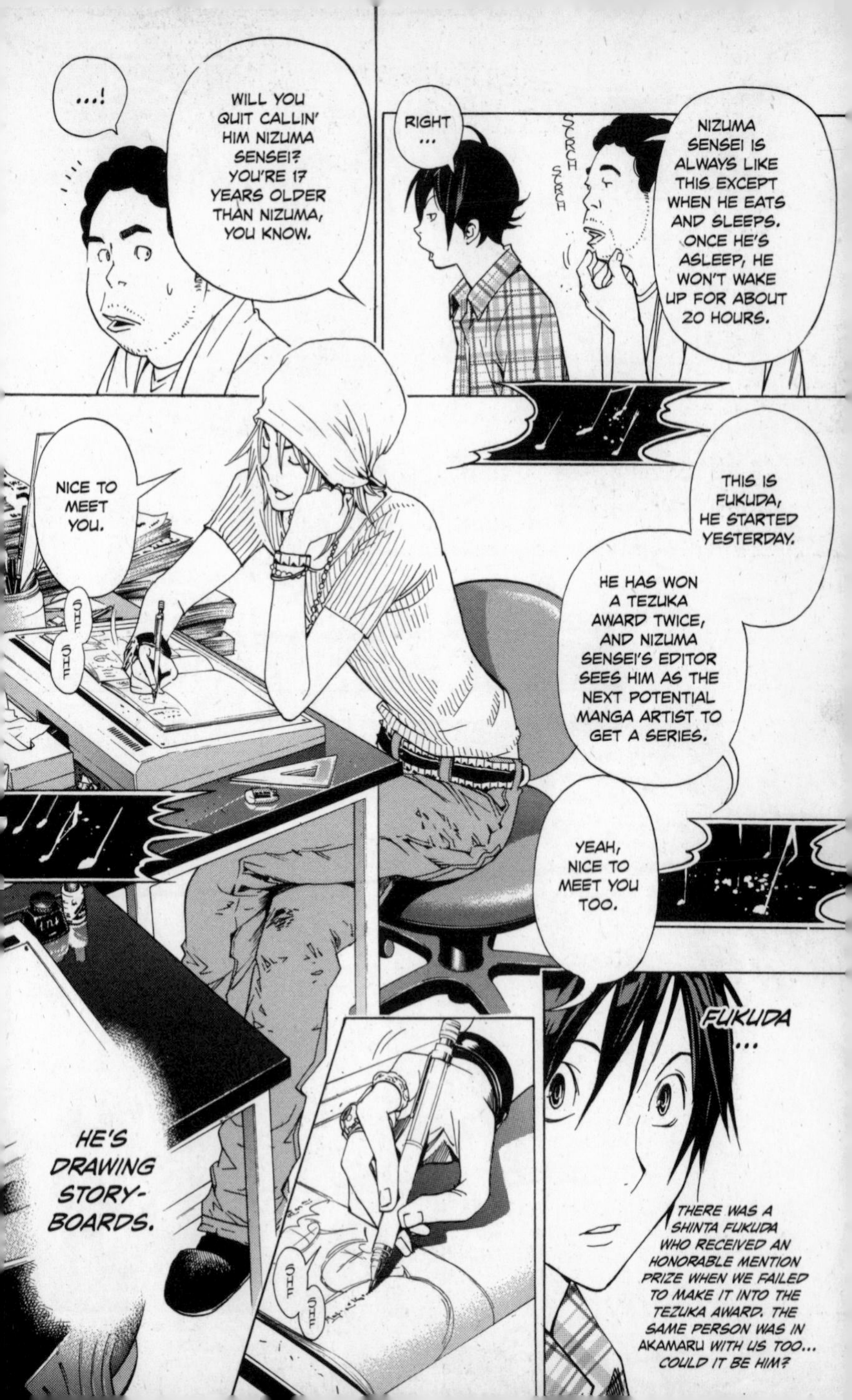
NIZUMA SENSEI IS ALWAYS LIKE THIS EXCEPT WHEN HE EATS AND SLEEPS. ONCE HE'S ASLEEP, HE WON'T WAKE UP FOR ABOUT 20 HOURS.
SCRCH SCRCH
RIGHT ...
WILL YOU QUIT CALLIN' HIM NIZUMA SENSEI? YOU'RE 17 YEARS OLDER THAN NIZUMA, YOU KNOW.
...!
THIS IS FUKUDA, HE STARTED YESTERDAY.
HE HAS WON A TEZUKA AWARD TWICE, AND NIZUMA SENSEI'S EDITOR SEES HIM AS THE NEXT POTENTIAL MANGA ARTIST TO GET A SERIES.
NICE TO MEET YOU.
SHF SHF
YEAH, NICE TO MEET YOU TOO.
FUKUDA ...
THERE WAS A SHINTA FUKUDA WHO RECEIVED AN HONORABLE MENTION PRIZE WHEN WE FAILED TO MAKE IT INTO THE TEZUKA AWARD. THE SAME PERSON WAS IN AKAMARU WITH US TOO... COULD IT BE HIM?
HE'S DRAWING STORY-BOARDS.
SHF SHF

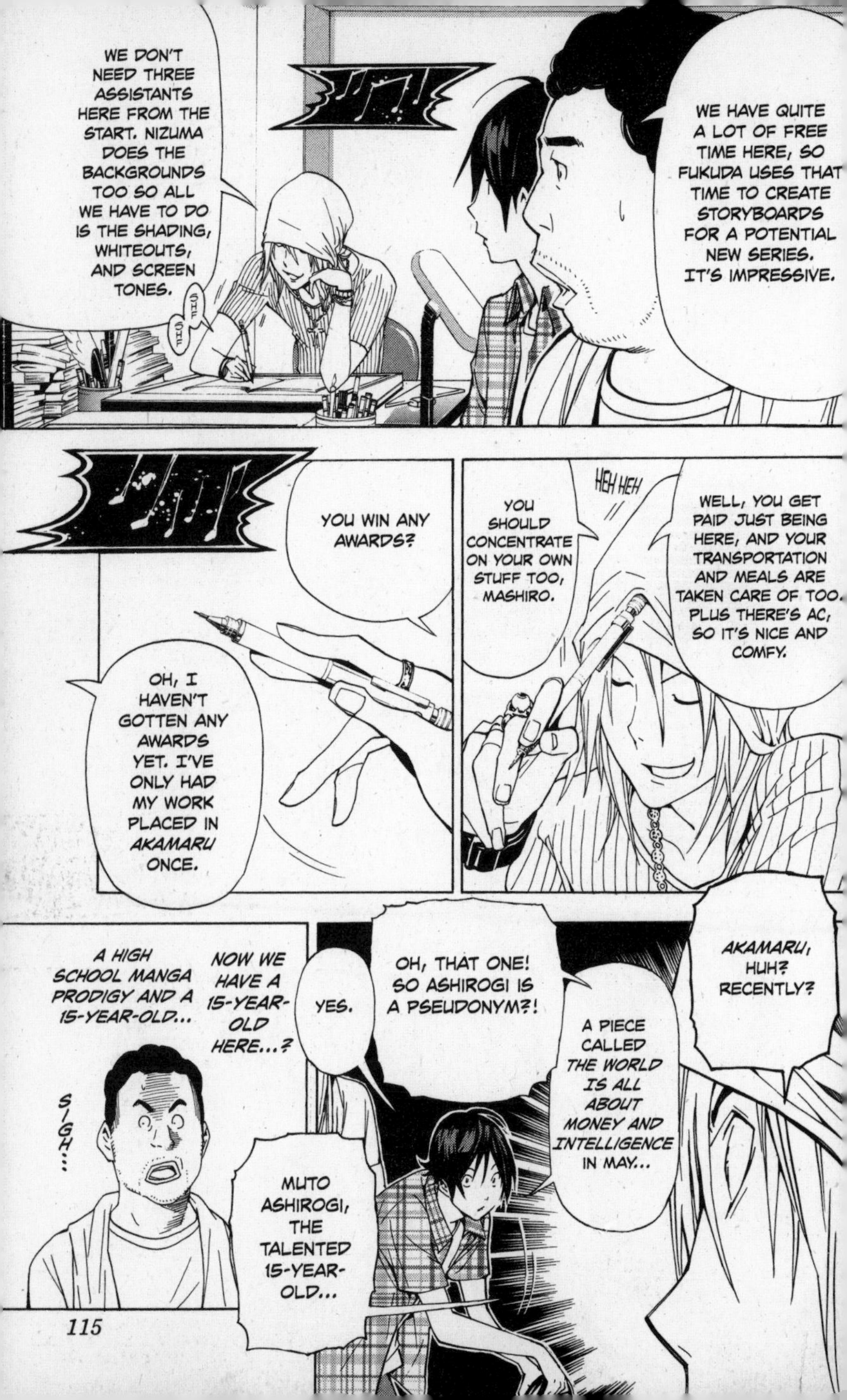

WE HAVE QUITE A LOT OF FREE TIME HERE, SO FUKUDA USES THAT TIME TO CREATE STORYBOARDS FOR A POTENTIAL NEW SERIES. IT'S IMPRESSIVE.
WE DON'T NEED THREE ASSISTANTS HERE FROM THE START. NIZUMA DOES THE BACKGROUNDS TOO SO ALL WE HAVE TO DO IS THE SHADING, WHITEOUTS, AND SCREEN TONES.
SHF SHF
HEH HEH
WELL, YOU GET PAID JUST BEING HERE, AND YOUR TRANSPORTATION AND MEALS ARE TAKEN CARE OF TOO. PLUS THERE'S AC, SO IT'S NICE AND COMFY.
YOU SHOULD CONCENTRATE ON YOUR OWN STUFF TOO, MASHIRO.
YOU WIN ANY AWARDS?
OH, I HAVEN'T GOTTEN ANY AWARDS YET. I'VE ONLY HAD MY WORK PLACED IN *AKAMARU* ONCE.
AKAMARU, HUH? RECENTLY?
A PIECE CALLED *THE WORLD IS ALL ABOUT MONEY AND INTELLIGENCE* IN MAY...
OH, THAT ONE! SO ASHIROGI IS A PSEUDONYM?!
YES.
MUTO ASHIROGI, THE TALENTED 15-YEAR-OLD...
NOW WE HAVE A 15-YEAR-OLD HERE...?
A HIGH SCHOOL MANGA PRODIGY AND A 15-YEAR-OLD...
SIGH...

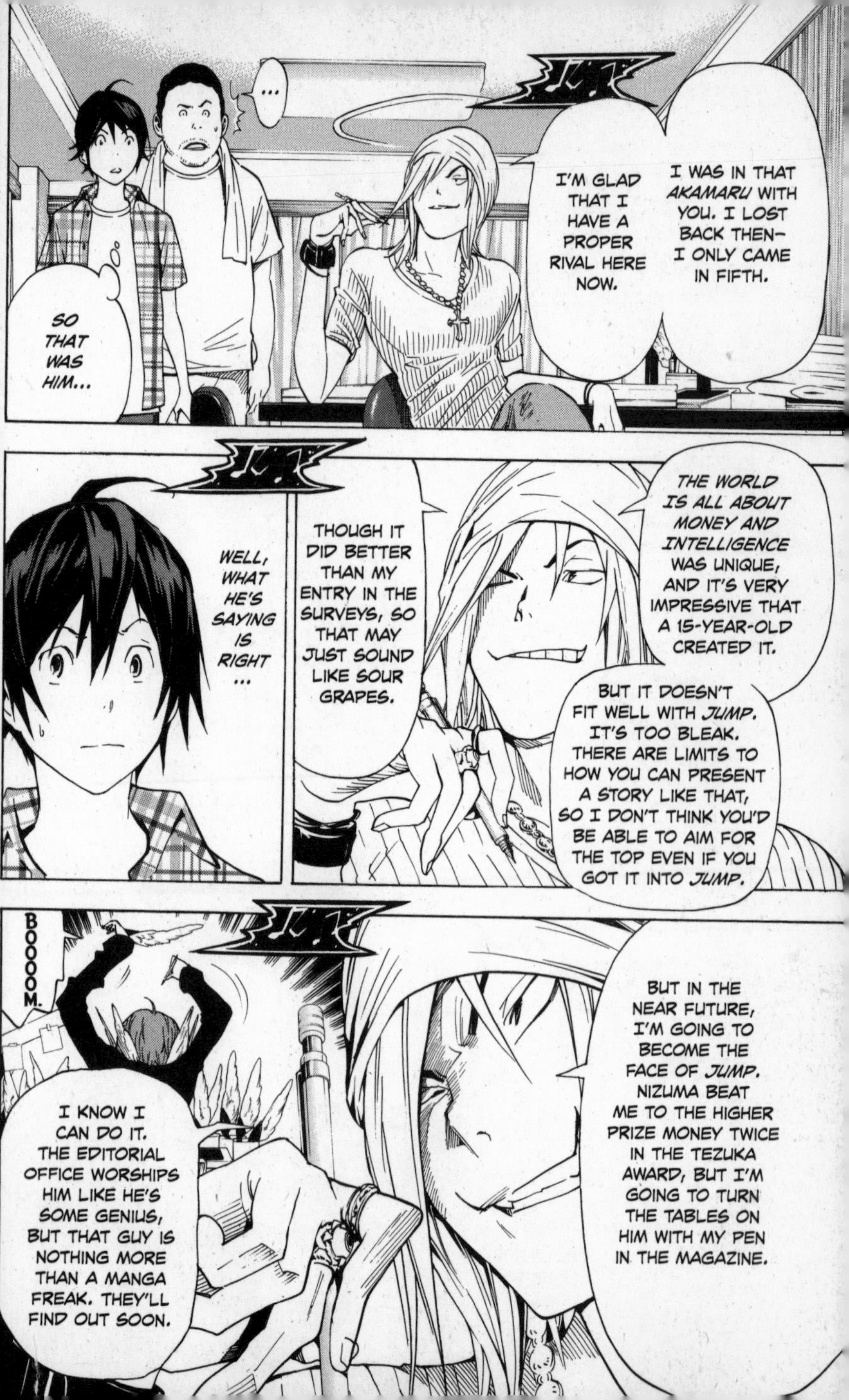
I WAS IN THAT AKAMARU WITH YOU. I LOST BACK THEN— I ONLY CAME IN FIFTH.
I'M GLAD THAT I HAVE A PROPER RIVAL HERE NOW.
...
SO THAT WAS HIM...
THE WORLD IS ALL ABOUT MONEY AND INTELLIGENCE WAS UNIQUE, AND IT'S VERY IMPRESSIVE THAT A 15-YEAR-OLD CREATED IT.
BUT IT DOESN'T FIT WELL WITH JUMP. IT'S TOO BLEAK. THERE ARE LIMITS TO HOW YOU CAN PRESENT A STORY LIKE THAT, SO I DON'T THINK YOU'D BE ABLE TO AIM FOR THE TOP EVEN IF YOU GOT IT INTO JUMP.
THOUGH IT DID BETTER THAN MY ENTRY IN THE SURVEYS, SO THAT MAY JUST SOUND LIKE SOUR GRAPES.
WELL, WHAT HE'S SAYING IS RIGHT...
BUT IN THE NEAR FUTURE, I'M GOING TO BECOME THE FACE OF JUMP. NIZUMA BEAT ME TO THE HIGHER PRIZE MONEY TWICE IN THE TEZUKA AWARD, BUT I'M GOING TO TURN THE TABLES ON HIM WITH MY PEN IN THE MAGAZINE.
I KNOW I CAN DO IT. THE EDITORIAL OFFICE WORSHIPS HIM LIKE HE'S SOME GENIUS, BUT THAT GUY IS NOTHING MORE THAN A MANGA FREAK. THEY'LL FIND OUT SOON.
BOOOOOM.

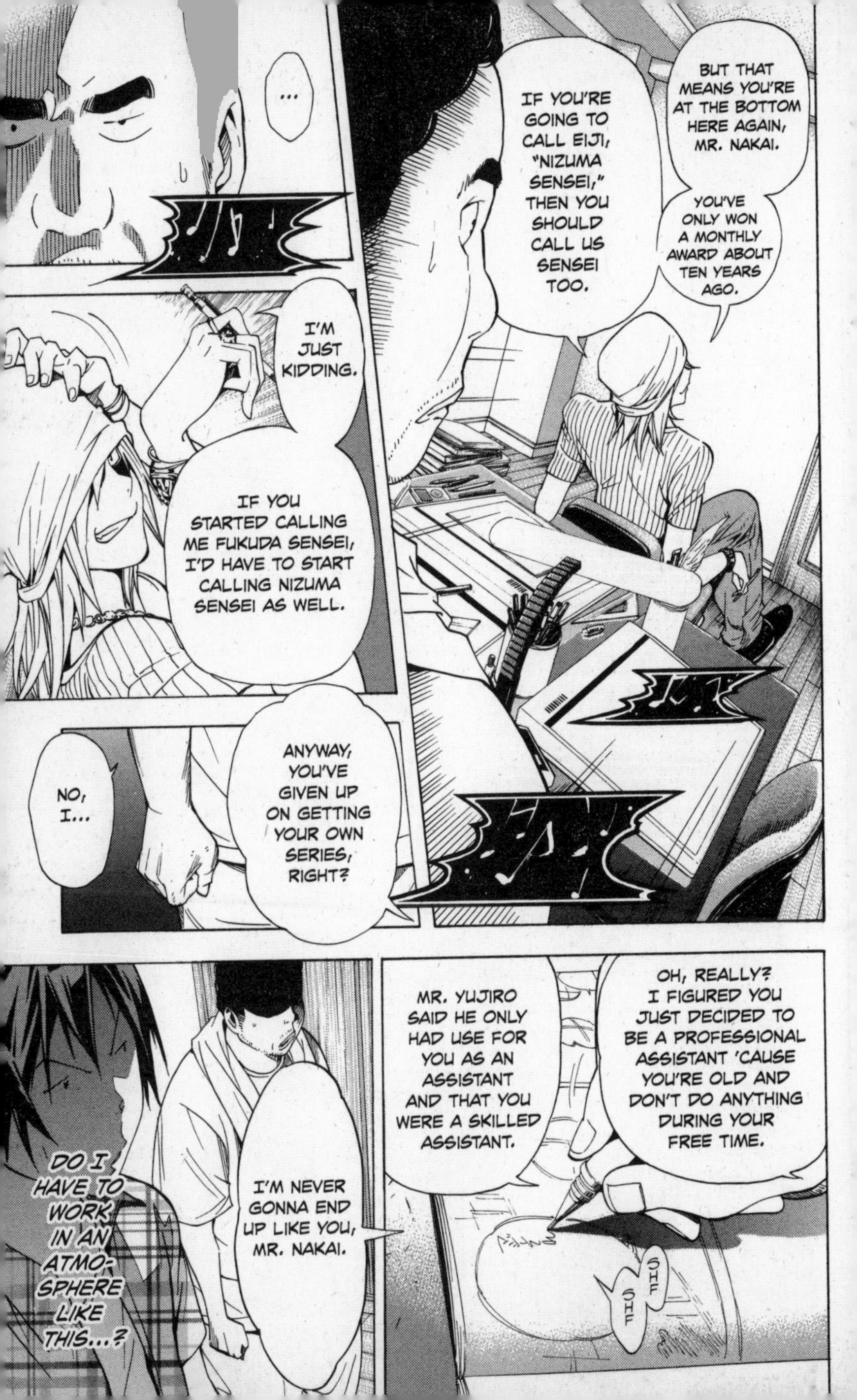
IF YOU'RE GOING TO CALL EIJI, "NIZUMA SENSEI," THEN YOU SHOULD CALL US SENSEI TOO.
BUT THAT MEANS YOU'RE AT THE BOTTOM HERE AGAIN, MR. NAKAI.
YOU'VE ONLY WON A MONTHLY AWARD ABOUT TEN YEARS AGO.
...
I'M JUST KIDDING.
IF YOU STARTED CALLING ME FUKUDA SENSEI, I'D HAVE TO START CALLING NIZUMA SENSEI AS WELL.
ANYWAY, YOU'VE GIVEN UP ON GETTING YOUR OWN SERIES, RIGHT?
NO, I...
OH, REALLY? I FIGURED YOU JUST DECIDED TO BE A PROFESSIONAL ASSISTANT 'CAUSE YOU'RE OLD AND DON'T DO ANYTHING DURING YOUR FREE TIME.
MR. YUJIRO SAID HE ONLY HAD USE FOR YOU AS AN ASSISTANT AND THAT YOU WERE A SKILLED ASSISTANT.
SHF
SHF
I'M NEVER GONNA END UP LIKE YOU, MR. NAKAI.
DO I HAVE TO WORK IN AN ATMOSPHERE LIKE THIS...?

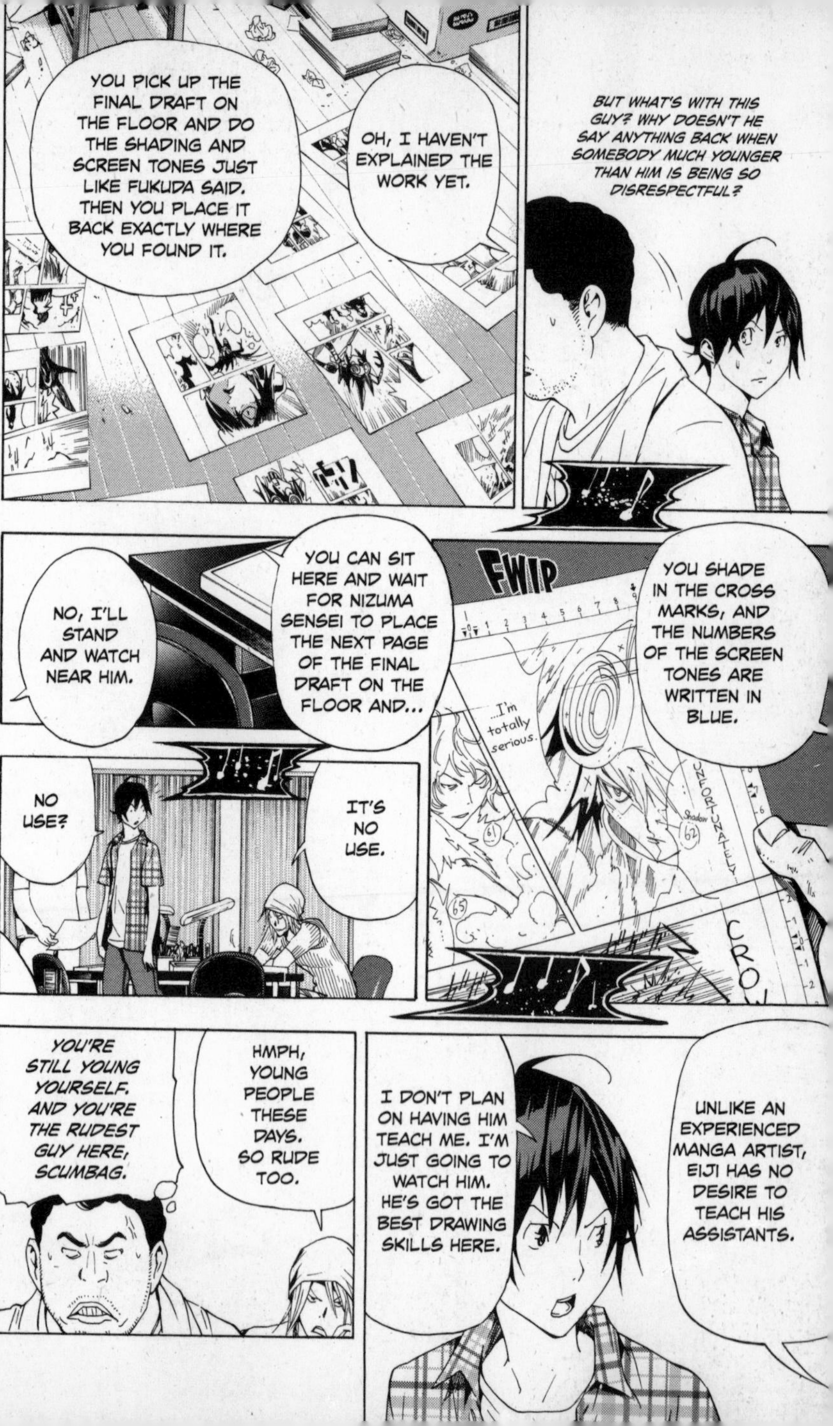
BUT WHAT'S WITH THIS GUY? WHY DOESN'T HE SAY ANYTHING BACK WHEN SOMEBODY MUCH YOUNGER THAN HIM IS BEING SO DISRESPECTFUL?
OH, I HAVEN'T EXPLAINED THE WORK YET.
YOU PICK UP THE FINAL DRAFT ON THE FLOOR AND DO THE SHADING AND SCREEN TONES JUST LIKE FUKUDA SAID. THEN YOU PLACE IT BACK EXACTLY WHERE YOU FOUND IT.
FWIP
YOU SHADE IN THE CROSS MARKS, AND THE NUMBERS OF THE SCREEN TONES ARE WRITTEN IN BLUE.
...I'm totally serious.
UNFORTUNATELY
Shadow
CROW
YOU CAN SIT HERE AND WAIT FOR NIZUMA SENSEI TO PLACE THE NEXT PAGE OF THE FINAL DRAFT ON THE FLOOR AND...
NO, I'LL STAND AND WATCH NEAR HIM.
IT'S NO USE.
NO USE?
UNLIKE AN EXPERIENCED MANGA ARTIST, EIJI HAS NO DESIRE TO TEACH HIS ASSISTANTS.
I DON'T PLAN ON HAVING HIM TEACH ME. I'M JUST GOING TO WATCH HIM. HE'S GOT THE BEST DRAWING SKILLS HERE.
HMPH, YOUNG PEOPLE THESE DAYS. SO RUDE TOO.
YOU'RE STILL YOUNG YOURSELF. AND YOU'RE THE RUDEST GUY HERE, SCUMBAG.

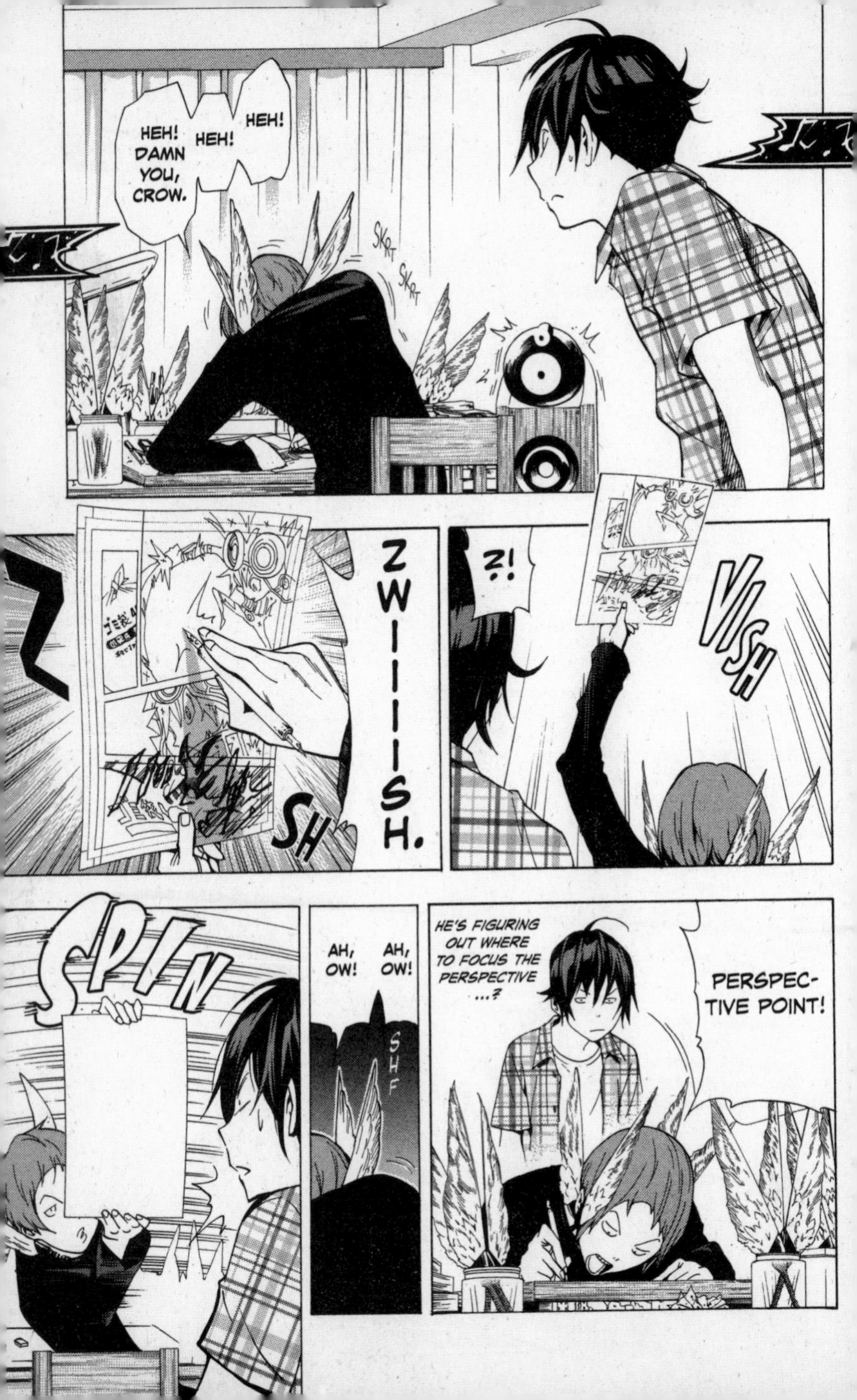
HEH!
HEH!
HEH! DAMN YOU, CROW.
SKRT
SKRT
?!
VISH
ZWIIIISH.
SH
PERSPEC-TIVE POINT!
HE'S FIGURING OUT WHERE TO FOCUS THE PERSPECTIVE ...?
AH, OW!
AH, OW!
SHF
SPIN

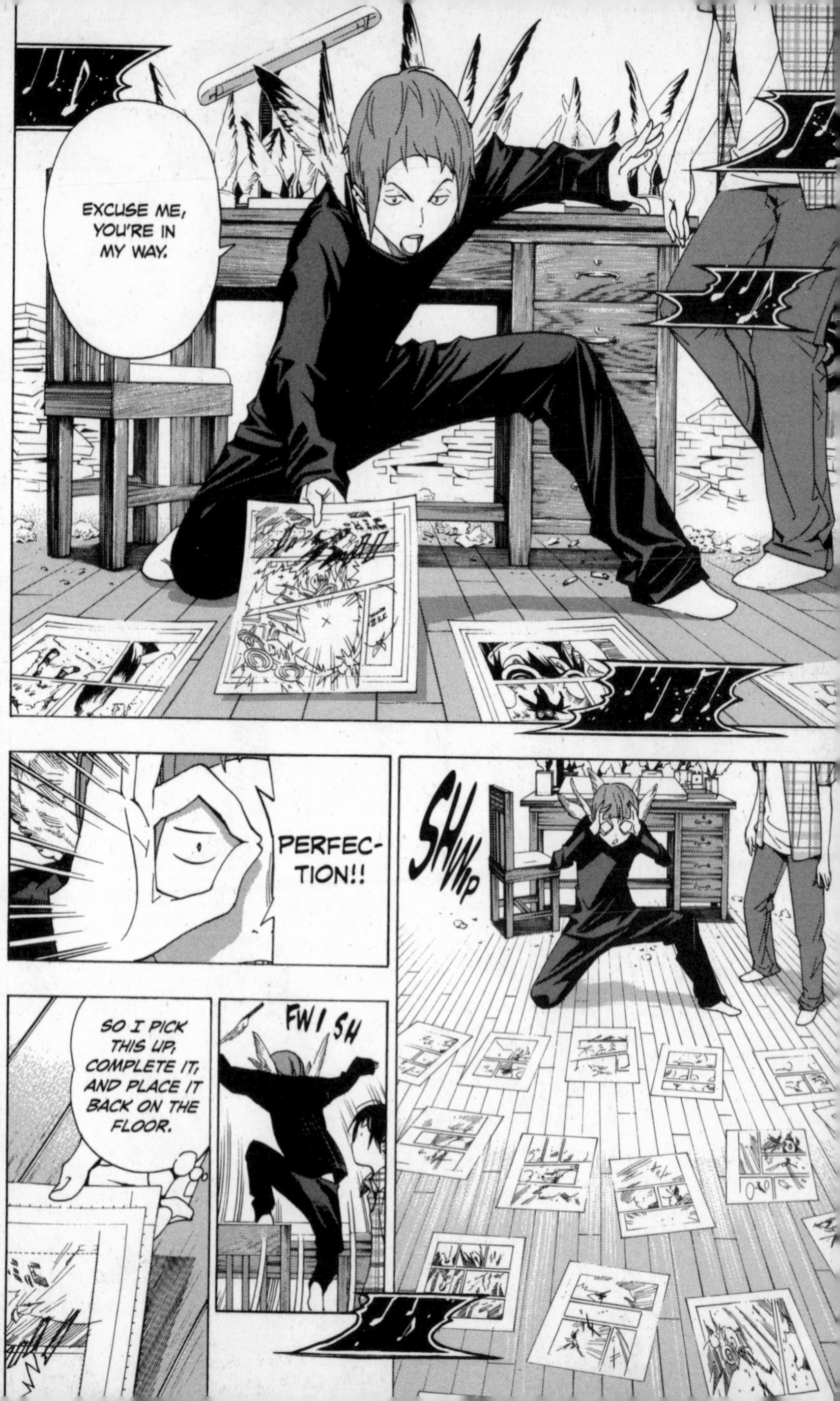
EXCUSE ME, YOU'RE IN MY WAY.
SHUNP
PERFEC-TION!!
FWISH
SO I PICK THIS UP, COMPLETE IT, AND PLACE IT BACK ON THE FLOOR.

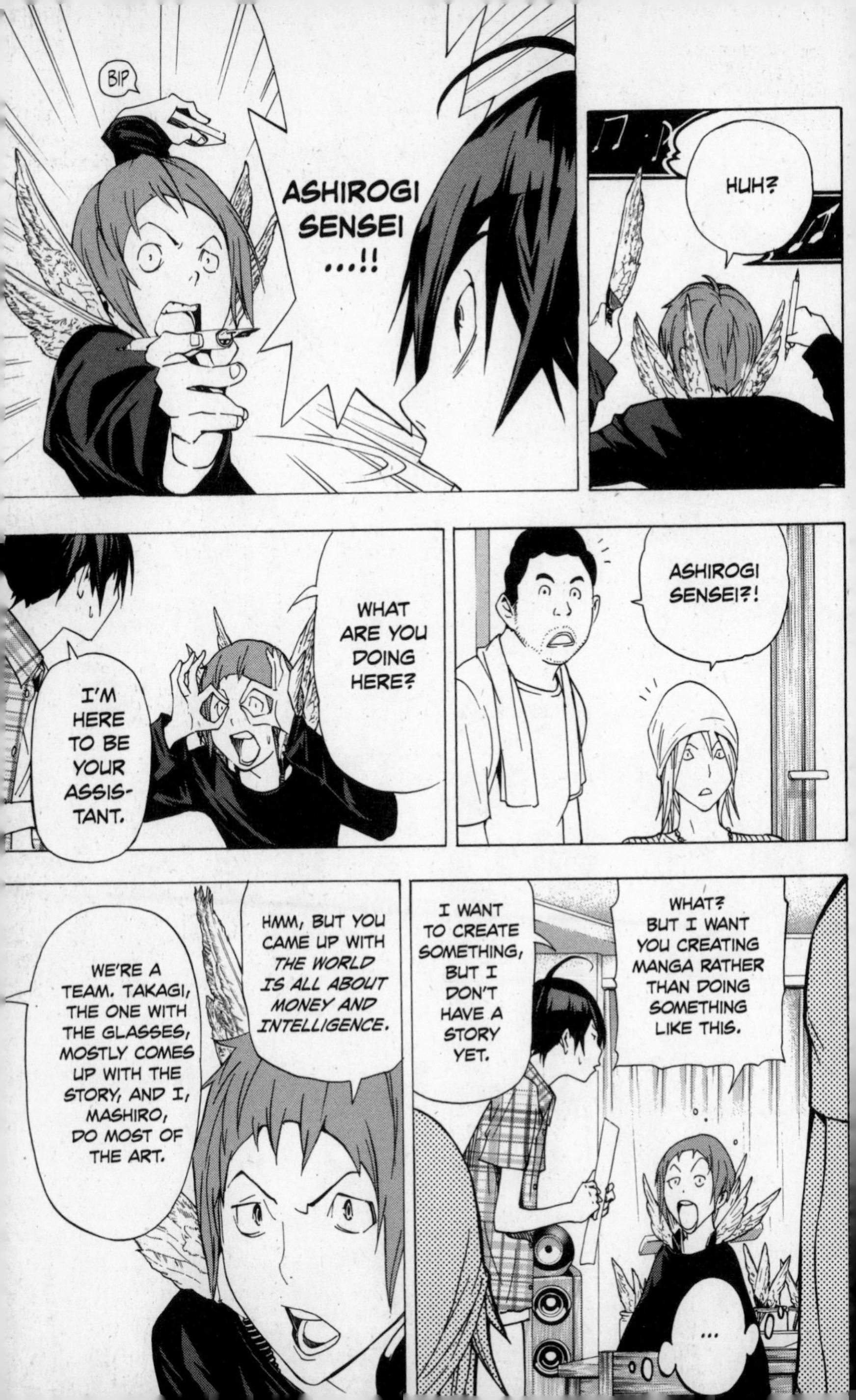
HUH?
BIP
ASHIROGI SENSEI ...!!
ASHIROGI SENSEI?!
WHAT ARE YOU DOING HERE?
I'M HERE TO BE YOUR ASSISTANT.
WHAT? BUT I WANT YOU CREATING MANGA RATHER THAN DOING SOMETHING LIKE THIS.
I WANT TO CREATE SOMETHING, BUT I DON'T HAVE A STORY YET.
...
HMM, BUT YOU CAME UP WITH *THE WORLD IS ALL ABOUT MONEY AND INTELLIGENCE*.
WE'RE A TEAM. TAKAGI, THE ONE WITH THE GLASSES, MOSTLY COMES UP WITH THE STORY, AND I, MASHIRO, DO MOST OF THE ART.

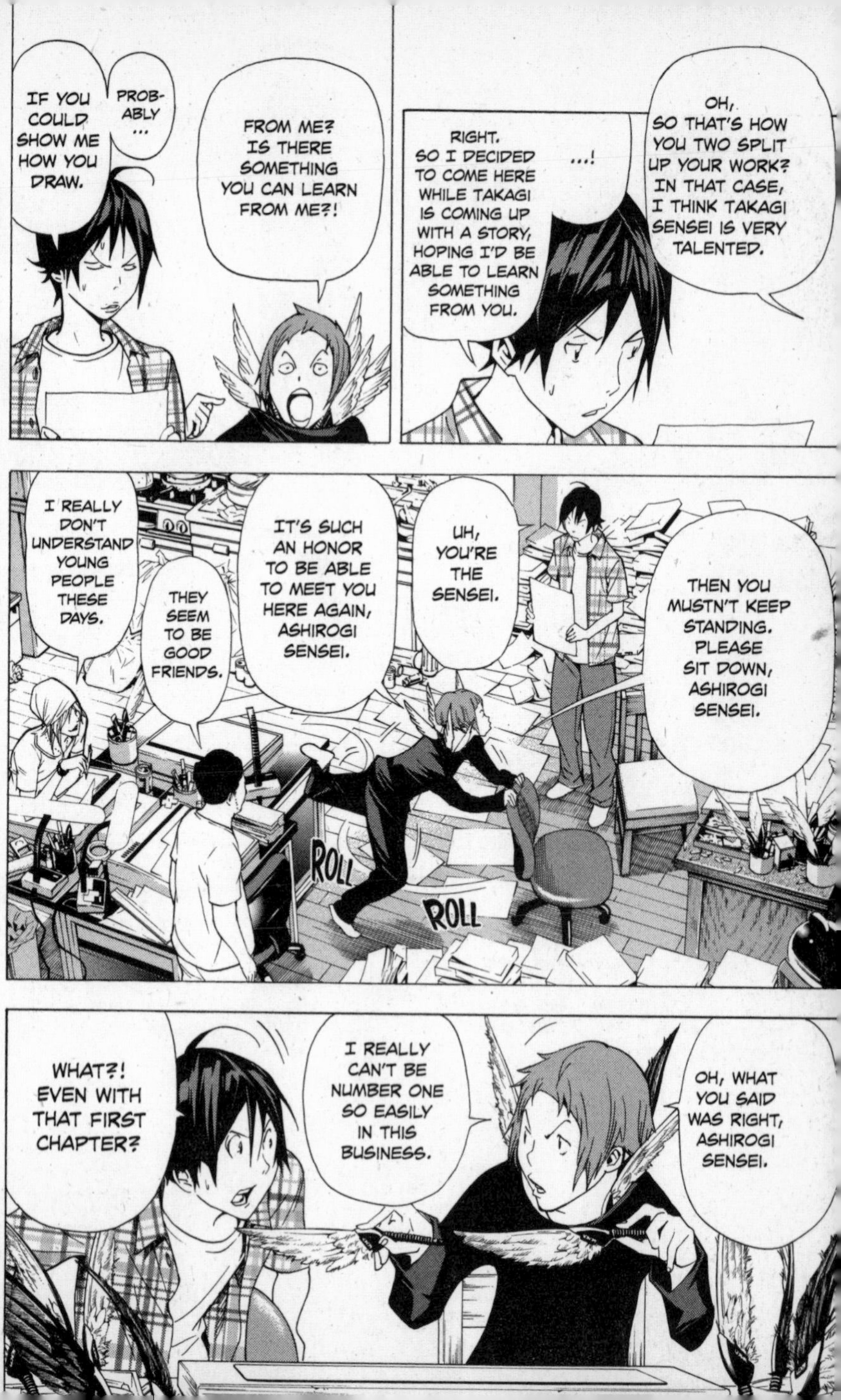
OH, SO THAT'S HOW YOU TWO SPLIT UP YOUR WORK? IN THAT CASE, I THINK TAKAGI SENSEI IS VERY TALENTED.
...!
RIGHT. SO I DECIDED TO COME HERE WHILE TAKAGI IS COMING UP WITH A STORY, HOPING I'D BE ABLE TO LEARN SOMETHING FROM YOU.
FROM ME? IS THERE SOMETHING YOU CAN LEARN FROM ME?!
PROB-ABLY ...
IF YOU COULD SHOW ME HOW YOU DRAW.
THEN YOU MUSTN'T KEEP STANDING. PLEASE SIT DOWN, ASHIROGI SENSEI.
UH, YOU'RE THE SENSEI.
IT'S SUCH AN HONOR TO BE ABLE TO MEET YOU HERE AGAIN, ASHIROGI SENSEI.
THEY SEEM TO BE GOOD FRIENDS.
I REALLY DON'T UNDERSTAND YOUNG PEOPLE THESE DAYS.
ROLL
ROLL
OH, WHAT YOU SAID WAS RIGHT, ASHIROGI SENSEI.
I REALLY CAN'T BE NUMBER ONE SO EASILY IN THIS BUSINESS.
WHAT?! EVEN WITH THAT FIRST CHAPTER?

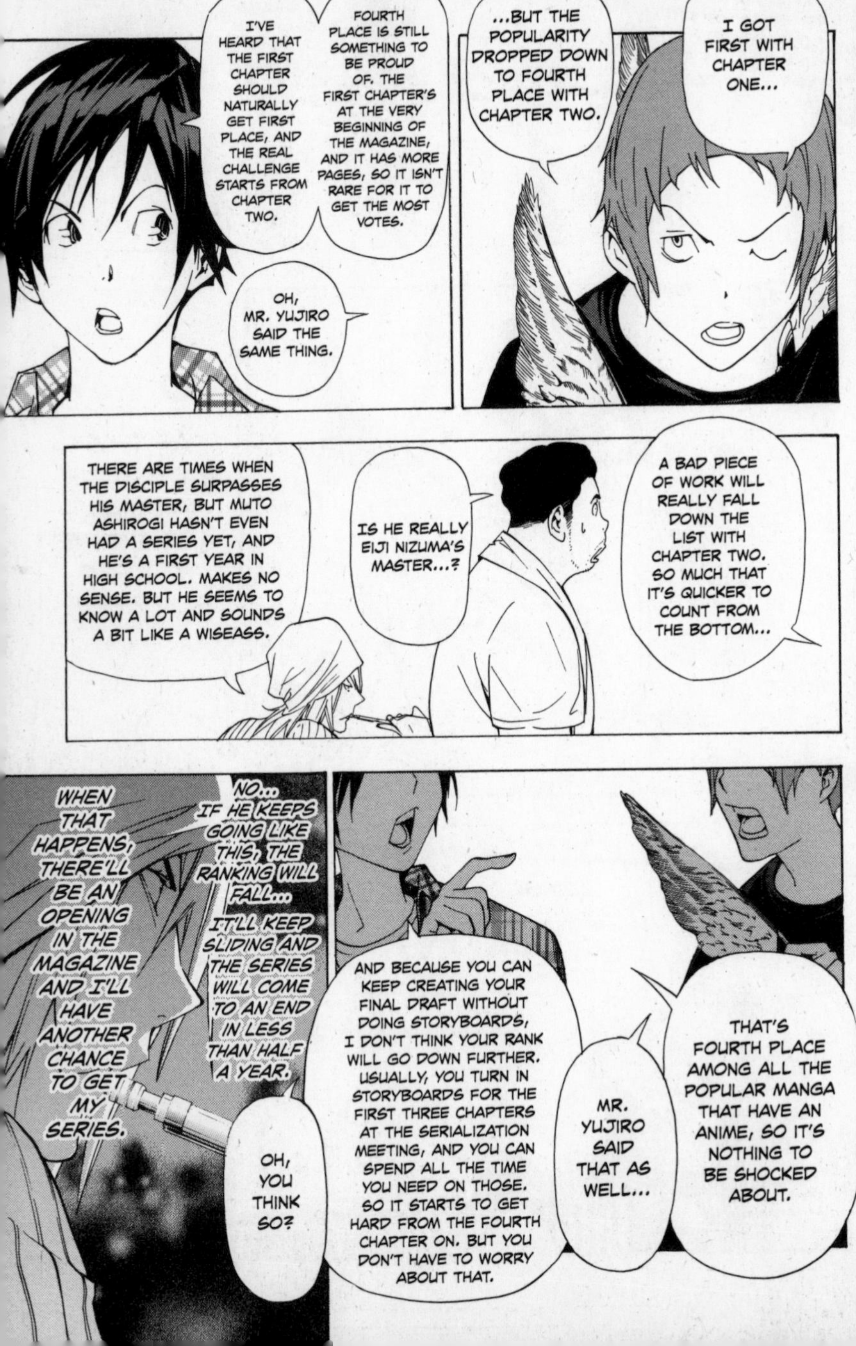

I GOT FIRST WITH CHAPTER ONE...
...BUT THE POPULARITY DROPPED DOWN TO FOURTH PLACE WITH CHAPTER TWO.
FOURTH PLACE IS STILL SOMETHING TO BE PROUD OF. THE FIRST CHAPTER'S AT THE VERY BEGINNING OF THE MAGAZINE, AND IT HAS MORE PAGES, SO IT ISN'T RARE FOR IT TO GET THE MOST VOTES.
I'VE HEARD THAT THE FIRST CHAPTER SHOULD NATURALLY GET FIRST PLACE, AND THE REAL CHALLENGE STARTS FROM CHAPTER TWO.
OH, MR. YUJIRO SAID THE SAME THING.
A BAD PIECE OF WORK WILL REALLY FALL DOWN THE LIST WITH CHAPTER TWO. SO MUCH THAT IT'S QUICKER TO COUNT FROM THE BOTTOM...
IS HE REALLY EIJI NIZUMA'S MASTER...?
THERE ARE TIMES WHEN THE DISCIPLE SURPASSES HIS MASTER, BUT MUTO ASHIROGI HASN'T EVEN HAD A SERIES YET, AND HE'S A FIRST YEAR IN HIGH SCHOOL. MAKES NO SENSE. BUT HE SEEMS TO KNOW A LOT AND SOUNDS A BIT LIKE A WISEASS.
THAT'S FOURTH PLACE AMONG ALL THE POPULAR MANGA THAT HAVE AN ANIME, SO IT'S NOTHING TO BE SHOCKED ABOUT.
MR. YUJIRO SAID THAT AS WELL...
AND BECAUSE YOU CAN KEEP CREATING YOUR FINAL DRAFT WITHOUT DOING STORYBOARDS, I DON'T THINK YOUR RANK WILL GO DOWN FURTHER. USUALLY, YOU TURN IN STORYBOARDS FOR THE FIRST THREE CHAPTERS AT THE SERIALIZATION MEETING, AND YOU CAN SPEND ALL THE TIME YOU NEED ON THOSE. SO IT STARTS TO GET HARD FROM THE FOURTH CHAPTER ON. BUT YOU DON'T HAVE TO WORRY ABOUT THAT.
OH, YOU THINK SO?
NO... IF HE KEEPS GOING LIKE THIS, THE RANKING WILL FALL...
IT'LL KEEP SLIDING AND THE SERIES WILL COME TO AN END IN LESS THAN HALF A YEAR.
WHEN THAT HAPPENS, THERE'LL BE AN OPENING IN THE MAGAZINE AND I'LL HAVE ANOTHER CHANCE TO GET MY SERIES.

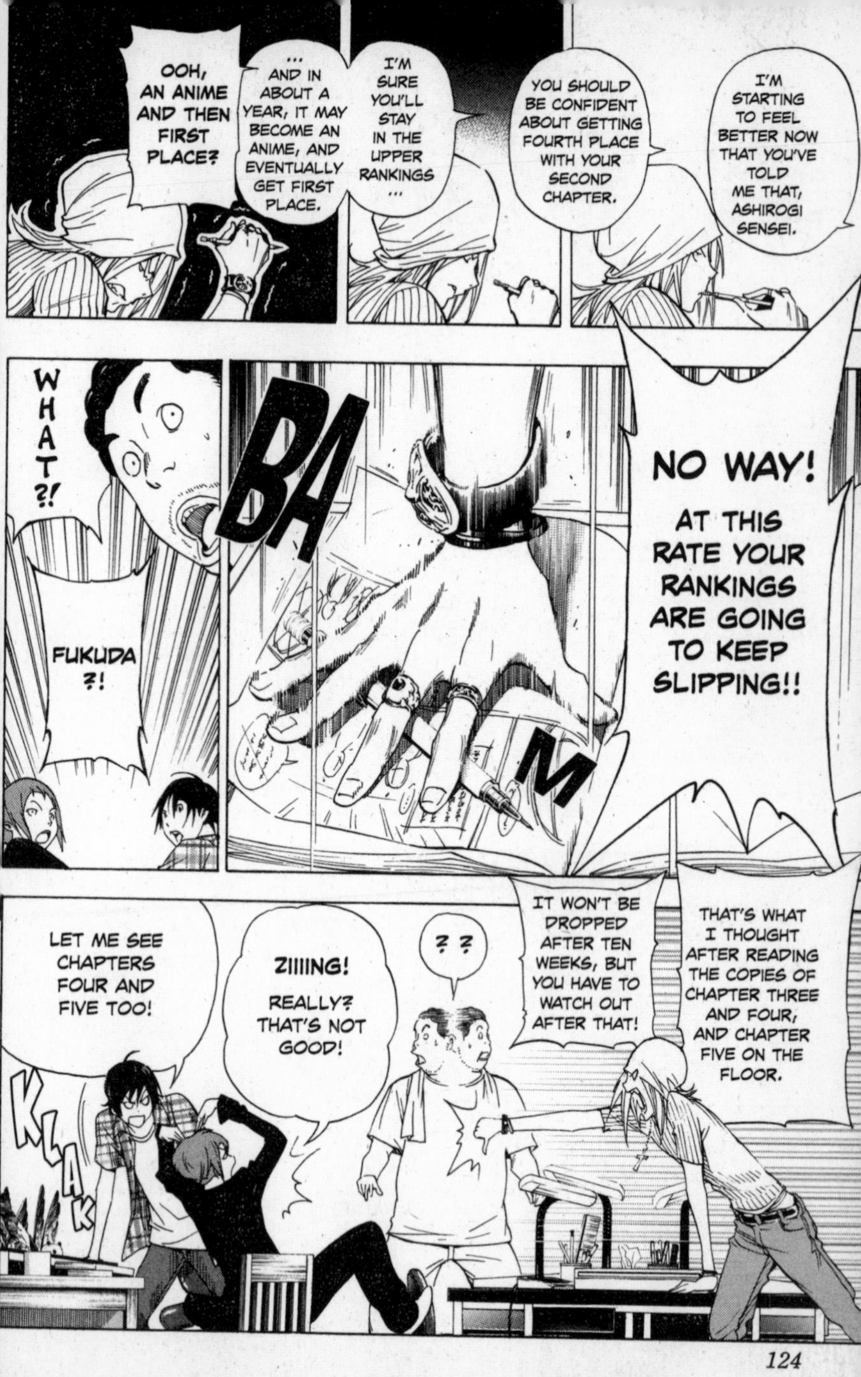
I'M STARTING TO FEEL BETTER NOW THAT YOU'VE TOLD ME THAT, ASHIROGI SENSEI.
YOU SHOULD BE CONFIDENT ABOUT GETTING FOURTH PLACE WITH YOUR SECOND CHAPTER.
I'M SURE YOU'LL STAY IN THE UPPER RANKINGS...
... AND IN ABOUT A YEAR, IT MAY BECOME AN ANIME, AND EVENTUALLY GET FIRST PLACE.
OOH, AN ANIME AND THEN FIRST PLACE?
NO WAY!
AT THIS RATE YOUR RANKINGS ARE GOING TO KEEP SLIPPING!!
BAM
WHAT?!
FUKUDA?!
THAT'S WHAT I THOUGHT AFTER READING THE COPIES OF CHAPTER THREE AND FOUR, AND CHAPTER FIVE ON THE FLOOR.
IT WON'T BE DROPPED AFTER TEN WEEKS, BUT YOU HAVE TO WATCH OUT AFTER THAT!
? ?
ZIIIING!
REALLY? THAT'S NOT GOOD!
LET ME SEE CHAPTERS FOUR AND FIVE TOO!
KLAK

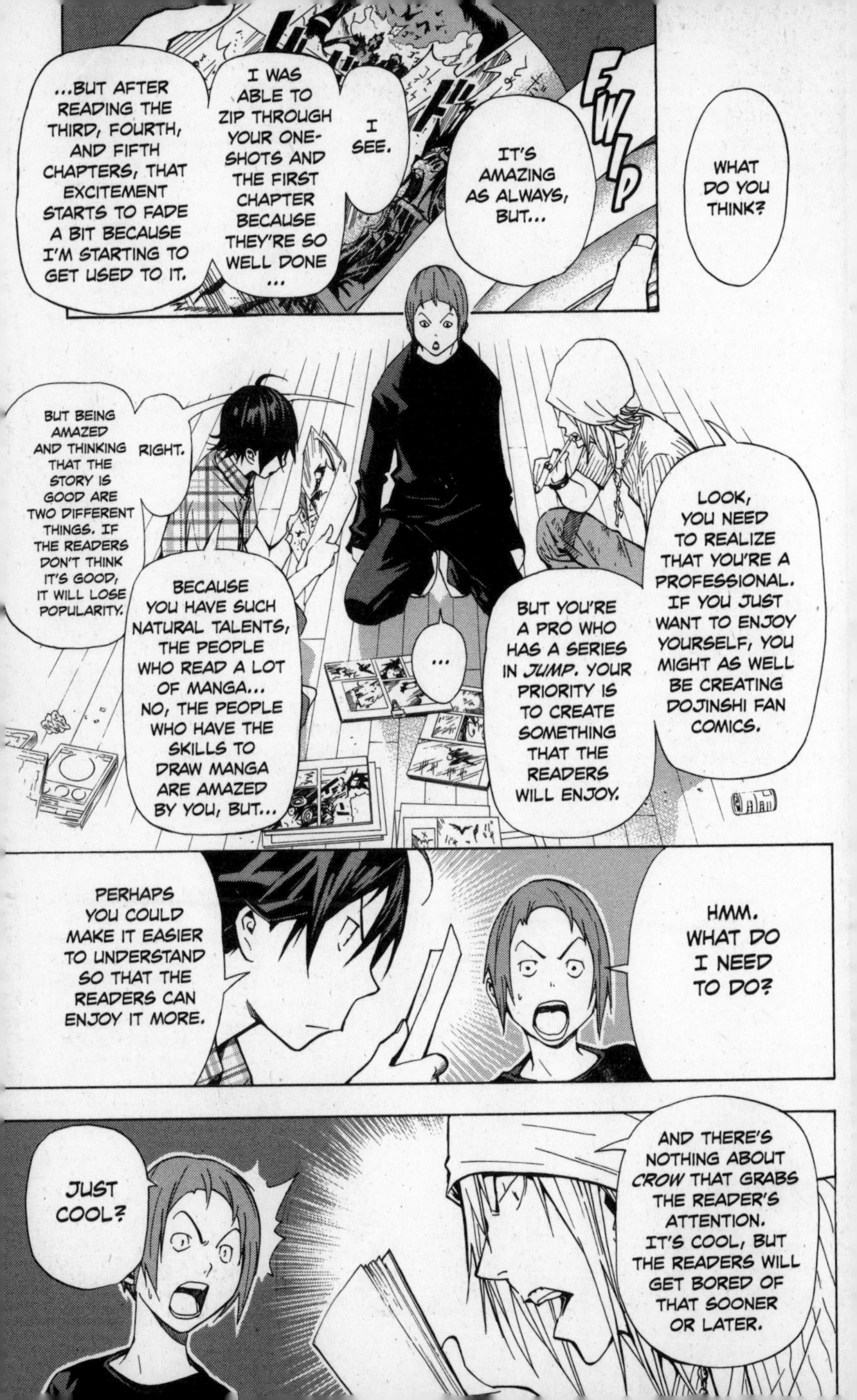
WHAT DO YOU THINK?
FWIP
IT'S AMAZING AS ALWAYS, BUT...
I SEE.
I WAS ABLE TO ZIP THROUGH YOUR ONE-SHOTS AND THE FIRST CHAPTER BECAUSE THEY'RE SO WELL DONE...
...BUT AFTER READING THE THIRD, FOURTH, AND FIFTH CHAPTERS, THAT EXCITEMENT STARTS TO FADE A BIT BECAUSE I'M STARTING TO GET USED TO IT.
BECAUSE YOU HAVE SUCH NATURAL TALENTS, THE PEOPLE WHO READ A LOT OF MANGA... NO, THE PEOPLE WHO HAVE THE SKILLS TO DRAW MANGA ARE AMAZED BY YOU, BUT...
RIGHT.
BUT BEING AMAZED AND THINKING THAT THE STORY IS GOOD ARE TWO DIFFERENT THINGS. IF THE READERS DON'T THINK IT'S GOOD, IT WILL LOSE POPULARITY.
...
LOOK, YOU NEED TO REALIZE THAT YOU'RE A PROFESSIONAL. IF YOU JUST WANT TO ENJOY YOURSELF, YOU MIGHT AS WELL BE CREATING DOJINSHI FAN COMICS.
BUT YOU'RE A PRO WHO HAS A SERIES IN *JUMP*. YOUR PRIORITY IS TO CREATE SOMETHING THAT THE READERS WILL ENJOY.
HMM. WHAT DO I NEED TO DO?
PERHAPS YOU COULD MAKE IT EASIER TO UNDERSTAND SO THAT THE READERS CAN ENJOY IT MORE.
AND THERE'S NOTHING ABOUT *CROW* THAT GRABS THE READER'S ATTENTION. IT'S COOL, BUT THE READERS WILL GET BORED OF THAT SOONER OR LATER.
JUST COOL?

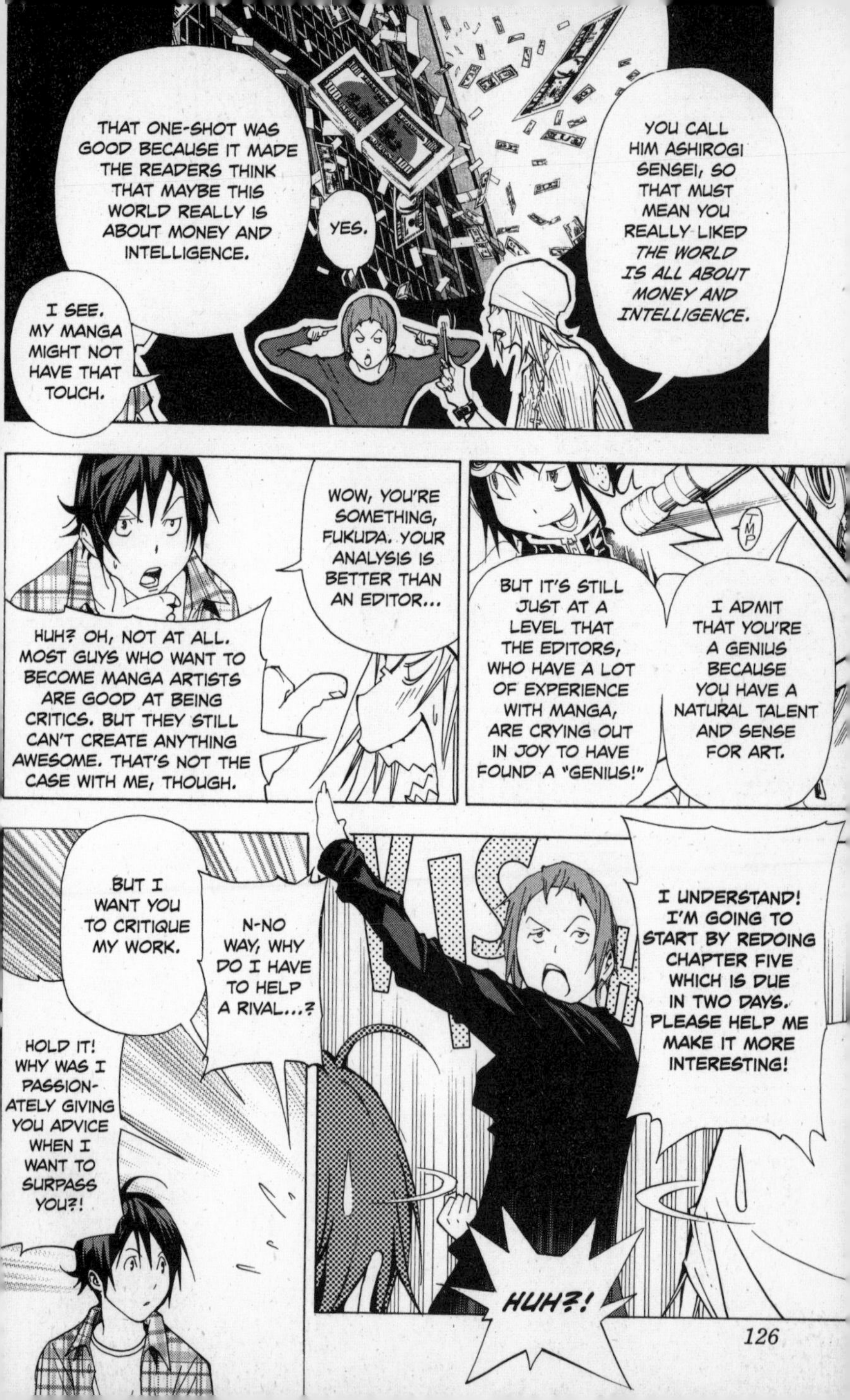
YOU CALL HIM ASHIROGI SENSEI, SO THAT MUST MEAN YOU REALLY LIKED *THE WORLD IS ALL ABOUT MONEY AND INTELLIGENCE.*
YES.
THAT ONE-SHOT WAS GOOD BECAUSE IT MADE THE READERS THINK THAT MAYBE THIS WORLD REALLY IS ABOUT MONEY AND INTELLIGENCE.
I SEE. MY MANGA MIGHT NOT HAVE THAT TOUCH.
TMP
I ADMIT THAT YOU'RE A GENIUS BECAUSE YOU HAVE A NATURAL TALENT AND SENSE FOR ART.
BUT IT'S STILL JUST AT A LEVEL THAT THE EDITORS, WHO HAVE A LOT OF EXPERIENCE WITH MANGA, ARE CRYING OUT IN JOY TO HAVE FOUND A "GENIUS!"
WOW, YOU'RE SOMETHING, FUKUDA. YOUR ANALYSIS IS BETTER THAN AN EDITOR...
HUH? OH, NOT AT ALL. MOST GUYS WHO WANT TO BECOME MANGA ARTISTS ARE GOOD AT BEING CRITICS. BUT THEY STILL CAN'T CREATE ANYTHING AWESOME. THAT'S NOT THE CASE WITH ME, THOUGH.
I UNDERSTAND! I'M GOING TO START BY REDOING CHAPTER FIVE WHICH IS DUE IN TWO DAYS. PLEASE HELP ME MAKE IT MORE INTERESTING!
BUT I WANT YOU TO CRITIQUE MY WORK.
N-NO WAY, WHY DO I HAVE TO HELP A RIVAL...?
HUH?!
HOLD IT! WHY WAS I PASSION-ATELY GIVING YOU ADVICE WHEN I WANT TO SURPASS YOU?!

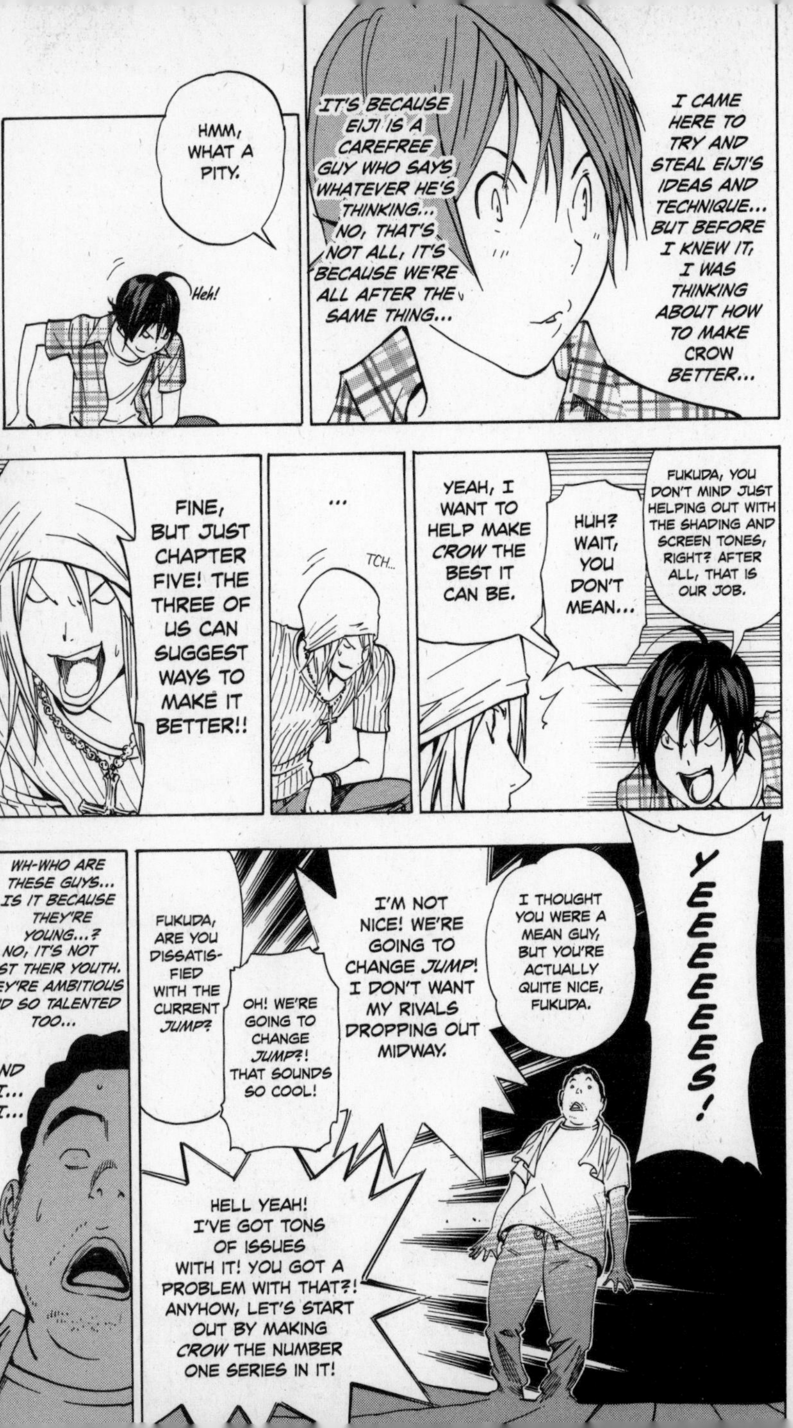
I CAME HERE TO TRY AND STEAL EIJI'S IDEAS AND TECHNIQUE... BUT BEFORE I KNEW IT, I WAS THINKING ABOUT HOW TO MAKE CROW BETTER...
IT'S BECAUSE EIJI IS A CAREFREE GUY WHO SAYS WHATEVER HE'S THINKING... NO, THAT'S NOT ALL, IT'S BECAUSE WE'RE ALL AFTER THE SAME THING...
HMM, WHAT A PITY.
Heh!
FUKUDA, YOU DON'T MIND JUST HELPING OUT WITH THE SHADING AND SCREEN TONES, RIGHT? AFTER ALL, THAT IS OUR JOB.
HUH? WAIT, YOU DON'T MEAN...
YEAH, I WANT TO HELP MAKE *CROW* THE BEST IT CAN BE.
...
TCH...
FINE, BUT JUST CHAPTER FIVE! THE THREE OF US CAN SUGGEST WAYS TO MAKE IT BETTER!!
YEEEEEES!
I THOUGHT YOU WERE A MEAN GUY, BUT YOU'RE ACTUALLY QUITE NICE, FUKUDA.
I'M NOT NICE! WE'RE GOING TO CHANGE *JUMP*! I DON'T WANT MY RIVALS DROPPING OUT MIDWAY.
FUKUDA, ARE YOU DISSATIS-FIED WITH THE CURRENT *JUMP*?
OH! WE'RE GOING TO CHANGE *JUMP*?! THAT SOUNDS SO COOL!
HELL YEAH! I'VE GOT TONS OF ISSUES WITH IT! YOU GOT A PROBLEM WITH THAT?! ANYHOW, LET'S START OUT BY MAKING *CROW* THE NUMBER ONE SERIES IN IT!
WH-WHO ARE THESE GUYS... IS IT BECAUSE THEY'RE YOUNG...? NO, IT'S NOT JUST THEIR YOUTH. THEY'RE AMBITIOUS AND SO TALENTED TOO...
AND I... I...

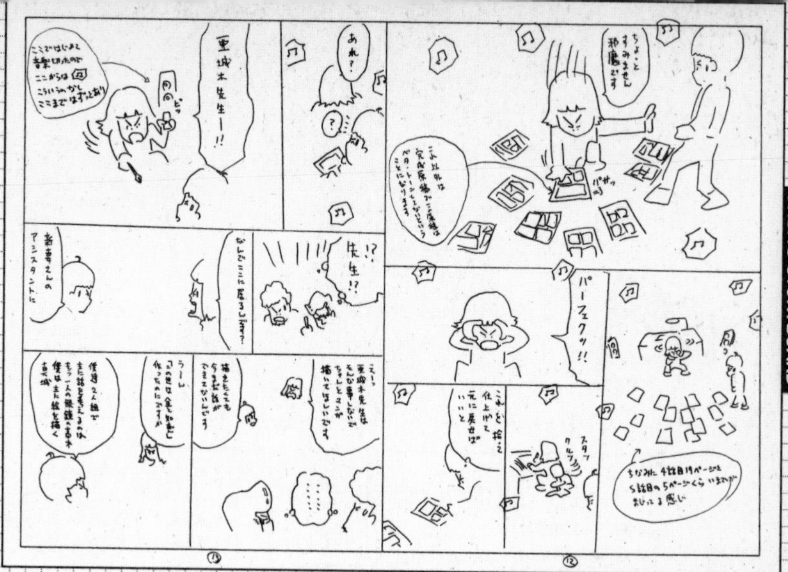
亜城木先生ー!!
あれ?
パーフェクッ!!

OHBA'S STORYBOARD

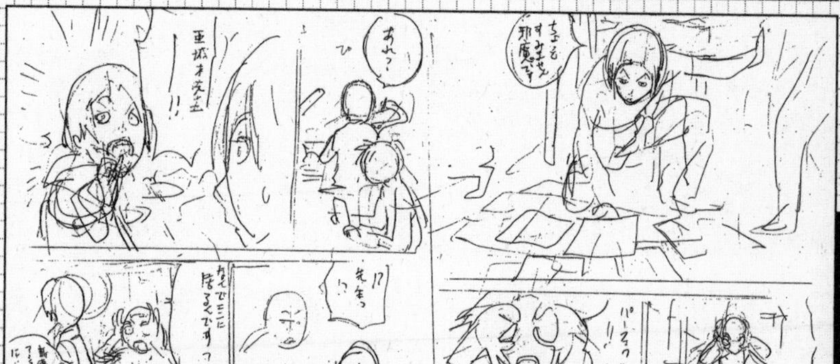

OBATA'S STORYBOARD

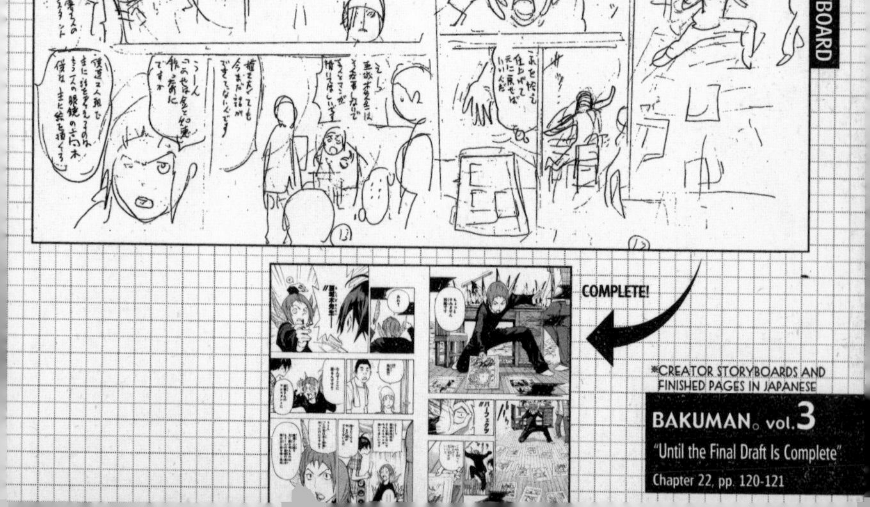

COMPLETE!

※CREATOR STORYBOARDS AND FINISHED PAGES IN JAPANESE

BAKUMAN。 vol.3

"Until the Final Draft Is Complete"

Chapter 22, pp. 120-121

CHAPTER 23 CONCEIT AND KINDNESS

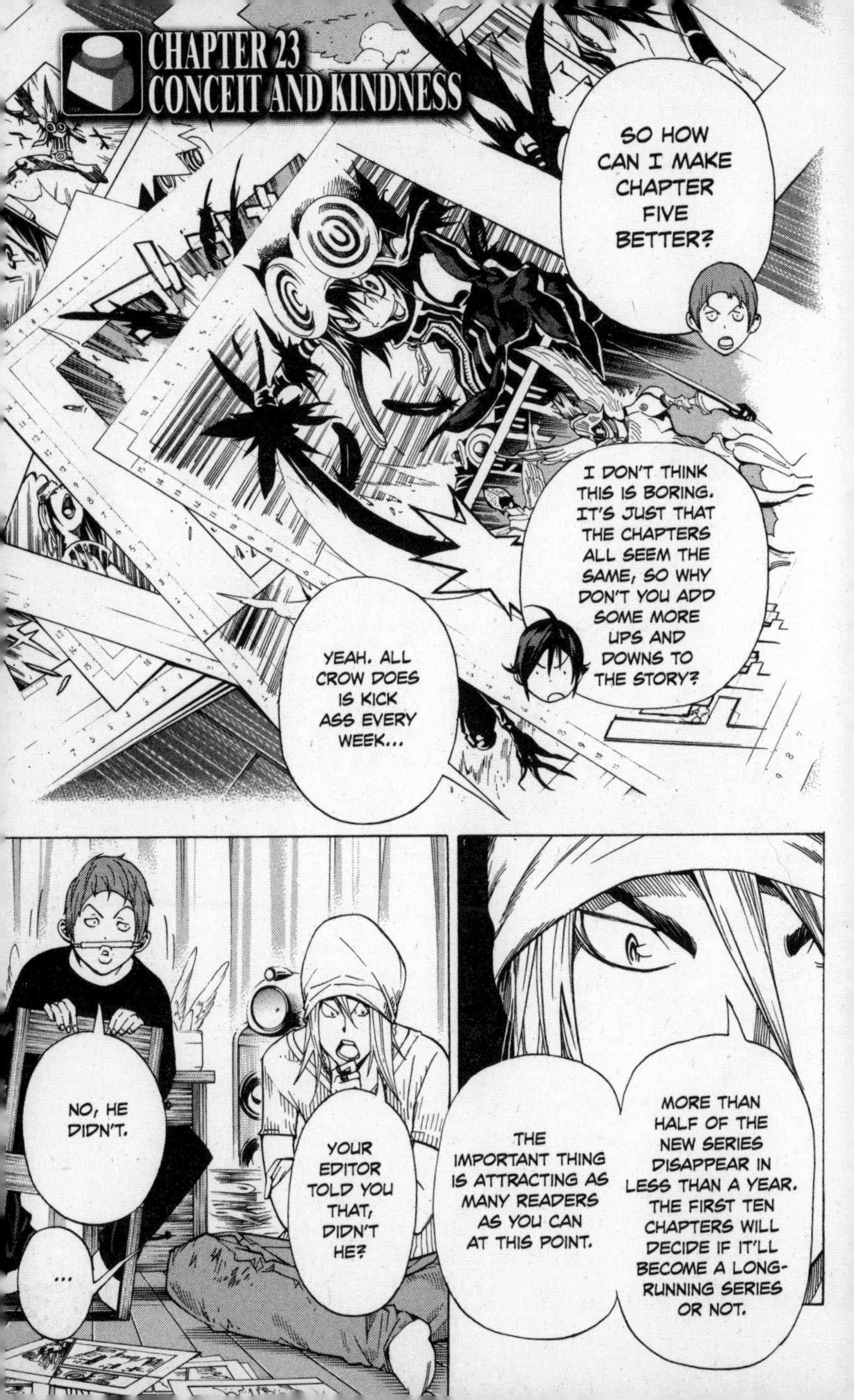

SO HOW CAN I MAKE CHAPTER FIVE BETTER?
I DON'T THINK THIS IS BORING. IT'S JUST THAT THE CHAPTERS ALL SEEM THE SAME, SO WHY DON'T YOU ADD SOME MORE UPS AND DOWNS TO THE STORY?
YEAH. ALL CROW DOES IS KICK ASS EVERY WEEK...
MORE THAN HALF OF THE NEW SERIES DISAPPEAR IN LESS THAN A YEAR. THE FIRST TEN CHAPTERS WILL DECIDE IF IT'LL BECOME A LONG-RUNNING SERIES OR NOT.
THE IMPORTANT THING IS ATTRACTING AS MANY READERS AS YOU CAN AT THIS POINT.
YOUR EDITOR TOLD YOU THAT, DIDN'T HE?
NO, HE DIDN'T.
...

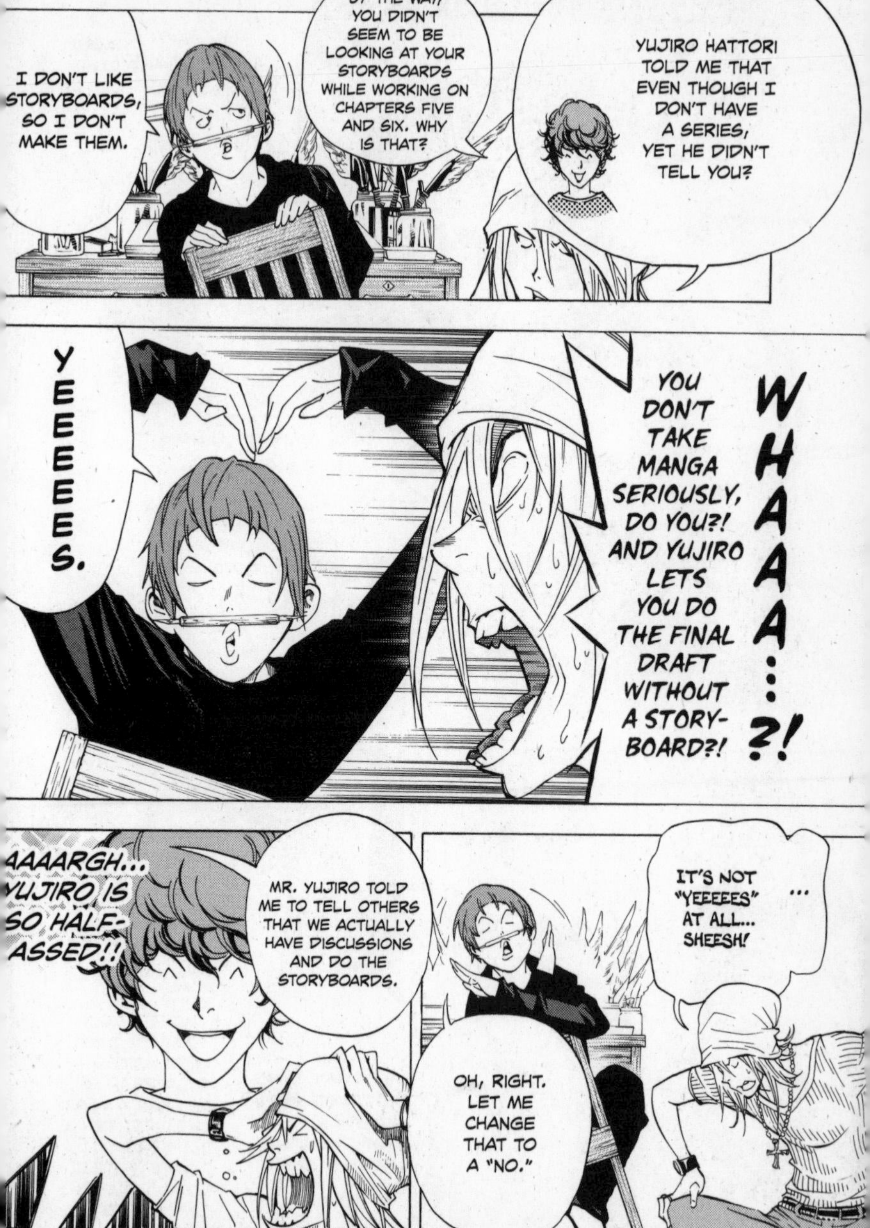
YUJIRO HATTORI TOLD ME THAT EVEN THOUGH I DON'T HAVE A SERIES, YET HE DIDN'T TELL YOU?
BY THE WAY, YOU DIDN'T SEEM TO BE LOOKING AT YOUR STORYBOARDS WHILE WORKING ON CHAPTERS FIVE AND SIX. WHY IS THAT?
I DON'T LIKE STORYBOARDS, SO I DON'T MAKE THEM.
WHAAAA...?!
YOU DON'T TAKE MANGA SERIOUSLY, DO YOU?! AND YUJIRO LETS YOU DO THE FINAL DRAFT WITHOUT A STORY-BOARD?!
YEEEEEES.
...
IT'S NOT "YEEEEES" AT ALL... SHEESH!
OH, RIGHT. LET ME CHANGE THAT TO A "NO."
MR. YUJIRO TOLD ME TO TELL OTHERS THAT WE ACTUALLY HAVE DISCUSSIONS AND DO THE STORYBOARDS.
AAAARGH... YUJIRO IS SO HALF-ASSED!!

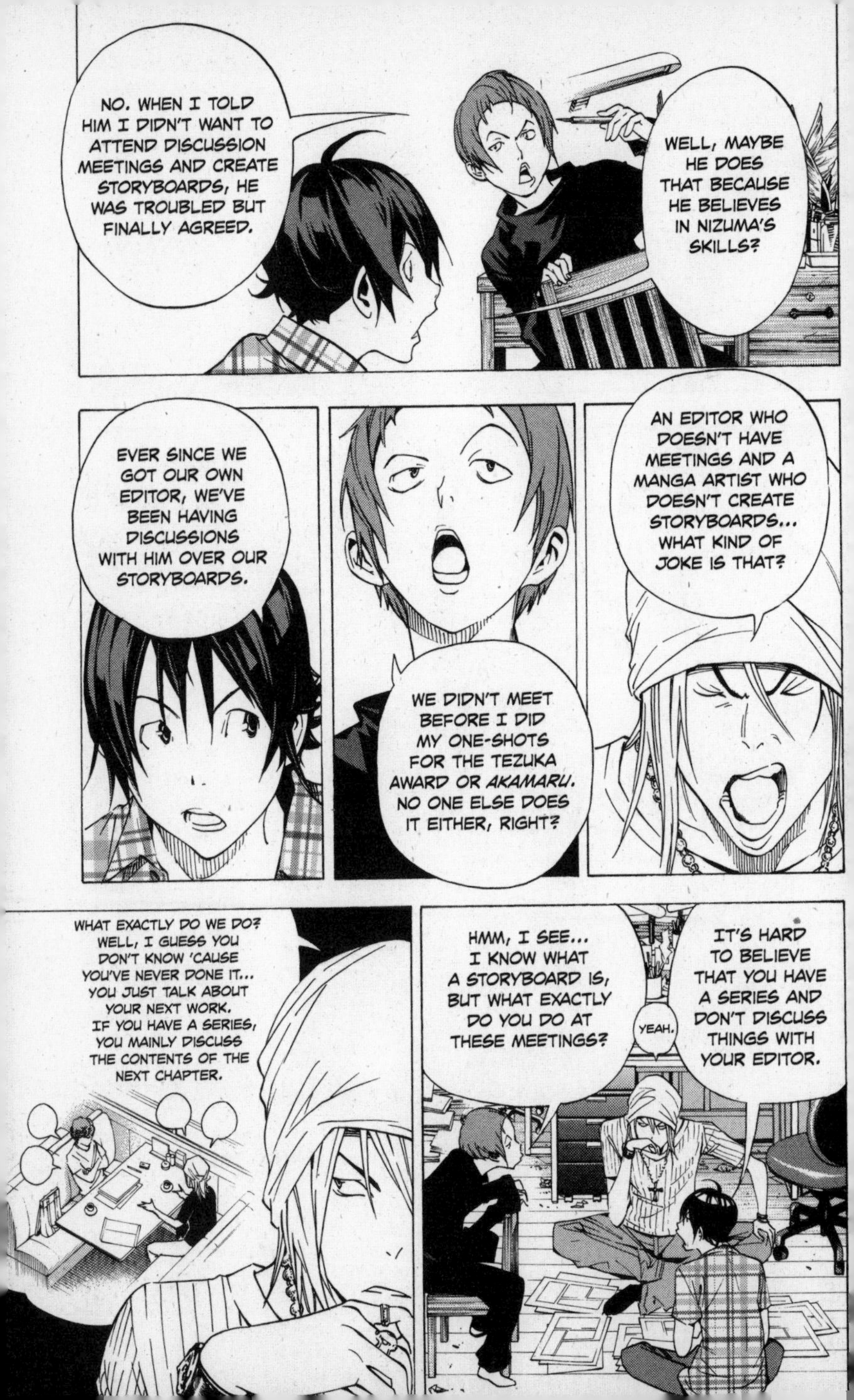

NO. WHEN I TOLD HIM I DIDN'T WANT TO ATTEND DISCUSSION MEETINGS AND CREATE STORYBOARDS, HE WAS TROUBLED BUT FINALLY AGREED.
WELL, MAYBE HE DOES THAT BECAUSE HE BELIEVES IN NIZUMA'S SKILLS?
AN EDITOR WHO DOESN'T HAVE MEETINGS AND A MANGA ARTIST WHO DOESN'T CREATE STORYBOARDS... WHAT KIND OF JOKE IS THAT?
WE DIDN'T MEET BEFORE I DID MY ONE-SHOTS FOR THE TEZUKA AWARD OR *AKAMARU*. NO ONE ELSE DOES IT EITHER, RIGHT?
EVER SINCE WE GOT OUR OWN EDITOR, WE'VE BEEN HAVING DISCUSSIONS WITH HIM OVER OUR STORYBOARDS.
IT'S HARD TO BELIEVE THAT YOU HAVE A SERIES AND DON'T DISCUSS THINGS WITH YOUR EDITOR.
YEAH.
HMM, I SEE... I KNOW WHAT A STORYBOARD IS, BUT WHAT EXACTLY DO YOU DO AT THESE MEETINGS?
WHAT EXACTLY DO WE DO? WELL, I GUESS YOU DON'T KNOW 'CAUSE YOU'VE NEVER DONE IT... YOU JUST TALK ABOUT YOUR NEXT WORK. IF YOU HAVE A SERIES, YOU MAINLY DISCUSS THE CONTENTS OF THE NEXT CHAPTER.

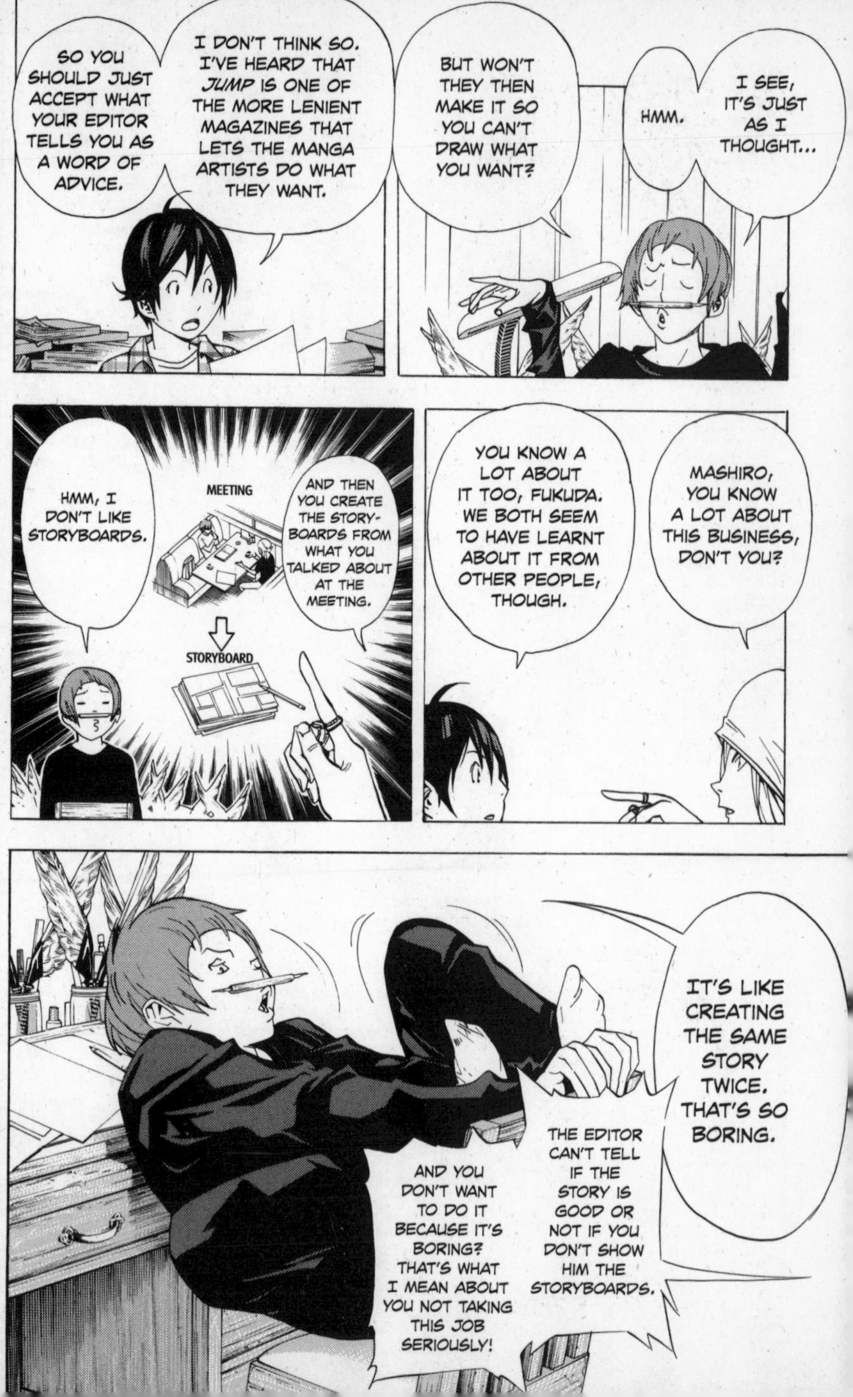
I SEE, IT'S JUST AS I THOUGHT...
HMM.
BUT WON'T THEY THEN MAKE IT SO YOU CAN'T DRAW WHAT YOU WANT?
I DON'T THINK SO. I'VE HEARD THAT *JUMP* IS ONE OF THE MORE LENIENT MAGAZINES THAT LETS THE MANGA ARTISTS DO WHAT THEY WANT.
SO YOU SHOULD JUST ACCEPT WHAT YOUR EDITOR TELLS YOU AS A WORD OF ADVICE.
MASHIRO, YOU KNOW A LOT ABOUT THIS BUSINESS, DON'T YOU?
YOU KNOW A LOT ABOUT IT TOO, FUKUDA. WE BOTH SEEM TO HAVE LEARNT ABOUT IT FROM OTHER PEOPLE, THOUGH.
AND THEN YOU CREATE THE STORY-BOARDS FROM WHAT YOU TALKED ABOUT AT THE MEETING.
MEETING
STORYBOARD
HMM, I DON'T LIKE STORYBOARDS.
IT'S LIKE CREATING THE SAME STORY TWICE. THAT'S SO BORING.
THE EDITOR CAN'T TELL IF THE STORY IS GOOD OR NOT IF YOU DON'T SHOW HIM THE STORYBOARDS.
AND YOU DON'T WANT TO DO IT BECAUSE IT'S BORING? THAT'S WHAT I MEAN ABOUT YOU NOT TAKING THIS JOB SERIOUSLY!

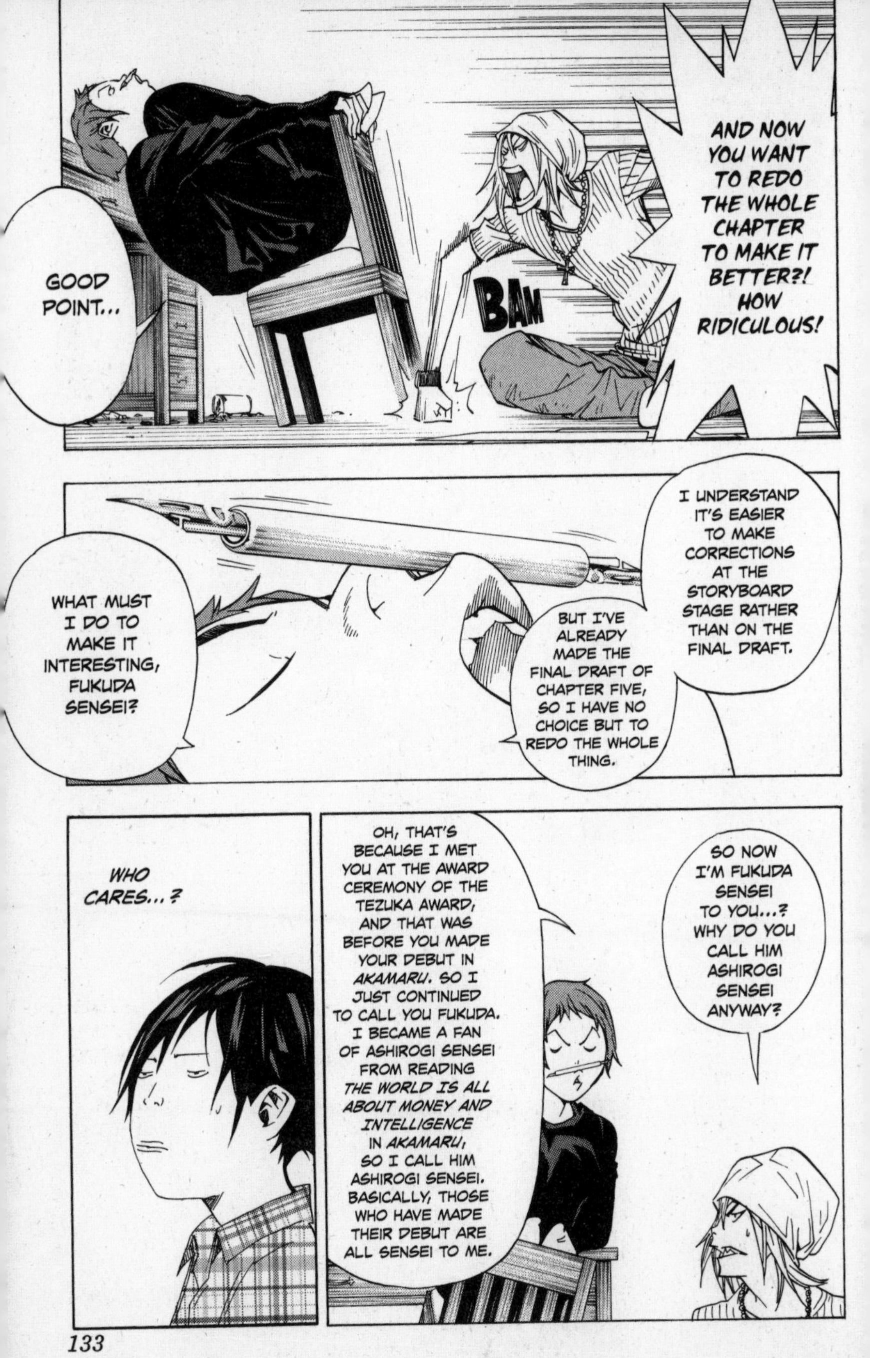
AND NOW YOU WANT TO REDO THE WHOLE CHAPTER TO MAKE IT BETTER?! HOW RIDICULOUS!
BAM
GOOD POINT...
I UNDERSTAND IT'S EASIER TO MAKE CORRECTIONS AT THE STORYBOARD STAGE RATHER THAN ON THE FINAL DRAFT.
BUT I'VE ALREADY MADE THE FINAL DRAFT OF CHAPTER FIVE, SO I HAVE NO CHOICE BUT TO REDO THE WHOLE THING.
WHAT MUST I DO TO MAKE IT INTERESTING, FUKUDA SENSEI?
SO NOW I'M FUKUDA SENSEI TO YOU...? WHY DO YOU CALL HIM ASHIROGI SENSEI ANYWAY?
OH, THAT'S BECAUSE I MET YOU AT THE AWARD CEREMONY OF THE TEZUKA AWARD, AND THAT WAS BEFORE YOU MADE YOUR DEBUT IN *AKAMARU*. SO I JUST CONTINUED TO CALL YOU FUKUDA. I BECAME A FAN OF ASHIROGI SENSEI FROM READING *THE WORLD IS ALL ABOUT MONEY AND INTELLIGENCE* IN *AKAMARU*, SO I CALL HIM ASHIROGI SENSEI. BASICALLY, THOSE WHO HAVE MADE THEIR DEBUT ARE ALL SENSEI TO ME.
WHO CARES...?

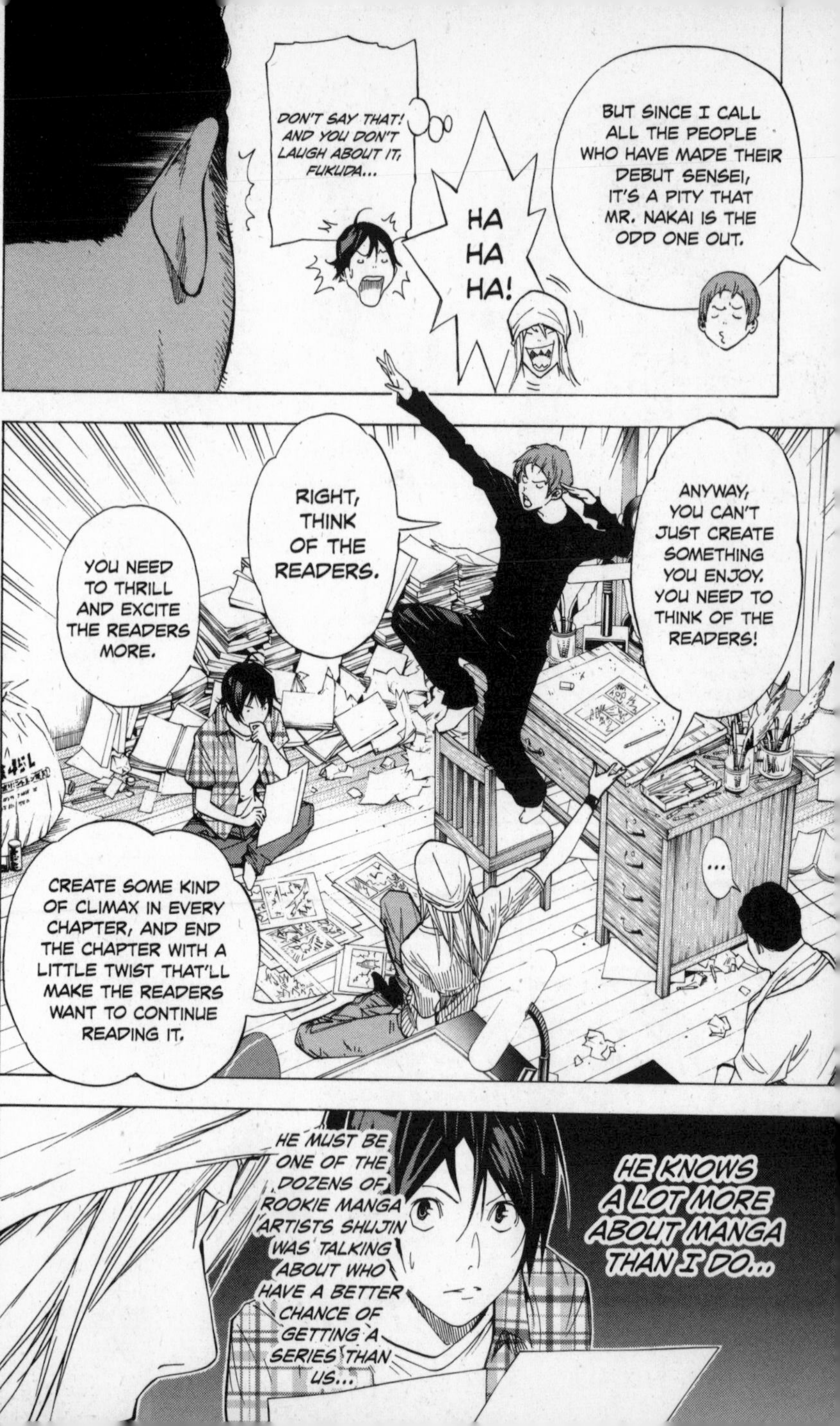
BUT SINCE I CALL ALL THE PEOPLE WHO HAVE MADE THEIR DEBUT SENSEI, IT'S A PITY THAT MR. NAKAI IS THE ODD ONE OUT.
HA HA HA!
DON'T SAY THAT! AND YOU DON'T LAUGH ABOUT IT, FUKUDA...
ANYWAY, YOU CAN'T JUST CREATE SOMETHING YOU ENJOY. YOU NEED TO THINK OF THE READERS!
RIGHT, THINK OF THE READERS.
YOU NEED TO THRILL AND EXCITE THE READERS MORE.
...
CREATE SOME KIND OF CLIMAX IN EVERY CHAPTER, AND END THE CHAPTER WITH A LITTLE TWIST THAT'LL MAKE THE READERS WANT TO CONTINUE READING IT.
HE KNOWS A LOT MORE ABOUT MANGA THAN I DO...
HE MUST BE ONE OF THE DOZENS OF ROOKIE MANGA ARTISTS SHUJIN WAS TALKING ABOUT WHO HAVE A BETTER CHANCE OF GETTING A SERIES THAN US...

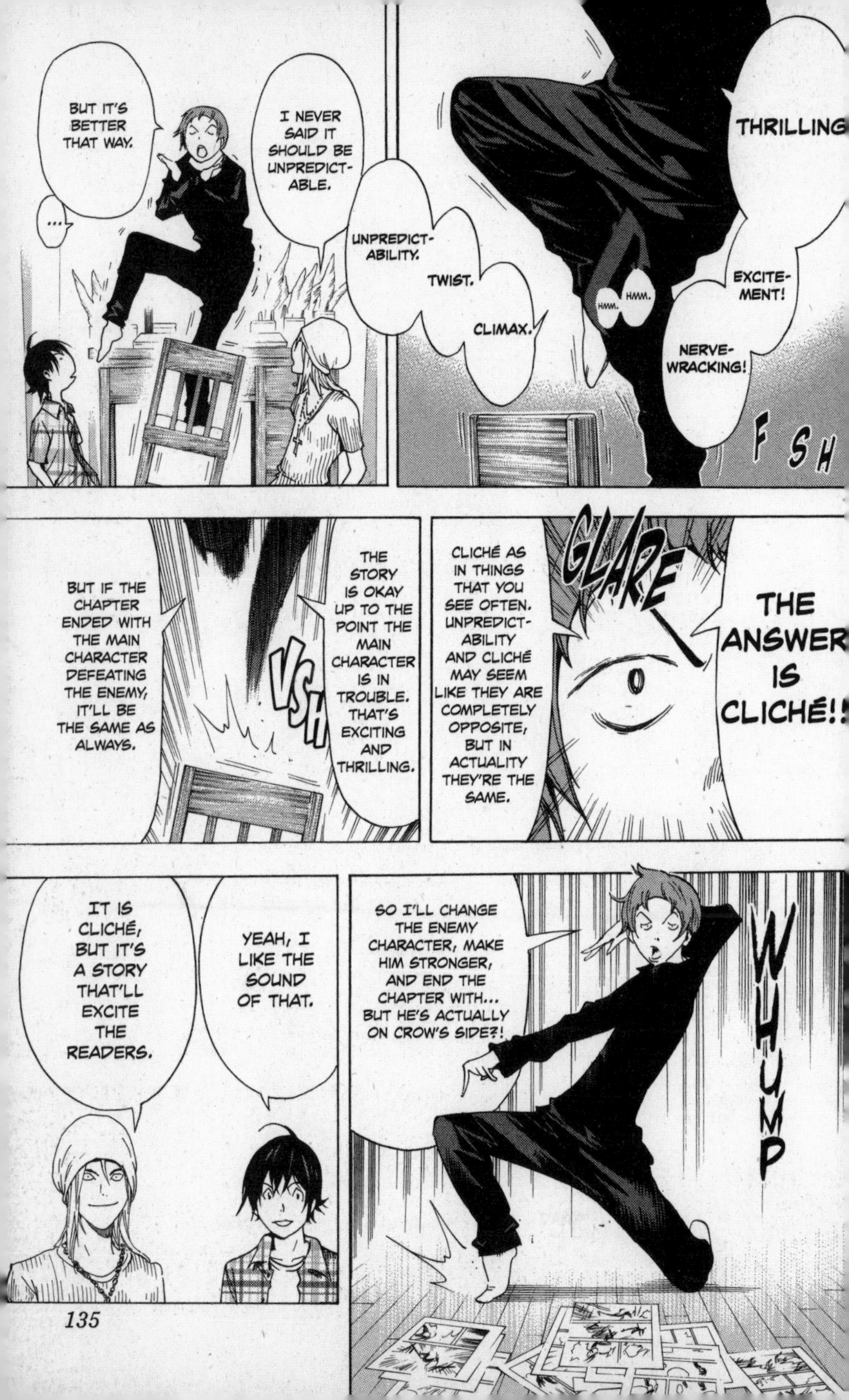
THRILLING
EXCITE-MENT!
HMM.
HMM.
NERVE-WRACKING!
F SH
UNPREDICT-ABILITY.
TWIST.
CLIMAX.
I NEVER SAID IT SHOULD BE UNPREDICT-ABLE.
BUT IT'S BETTER THAT WAY.
...
GLARE
THE ANSWER IS CLICHÉ!!
CLICHÉ AS IN THINGS THAT YOU SEE OFTEN. UNPREDICT-ABILITY AND CLICHÉ MAY SEEM LIKE THEY ARE COMPLETELY OPPOSITE, BUT IN ACTUALITY THEY'RE THE SAME.
THE STORY IS OKAY UP TO THE POINT THE MAIN CHARACTER IS IN TROUBLE. THAT'S EXCITING AND THRILLING.
VSH
BUT IF THE CHAPTER ENDED WITH THE MAIN CHARACTER DEFEATING THE ENEMY, IT'LL BE THE SAME AS ALWAYS.
WHUMP
SO I'LL CHANGE THE ENEMY CHARACTER, MAKE HIM STRONGER, AND END THE CHAPTER WITH... BUT HE'S ACTUALLY ON CROW'S SIDE?!
YEAH, I LIKE THE SOUND OF THAT.
IT IS CLICHÉ, BUT IT'S A STORY THAT'LL EXCITE THE READERS.

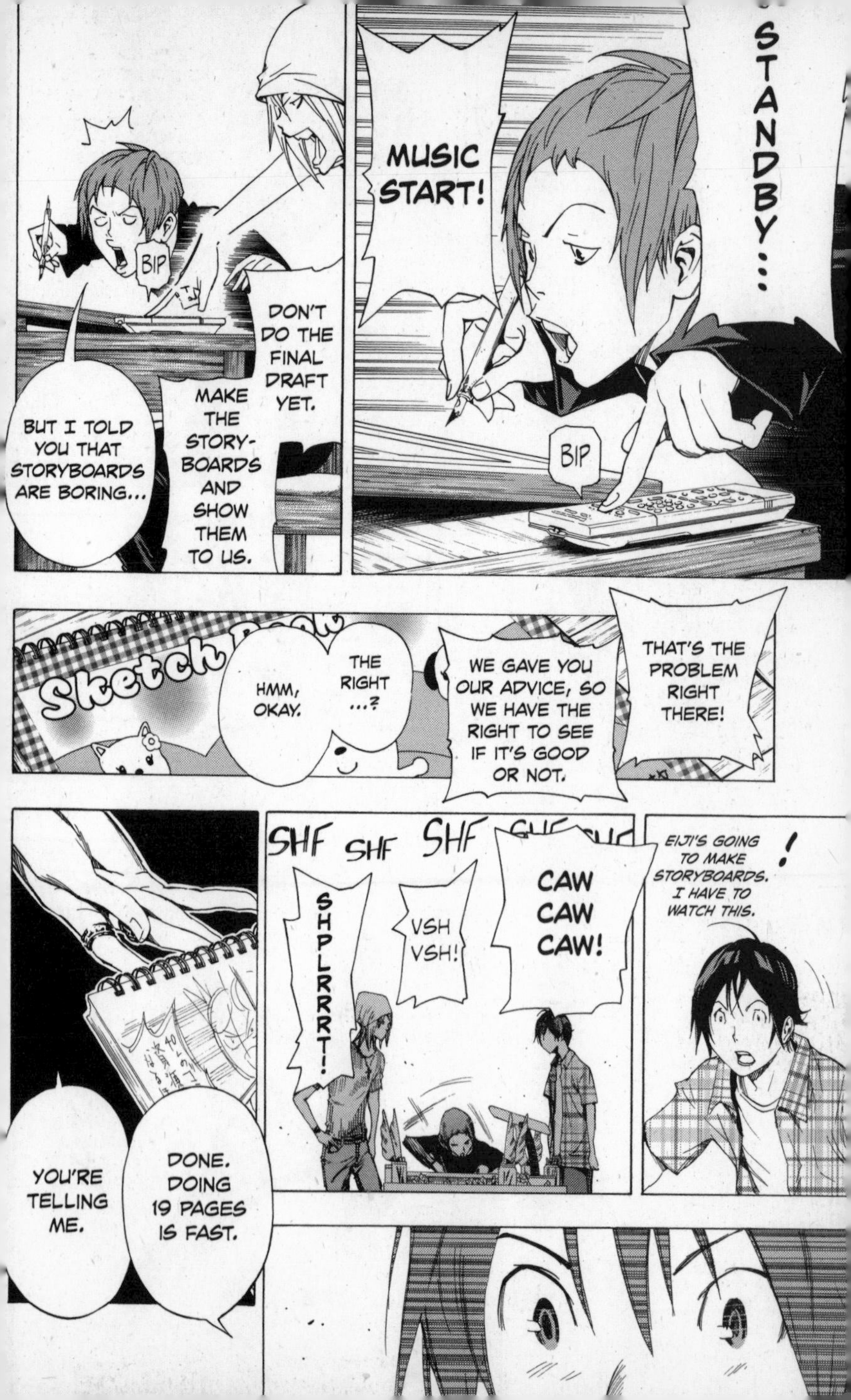
STANDBY...
MUSIC START!
BIP
BIP
DON'T DO THE FINAL DRAFT YET.
MAKE THE STORY-BOARDS AND SHOW THEM TO US.
BUT I TOLD YOU THAT STORYBOARDS ARE BORING...
THAT'S THE PROBLEM RIGHT THERE!
WE GAVE YOU OUR ADVICE, SO WE HAVE THE RIGHT TO SEE IF IT'S GOOD OR NOT.
THE RIGHT ...?
HMM, OKAY.
EIJI'S GOING TO MAKE STORYBOARDS. I HAVE TO WATCH THIS.
!
SHF SHF SHF
CAW CAW CAW!
VSH VSH!
SHPLRRRT!
DONE. DOING 19 PAGES IS FAST.
YOU'RE TELLING ME.

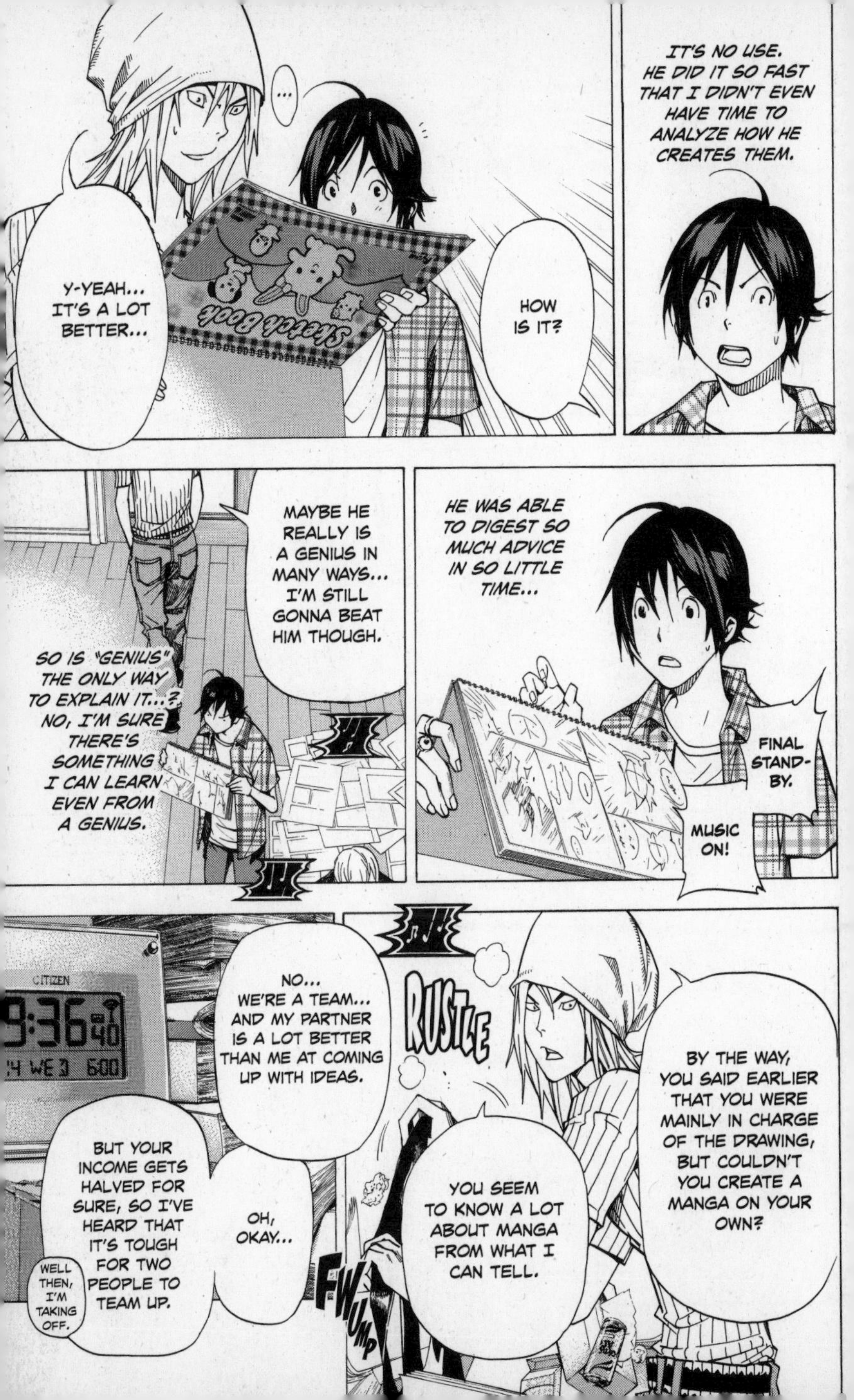
IT'S NO USE. HE DID IT SO FAST THAT I DIDN'T EVEN HAVE TIME TO ANALYZE HOW HE CREATES THEM.
HOW IS IT?
...
Y-YEAH... IT'S A LOT BETTER...
Sketch Book
HE WAS ABLE TO DIGEST SO MUCH ADVICE IN SO LITTLE TIME...
FINAL STAND-BY.
MUSIC ON!
MAYBE HE REALLY IS A GENIUS IN MANY WAYS... I'M STILL GONNA BEAT HIM THOUGH.
SO IS "GENIUS" THE ONLY WAY TO EXPLAIN IT...? NO, I'M SURE THERE'S SOMETHING I CAN LEARN EVEN FROM A GENIUS.
RUSTLE
BY THE WAY, YOU SAID EARLIER THAT YOU WERE MAINLY IN CHARGE OF THE DRAWING, BUT COULDN'T YOU CREATE A MANGA ON YOUR OWN?
YOU SEEM TO KNOW A LOT ABOUT MANGA FROM WHAT I CAN TELL.
NO... WE'RE A TEAM... AND MY PARTNER IS A LOT BETTER THAN ME AT COMING UP WITH IDEAS.
BUT YOUR INCOME GETS HALVED FOR SURE, SO I'VE HEARD THAT IT'S TOUGH FOR TWO PEOPLE TO TEAM UP.
OH, OKAY...
WELL THEN, I'M TAKING OFF.
FWUMP
CITIZEN

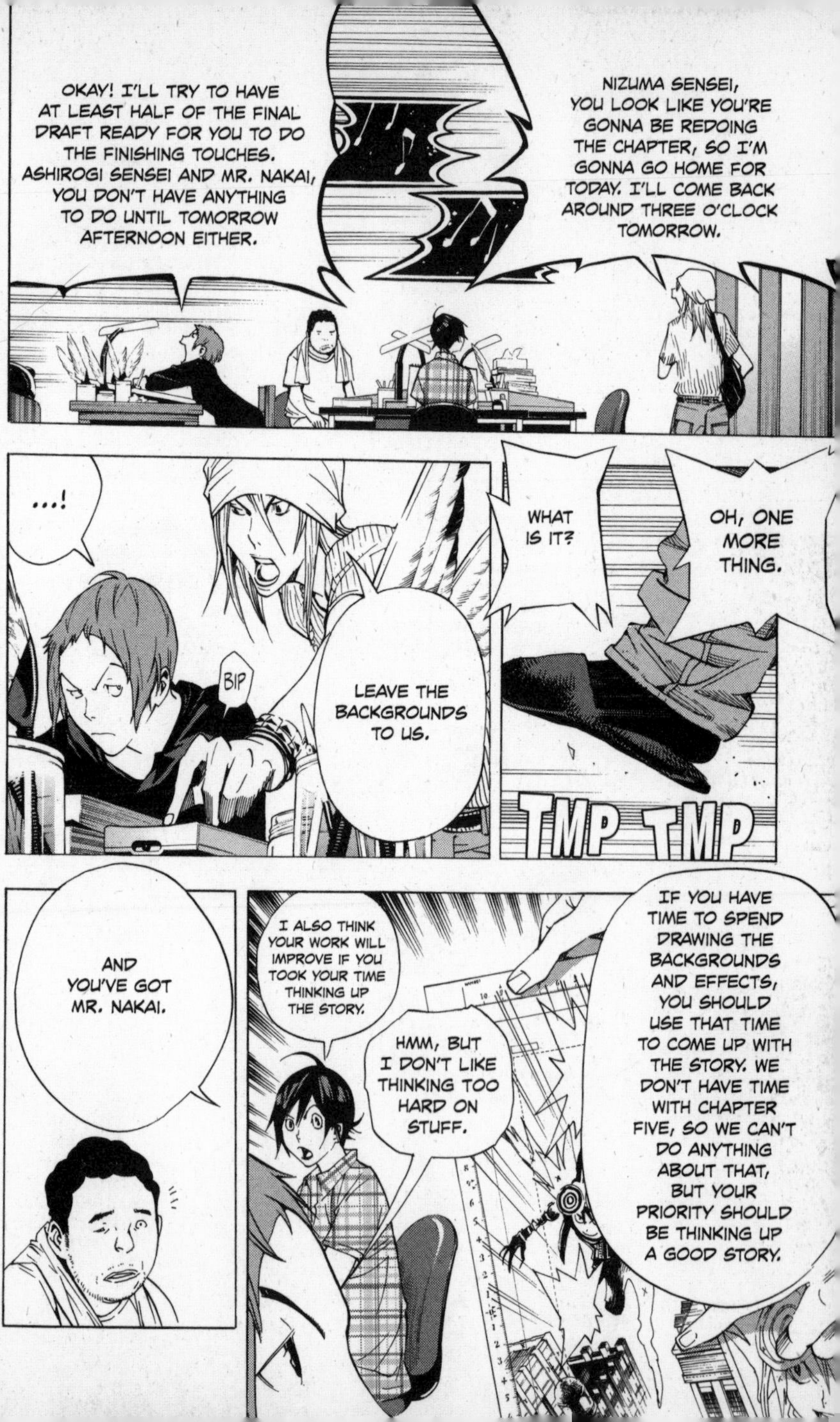
NIZUMA SENSEI, YOU LOOK LIKE YOU'RE GONNA BE REDOING THE CHAPTER, SO I'M GONNA GO HOME FOR TODAY. I'LL COME BACK AROUND THREE O'CLOCK TOMORROW.
OKAY! I'LL TRY TO HAVE AT LEAST HALF OF THE FINAL DRAFT READY FOR YOU TO DO THE FINISHING TOUCHES. ASHIROGI SENSEI AND MR. NAKAI, YOU DON'T HAVE ANYTHING TO DO UNTIL TOMORROW AFTERNOON EITHER.
OH, ONE MORE THING.
WHAT IS IT?
TMP TMP
LEAVE THE BACKGROUNDS TO US.
BIP
...!
IF YOU HAVE TIME TO SPEND DRAWING THE BACKGROUNDS AND EFFECTS, YOU SHOULD USE THAT TIME TO COME UP WITH THE STORY. WE DON'T HAVE TIME WITH CHAPTER FIVE, SO WE CAN'T DO ANYTHING ABOUT THAT, BUT YOUR PRIORITY SHOULD BE THINKING UP A GOOD STORY.
I ALSO THINK YOUR WORK WILL IMPROVE IF YOU TOOK YOUR TIME THINKING UP THE STORY.
HMM, BUT I DON'T LIKE THINKING TOO HARD ON STUFF.
AND YOU'VE GOT MR. NAKAI.

YEAH. I CAN DRAW OR ANYTHING OR ANY PLACE FROM ANY ANGLE YOU WANT ME TO WITHOUT LOOKING AT THE ACTUAL IMAGE. AND I'M PROBABLY THE FASTEST PERSON AROUND WHEN IT COMES TO DOING EFFECT-LINES, SHADE-FLASHES, AND TONE-FLASHES.

ISN'T THAT RIGHT?

MR. NAKAI HAS BEEN AN ASSISTANT FOR MORE THAN TEN YEARS. HIS SKILLS ARE AMAZING AND HE CAN DRAW SOMETHING EVEN BETTER THAN YOU WHEN IT COMES TO THE BACKGROUNDS.

FUKUDA ALWAYS SAYS ONE THING TOO MANY... AND MR. NAKAI GETS DEPRESSED EVERY TIME HE HEARS IT...

!

IT'S NOT SOMETHING A PERSON WHO WANTS TO GET HIS OWN SERIES SHOULD BE PROUD OF, THOUGH.

HE'S FORCED HIMSELF INTO A CORNER ON PURPOSE... HE SEEMS LIKE HE'S JUST HAVING FUN BUT HE'S ACTUALLY GOT GUTS...

I'M BALANCING MANGA AND WORK AS MUCH AS POSSIBLE. I GOTTA FOLLOW MY DREAM.

SEE YA.

YEAH, I TOOK MY CHANCES AND CAME UP TO TOKYO FROM HIROSHIMA AFTER GRADUATING HIGH SCHOOL, BUT I CAN'T MAKE A LIVING OUT OF JUST BEING AN ASSISTANT. SO I WORK AT A CONVENIENCE STORE DURING THE EARLY MORNING.

KLAK

PART-TIME JOB?

CRAP, I GOTTA GO HOME AND GET SOME SLEEP! I HAVE A PART-TIME JOB TOO.

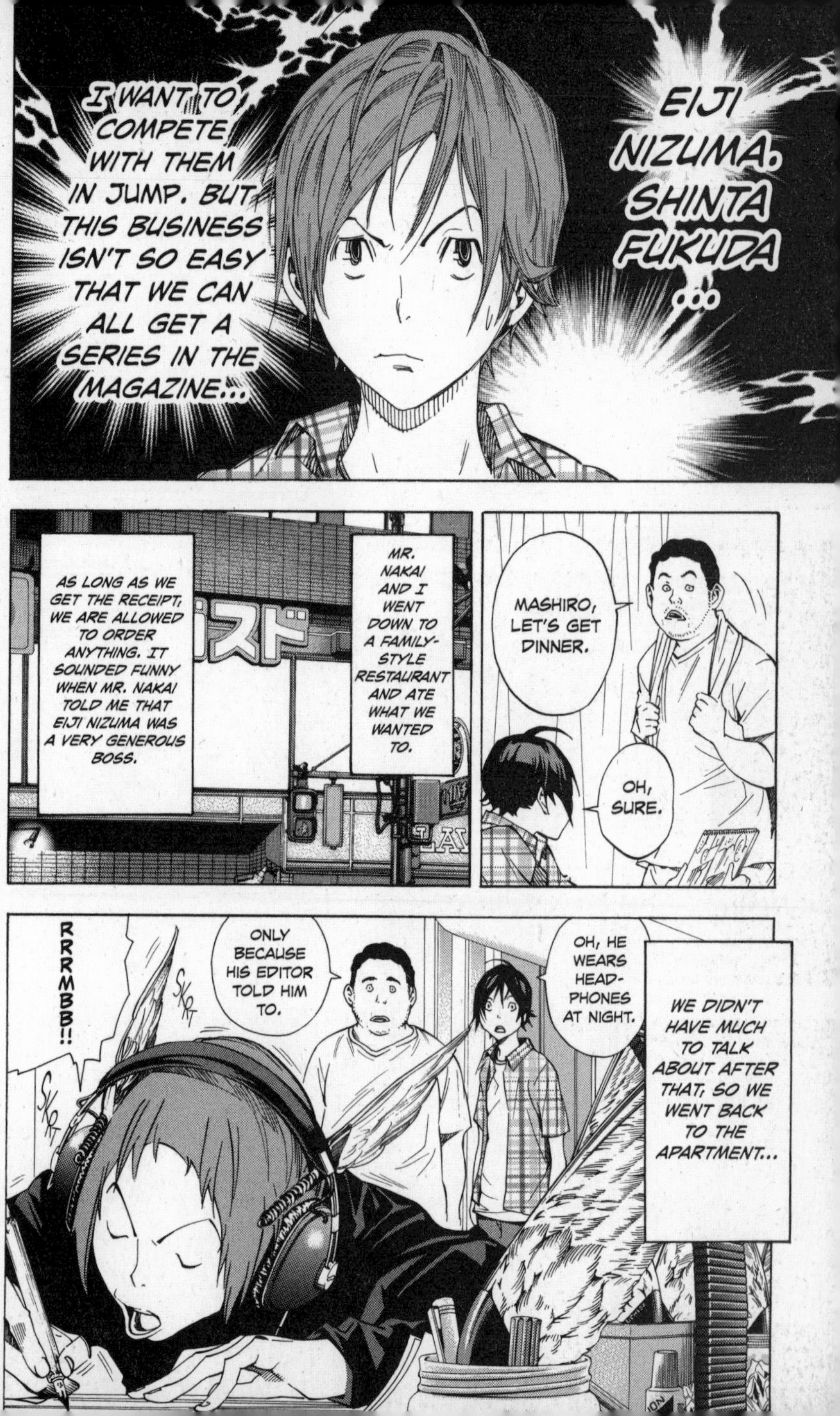
EIJI NIZUMA. SHINTA FUKUDA...
I WANT TO COMPETE WITH THEM IN JUMP. BUT THIS BUSINESS ISN'T SO EASY THAT WE CAN ALL GET A SERIES IN THE MAGAZINE...
MASHIRO, LET'S GET DINNER.
OH, SURE.
MR. NAKAI AND I WENT DOWN TO A FAMILY-STYLE RESTAURANT AND ATE WHAT WE WANTED TO.
AS LONG AS WE GET THE RECEIPT, WE ARE ALLOWED TO ORDER ANYTHING. IT SOUNDED FUNNY WHEN MR. NAKAI TOLD ME THAT EIJI NIZUMA WAS A VERY GENEROUS BOSS.
WE DIDN'T HAVE MUCH TO TALK ABOUT AFTER THAT, SO WE WENT BACK TO THE APARTMENT...
OH, HE WEARS HEAD-PHONES AT NIGHT.
ONLY BECAUSE HIS EDITOR TOLD HIM TO.
SKRT
RRRMBB!!
SKRT

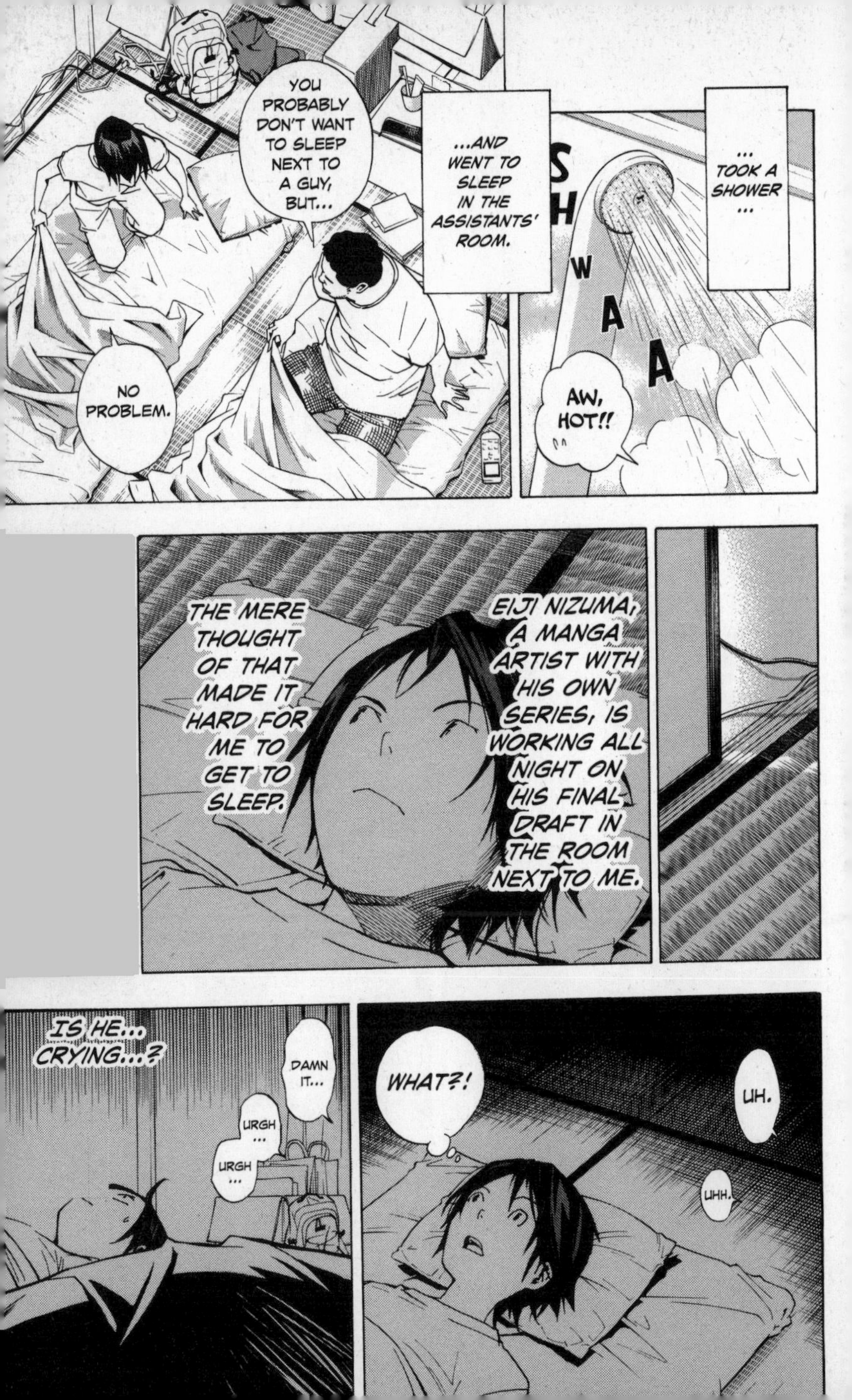
... TOOK A SHOWER ...
SHWAAA
AW, HOT!!
...AND WENT TO SLEEP IN THE ASSISTANTS' ROOM.
YOU PROBABLY DON'T WANT TO SLEEP NEXT TO A GUY, BUT...
NO PROBLEM.
EIJI NIZUMA, A MANGA ARTIST WITH HIS OWN SERIES, IS WORKING ALL NIGHT ON HIS FINAL DRAFT IN THE ROOM NEXT TO ME.
THE MERE THOUGHT OF THAT MADE IT HARD FOR ME TO GET TO SLEEP.
UH.
WHAT?!
UHH.
DAMN IT...
IS HE... CRYING...?
URGH ...
URGH ...

SO, HE IS FRUSTRATED ABOUT FUKUDA TREATING HIM LIKE THAT AFTER ALL...

WELL, AT LEAST I DON'T HAVE TO WORRY ABOUT HIM COMING ON TO ME...

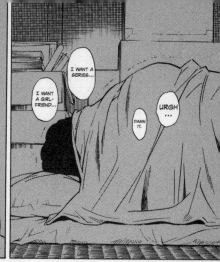

I WANT A SERIES...

I WANT A GIRL-FRIEND...

URGH...

DAMN IT.

I KNEW YOU WERE AWAKE BECAUSE YOU WEREN'T SNORING, BUT...

YES.

HUH?!

YES.

MASHIRO.

PHEW, HE'S NOW QUIET, IT'S OVER AT LAST...

O-OH... I'M SORRY.

THAT ACTUALLY JUST MAKES IT WORSE...

NO... I KIND OF UNDERSTAND HOW YOU FEEL.

I'M SORRY, THERE ARE TIMES WHEN I JUST CAN'T STAND IT ANYMORE...

OH... RIGHT, I UNDERSTAND. I'M ONLY DOING THIS FOR MY SUMMER BREAK.

DON'T WORK AS AN ASSISTANT FOR A LONG TIME.

SHUP

BUT I JUST CAN'T GIVE UP ON MY DREAM OF BECOMING A MANGA ARTIST.

I'M SURE THINGS WOULD BE EASIER FOR ME IF I JUST ACCEPTED MYSELF BEING A PROFESSIONAL ASSISTANT.

OH, I SEE...

YOU CAN DO IT. THE ONLY IMPORTANT THING IN THE MANGA WORLD IS TALENT.

AGE SHOULDN'T HAVE ANYTHING TO DO WITH IT.

BUT I JUST CAN'T GIVE IT UP... DAMMIT...

I KEEP WORKING UNDER MANY MANGA ARTISTS WHILE TELLING MYSELF I CAN STILL DO IT ON MY OWN SOMEDAY. I FEEL SO MISERABLE...

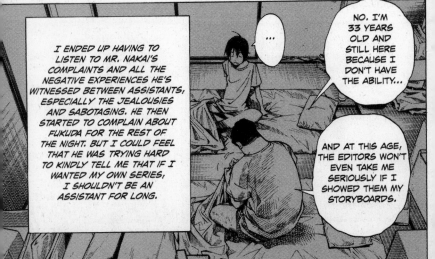

...

NO. I'M 33 YEARS OLD AND STILL HERE BECAUSE I DON'T HAVE THE ABILITY...

I ENDED UP HAVING TO LISTEN TO MR. NAKAI'S COMPLAINTS AND ALL THE NEGATIVE EXPERIENCES HE'S WITNESSED BETWEEN ASSISTANTS, ESPECIALLY THE JEALOUSIES AND SABOTAGING. HE THEN STARTED TO COMPLAIN ABOUT FUKUDA FOR THE REST OF THE NIGHT. BUT I COULD FEEL THAT HE WAS TRYING HARD TO KINDLY TELL ME THAT IF I WANTED MY OWN SERIES, I SHOULDN'T BE AN ASSISTANT FOR LONG.

AND AT THIS AGE, THE EDITORS WON'T EVEN TAKE ME SERIOUSLY IF I SHOWED THEM MY STORYBOARDS.

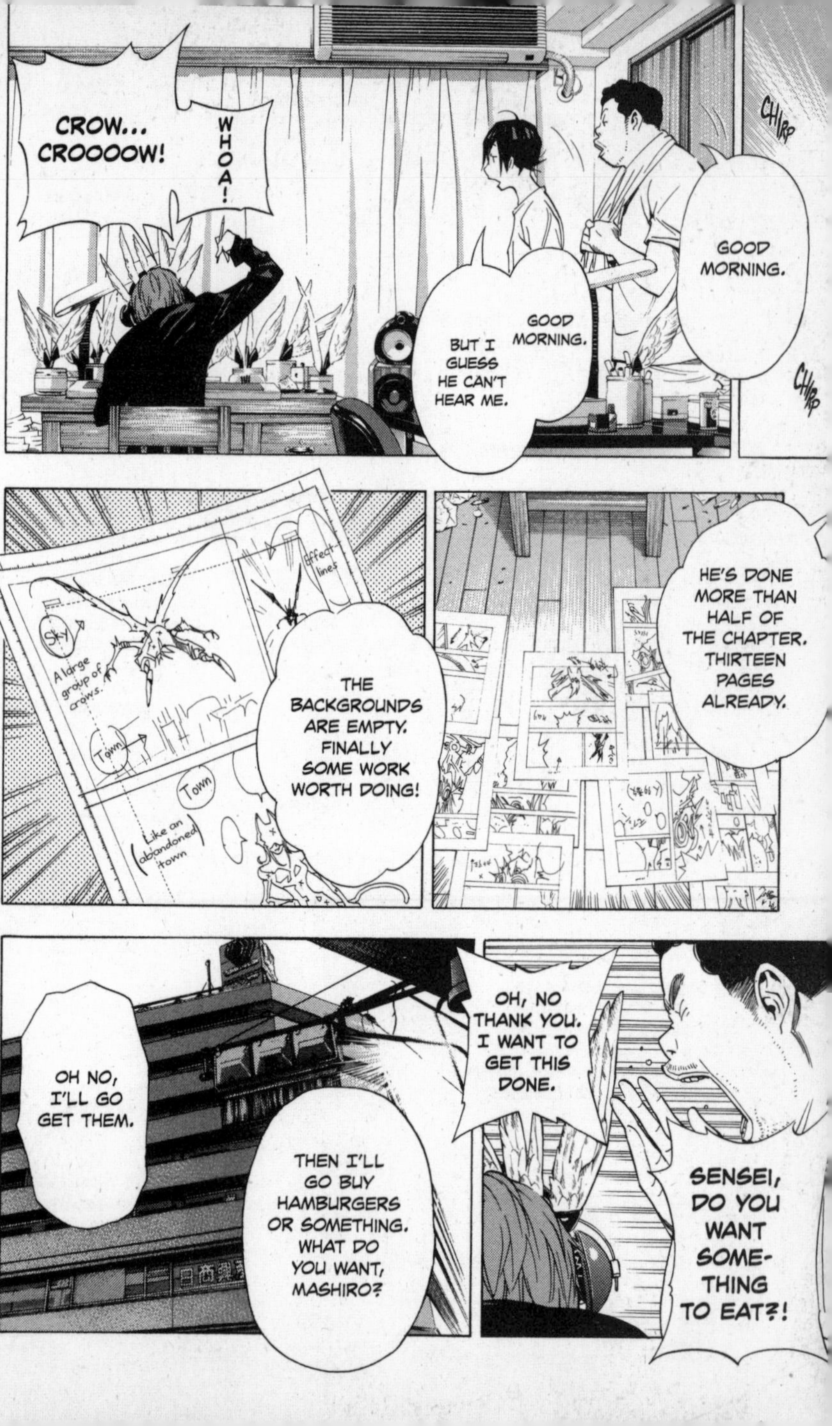
CHIRP
GOOD MORNING.
GOOD MORNING.
BUT I GUESS HE CAN'T HEAR ME.
WHOA!
CROW... CROOOOW!
CHIRP
HE'S DONE MORE THAN HALF OF THE CHAPTER. THIRTEEN PAGES ALREADY.
THE BACKGROUNDS ARE EMPTY. FINALLY SOME WORK WORTH DOING!
Effect lines
Sky
A large group of crows.
Town
Town
Like an abandoned town
SENSEI, DO YOU WANT SOME-THING TO EAT?!
OH, NO THANK YOU. I WANT TO GET THIS DONE.
THEN I'LL GO BUY HAMBURGERS OR SOMETHING. WHAT DO YOU WANT, MASHIRO?
OH NO, I'LL GO GET THEM.

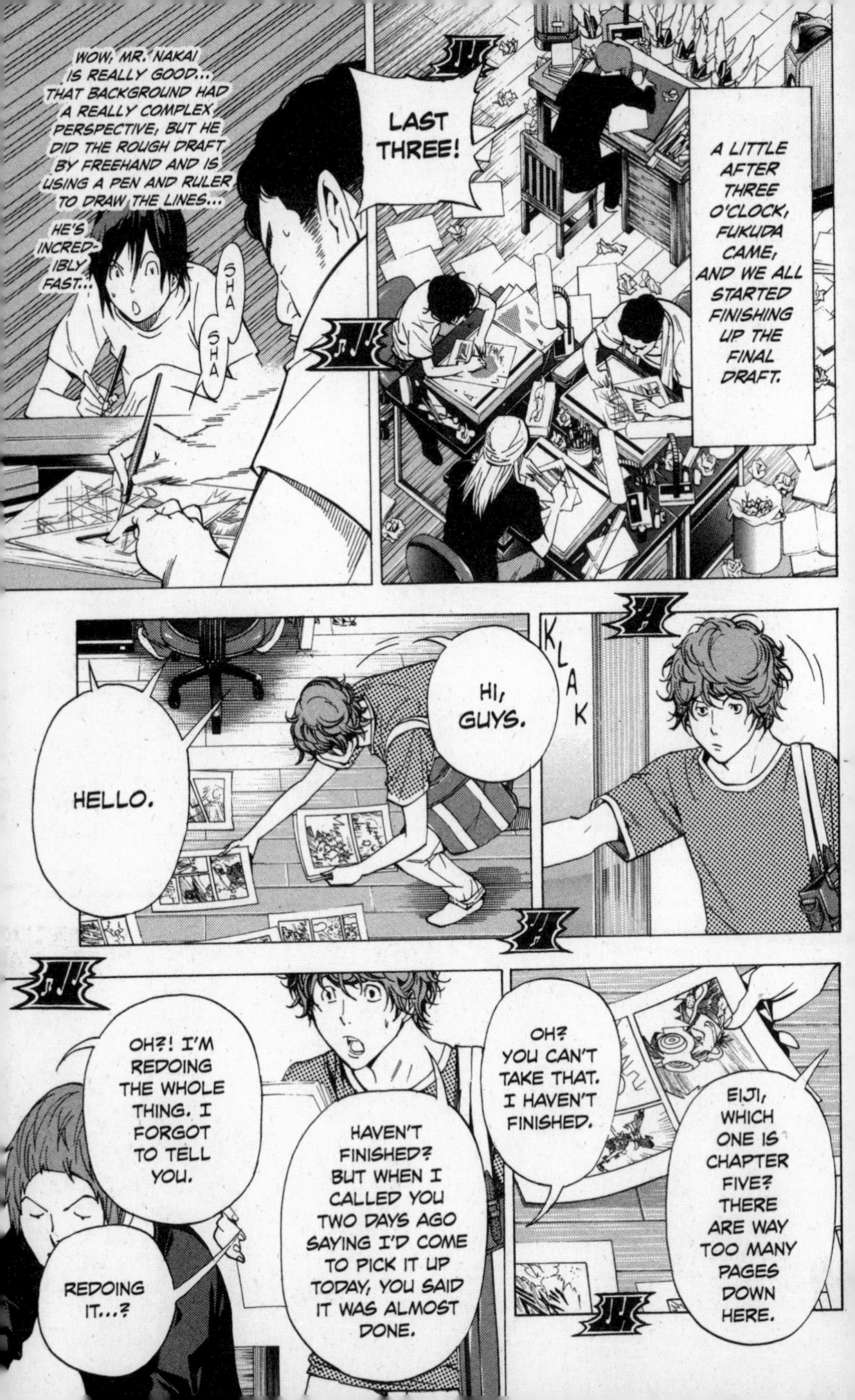
A LITTLE AFTER THREE O'CLOCK, FUKUDA CAME, AND WE ALL STARTED FINISHING UP THE FINAL DRAFT.
LAST THREE!
SHA SHA
WOW, MR. NAKAI IS REALLY GOOD... THAT BACKGROUND HAD A REALLY COMPLEX PERSPECTIVE, BUT HE DID THE ROUGH DRAFT BY FREEHAND AND IS USING A PEN AND RULER TO DRAW THE LINES...
HE'S INCREDIBLY FAST...
KLAK
HI, GUYS.
HELLO.
EIJI, WHICH ONE IS CHAPTER FIVE? THERE ARE WAY TOO MANY PAGES DOWN HERE.
OH? YOU CAN'T TAKE THAT. I HAVEN'T FINISHED.
HAVEN'T FINISHED? BUT WHEN I CALLED YOU TWO DAYS AGO SAYING I'D COME TO PICK IT UP TODAY, YOU SAID IT WAS ALMOST DONE.
OH?! I'M REDOING THE WHOLE THING. I FORGOT TO TELL YOU.
REDOING IT...?

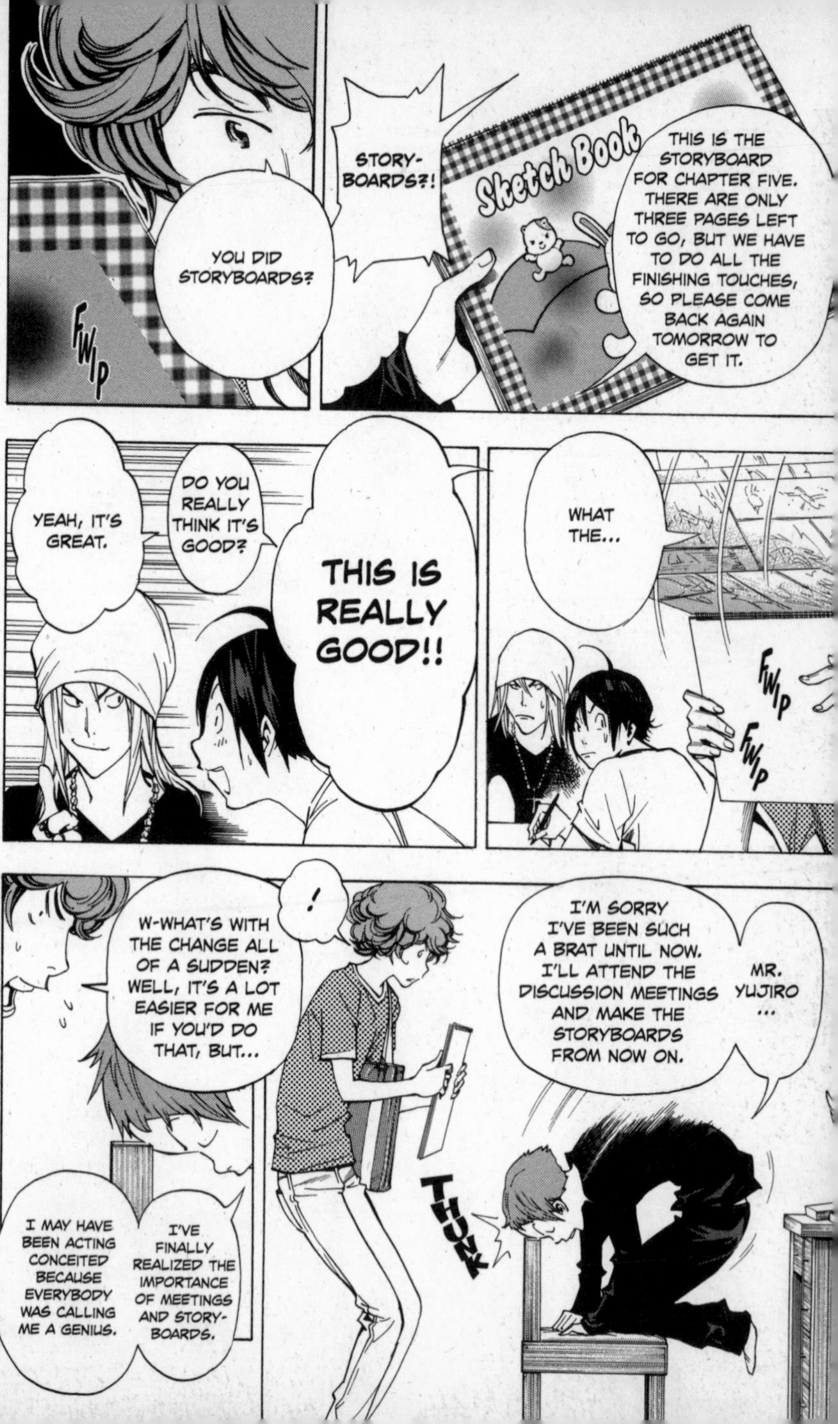
Sketch Book
THIS IS THE STORYBOARD FOR CHAPTER FIVE. THERE ARE ONLY THREE PAGES LEFT TO GO, BUT WE HAVE TO DO ALL THE FINISHING TOUCHES, SO PLEASE COME BACK AGAIN TOMORROW TO GET IT.
STORY-BOARDS?!
YOU DID STORYBOARDS?
FWIP
WHAT THE...
FWIP
FWIP
THIS IS REALLY GOOD!!
DO YOU REALLY THINK IT'S GOOD?
YEAH, IT'S GREAT.
MR. YUJIRO...
I'M SORRY I'VE BEEN SUCH A BRAT UNTIL NOW. I'LL ATTEND THE DISCUSSION MEETINGS AND MAKE THE STORYBOARDS FROM NOW ON.
THUNK
!
W-WHAT'S WITH THE CHANGE ALL OF A SUDDEN? WELL, IT'S A LOT EASIER FOR ME IF YOU'D DO THAT, BUT...
I'VE FINALLY REALIZED THE IMPORTANCE OF MEETINGS AND STORY-BOARDS.
I MAY HAVE BEEN ACTING CONCEITED BECAUSE EVERYBODY WAS CALLING ME A GENIUS.

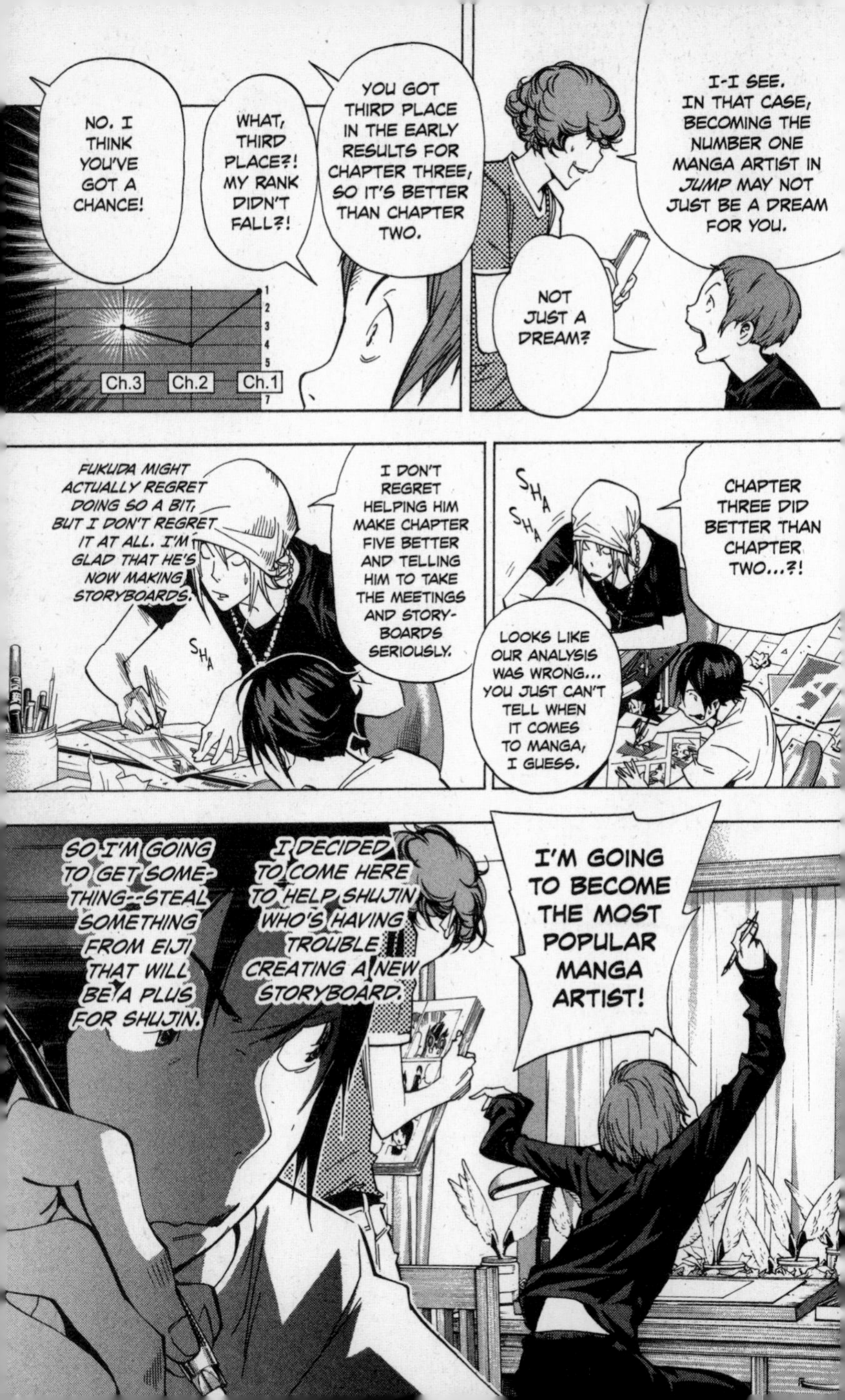
I-I SEE. IN THAT CASE, BECOMING THE NUMBER ONE MANGA ARTIST IN *JUMP* MAY NOT JUST BE A DREAM FOR YOU.
NOT JUST A DREAM?
YOU GOT THIRD PLACE IN THE EARLY RESULTS FOR CHAPTER THREE, SO IT'S BETTER THAN CHAPTER TWO.
WHAT, THIRD PLACE?! MY RANK DIDN'T FALL?!
NO. I THINK YOU'VE GOT A CHANCE!
Ch.3
Ch.2
Ch.1
CHAPTER THREE DID BETTER THAN CHAPTER TWO...?!
SHA
SHA
LOOKS LIKE OUR ANALYSIS WAS WRONG... YOU JUST CAN'T TELL WHEN IT COMES TO MANGA, I GUESS.
I DON'T REGRET HELPING HIM MAKE CHAPTER FIVE BETTER AND TELLING HIM TO TAKE THE MEETINGS AND STORY-BOARDS SERIOUSLY.
FUKUDA MIGHT ACTUALLY REGRET DOING SO A BIT, BUT I DON'T REGRET IT AT ALL. I'M GLAD THAT HE'S NOW MAKING STORYBOARDS.
SHA
I'M GOING TO BECOME THE MOST POPULAR MANGA ARTIST!
I DECIDED TO COME HERE TO HELP SHUJIN WHO'S HAVING TROUBLE CREATING A NEW STORYBOARD.
SO I'M GOING TO GET SOME-THING--STEAL SOMETHING FROM EIJI THAT WILL BE A PLUS FOR SHUJIN.

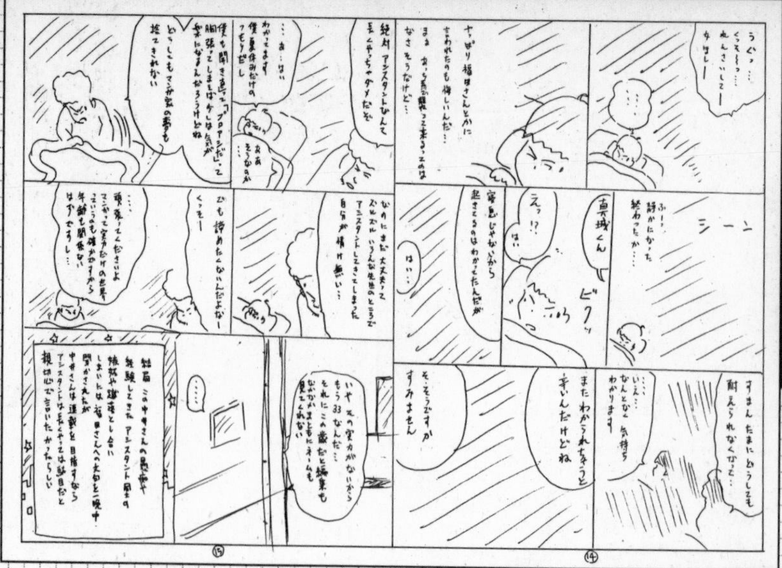
うぐっ…くっそ〜っ…れんさいしてーなぁー
…………
やっぱり福田さんとかにまわれたのも悔しいんだ…
まぁ おっちゃん頑張って来るってのはなさそうだけど…
シーン
ふーっ 静かになった 終わったか…
真城くん
ビクッ
えっ!? はい
寝息じゃないから起きてるのはわかってたんだが
はい…
すまん たまにどうしても耐えられなくなって…
…いえ… なんとなく気持ちわかります
またわかられちゃうと辛いんだけどね
そ・そうですか すみません
絶対アシスタントなんて長くやっちゃダメだぞ
…あ…はい わかってます 僕夏休みだけのつもりだし
ああ そうなのか
僕も聞き直って「プロアシだ」って頑張ってしまえば少しは気が楽になるんだろうけどね
どうしてもマンガ家の夢も捨てきれない
なのにまだ大丈夫って ズルズルいろんな先生のところで アシスタントしてきてしまった 自分が情け無い…
でも諦めたくないんだよなー くっそー
…頑張ってくださいよ マンガって実力だけの世界って いうのも確かですから 年齢も関係ない はずですし…
いや その実力がないから もう33なんだ… それにこの歳だと編集も なかなかまともにネームも 見てくれない
……
結局 この中井さんの愚痴や 経験してきた アシスタント同士の 嫉妬や蹴落とし合い しまいには 福田さんへの文句と一晩中 聞かされたが 中井さんは連載を 目指すなら アシスタントは長くやっては駄目だと 親切心で言いたかったらしい
⑭
⑮

OHBA'S STORYBOARD

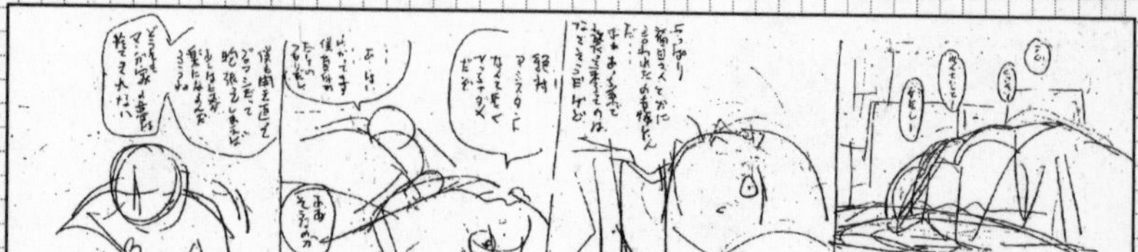

OBATA'S STORYBOARD

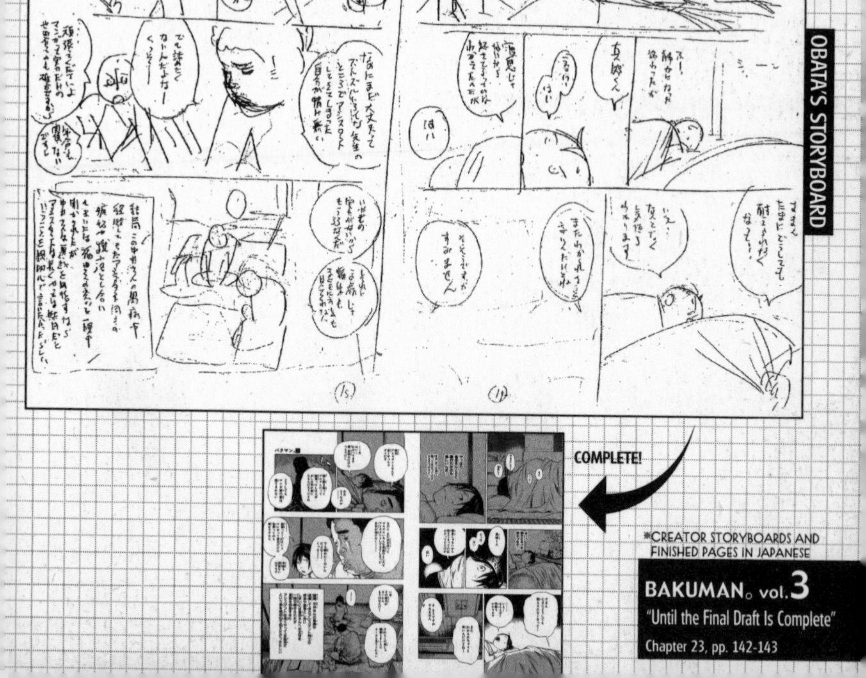

COMPLETE!

*CREATOR STORYBOARDS AND FINISHED PAGES IN JAPANESE

BAKUMAN。 vol. 3

"Until the Final Draft Is Complete"

Chapter 23, pp. 142-143

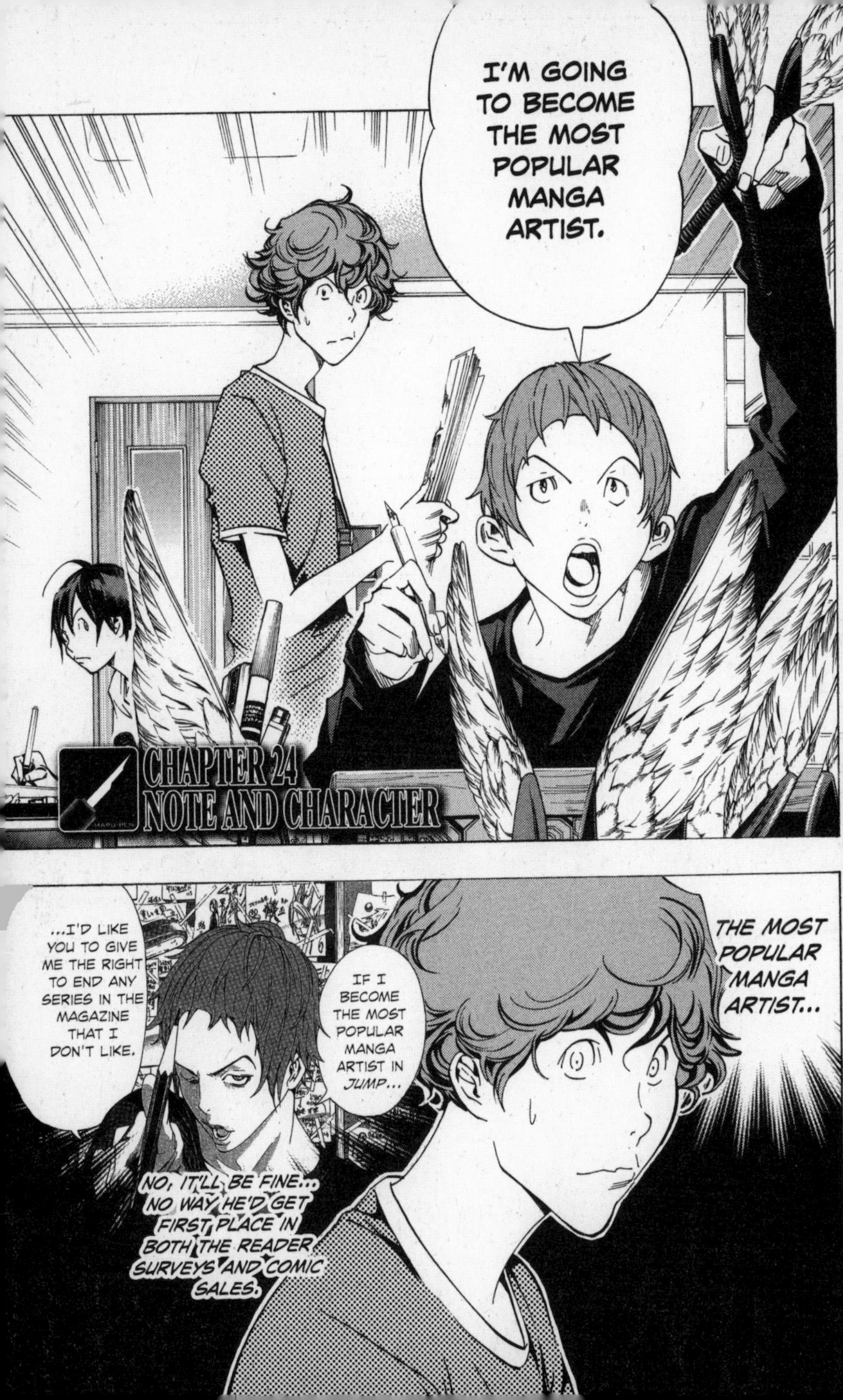

I'M GOING TO BECOME THE MOST POPULAR MANGA ARTIST.
CHAPTER 24
NOTE AND CHARACTER
THE MOST POPULAR MANGA ARTIST...
IF I BECOME THE MOST POPULAR MANGA ARTIST IN *JUMP*...
...I'D LIKE YOU TO GIVE ME THE RIGHT TO END ANY SERIES IN THE MAGAZINE THAT I DON'T LIKE.
NO, IT'LL BE FINE... NO WAY HE'D GET FIRST PLACE IN BOTH THE READER SURVEYS AND COMIC SALES.

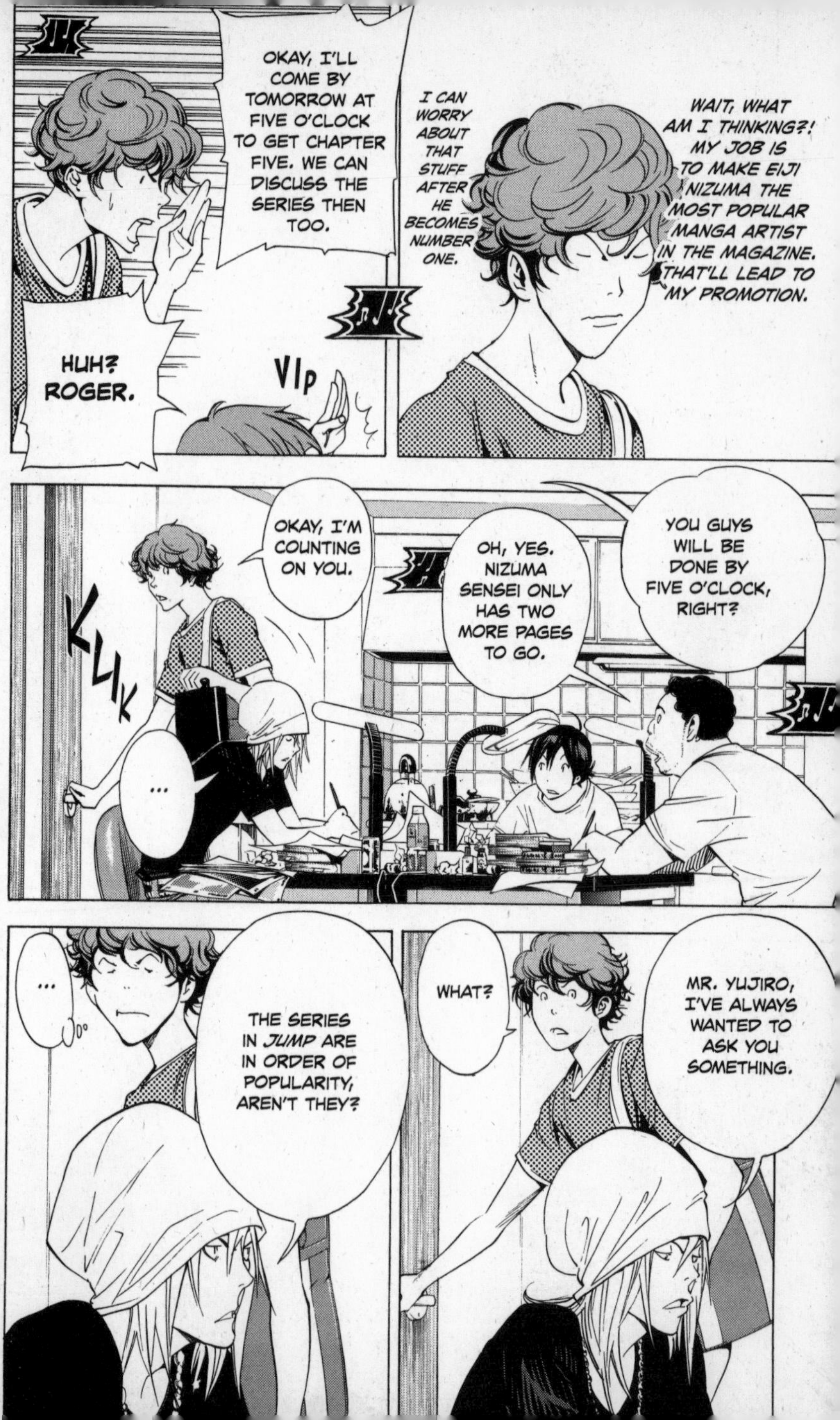
WAIT, WHAT AM I THINKING?! MY JOB IS TO MAKE EIJI NIZUMA THE MOST POPULAR MANGA ARTIST IN THE MAGAZINE. THAT'LL LEAD TO MY PROMOTION.
I CAN WORRY ABOUT THAT STUFF AFTER HE BECOMES NUMBER ONE.
OKAY, I'LL COME BY TOMORROW AT FIVE O'CLOCK TO GET CHAPTER FIVE. WE CAN DISCUSS THE SERIES THEN TOO.
HUH? ROGER.
VIP
YOU GUYS WILL BE DONE BY FIVE O'CLOCK, RIGHT?
OH, YES. NIZUMA SENSEI ONLY HAS TWO MORE PAGES TO GO.
OKAY, I'M COUNTING ON YOU.
KLIK
...
MR. YUJIRO, I'VE ALWAYS WANTED TO ASK YOU SOMETHING.
WHAT?
THE SERIES IN *JUMP* ARE IN ORDER OF POPULARITY, AREN'T THEY?
...

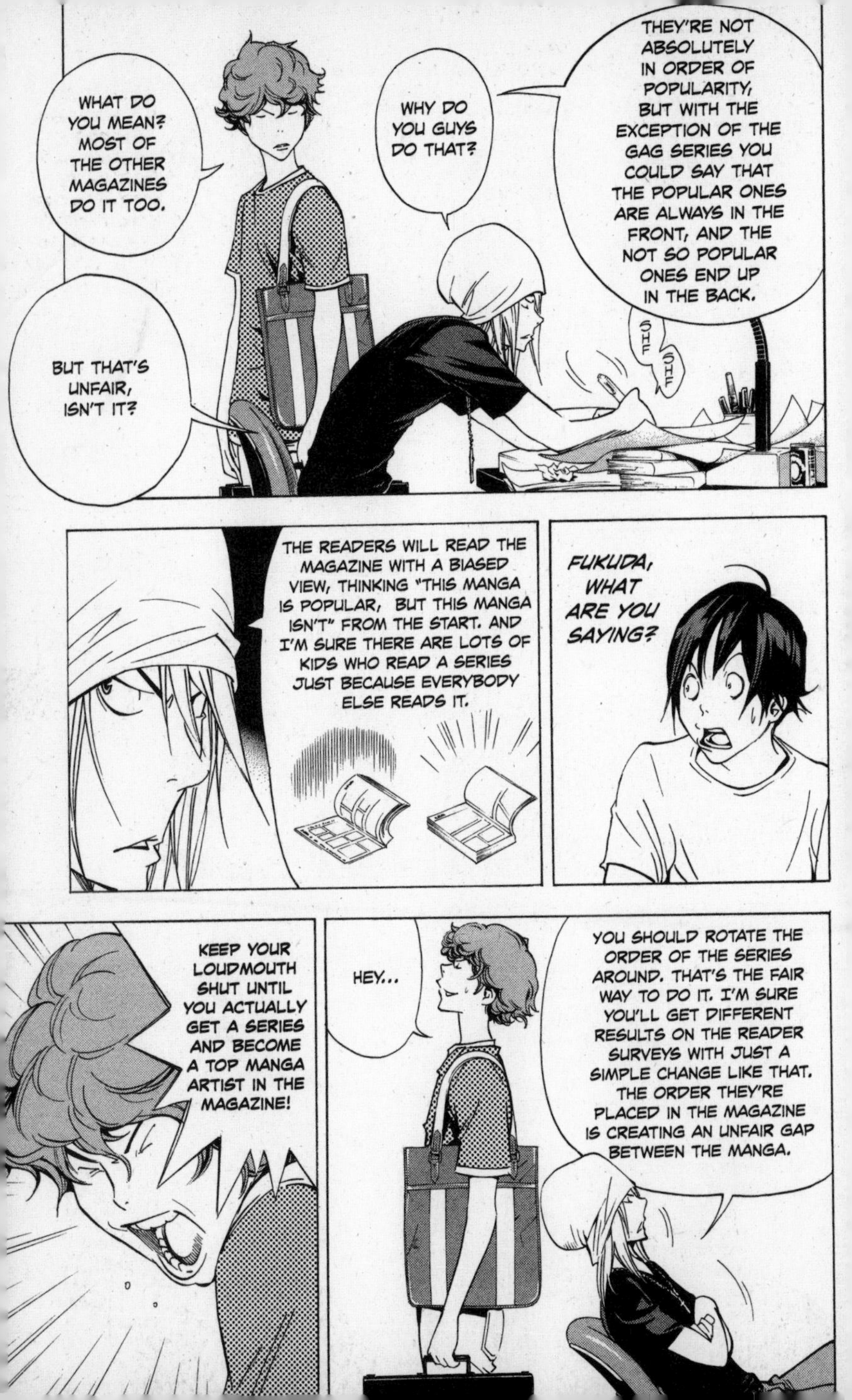
THEY'RE NOT ABSOLUTELY IN ORDER OF POPULARITY, BUT WITH THE EXCEPTION OF THE GAG SERIES YOU COULD SAY THAT THE POPULAR ONES ARE ALWAYS IN THE FRONT, AND THE NOT SO POPULAR ONES END UP IN THE BACK.
WHY DO YOU GUYS DO THAT?
WHAT DO YOU MEAN? MOST OF THE OTHER MAGAZINES DO IT TOO.
SHF
SHF
BUT THAT'S UNFAIR, ISN'T IT?
FUKUDA, WHAT ARE YOU SAYING?
THE READERS WILL READ THE MAGAZINE WITH A BIASED VIEW, THINKING "THIS MANGA IS POPULAR, BUT THIS MANGA ISN'T" FROM THE START. AND I'M SURE THERE ARE LOTS OF KIDS WHO READ A SERIES JUST BECAUSE EVERYBODY ELSE READS IT.
YOU SHOULD ROTATE THE ORDER OF THE SERIES AROUND. THAT'S THE FAIR WAY TO DO IT. I'M SURE YOU'LL GET DIFFERENT RESULTS ON THE READER SURVEYS WITH JUST A SIMPLE CHANGE LIKE THAT. THE ORDER THEY'RE PLACED IN THE MAGAZINE IS CREATING AN UNFAIR GAP BETWEEN THE MANGA.
HEY...
KEEP YOUR LOUDMOUTH SHUT UNTIL YOU ACTUALLY GET A SERIES AND BECOME A TOP MANGA ARTIST IN THE MAGAZINE!

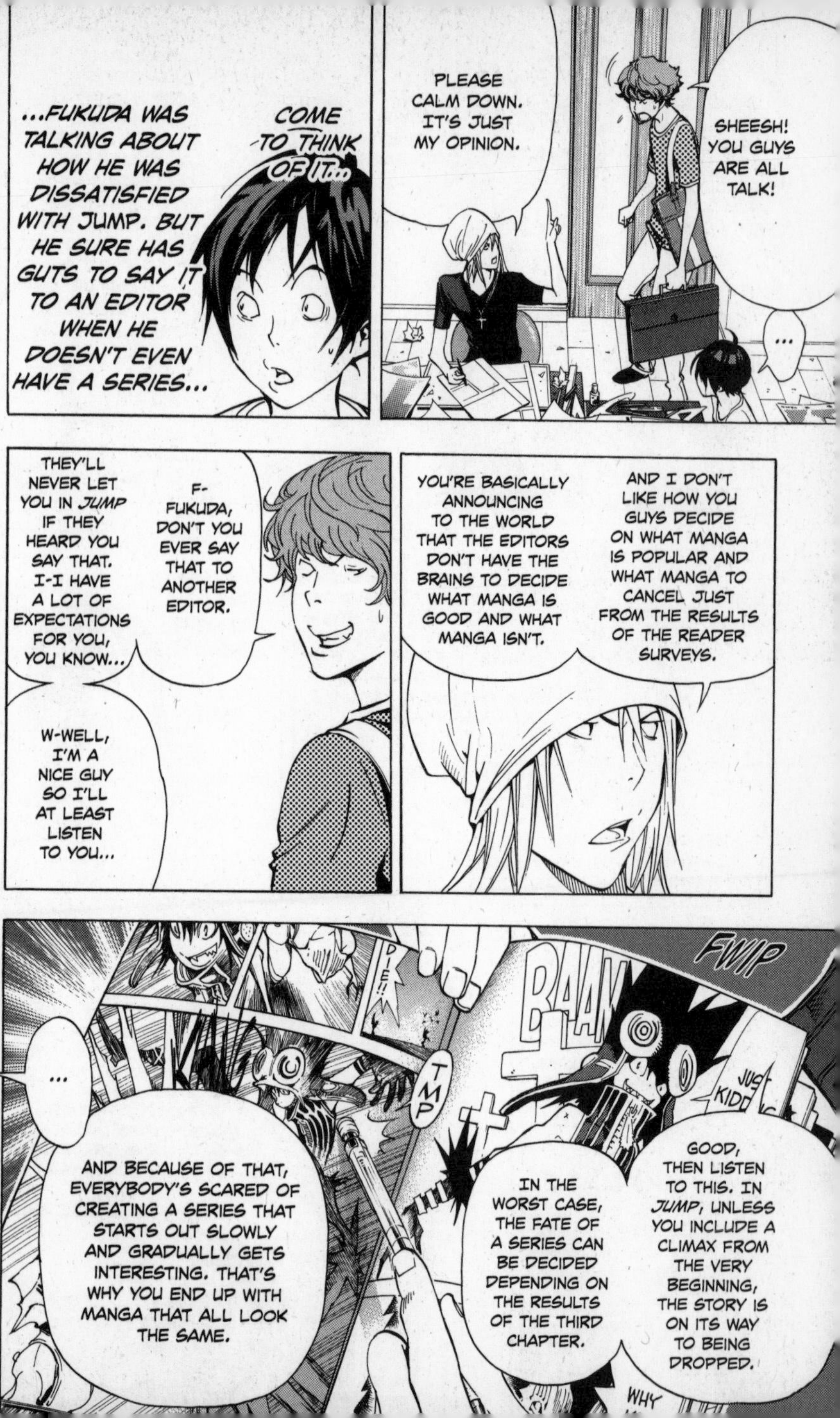
SHEESH! YOU GUYS ARE ALL TALK!
PLEASE CALM DOWN. IT'S JUST MY OPINION.
...
COME TO THINK OF IT...
...FUKUDA WAS TALKING ABOUT HOW HE WAS DISSATISFIED WITH JUMP. BUT HE SURE HAS GUTS TO SAY IT TO AN EDITOR WHEN HE DOESN'T EVEN HAVE A SERIES...
AND I DON'T LIKE HOW YOU GUYS DECIDE ON WHAT MANGA IS POPULAR AND WHAT MANGA TO CANCEL JUST FROM THE RESULTS OF THE READER SURVEYS.
YOU'RE BASICALLY ANNOUNCING TO THE WORLD THAT THE EDITORS DON'T HAVE THE BRAINS TO DECIDE WHAT MANGA IS GOOD AND WHAT MANGA ISN'T.
F-FUKUDA, DON'T YOU EVER SAY THAT TO ANOTHER EDITOR.
THEY'LL NEVER LET YOU IN *JUMP* IF THEY HEARD YOU SAY THAT. I-I HAVE A LOT OF EXPECTATIONS FOR YOU, YOU KNOW...
W-WELL, I'M A NICE GUY SO I'LL AT LEAST LISTEN TO YOU...
FWIP
GOOD, THEN LISTEN TO THIS. IN *JUMP*, UNLESS YOU INCLUDE A CLIMAX FROM THE VERY BEGINNING, THE STORY IS ON ITS WAY TO BEING DROPPED.
IN THE WORST CASE, THE FATE OF A SERIES CAN BE DECIDED DEPENDING ON THE RESULTS OF THE THIRD CHAPTER.
TMP
AND BECAUSE OF THAT, EVERYBODY'S SCARED OF CREATING A SERIES THAT STARTS OUT SLOWLY AND GRADUALLY GETS INTERESTING. THAT'S WHY YOU END UP WITH MANGA THAT ALL LOOK THE SAME.
...

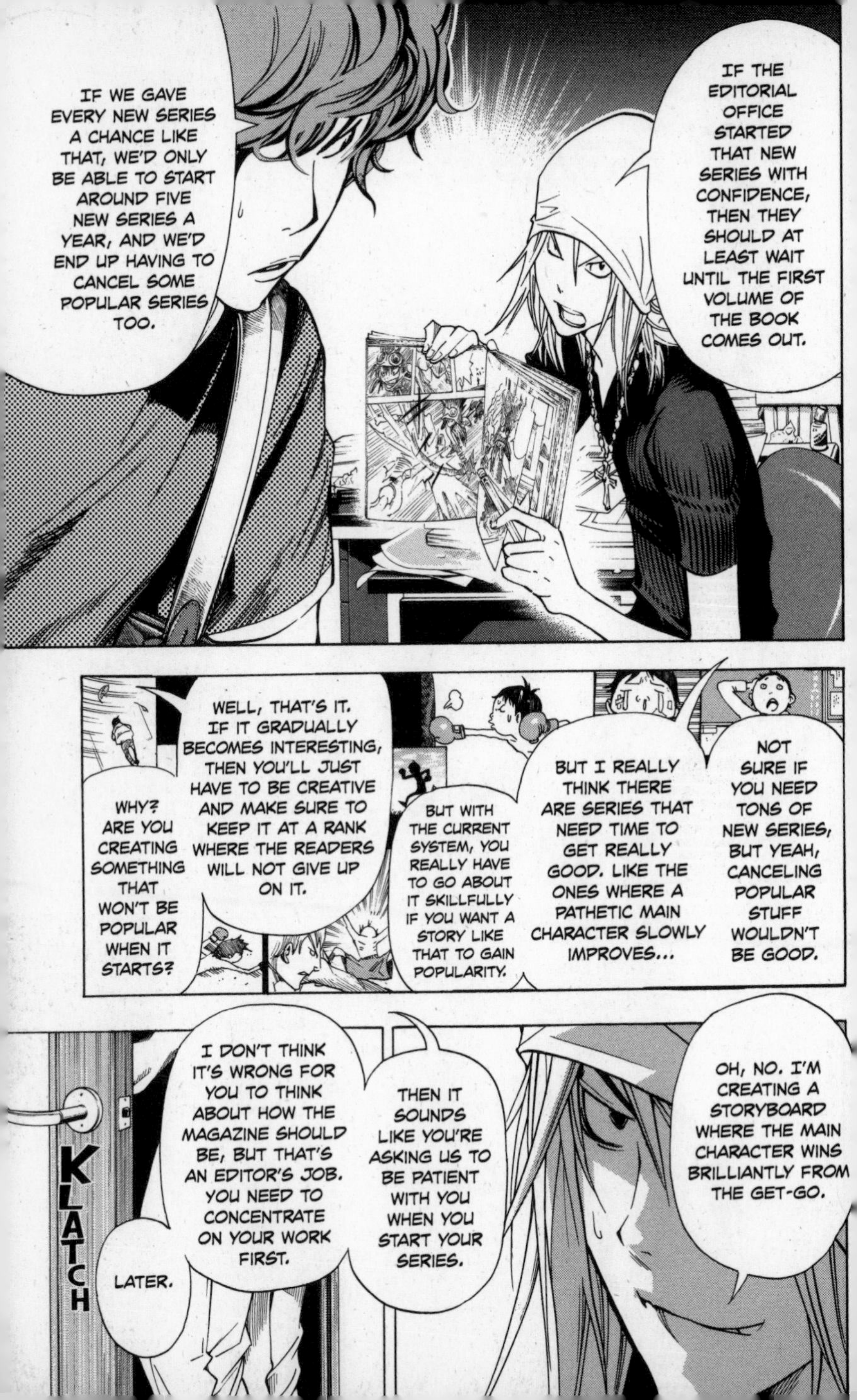
IF THE EDITORIAL OFFICE STARTED THAT NEW SERIES WITH CONFIDENCE, THEN THEY SHOULD AT LEAST WAIT UNTIL THE FIRST VOLUME OF THE BOOK COMES OUT.
IF WE GAVE EVERY NEW SERIES A CHANCE LIKE THAT, WE'D ONLY BE ABLE TO START AROUND FIVE NEW SERIES A YEAR, AND WE'D END UP HAVING TO CANCEL SOME POPULAR SERIES TOO.
NOT SURE IF YOU NEED TONS OF NEW SERIES, BUT YEAH, CANCELING POPULAR STUFF WOULDN'T BE GOOD.
BUT I REALLY THINK THERE ARE SERIES THAT NEED TIME TO GET REALLY GOOD. LIKE THE ONES WHERE A PATHETIC MAIN CHARACTER SLOWLY IMPROVES...
BUT WITH THE CURRENT SYSTEM, YOU REALLY HAVE TO GO ABOUT IT SKILLFULLY IF YOU WANT A STORY LIKE THAT TO GAIN POPULARITY.
WELL, THAT'S IT. IF IT GRADUALLY BECOMES INTERESTING, THEN YOU'LL JUST HAVE TO BE CREATIVE AND MAKE SURE TO KEEP IT AT A RANK WHERE THE READERS WILL NOT GIVE UP ON IT.
WHY? ARE YOU CREATING SOMETHING THAT WON'T BE POPULAR WHEN IT STARTS?
OH, NO. I'M CREATING A STORYBOARD WHERE THE MAIN CHARACTER WINS BRILLIANTLY FROM THE GET-GO.
THEN IT SOUNDS LIKE YOU'RE ASKING US TO BE PATIENT WITH YOU WHEN YOU START YOUR SERIES.
I DON'T THINK IT'S WRONG FOR YOU TO THINK ABOUT HOW THE MAGAZINE SHOULD BE, BUT THAT'S AN EDITOR'S JOB. YOU NEED TO CONCENTRATE ON YOUR WORK FIRST.
LATER.
KLATCH

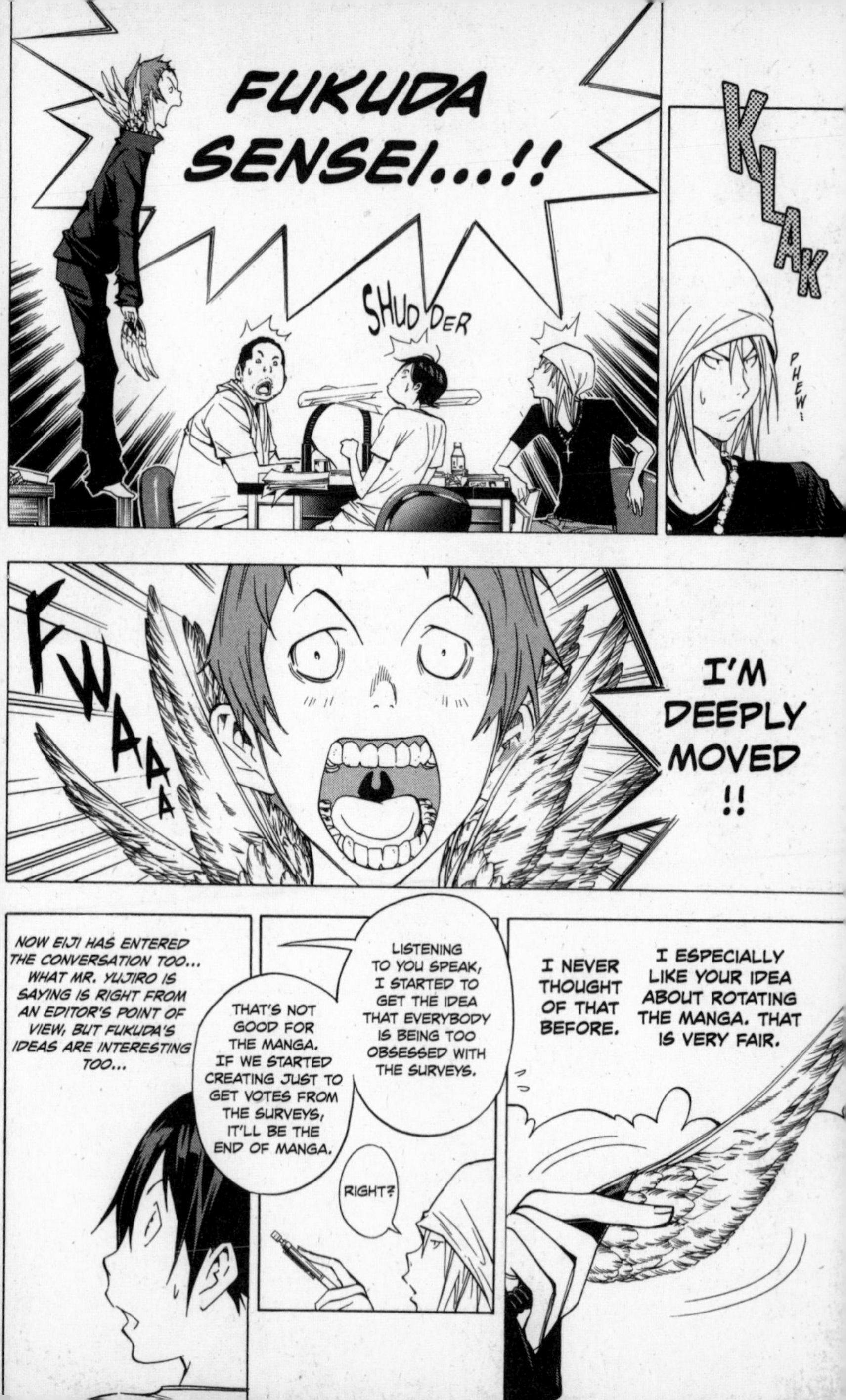
KLLAK
PHEW!!
FUKUDA SENSEI...!!
SHUDDER
I'M DEEPLY MOVED !!
FWAAAA
I ESPECIALLY LIKE YOUR IDEA ABOUT ROTATING THE MANGA. THAT IS VERY FAIR.
I NEVER THOUGHT OF THAT BEFORE.
LISTENING TO YOU SPEAK, I STARTED TO GET THE IDEA THAT EVERYBODY IS BEING TOO OBSESSED WITH THE SURVEYS.
THAT'S NOT GOOD FOR THE MANGA. IF WE STARTED CREATING JUST TO GET VOTES FROM THE SURVEYS, IT'LL BE THE END OF MANGA.
RIGHT?
NOW EIJI HAS ENTERED THE CONVERSATION TOO... WHAT MR. YUJIRO IS SAYING IS RIGHT FROM AN EDITOR'S POINT OF VIEW, BUT FUKUDA'S IDEAS ARE INTERESTING TOO...

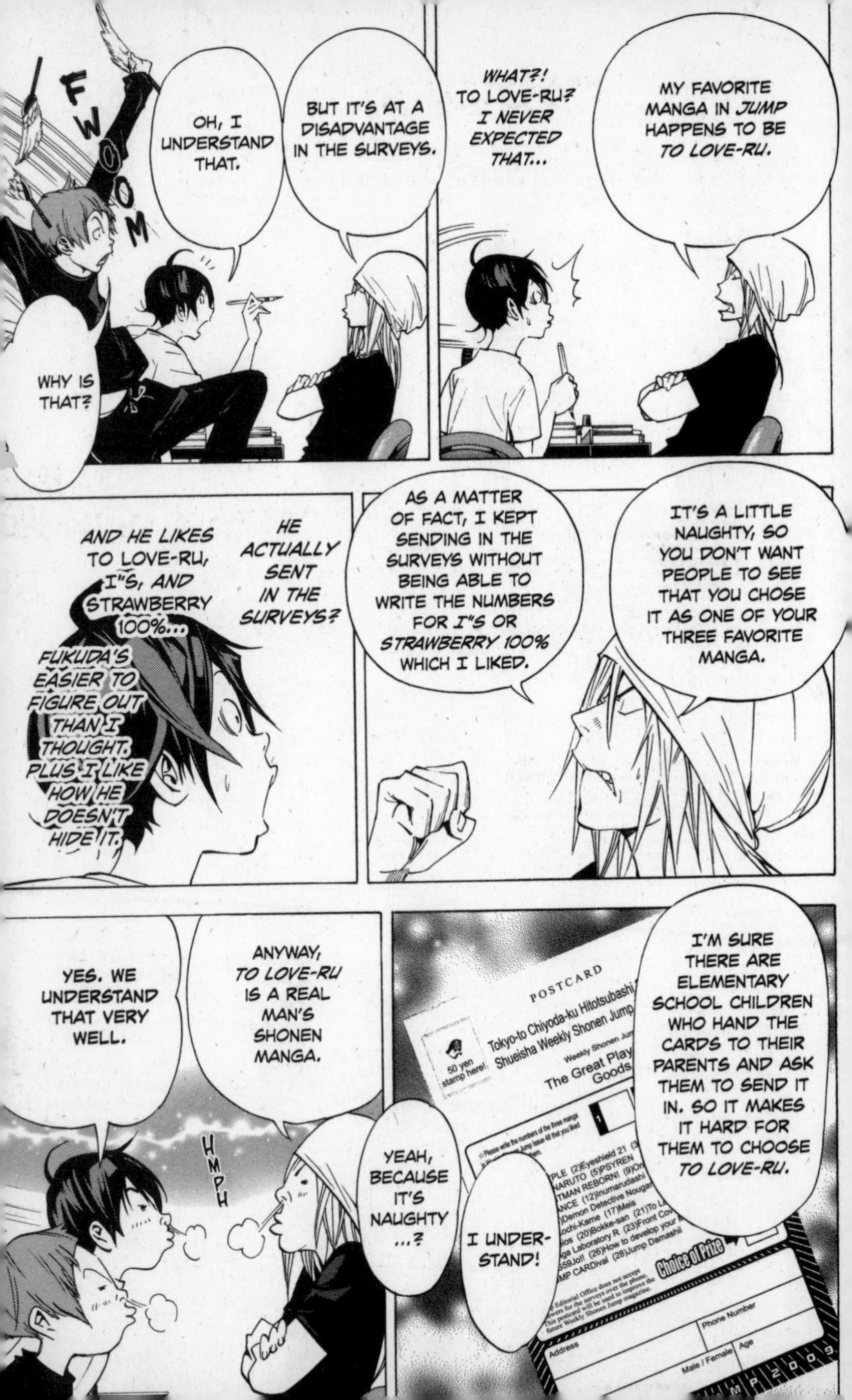
MY FAVORITE MANGA IN JUMP HAPPENS TO BE TO LOVE-RU.
WHAT?! TO LOVE-RU? I NEVER EXPECTED THAT...
BUT IT'S AT A DISADVANTAGE IN THE SURVEYS.
OH, I UNDERSTAND THAT.
FWOOM
WHY IS THAT?
IT'S A LITTLE NAUGHTY, SO YOU DON'T WANT PEOPLE TO SEE THAT YOU CHOSE IT AS ONE OF YOUR THREE FAVORITE MANGA.
AS A MATTER OF FACT, I KEPT SENDING IN THE SURVEYS WITHOUT BEING ABLE TO WRITE THE NUMBERS FOR I"S OR STRAWBERRY 100% WHICH I LIKED.
HE ACTUALLY SENT IN THE SURVEYS?
AND HE LIKES TO LOVE-RU, I"S, AND STRAWBERRY 100%...
FUKUDA'S EASIER TO FIGURE OUT THAN I THOUGHT. PLUS I LIKE HOW HE DOESN'T HIDE IT.
I'M SURE THERE ARE ELEMENTARY SCHOOL CHILDREN WHO HAND THE CARDS TO THEIR PARENTS AND ASK THEM TO SEND IT IN. SO IT MAKES IT HARD FOR THEM TO CHOOSE TO LOVE-RU.
POSTCARD
50 yen stamp here!
Tokyo-to Chiyoda-ku Hitotsubashi
Shueisha Weekly Shonen Jump
Choice of Prize
Address
Phone Number
Male / Female
Age
I UNDER-STAND!
YEAH, BECAUSE IT'S NAUGHTY...?
ANYWAY, TO LOVE-RU IS A REAL MAN'S SHONEN MANGA.
YES. WE UNDERSTAND THAT VERY WELL.
HMPH

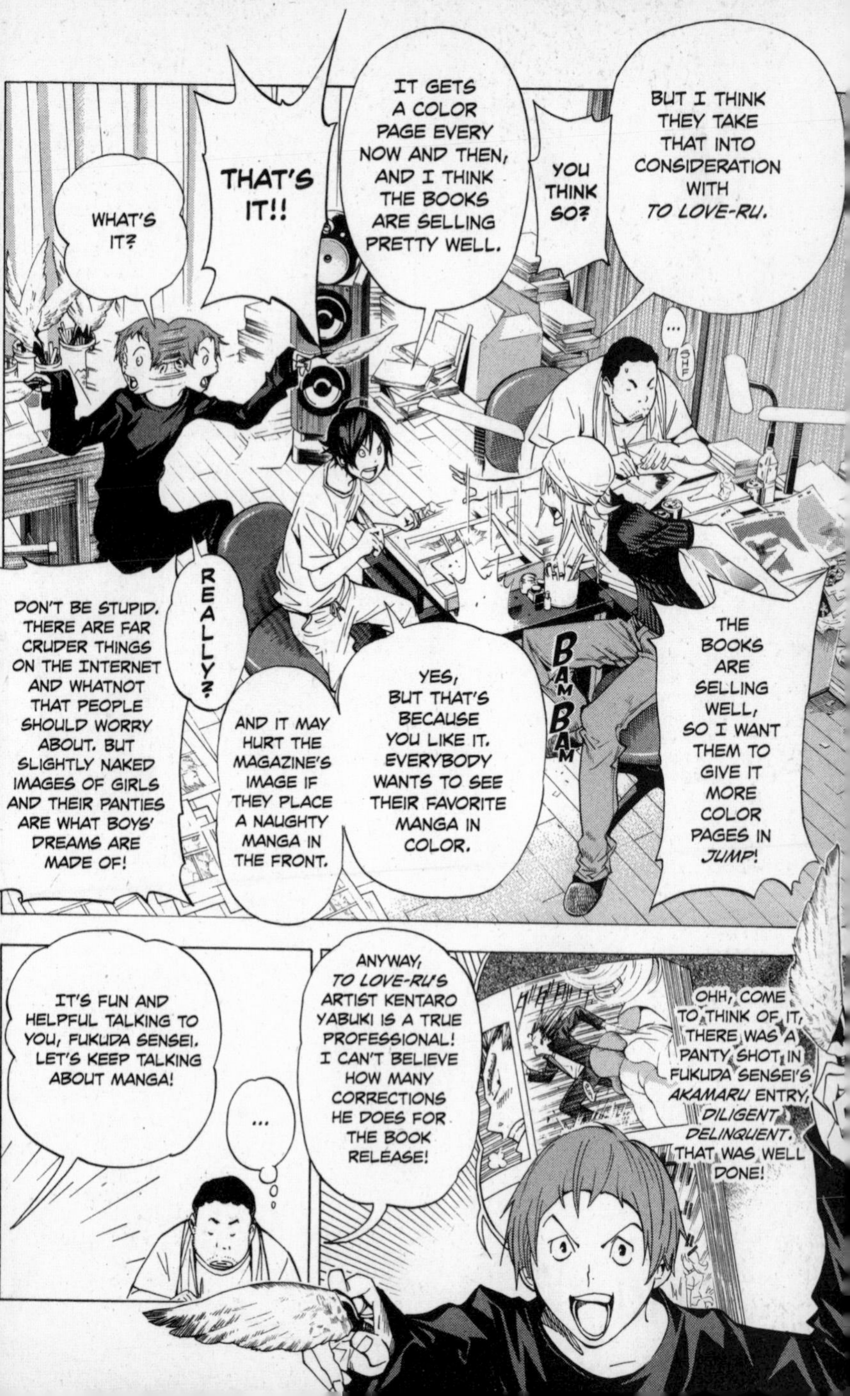
BUT I THINK THEY TAKE THAT INTO CONSIDERATION WITH *TO LOVE-RU*.
YOU THINK SO?
IT GETS A COLOR PAGE EVERY NOW AND THEN, AND I THINK THE BOOKS ARE SELLING PRETTY WELL.
THAT'S IT!!
WHAT'S IT?
...
SHF
THE BOOKS ARE SELLING WELL, SO I WANT THEM TO GIVE IT MORE COLOR PAGES IN *JUMP*!
BAM BAM
YES, BUT THAT'S BECAUSE YOU LIKE IT. EVERYBODY WANTS TO SEE THEIR FAVORITE MANGA IN COLOR.
AND IT MAY HURT THE MAGAZINE'S IMAGE IF THEY PLACE A NAUGHTY MANGA IN THE FRONT.
REALLY?
DON'T BE STUPID. THERE ARE FAR CRUDER THINGS ON THE INTERNET AND WHATNOT THAT PEOPLE SHOULD WORRY ABOUT. BUT SLIGHTLY NAKED IMAGES OF GIRLS AND THEIR PANTIES ARE WHAT BOYS' DREAMS ARE MADE OF!
OHH, COME TO THINK OF IT, THERE WAS A PANTY SHOT IN FUKUDA SENSEI'S *AKAMARU* ENTRY, *DILIGENT DELINQUENT*. THAT WAS WELL DONE!
ANYWAY, *TO LOVE-RU'S* ARTIST KENTARO YABUKI IS A TRUE PROFESSIONAL! I CAN'T BELIEVE HOW MANY CORRECTIONS HE DOES FOR THE BOOK RELEASE!
IT'S FUN AND HELPFUL TALKING TO YOU, FUKUDA SENSEI. LET'S KEEP TALKING ABOUT MANGA!
...

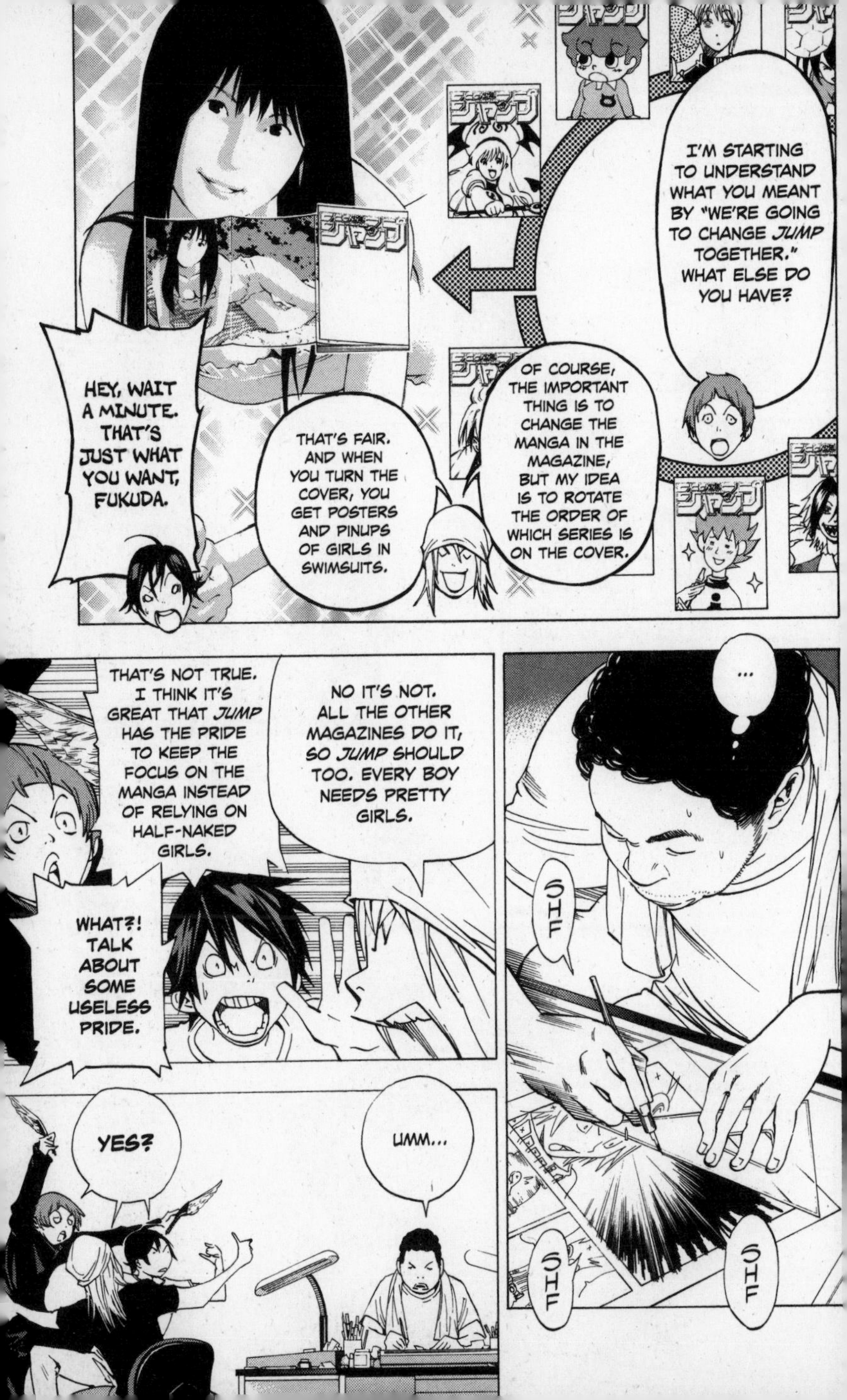
I'M STARTING TO UNDERSTAND WHAT YOU MEANT BY "WE'RE GOING TO CHANGE *JUMP* TOGETHER." WHAT ELSE DO YOU HAVE?
OF COURSE, THE IMPORTANT THING IS TO CHANGE THE MANGA IN THE MAGAZINE, BUT MY IDEA IS TO ROTATE THE ORDER OF WHICH SERIES IS ON THE COVER.
THAT'S FAIR. AND WHEN YOU TURN THE COVER, YOU GET POSTERS AND PINUPS OF GIRLS IN SWIMSUITS.
HEY, WAIT A MINUTE. THAT'S JUST WHAT YOU WANT, FUKUDA.
...
SHF
SHF
SHF
NO IT'S NOT. ALL THE OTHER MAGAZINES DO IT, SO *JUMP* SHOULD TOO. EVERY BOY NEEDS PRETTY GIRLS.
THAT'S NOT TRUE. I THINK IT'S GREAT THAT *JUMP* HAS THE PRIDE TO KEEP THE FOCUS ON THE MANGA INSTEAD OF RELYING ON HALF-NAKED GIRLS.
WHAT?! TALK ABOUT SOME USELESS PRIDE.
UMM...
YES?

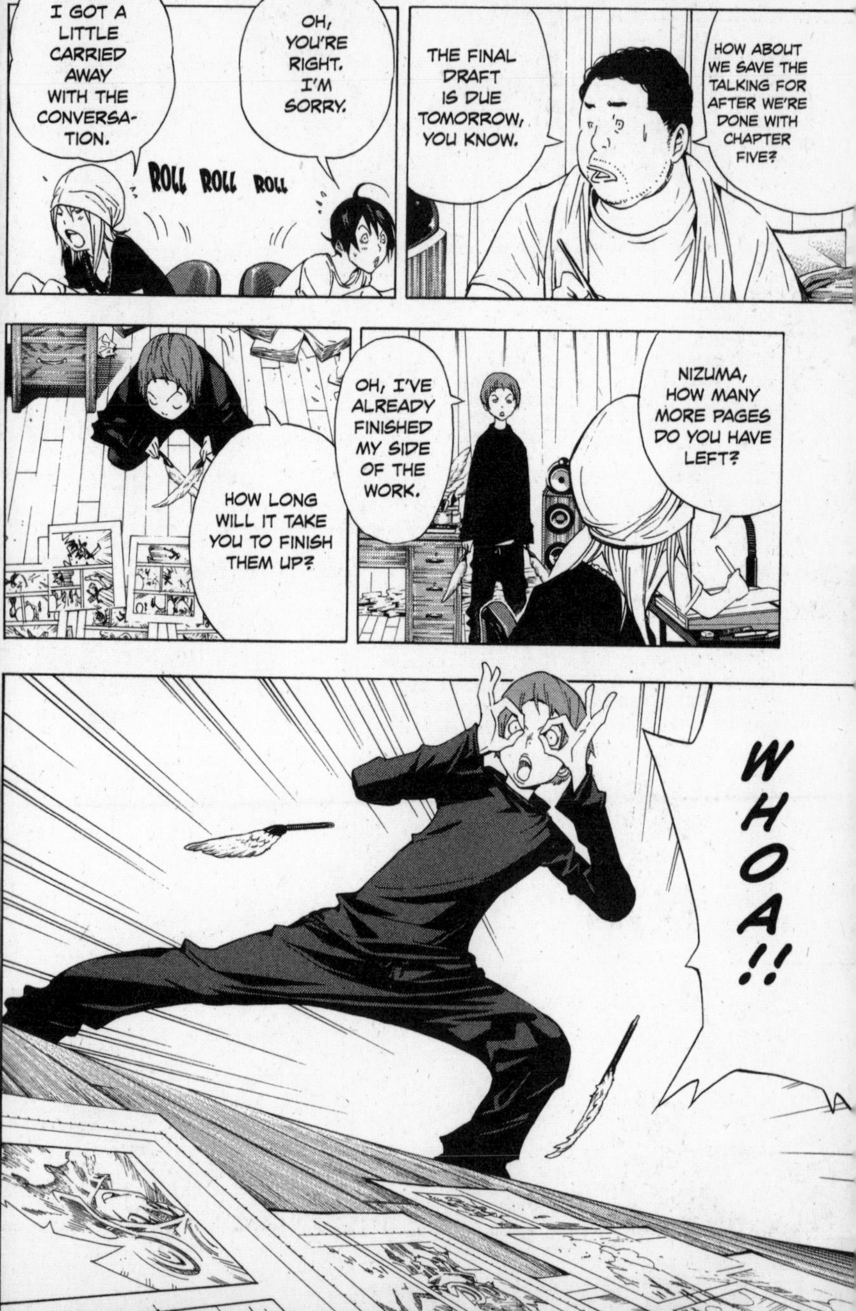
HOW ABOUT WE SAVE THE TALKING FOR AFTER WE'RE DONE WITH CHAPTER FIVE?
THE FINAL DRAFT IS DUE TOMORROW, YOU KNOW.
OH, YOU'RE RIGHT. I'M SORRY.
SORRY... I GOT A LITTLE CARRIED AWAY WITH THE CONVERSATION.
ROLL ROLL ROLL
NIZUMA, HOW MANY MORE PAGES DO YOU HAVE LEFT?
OH, I'VE ALREADY FINISHED MY SIDE OF THE WORK.
HOW LONG WILL IT TAKE YOU TO FINISH THEM UP?
WHOA!!

READ THIS WAY

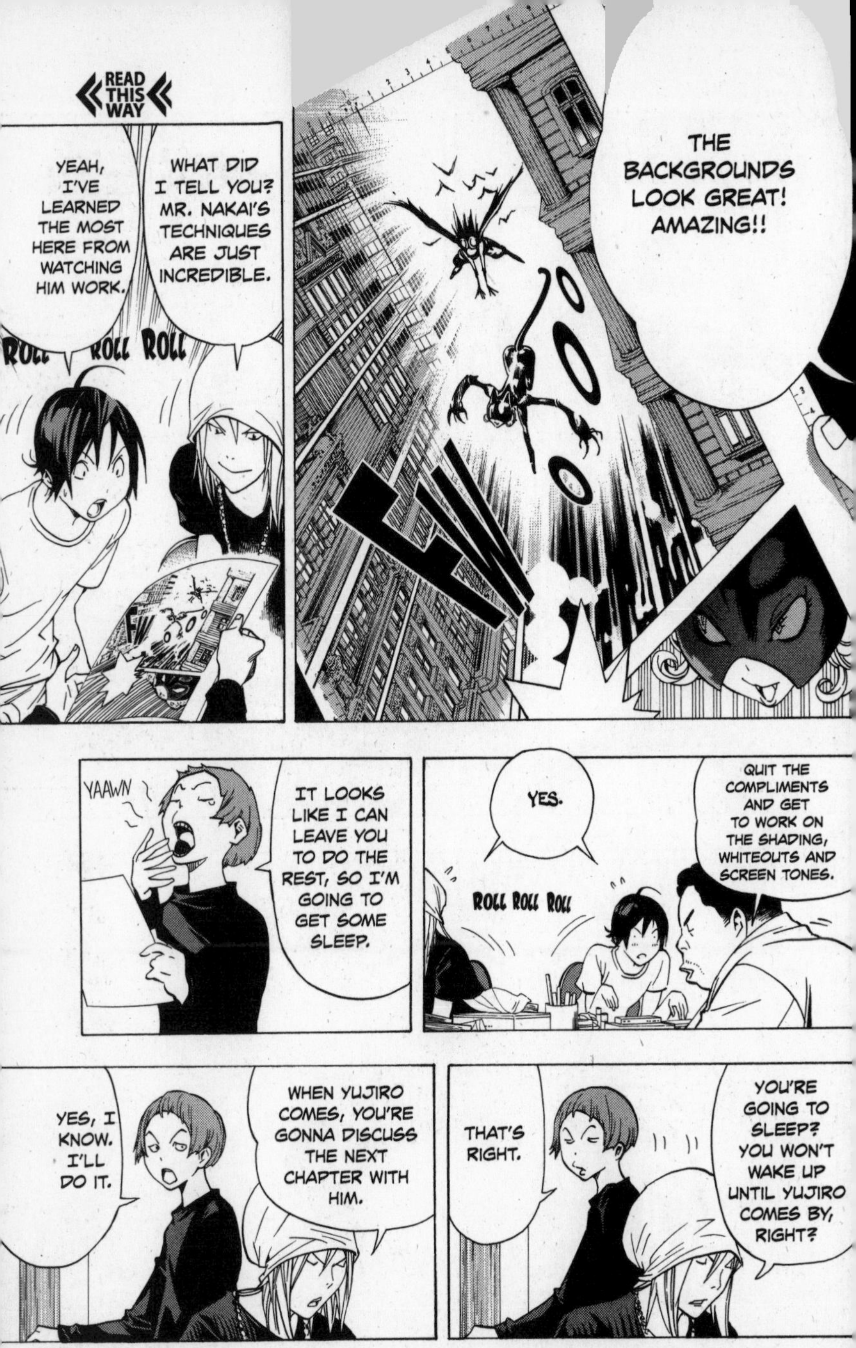
THE BACKGROUNDS LOOK GREAT! AMAZING!!
FW
ROLL ROLL ROLL
WHAT DID I TELL YOU? MR. NAKAI'S TECHNIQUES ARE JUST INCREDIBLE.
YEAH, I'VE LEARNED THE MOST HERE FROM WATCHING HIM WORK.
QUIT THE COMPLIMENTS AND GET TO WORK ON THE SHADING, WHITEOUTS AND SCREEN TONES.
YES.
ROLL ROLL ROLL
YAAWN
IT LOOKS LIKE I CAN LEAVE YOU TO DO THE REST, SO I'M GOING TO GET SOME SLEEP.
YOU'RE GOING TO SLEEP? YOU WON'T WAKE UP UNTIL YUJIRO COMES BY, RIGHT?
THAT'S RIGHT.
WHEN YUJIRO COMES, YOU'RE GONNA DISCUSS THE NEXT CHAPTER WITH HIM.
YES, I KNOW. I'LL DO IT.

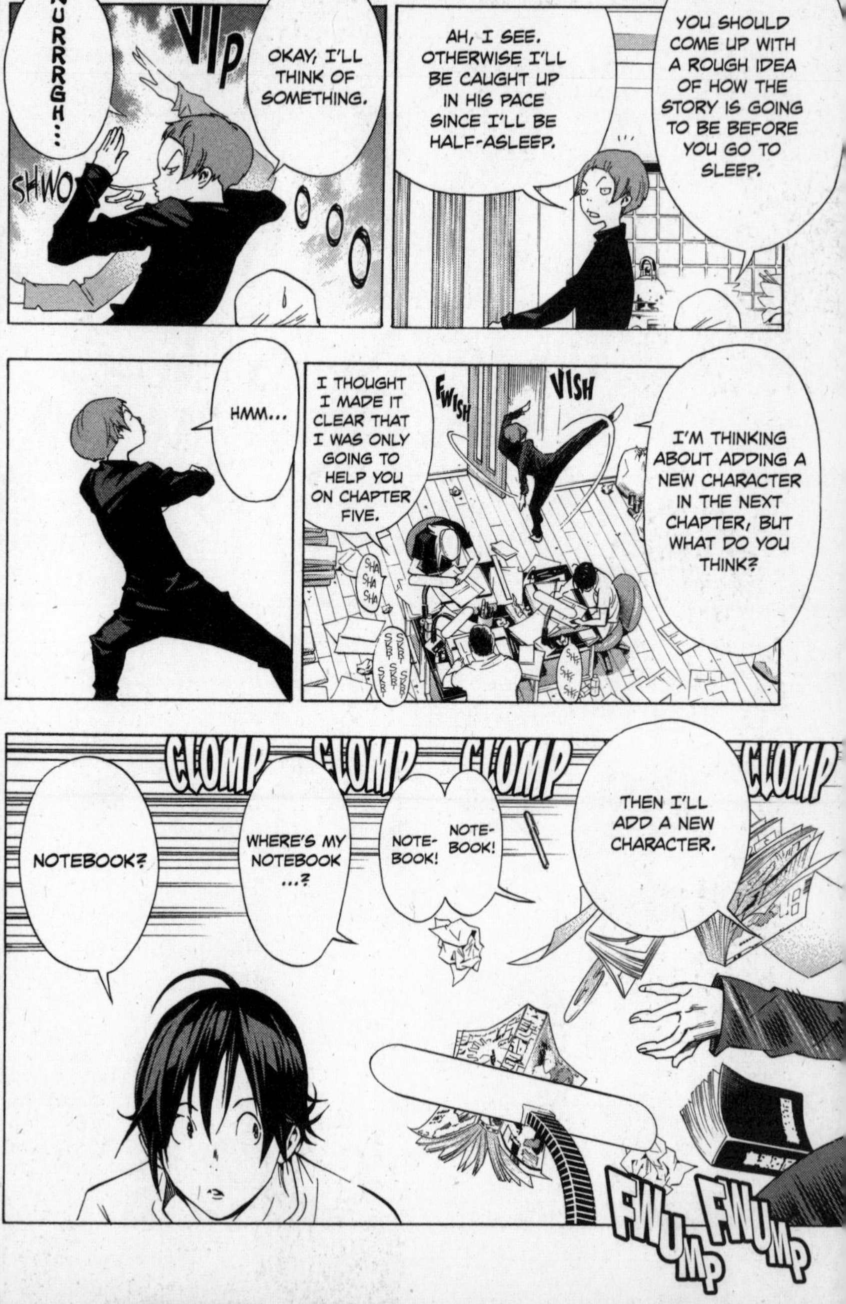
YOU SHOULD COME UP WITH A ROUGH IDEA OF HOW THE STORY IS GOING TO BE BEFORE YOU GO TO SLEEP.
AH, I SEE. OTHERWISE I'LL BE CAUGHT UP IN HIS PACE SINCE I'LL BE HALF-ASLEEP.
VIP
OKAY, I'LL THINK OF SOMETHING.
NURRRGH...
SHWO
I'M THINKING ABOUT ADDING A NEW CHARACTER IN THE NEXT CHAPTER, BUT WHAT DO YOU THINK?
VISH
FWISH
I THOUGHT I MADE IT CLEAR THAT I WAS ONLY GOING TO HELP YOU ON CHAPTER FIVE.
SHA SHA SHA
HMM...
CLOMP
CLOMP
THEN I'LL ADD A NEW CHARACTER.
CLOMP
NOTE-BOOK!
NOTE-BOOK!
CLOMP
WHERE'S MY NOTEBOOK ...?
NOTEBOOK?
FWUMP FWUMP

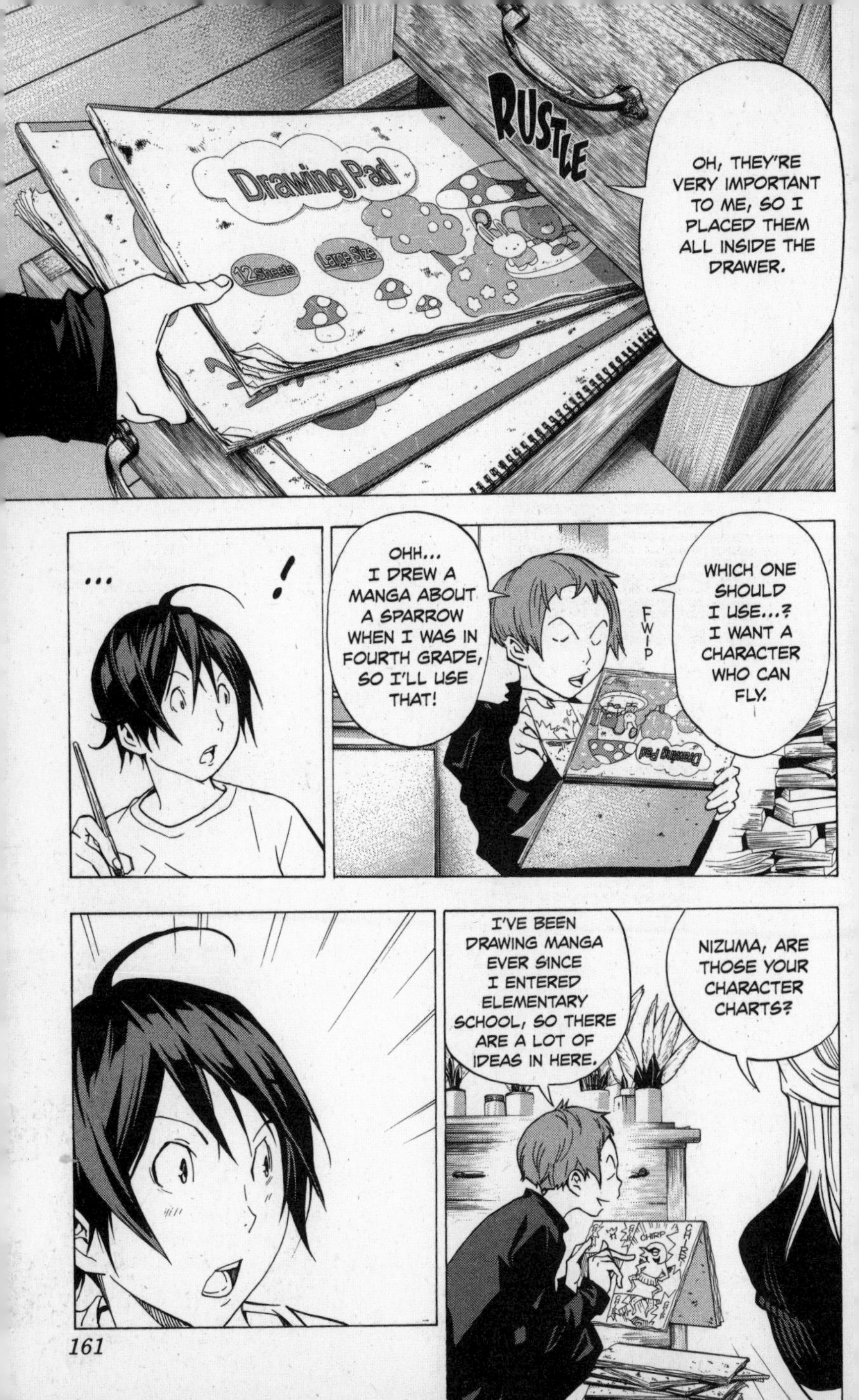
RUSTLE
OH, THEY'RE VERY IMPORTANT TO ME, SO I PLACED THEM ALL INSIDE THE DRAWER.
Drawing Pad
12 Sheets
Large Size
WHICH ONE SHOULD I USE...? I WANT A CHARACTER WHO CAN FLY.
OHH... I DREW A MANGA ABOUT A SPARROW WHEN I WAS IN FOURTH GRADE, SO I'LL USE THAT!
FWIP
...
!
NIZUMA, ARE THOSE YOUR CHARACTER CHARTS?
I'VE BEEN DRAWING MANGA EVER SINCE I ENTERED ELEMENTARY SCHOOL, SO THERE ARE A LOT OF IDEAS IN HERE.
CHIRP

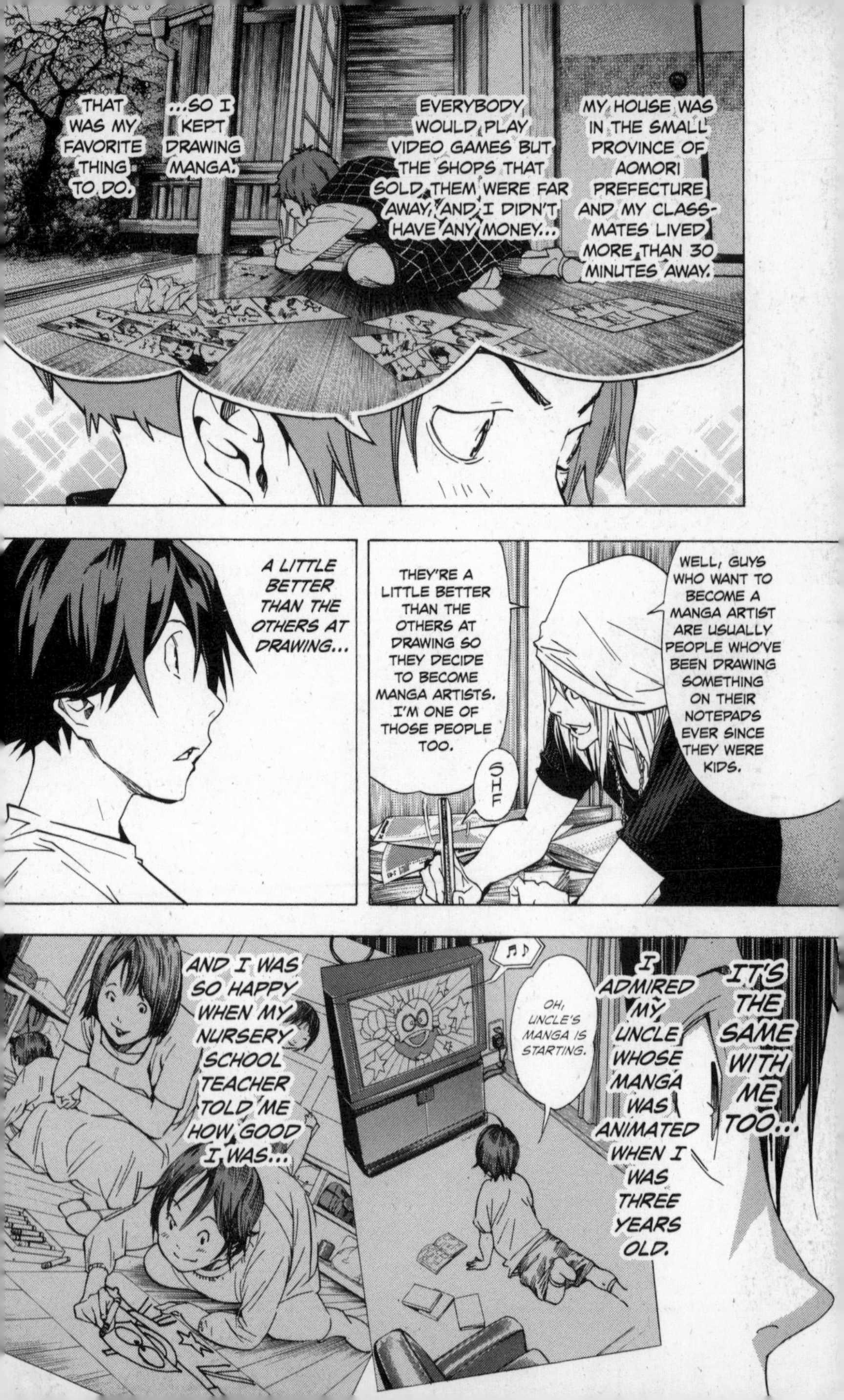
MY HOUSE WAS IN THE SMALL PROVINCE OF AOMORI PREFECTURE AND MY CLASSMATES LIVED MORE THAN 30 MINUTES AWAY.
EVERYBODY WOULD PLAY VIDEO GAMES BUT THE SHOPS THAT SOLD THEM WERE FAR AWAY, AND I DIDN'T HAVE ANY MONEY...
...SO I KEPT DRAWING MANGA.
THAT WAS MY FAVORITE THING TO DO.
WELL, GUYS WHO WANT TO BECOME A MANGA ARTIST ARE USUALLY PEOPLE WHO'VE BEEN DRAWING SOMETHING ON THEIR NOTEPADS EVER SINCE THEY WERE KIDS.
THEY'RE A LITTLE BETTER THAN THE OTHERS AT DRAWING SO THEY DECIDE TO BECOME MANGA ARTISTS. I'M ONE OF THOSE PEOPLE TOO.
SHF
A LITTLE BETTER THAN THE OTHERS AT DRAWING...
IT'S THE SAME WITH ME TOO...
I ADMIRED MY UNCLE WHOSE MANGA WAS ANIMATED WHEN I WAS THREE YEARS OLD.
OH, UNCLE'S MANGA IS STARTING.
AND I WAS SO HAPPY WHEN MY NURSERY SCHOOL TEACHER TOLD ME HOW GOOD I WAS...

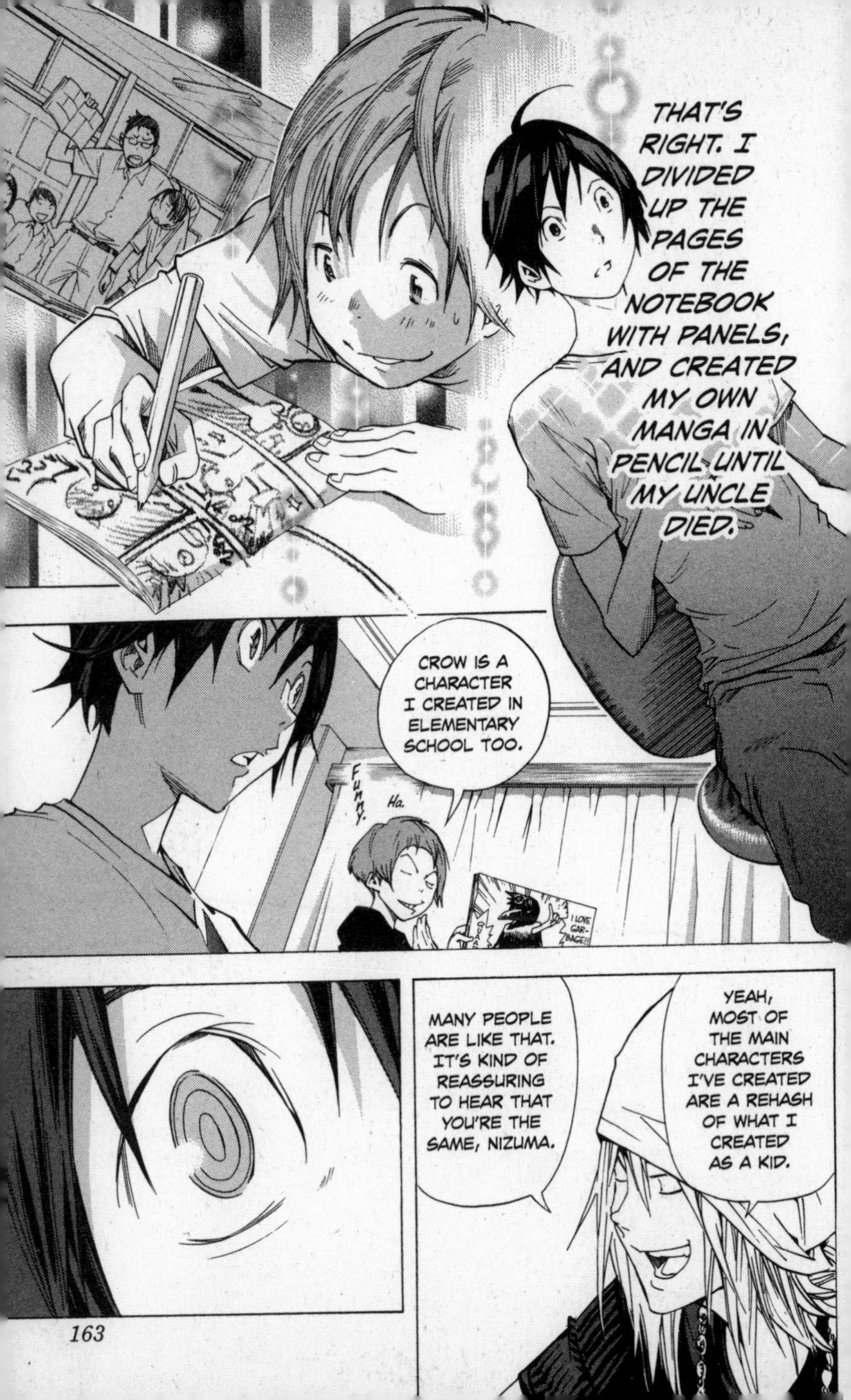
THAT'S RIGHT. I DIVIDED UP THE PAGES OF THE NOTEBOOK WITH PANELS, AND CREATED MY OWN MANGA IN PENCIL UNTIL MY UNCLE DIED.
CROW IS A CHARACTER I CREATED IN ELEMENTARY SCHOOL TOO.
Ha.
Funny.
I LOVE GARBAGE!!
YEAH, MOST OF THE MAIN CHARACTERS I'VE CREATED ARE A REHASH OF WHAT I CREATED AS A KID.
MANY PEOPLE ARE LIKE THAT. IT'S KIND OF REASSURING TO HEAR THAT YOU'RE THE SAME, NIZUMA.

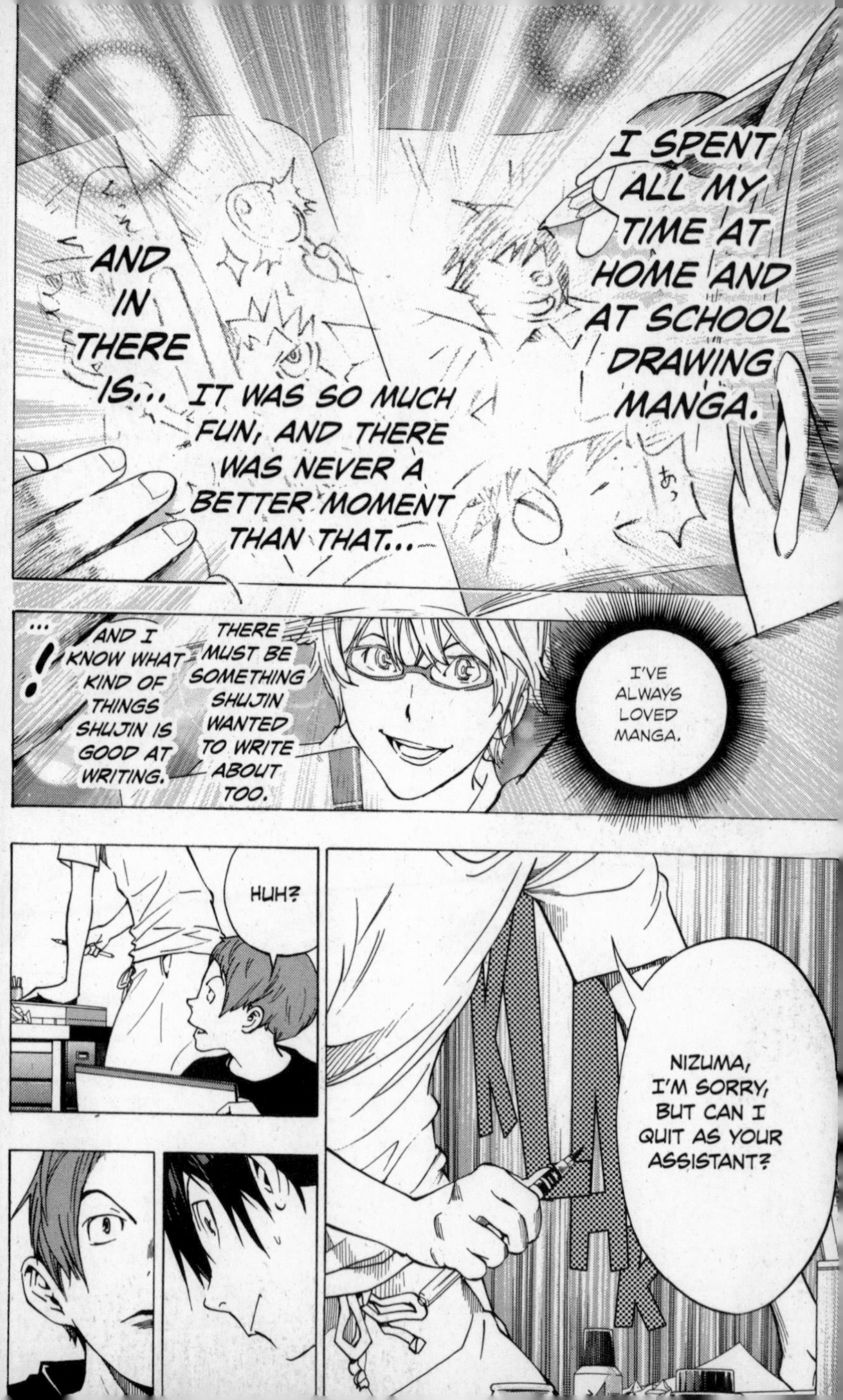
I SPENT ALL MY TIME AT HOME AND AT SCHOOL DRAWING MANGA.
AND IN THERE IS...
IT WAS SO MUCH FUN, AND THERE WAS NEVER A BETTER MOMENT THAN THAT...
I'VE ALWAYS LOVED MANGA.
THERE MUST BE SOMETHING SHUJIN WANTED TO WRITE ABOUT TOO.
AND I KNOW WHAT KIND OF THINGS SHUJIN IS GOOD AT WRITING.
...!
NIZUMA, I'M SORRY, BUT CAN I QUIT AS YOUR ASSISTANT?
HUH?

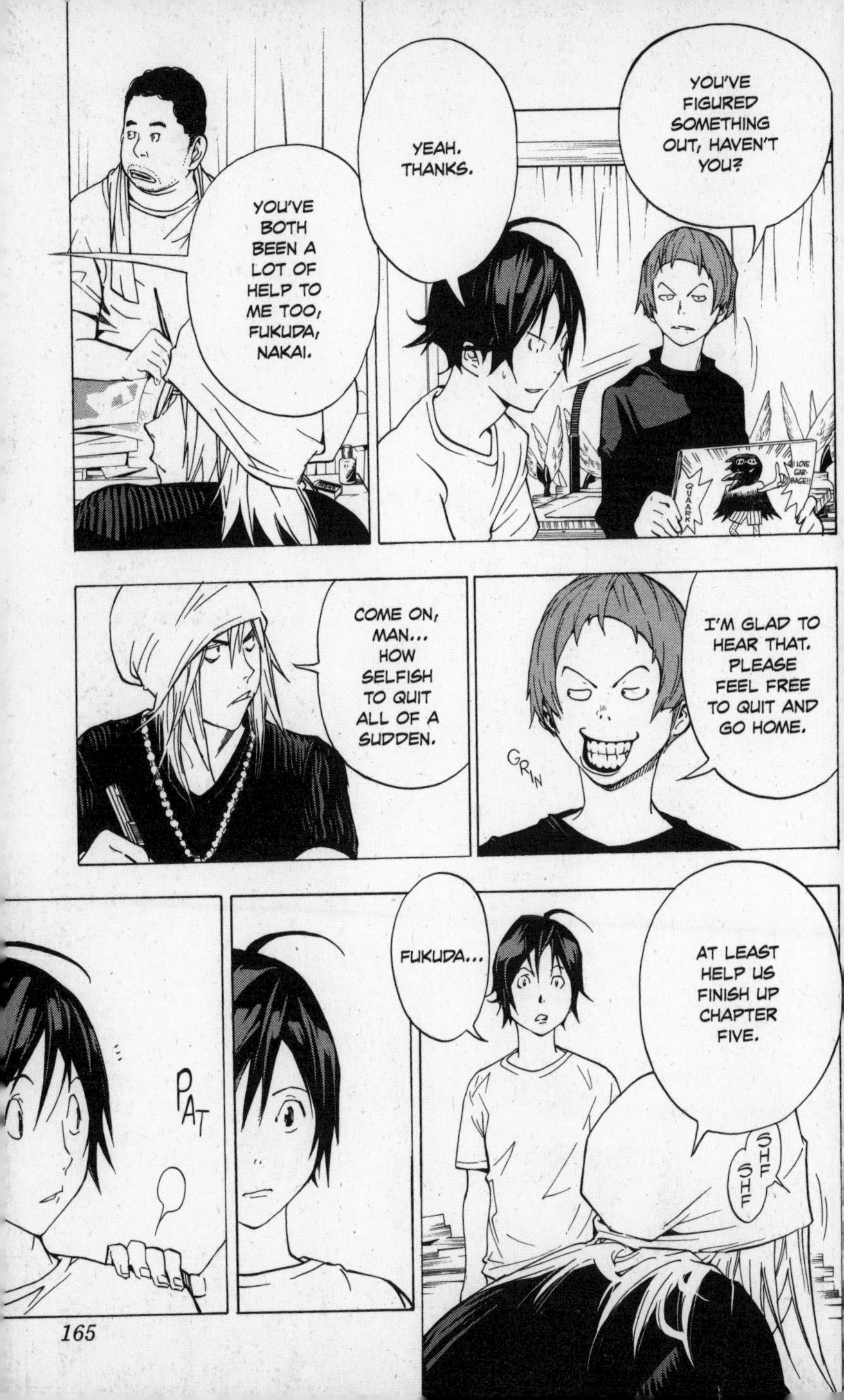
YOU'VE FIGURED SOMETHING OUT, HAVEN'T YOU?
QUAARK
I LOVE GAR-BAGE!!
YEAH. THANKS.
YOU'VE BOTH BEEN A LOT OF HELP TO ME TOO, FUKUDA, NAKAI.
I'M GLAD TO HEAR THAT. PLEASE FEEL FREE TO QUIT AND GO HOME.
GRIN
COME ON, MAN... HOW SELFISH TO QUIT ALL OF A SUDDEN.
AT LEAST HELP US FINISH UP CHAPTER FIVE.
SHF SHF
FUKUDA...
PAT

SHUP

TH-THANK YOU VERY MUCH.

HMPH. I FEEL SORRY FOR YOU, SO I'LL WORK HERE UNTIL I GET MY OWN SERIES.

YOU CAN QUIT WHENEVER YOU WANT TO TOO, FUKUDA.

DON'T WORRY. I CAN SUPPORT NIZUMA SENSEI ON MY OWN. LEAVE THE REST TO ME.

WHAT A MANGA ARTIST ULTIMATELY NEEDS IS THE GUTS AND STAMINA TO KEEP ON DRAWING. ALL THE MANGA ARTISTS WHO I'VE WORKED FOR SAID THAT, AND I'M NEVER GOING TO GIVE UP.

BUT I'M GOING TO GET MY OWN SERIES TOO. I'M NOT GOING TO END AS A MERE ASSISTANT, I PROMISE YOU THAT.

OKAY, LET'S GET THIS OVER WITH.

YES!

AND YOU TOO, FUKUDA,

TISS

I WANT TO BE IN *JUMP* WITH YOU, MR. NAKAI.

YEAH! GOOD LUCK. I'LL GET MY OWN SERIES TOO SOMEDAY.

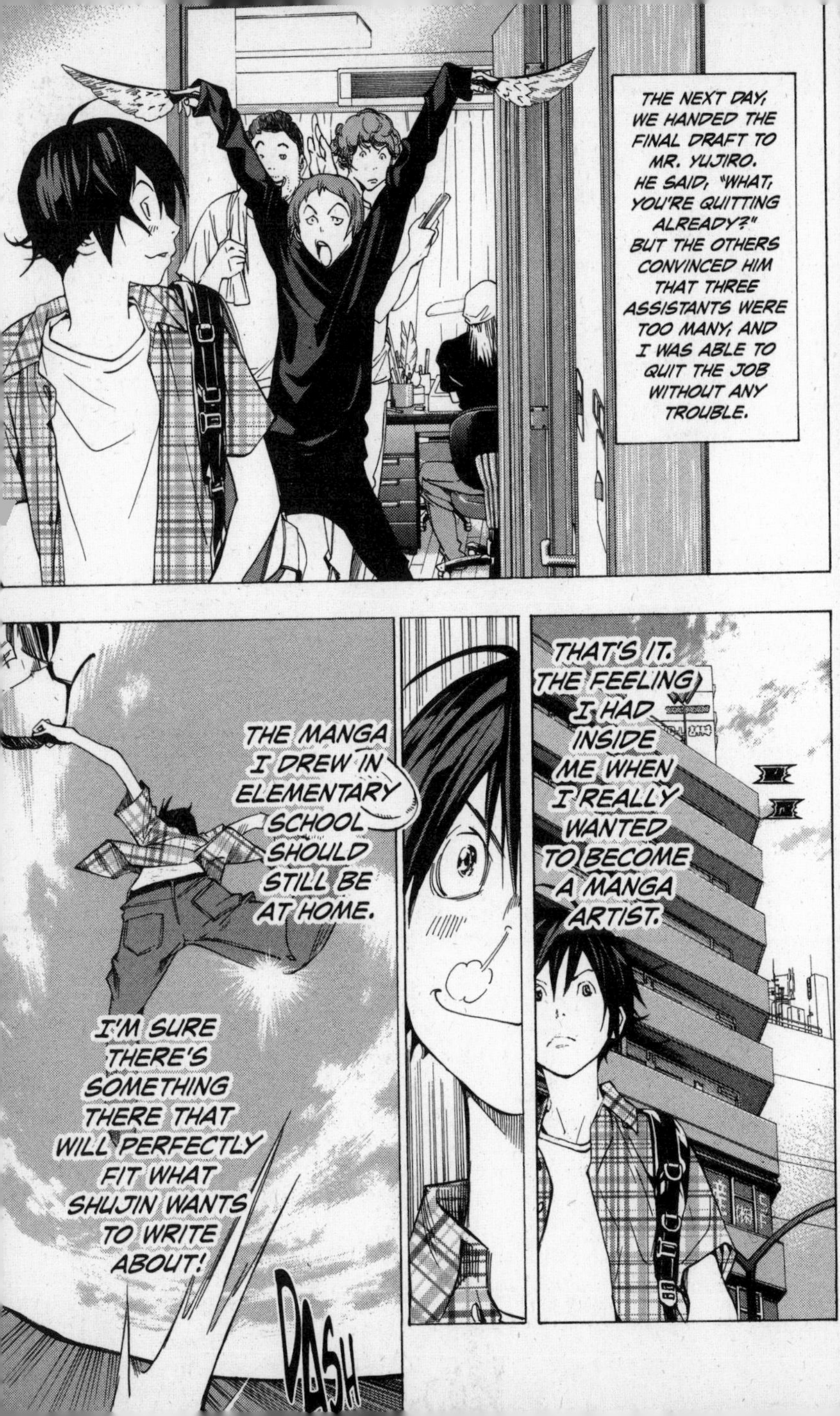
THE NEXT DAY, WE HANDED THE FINAL DRAFT TO MR. YUJIRO. HE SAID, "WHAT, YOU'RE QUITTING ALREADY?" BUT THE OTHERS CONVINCED HIM THAT THREE ASSISTANTS WERE TOO MANY, AND I WAS ABLE TO QUIT THE JOB WITHOUT ANY TROUBLE.
THAT'S IT. THE FEELING I HAD INSIDE ME WHEN I REALLY WANTED TO BECOME A MANGA ARTIST.
THE MANGA I DREW IN ELEMENTARY SCHOOL SHOULD STILL BE AT HOME.
I'M SURE THERE'S SOMETHING THERE THAT WILL PERFECTLY FIT WHAT SHUJIN WANTS TO WRITE ABOUT!
DASH

OHBA'S STORYBOARD

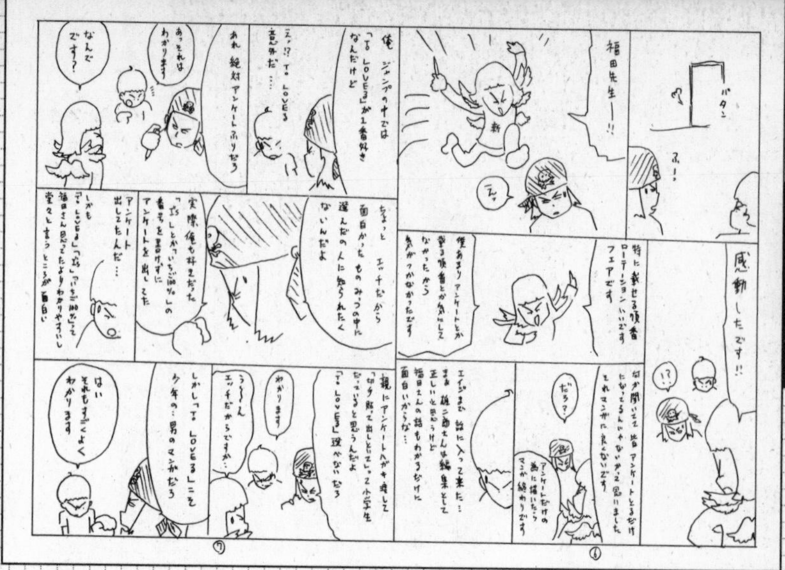
バタン
ふ!
福田先生ー!!
え…
感動したです!!
特に載せる順番ローテーションいいです フェアです
僕あまりアンケートとか載る順番とか気にしてなかったから気がつかなかったです
なぜ聞いて皆アンケートとるだけになってるんじゃないかと思いました それマンガに良くないです
!?
だろ?
アンケートだけの為に描いたらマンガが終わりです
エイジまで話に入って来た… まあ雄二郎さんは編集として正しいと思うけど 福田さんの話もわかるなあ 面白いからな…
⑥
俺 ジャンプの中では「To LOVEる」が1番好きなんだけど
えっ!? To LOVEる 意外だ…
あれ 絶対アンケートふりだろ
あっそれはわかります
なんでです?
ちょっとエッチなから面白かったものみっつの中に選んだの人に知られたくないんだよ
実際俺も好きだった「ToLOVEる」とか「いちご100%」の番号を書けずにアンケートを出してた
アンケート出してたんだ…
しかも「To LOVEる」「To」「いちご100%」って福田さん思ってたよりわかりやすいし堂々と言うところが面白い
親にアンケートハガキ渡して「切手貼って出しといて」って小学生だっていると思うんだよ「To LOVEる」選べないだろ
わかります
う〜ん エッチだからですか…
しかし「To LOVEる」こそ少年の…男のマンガだろ
はい それもすごくよくわかります
⑦

OBATA'S STORYBOARD

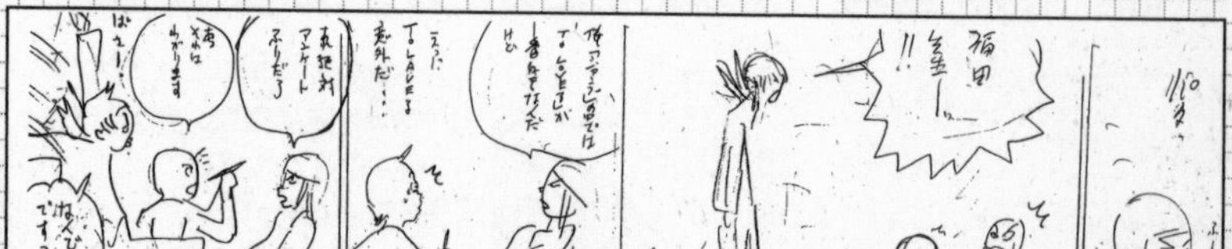
福田先生ー!!
感動したです!!
ぶわっ

COMPLETE!

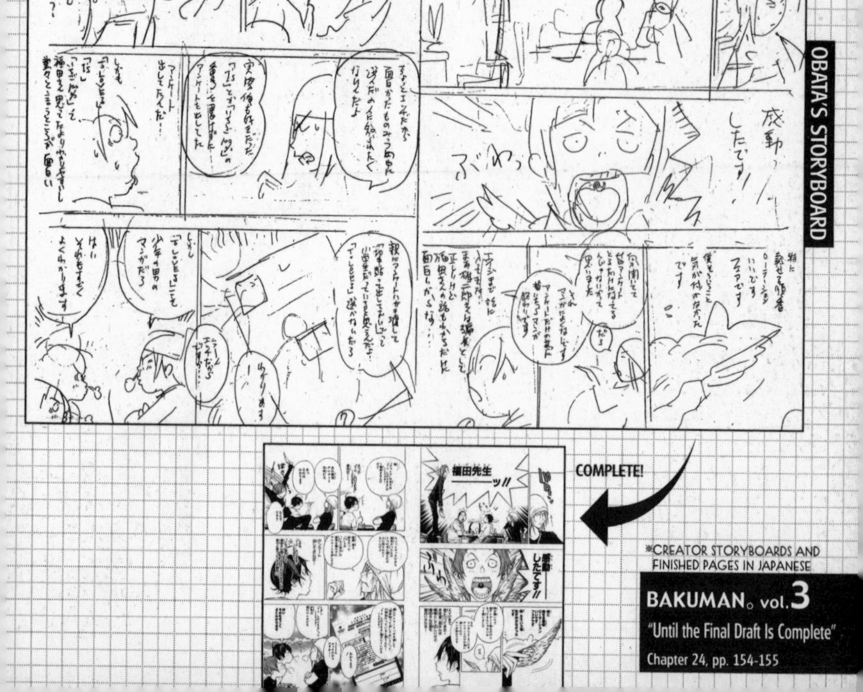
福田先生ーッ!!
感動したです!!

※CREATOR STORYBOARDS AND FINISHED PAGES IN JAPANESE

BAKUMAN。vol.3

"Until the Final Draft Is Complete"

Chapter 24, pp. 154-155

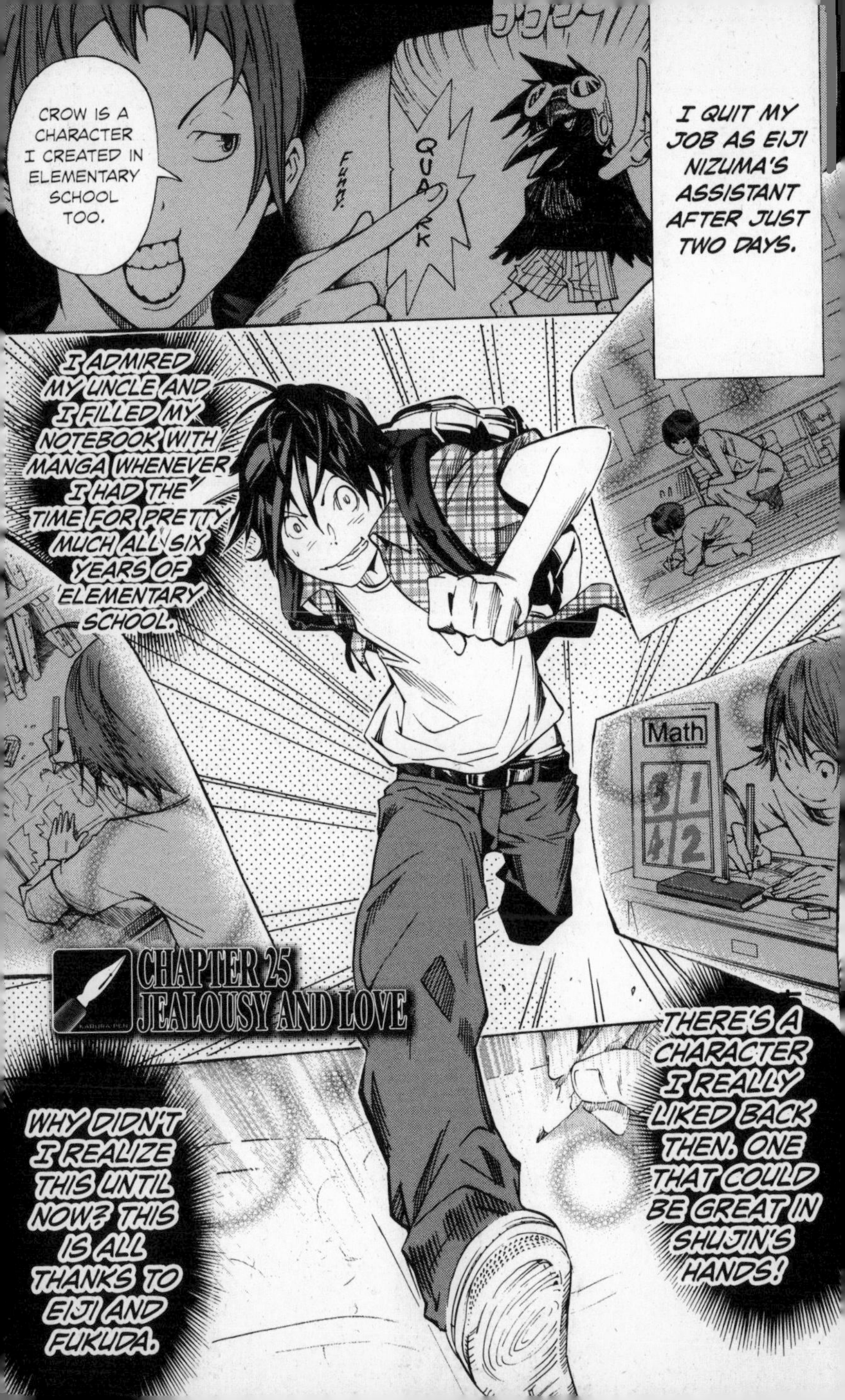
I QUIT MY JOB AS EIJI NIZUMA'S ASSISTANT AFTER JUST TWO DAYS.
QUARK
FUNNY
CROW IS A CHARACTER I CREATED IN ELEMENTARY SCHOOL TOO.
Math
I ADMIRED MY UNCLE AND I FILLED MY NOTEBOOK WITH MANGA WHENEVER I HAD THE TIME FOR PRETTY MUCH ALL SIX YEARS OF ELEMENTARY SCHOOL.
CHAPTER 25
JEALOUSY AND LOVE
THERE'S A CHARACTER I REALLY LIKED BACK THEN. ONE THAT COULD BE GREAT IN SHUJIN'S HANDS!
WHY DIDN'T I REALIZE THIS UNTIL NOW? THIS IS ALL THANKS TO EIJI AND FUKUDA.

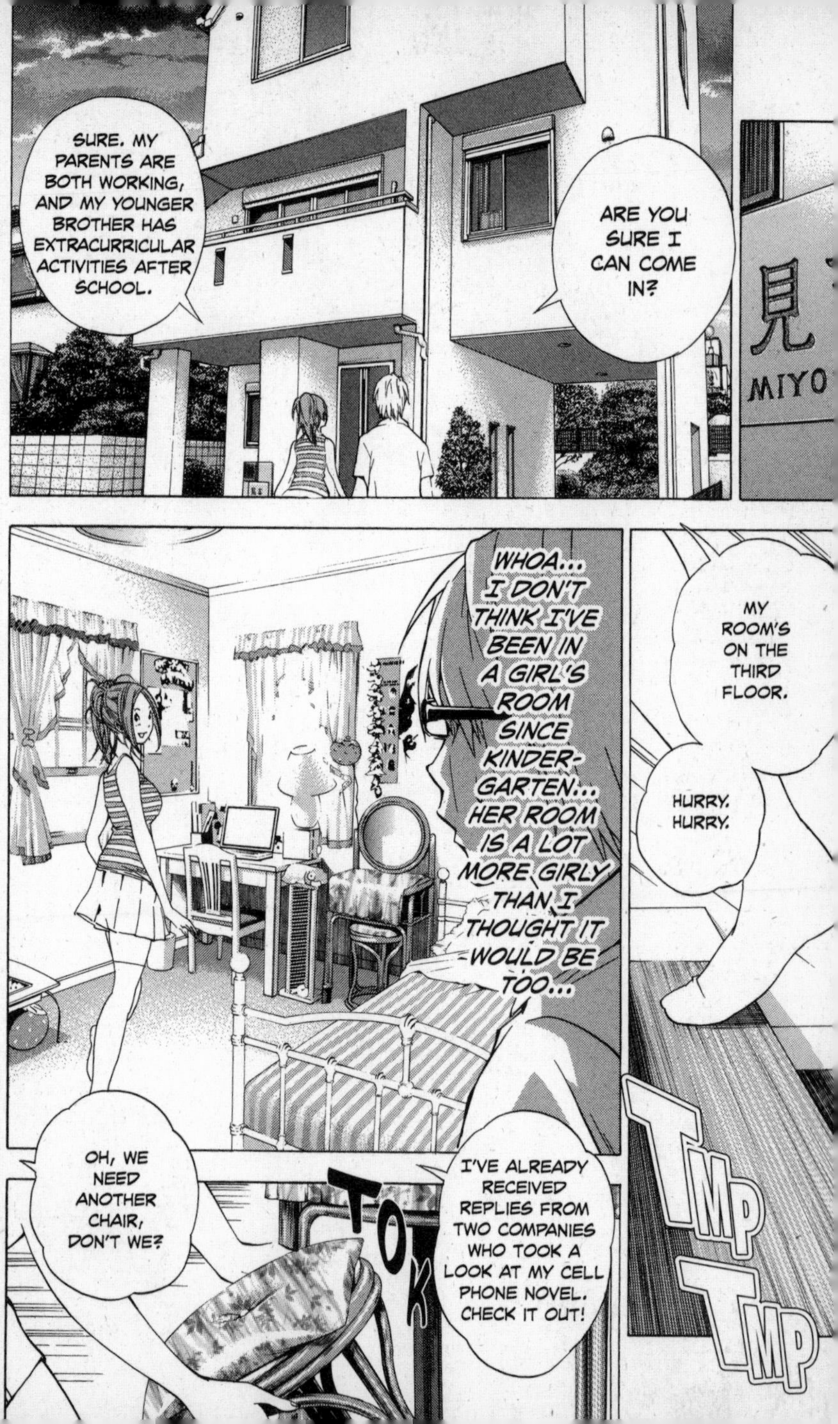
ARE YOU SURE I CAN COME IN?
SURE. MY PARENTS ARE BOTH WORKING, AND MY YOUNGER BROTHER HAS EXTRACURRICULAR ACTIVITIES AFTER SCHOOL.
見
MIYO
MY ROOM'S ON THE THIRD FLOOR.
HURRY. HURRY.
TMP TMP
WHOA... I DON'T THINK I'VE BEEN IN A GIRL'S ROOM SINCE KINDER-GARTEN... HER ROOM IS A LOT MORE GIRLY THAN I THOUGHT IT WOULD BE TOO...
OH, WE NEED ANOTHER CHAIR, DON'T WE?
TOK
I'VE ALREADY RECEIVED REPLIES FROM TWO COMPANIES WHO TOOK A LOOK AT MY CELL PHONE NOVEL. CHECK IT OUT!

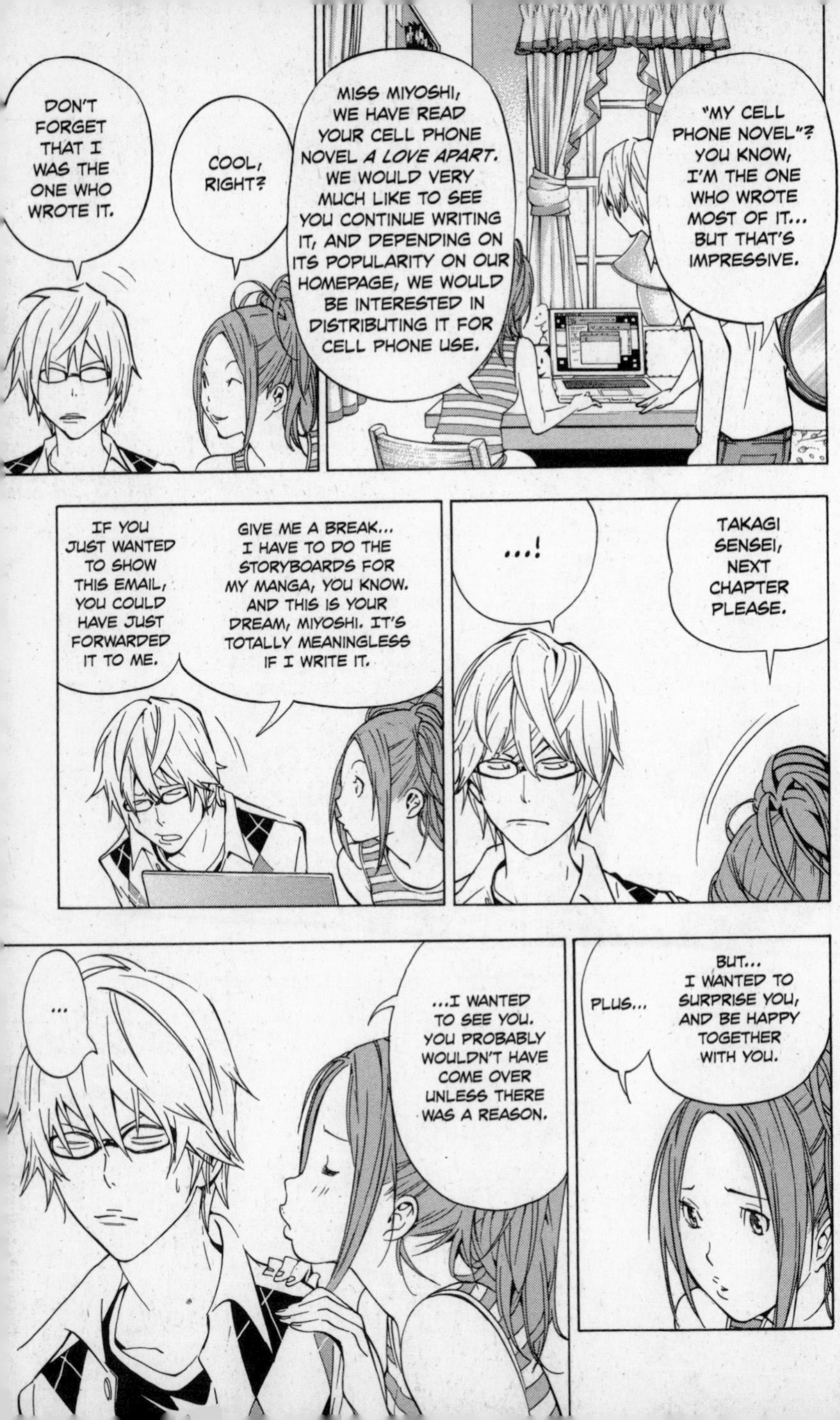
"MY CELL PHONE NOVEL"? YOU KNOW, I'M THE ONE WHO WROTE MOST OF IT... BUT THAT'S IMPRESSIVE.
MISS MIYOSHI, WE HAVE READ YOUR CELL PHONE NOVEL *A LOVE APART*. WE WOULD VERY MUCH LIKE TO SEE YOU CONTINUE WRITING IT, AND DEPENDING ON ITS POPULARITY ON OUR HOMEPAGE, WE WOULD BE INTERESTED IN DISTRIBUTING IT FOR CELL PHONE USE.
COOL, RIGHT?
DON'T FORGET THAT I WAS THE ONE WHO WROTE IT.
TAKAGI SENSEI, NEXT CHAPTER PLEASE.
...!
GIVE ME A BREAK... I HAVE TO DO THE STORYBOARDS FOR MY MANGA, YOU KNOW. AND THIS IS YOUR DREAM, MIYOSHI. IT'S TOTALLY MEANINGLESS IF I WRITE IT.
IF YOU JUST WANTED TO SHOW THIS EMAIL, YOU COULD HAVE JUST FORWARDED IT TO ME.
BUT... I WANTED TO SURPRISE YOU, AND BE HAPPY TOGETHER WITH YOU.
PLUS...
...I WANTED TO SEE YOU. YOU PROBABLY WOULDN'T HAVE COME OVER UNLESS THERE WAS A REASON.
...

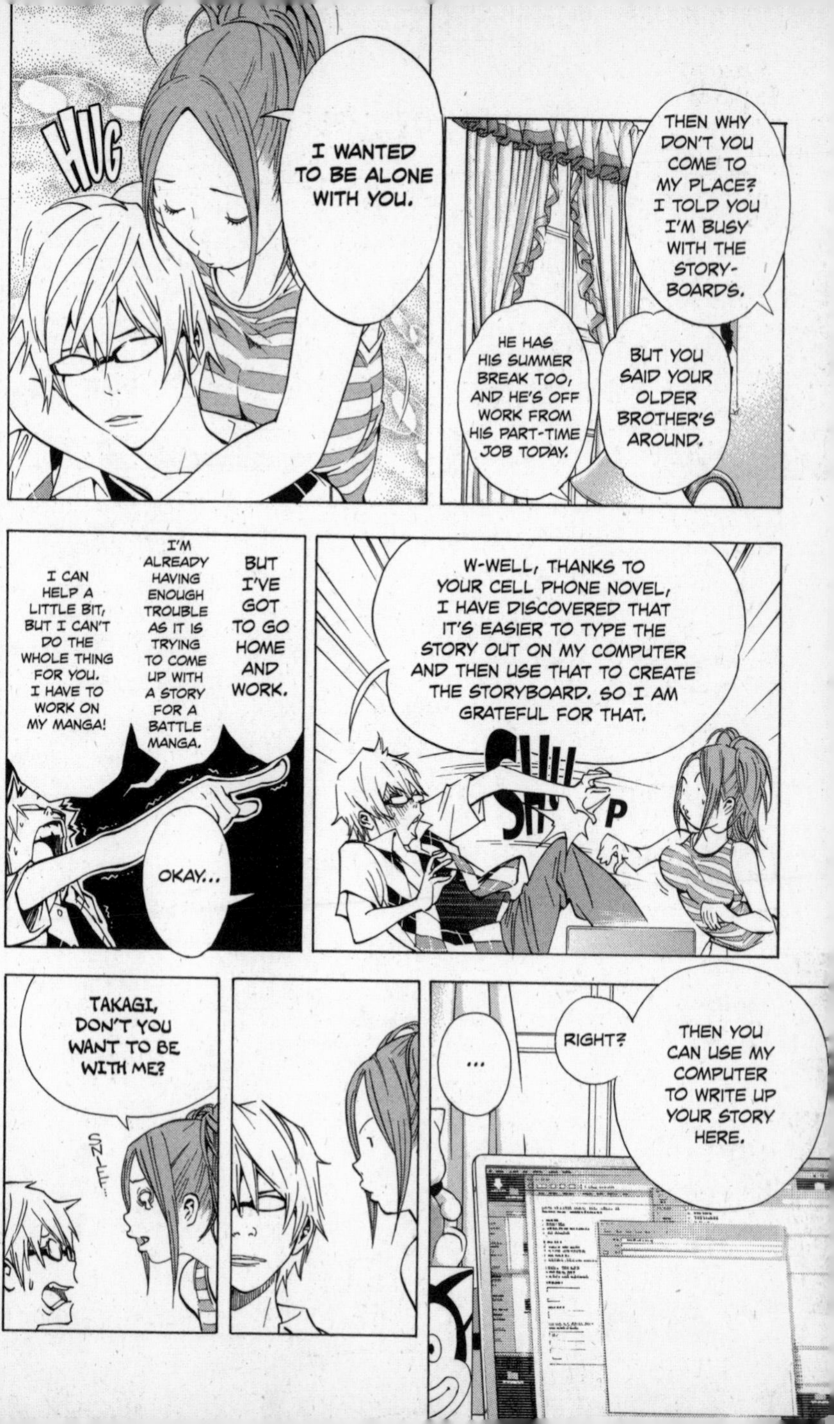
THEN WHY DON'T YOU COME TO MY PLACE? I TOLD YOU I'M BUSY WITH THE STORY-BOARDS.
BUT YOU SAID YOUR OLDER BROTHER'S AROUND.
HE HAS HIS SUMMER BREAK TOO, AND HE'S OFF WORK FROM HIS PART-TIME JOB TODAY.
HUG
I WANTED TO BE ALONE WITH YOU.
W-WELL, THANKS TO YOUR CELL PHONE NOVEL, I HAVE DISCOVERED THAT IT'S EASIER TO TYPE THE STORY OUT ON MY COMPUTER AND THEN USE THAT TO CREATE THE STORYBOARD. SO I AM GRATEFUL FOR THAT.
SHUP
BUT I'VE GOT TO GO HOME AND WORK.
I'M ALREADY HAVING ENOUGH TROUBLE AS IT IS TRYING TO COME UP WITH A STORY FOR A BATTLE MANGA.
I CAN HELP A LITTLE BIT, BUT I CAN'T DO THE WHOLE THING FOR YOU. I HAVE TO WORK ON MY MANGA!
OKAY...
THEN YOU CAN USE MY COMPUTER TO WRITE UP YOUR STORY HERE.
RIGHT?
...
TAKAGI, DON'T YOU WANT TO BE WITH ME?
SNIFF...

READ THIS WAY

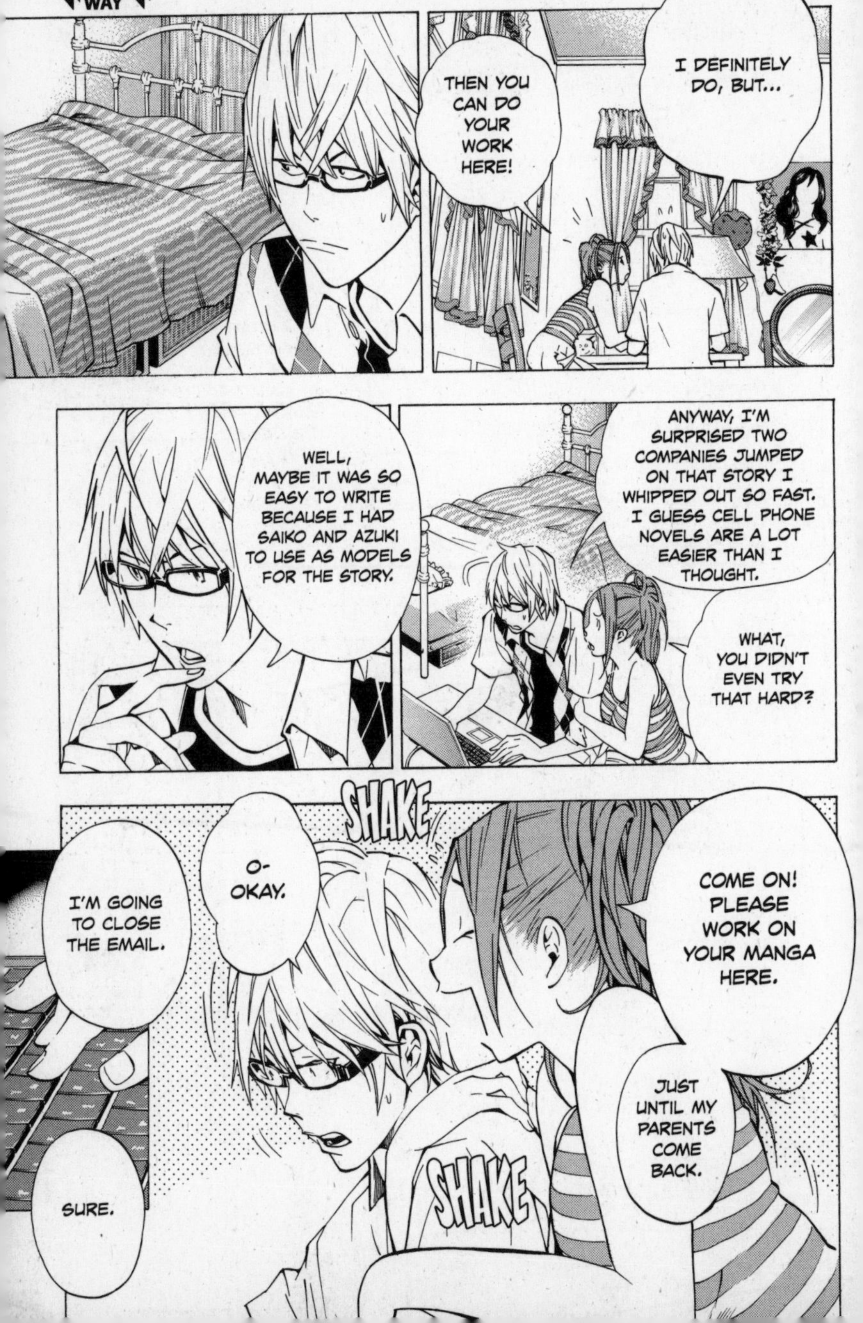
I DEFINITELY DO, BUT...
THEN YOU CAN DO YOUR WORK HERE!
ANYWAY, I'M SURPRISED TWO COMPANIES JUMPED ON THAT STORY I WHIPPED OUT SO FAST. I GUESS CELL PHONE NOVELS ARE A LOT EASIER THAN I THOUGHT.
WHAT, YOU DIDN'T EVEN TRY THAT HARD?
WELL, MAYBE IT WAS SO EASY TO WRITE BECAUSE I HAD SAIKO AND AZUKI TO USE AS MODELS FOR THE STORY.
COME ON! PLEASE WORK ON YOUR MANGA HERE.
JUST UNTIL MY PARENTS COME BACK.
SHAKE
SHAKE
O-OKAY.
I'M GOING TO CLOSE THE EMAIL.
SURE.

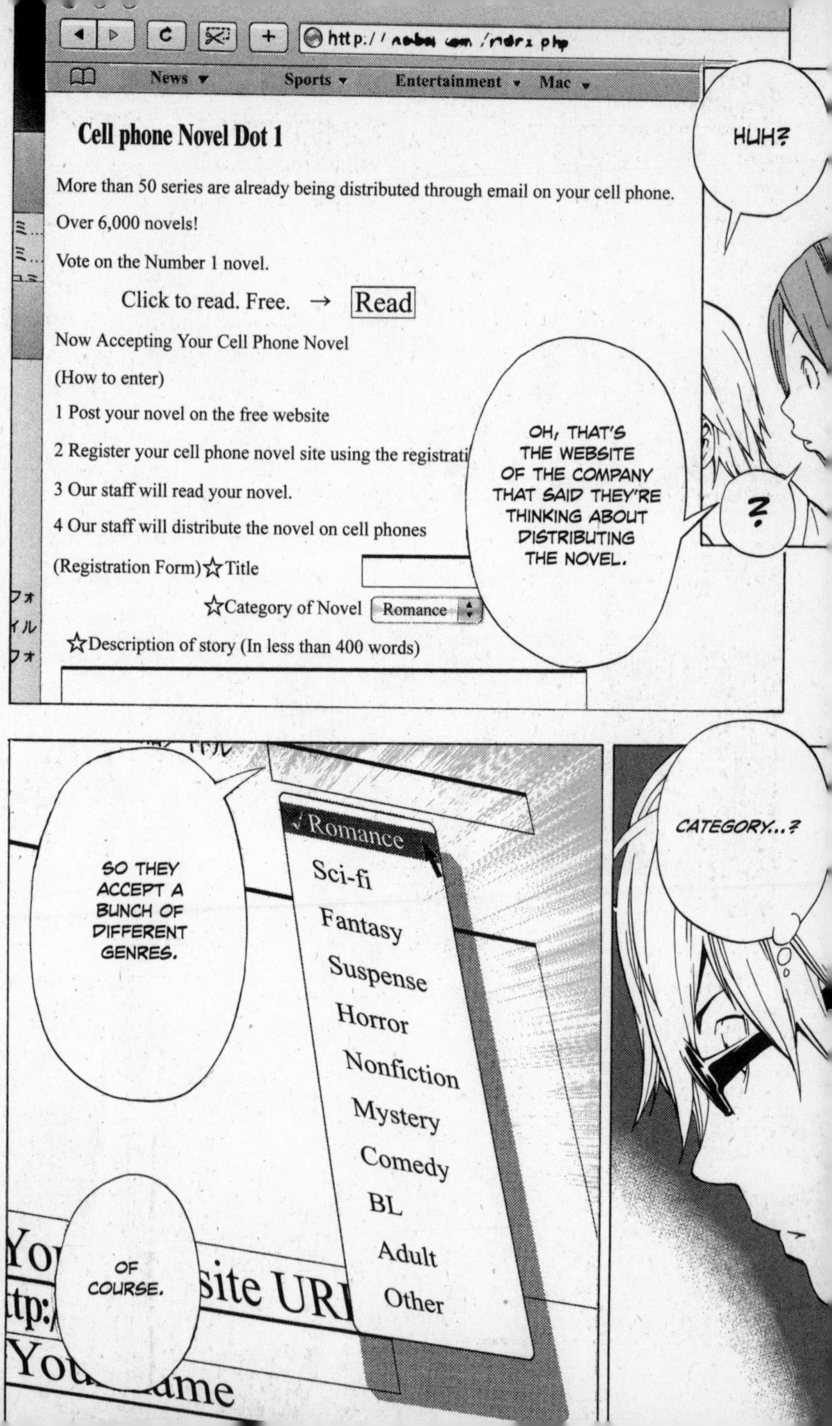
HUH?
News
Sports
Entertainment
Mac
Cell phone Novel Dot 1
More than 50 series are already being distributed through email on your cell phone.
Over 6,000 novels!
Vote on the Number 1 novel.
Click to read. Free. → Read
Now Accepting Your Cell Phone Novel
(How to enter)
1 Post your novel on the free website
2 Register your cell phone novel site using the registrati
3 Our staff will read your novel.
4 Our staff will distribute the novel on cell phones
(Registration Form)☆Title
☆Category of Novel Romance
☆Description of story (In less than 400 words)
OH, THAT'S THE WEBSITE OF THE COMPANY THAT SAID THEY'RE THINKING ABOUT DISTRIBUTING THE NOVEL.
?
CATEGORY...?
√Romance
Sci-fi
Fantasy
Suspense
Horror
Nonfiction
Mystery
Comedy
BL
Adult
Other
SO THEY ACCEPT A BUNCH OF DIFFERENT GENRES.
OF COURSE.

READ THIS WAY

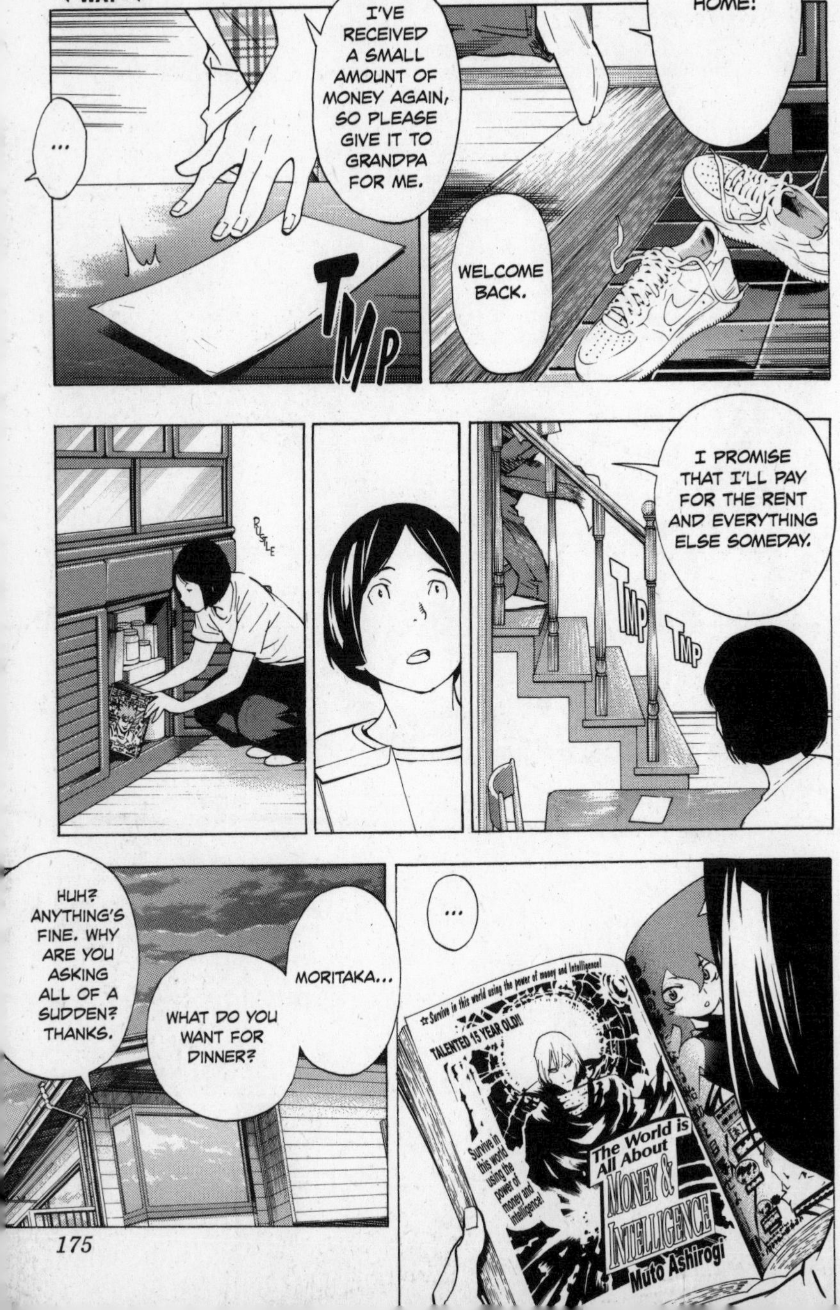
I'M HOME!
WELCOME BACK.
I'VE RECEIVED A SMALL AMOUNT OF MONEY AGAIN, SO PLEASE GIVE IT TO GRANDPA FOR ME.
TMP
...
I PROMISE THAT I'LL PAY FOR THE RENT AND EVERYTHING ELSE SOMEDAY.
TMP
TMP
RUSTLE
...
Survive in this world using the power of money and Intelligence!
☆ Survive in this world using the power of money and Intelligence!
TALENTED 15 YEAR OLD!!
Survive in this world using the power of money and intelligence!
The World is All About
MONEY &
INTELLIGENCE
Muto Ashirogi
MORITAKA...
WHAT DO YOU WANT FOR DINNER?
HUH? ANYTHING'S FINE. WHY ARE YOU ASKING ALL OF A SUDDEN? THANKS.

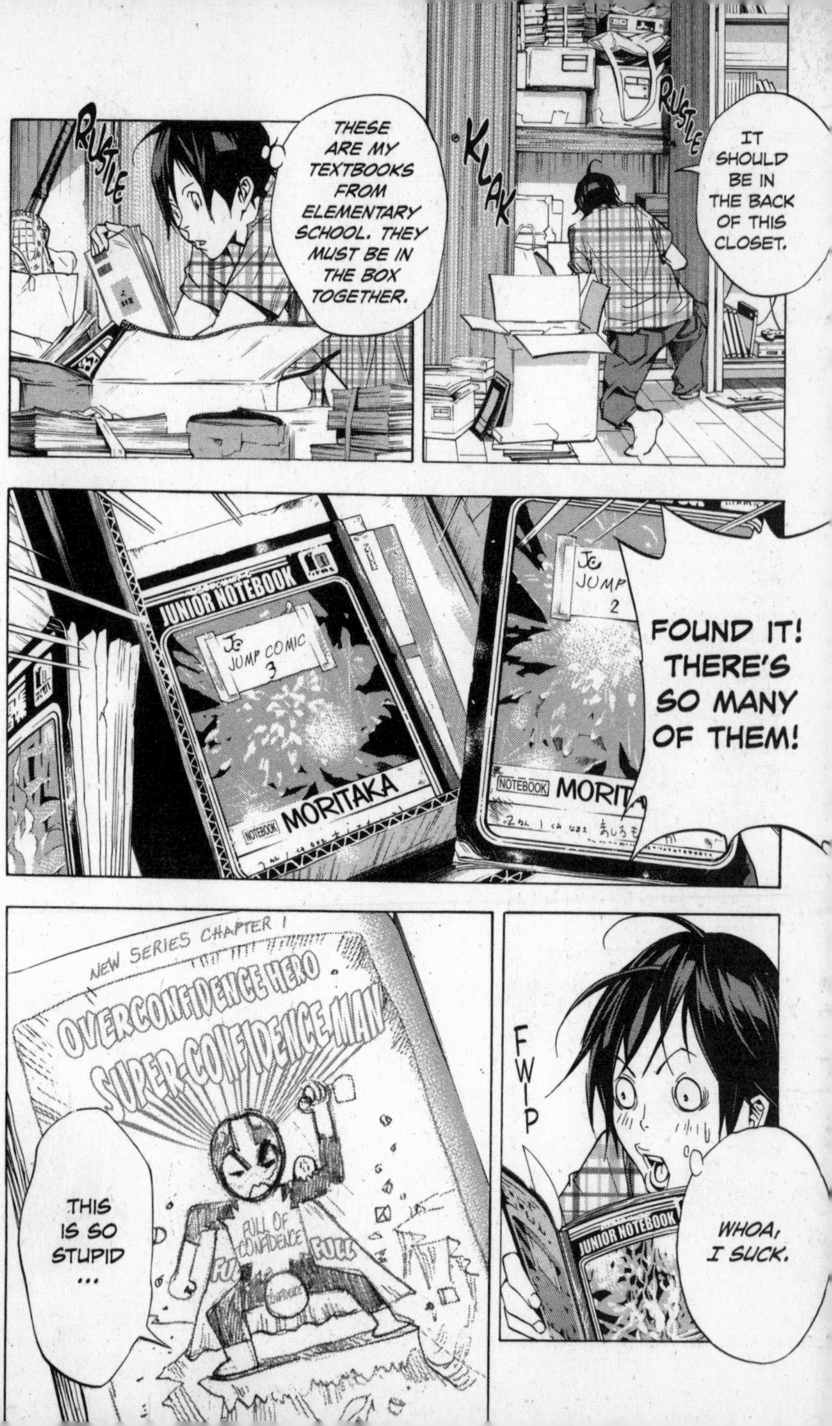
RUSTLE
IT SHOULD BE IN THE BACK OF THIS CLOSET.
KLAK
RUSTLE
THESE ARE MY TEXTBOOKS FROM ELEMENTARY SCHOOL. THEY MUST BE IN THE BOX TOGETHER.
FOUND IT! THERE'S SO MANY OF THEM!
JUMP 2
NOTEBOOK MORITA
JUNIOR NOTEBOOK
JUMP COMIC 3
NOTEBOOK MORITAKA
FWIP
WHOA, I SUCK.
JUNIOR NOTEBOOK
NEW SERIES CHAPTER 1
OVERCONFIDENCE HERO
SUPER-CONFIDENCE MAN
FULL OF CONFIDENCE
THIS IS SO STUPID ...

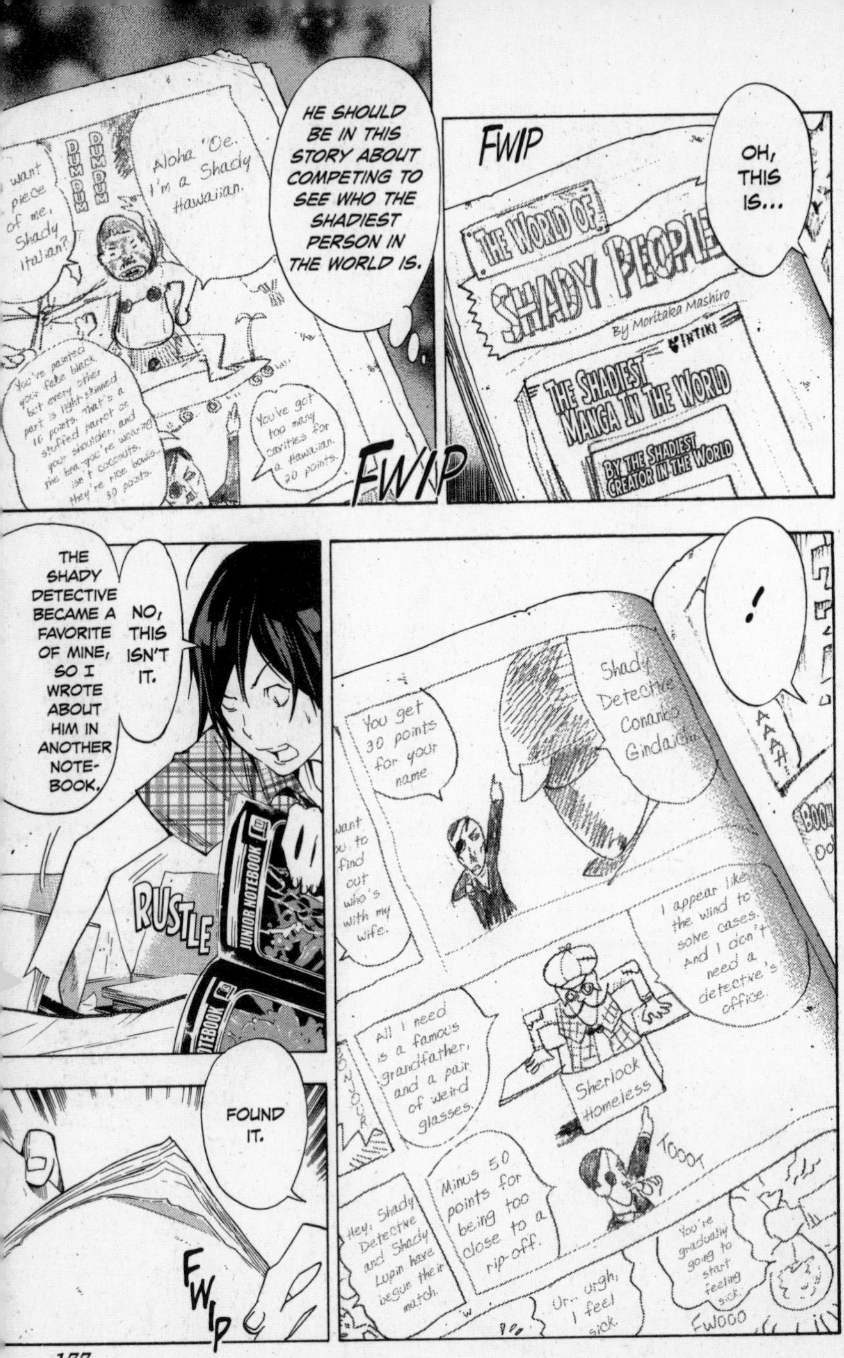
OH, THIS IS...
FWIP
THE WORLD OF SHADY PEOPLE
By Moritaka Mashiro
THE SHADIEST MANGA IN THE WORLD
BY THE SHADIEST CREATOR IN THE WORLD
HE SHOULD BE IN THIS STORY ABOUT COMPETING TO SEE WHO THE SHADIEST PERSON IN THE WORLD IS.
Aloha 'Oe. I'm a Shady Hawaiian.
DUM DUM DUM
DUM DUM DUM
want piece of me, Shady Italian?
You've got too many cavities for a Hawaiian. 20 points.
You've painted your face black, but every other part is light-skinned. 10 points. That's a stuffed parrot on your shoulder, and the bra you're wearing isn't coconuts, they're rice bowls. 30 points.
FWIP
!
Shady Detective Conanko Gind
AAAH
You get 30 points for your name.
want ...u to find out who's with my wife.
I appear like the wind to solve cases. And I don't need a detective's office.
All I need is a famous grandfather, and a pair of weird glasses.
Sherlock Homeless
BONJOUR
TOOOT
Minus 50 points for being too close to a rip-off.
Hey, Shady Detective and Shady Lupin have begun their match.
You're gradually going to start feeling sick.
Ur... urgh, I feel sick.
FWOOO
NO, THIS ISN'T IT.
THE SHADY DETECTIVE BECAME A FAVORITE OF MINE, SO I WROTE ABOUT HIM IN ANOTHER NOTEBOOK.
RUSTLE
JUNIOR NOTEBOOK
FOUND IT.
FWIP

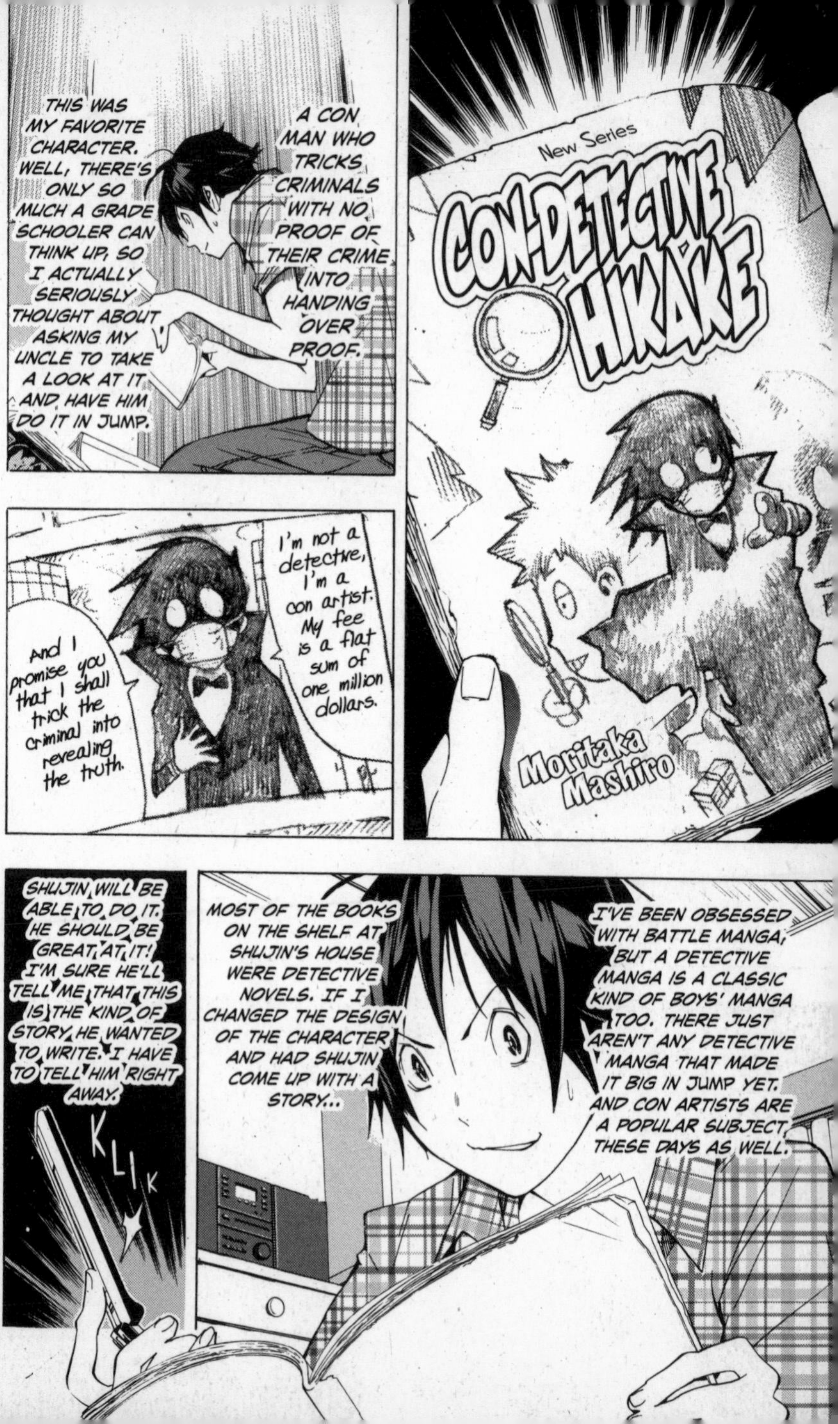
New Series
CON-DETECTIVE HIKAKE
Moritaka Mashiro
A CON MAN WHO TRICKS CRIMINALS WITH NO PROOF OF THEIR CRIME INTO HANDING OVER PROOF.
THIS WAS MY FAVORITE CHARACTER. WELL, THERE'S ONLY SO MUCH A GRADE SCHOOLER CAN THINK UP, SO I ACTUALLY SERIOUSLY THOUGHT ABOUT ASKING MY UNCLE TO TAKE A LOOK AT IT AND HAVE HIM DO IT IN JUMP.
I'm not a detective, I'm a con artist. My fee is a flat sum of one million dollars.
And I promise you that I shall trick the criminal into revealing the truth.
I'VE BEEN OBSESSED WITH BATTLE MANGA, BUT A DETECTIVE MANGA IS A CLASSIC KIND OF BOYS' MANGA TOO. THERE JUST AREN'T ANY DETECTIVE MANGA THAT MADE IT BIG IN JUMP YET. AND CON ARTISTS ARE A POPULAR SUBJECT THESE DAYS AS WELL.
MOST OF THE BOOKS ON THE SHELF AT SHUJIN'S HOUSE WERE DETECTIVE NOVELS. IF I CHANGED THE DESIGN OF THE CHARACTER AND HAD SHUJIN COME UP WITH A STORY...
SHUJIN WILL BE ABLE TO DO IT. HE SHOULD BE GREAT AT IT! I'M SURE HE'LL TELL ME THAT THIS IS THE KIND OF STORY HE WANTED TO WRITE. I HAVE TO TELL HIM RIGHT AWAY.
KLIK

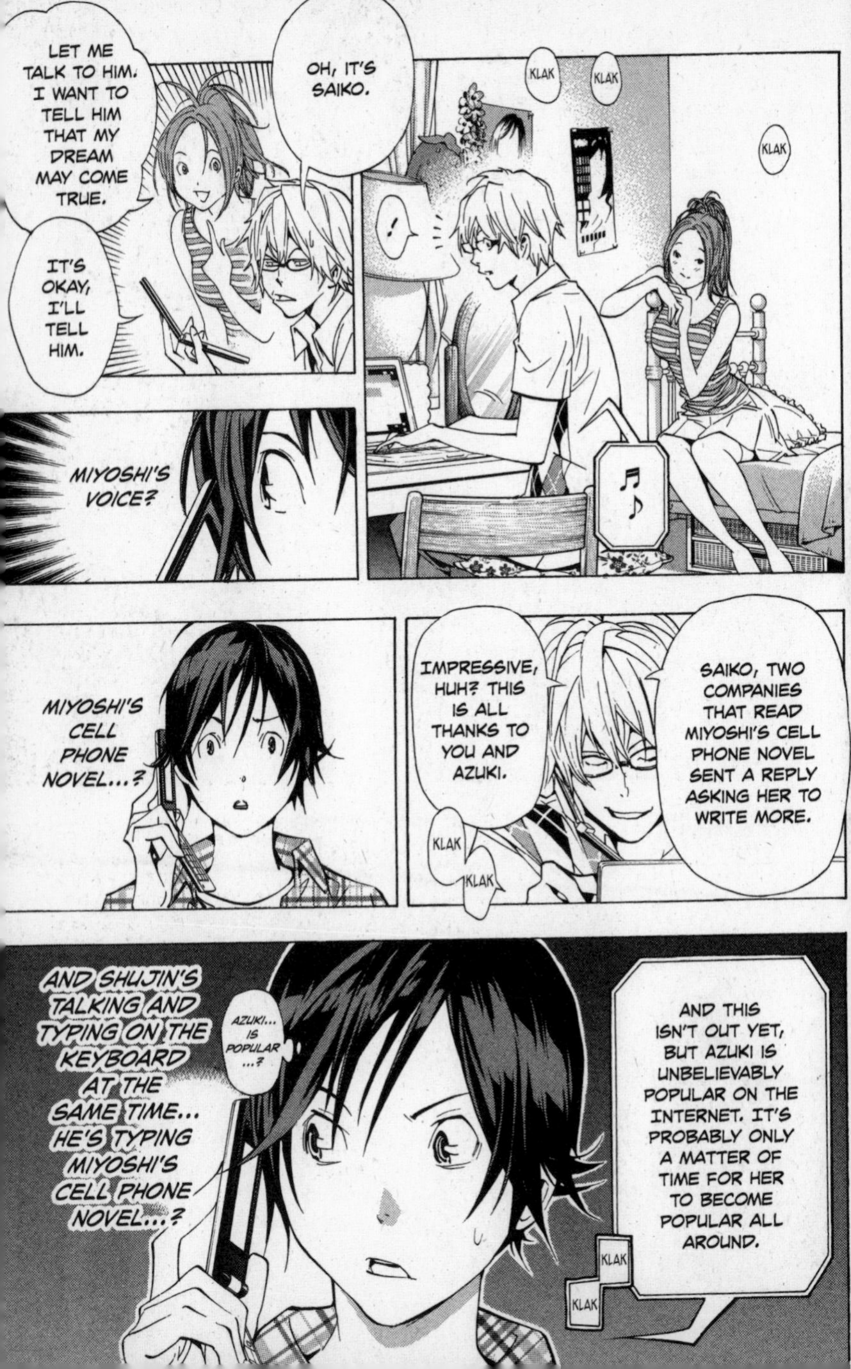
KLAK
KLAK
KLAK
!
♪
OH, IT'S SAIKO.
LET ME TALK TO HIM. I WANT TO TELL HIM THAT MY DREAM MAY COME TRUE.
IT'S OKAY, I'LL TELL HIM.
MIYOSHI'S VOICE?
SAIKO, TWO COMPANIES THAT READ MIYOSHI'S CELL PHONE NOVEL SENT A REPLY ASKING HER TO WRITE MORE.
IMPRESSIVE, HUH? THIS IS ALL THANKS TO YOU AND AZUKI.
KLAK
KLAK
MIYOSHI'S CELL PHONE NOVEL...?
AND THIS ISN'T OUT YET, BUT AZUKI IS UNBELIEVABLY POPULAR ON THE INTERNET. IT'S PROBABLY ONLY A MATTER OF TIME FOR HER TO BECOME POPULAR ALL AROUND.
KLAK
KLAK
AZUKI... IS POPULAR...?
AND SHUJIN'S TALKING AND TYPING ON THE KEYBOARD AT THE SAME TIME... HE'S TYPING MIYOSHI'S CELL PHONE NOVEL...?

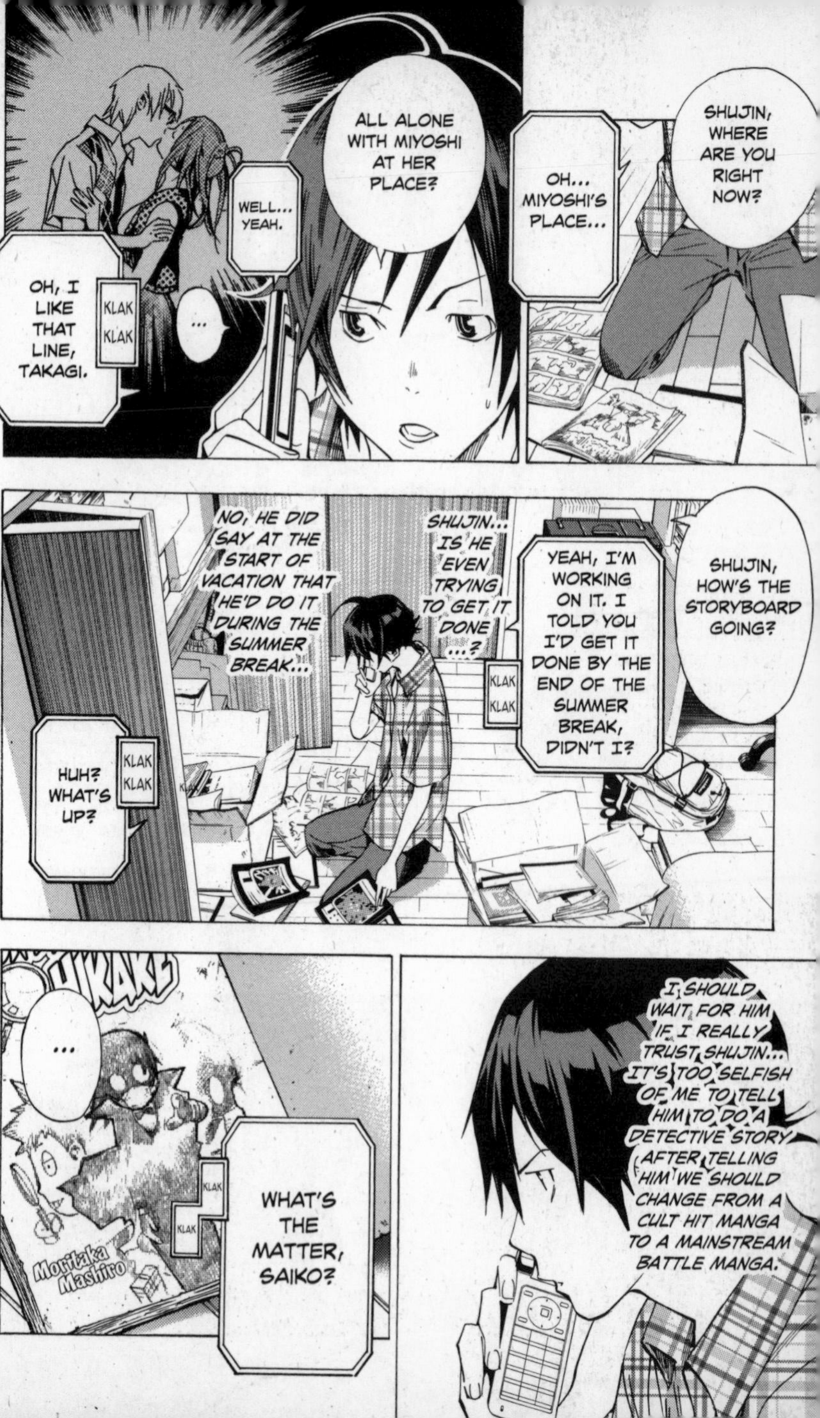
SHUJIN, WHERE ARE YOU RIGHT NOW?
OH... MIYOSHI'S PLACE...
ALL ALONE WITH MIYOSHI AT HER PLACE?
WELL... YEAH.
...
KLAK KLAK
OH, I LIKE THAT LINE, TAKAGI.
SHUJIN, HOW'S THE STORYBOARD GOING?
YEAH, I'M WORKING ON IT. I TOLD YOU I'D GET IT DONE BY THE END OF THE SUMMER BREAK, DIDN'T I?
KLAK KLAK
SHUJIN... IS HE EVEN TRYING TO GET IT DONE...?
NO, HE DID SAY AT THE START OF VACATION THAT HE'D DO IT DURING THE SUMMER BREAK...
KLAK KLAK
HUH? WHAT'S UP?
I SHOULD WAIT FOR HIM IF I REALLY TRUST SHUJIN... IT'S TOO SELFISH OF ME TO TELL HIM TO DO A DETECTIVE STORY AFTER TELLING HIM WE SHOULD CHANGE FROM A CULT HIT MANGA TO A MAINSTREAM BATTLE MANGA.
...
KLAK
KLAK
WHAT'S THE MATTER, SAIKO?
Moritaka Mashiro

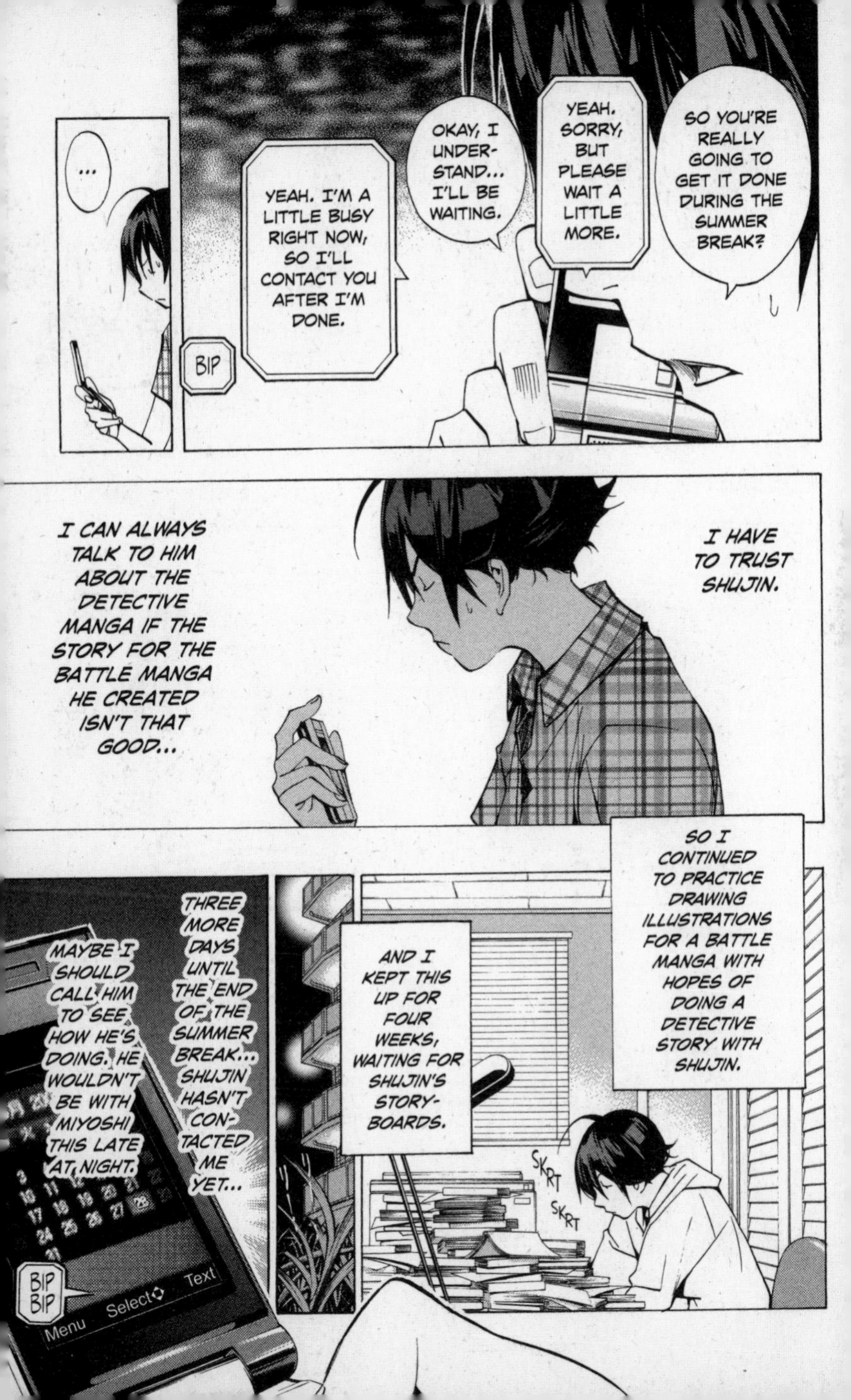
SO YOU'RE REALLY GOING TO GET IT DONE DURING THE SUMMER BREAK?
YEAH. SORRY, BUT PLEASE WAIT A LITTLE MORE.
OKAY, I UNDERSTAND... I'LL BE WAITING.
YEAH. I'M A LITTLE BUSY RIGHT NOW, SO I'LL CONTACT YOU AFTER I'M DONE.
BIP
...
I HAVE TO TRUST SHUJIN.
I CAN ALWAYS TALK TO HIM ABOUT THE DETECTIVE MANGA IF THE STORY FOR THE BATTLE MANGA HE CREATED ISN'T THAT GOOD...
SO I CONTINUED TO PRACTICE DRAWING ILLUSTRATIONS FOR A BATTLE MANGA WITH HOPES OF DOING A DETECTIVE STORY WITH SHUJIN.
AND I KEPT THIS UP FOR FOUR WEEKS, WAITING FOR SHUJIN'S STORYBOARDS.
SKRT
SKRT
THREE MORE DAYS UNTIL THE END OF THE SUMMER BREAK... SHUJIN HASN'T CONTACTED ME YET...
MAYBE I SHOULD CALL HIM TO SEE HOW HE'S DOING. HE WOULDN'T BE WITH MIYOSHI THIS LATE AT NIGHT.
BIP BIP
Text
Select
Menu

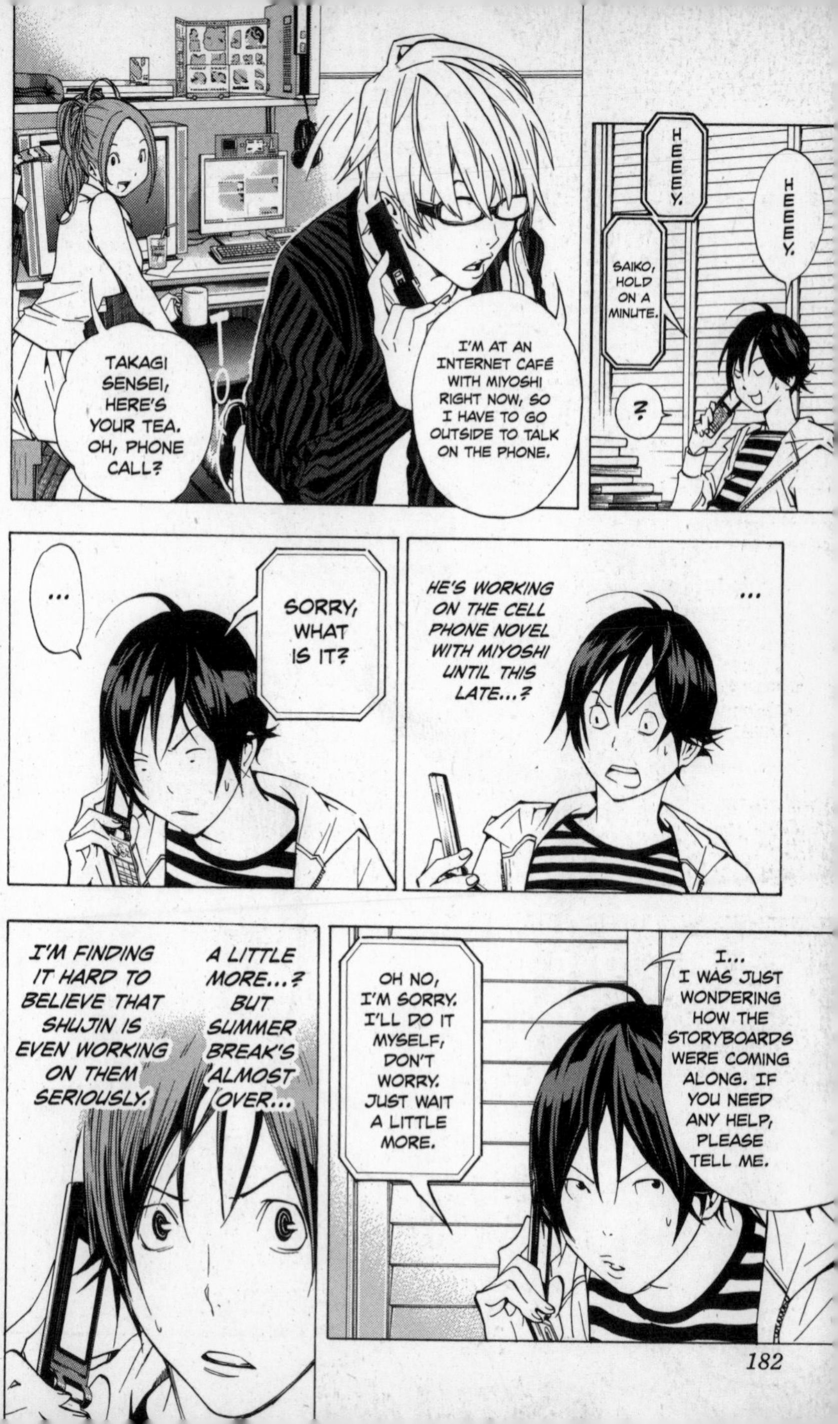
HEEEY.
HEEEY.
SAIKO, HOLD ON A MINUTE.
?
I'M AT AN INTERNET CAFÉ WITH MIYOSHI RIGHT NOW, SO I HAVE TO GO OUTSIDE TO TALK ON THE PHONE.
TAKAGI SENSEI, HERE'S YOUR TEA. OH, PHONE CALL?
...
HE'S WORKING ON THE CELL PHONE NOVEL WITH MIYOSHI UNTIL THIS LATE...?
SORRY, WHAT IS IT?
...
I... I WAS JUST WONDERING HOW THE STORYBOARDS WERE COMING ALONG. IF YOU NEED ANY HELP, PLEASE TELL ME.
OH NO, I'M SORRY. I'LL DO IT MYSELF, DON'T WORRY. JUST WAIT A LITTLE MORE.
A LITTLE MORE...? BUT SUMMER BREAK'S ALMOST OVER...
I'M FINDING IT HARD TO BELIEVE THAT SHUJIN IS EVEN WORKING ON THEM SERIOUSLY.

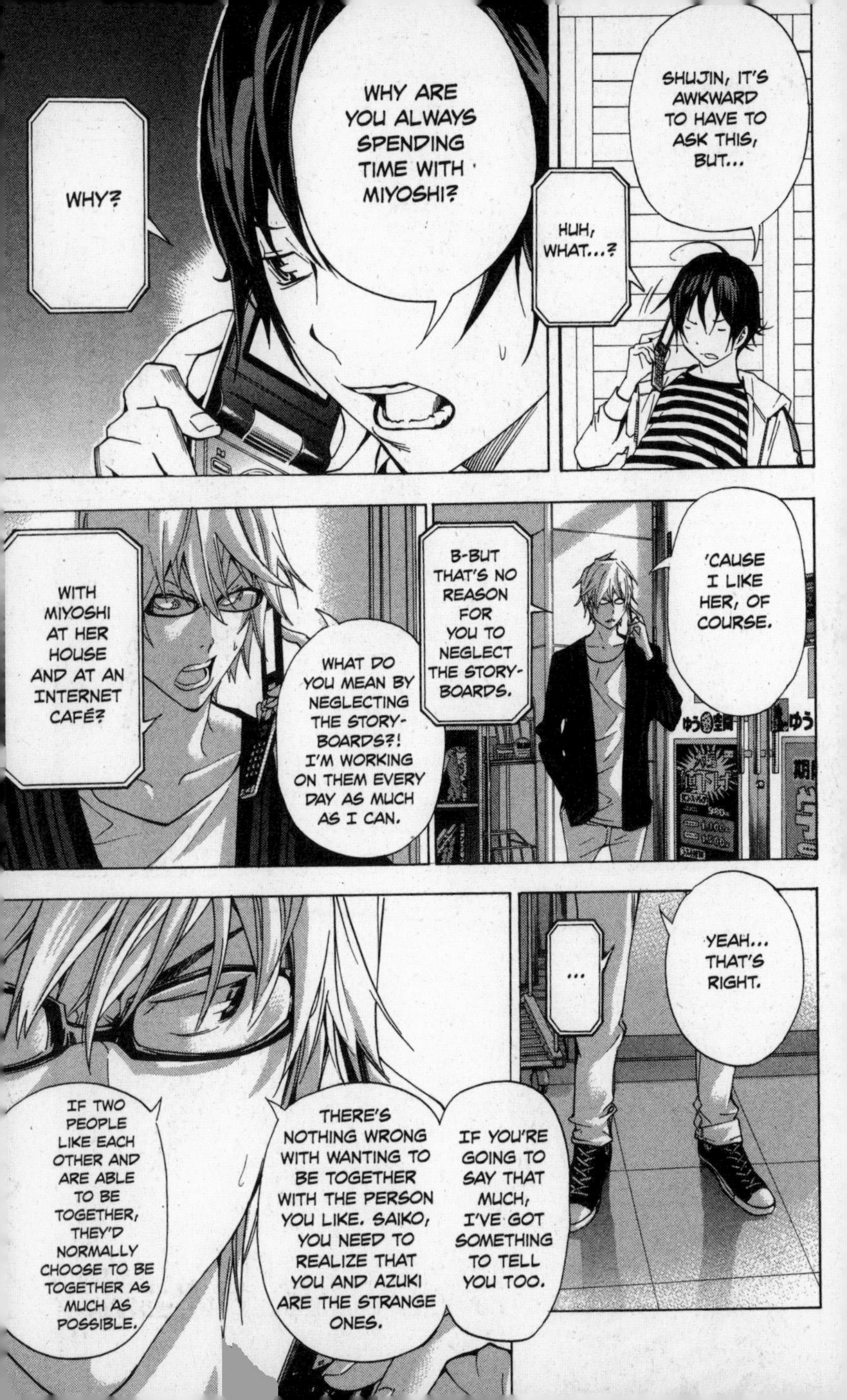
SHUJIN, IT'S AWKWARD TO HAVE TO ASK THIS, BUT...
HUH, WHAT...?
WHY ARE YOU ALWAYS SPENDING TIME WITH MIYOSHI?
WHY?
'CAUSE I LIKE HER, OF COURSE.
B-BUT THAT'S NO REASON FOR YOU TO NEGLECT THE STORY-BOARDS.
WHAT DO YOU MEAN BY NEGLECTING THE STORY-BOARDS?! I'M WORKING ON THEM EVERY DAY AS MUCH AS I CAN.
WITH MIYOSHI AT HER HOUSE AND AT AN INTERNET CAFÉ?
YEAH... THAT'S RIGHT.
...
IF YOU'RE GOING TO SAY THAT MUCH, I'VE GOT SOMETHING TO TELL YOU TOO.
THERE'S NOTHING WRONG WITH WANTING TO BE TOGETHER WITH THE PERSON YOU LIKE. SAIKO, YOU NEED TO REALIZE THAT YOU AND AZUKI ARE THE STRANGE ONES.
IF TWO PEOPLE LIKE EACH OTHER AND ARE ABLE TO BE TOGETHER, THEY'D NORMALLY CHOOSE TO BE TOGETHER AS MUCH AS POSSIBLE.

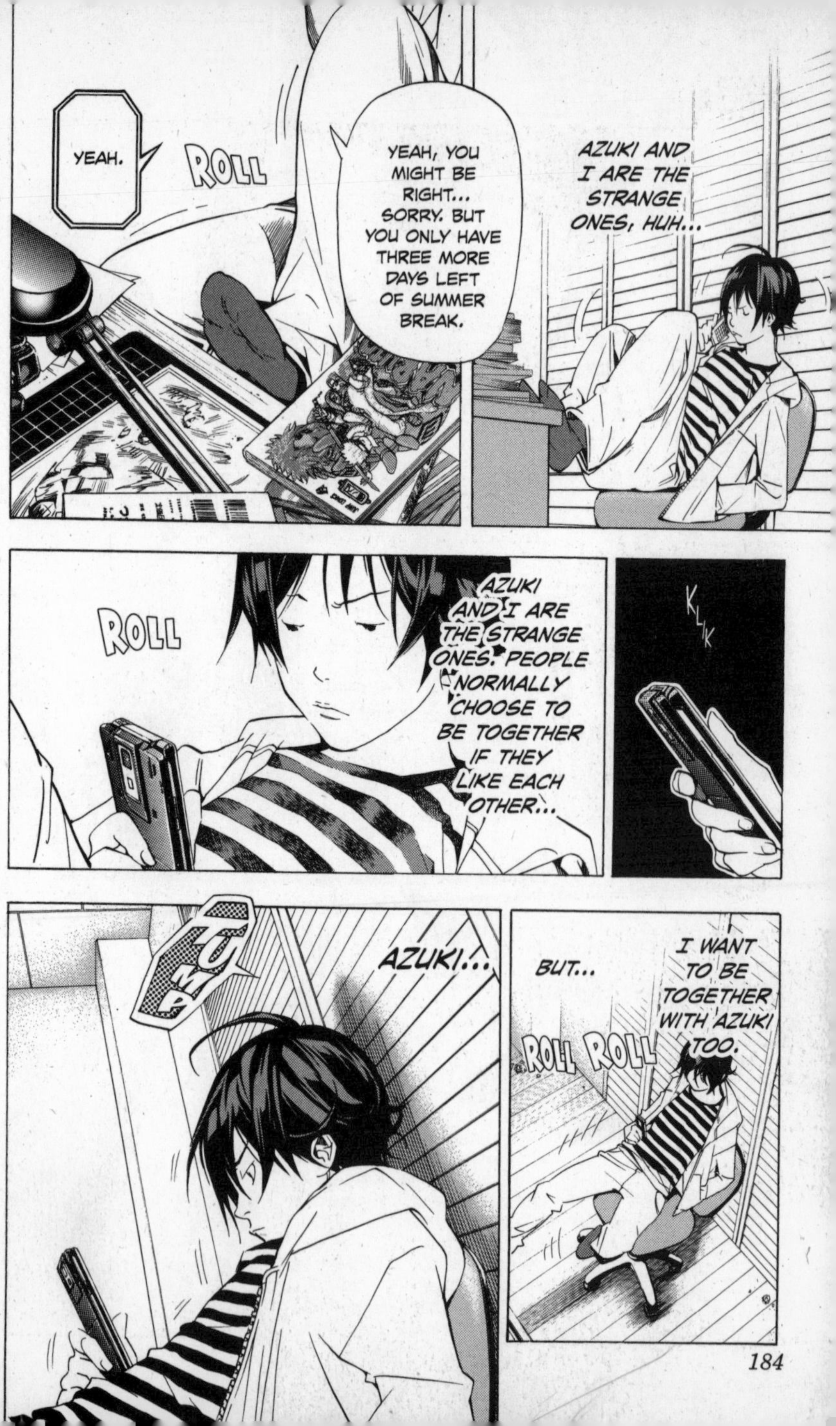
AZUKI AND I ARE THE STRANGE ONES, HUH...
YEAH, YOU MIGHT BE RIGHT... SORRY. BUT YOU ONLY HAVE THREE MORE DAYS LEFT OF SUMMER BREAK.
ROLL
YEAH.
KLIK
AZUKI AND I ARE THE STRANGE ONES. PEOPLE NORMALLY CHOOSE TO BE TOGETHER IF THEY LIKE EACH OTHER...
ROLL
I WANT TO BE TOGETHER WITH AZUKI TOO.
BUT...
ROLL ROLL
AZUKI...
TUMP

READ THIS WAY

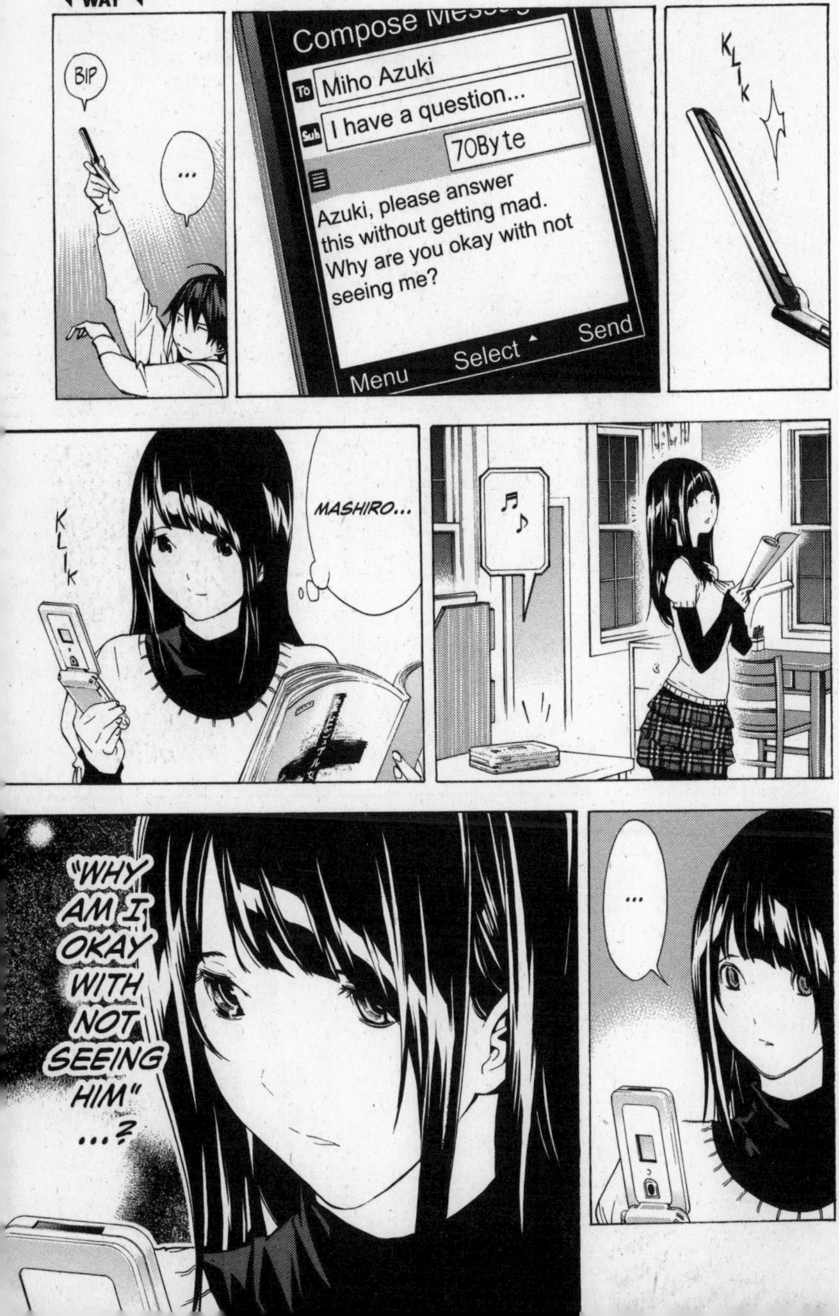
KLIK
Compose
To Miho Azuki
Sub I have a question...
70Byte
Azuki, please answer this without getting mad. Why are you okay with not seeing me?
Menu
Select
Send
BIP
...
MASHIRO...
KLIK
...
"WHY AM I OKAY WITH NOT SEEING HIM" ...?

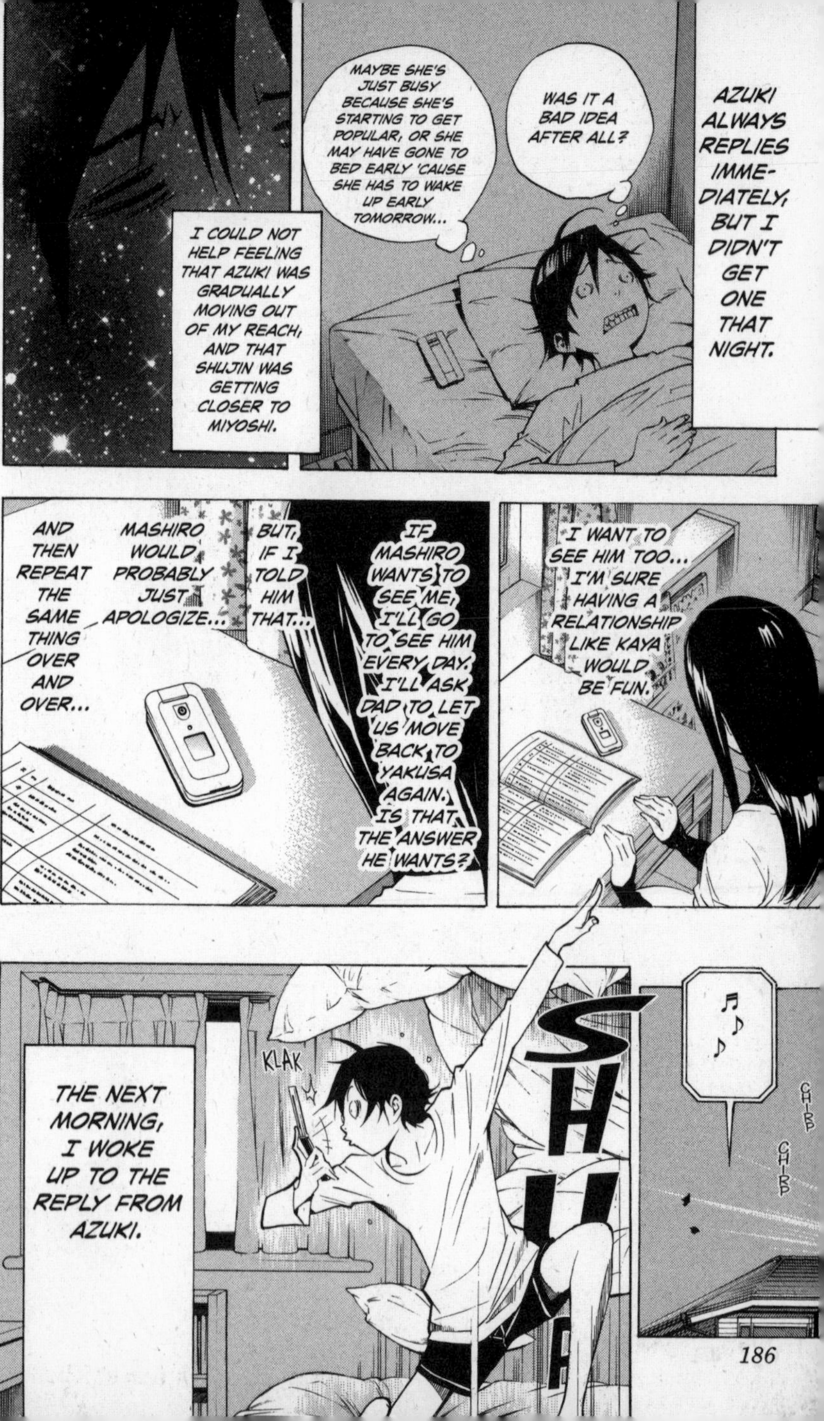
AZUKI ALWAYS REPLIES IMMEDIATELY, BUT I DIDN'T GET ONE THAT NIGHT.
WAS IT A BAD IDEA AFTER ALL?
MAYBE SHE'S JUST BUSY BECAUSE SHE'S STARTING TO GET POPULAR, OR SHE MAY HAVE GONE TO BED EARLY 'CAUSE SHE HAS TO WAKE UP EARLY TOMORROW...
I COULD NOT HELP FEELING THAT AZUKI WAS GRADUALLY MOVING OUT OF MY REACH, AND THAT SHUJIN WAS GETTING CLOSER TO MIYOSHI.
I WANT TO SEE HIM TOO... I'M SURE HAVING A RELATIONSHIP LIKE KAYA WOULD BE FUN.
IF MASHIRO WANTS TO SEE ME, I'LL GO TO SEE HIM EVERY DAY. I'LL ASK DAD TO LET US MOVE BACK TO YAKUSA AGAIN. IS THAT THE ANSWER HE WANTS?
BUT, IF I TOLD HIM THAT...
MASHIRO WOULD PROBABLY JUST APOLOGIZE...
AND THEN REPEAT THE SAME THING OVER AND OVER...
♪ ♪ ♪
CHIRP
CHIRP
SHU
KLAK
THE NEXT MORNING, I WOKE UP TO THE REPLY FROM AZUKI.

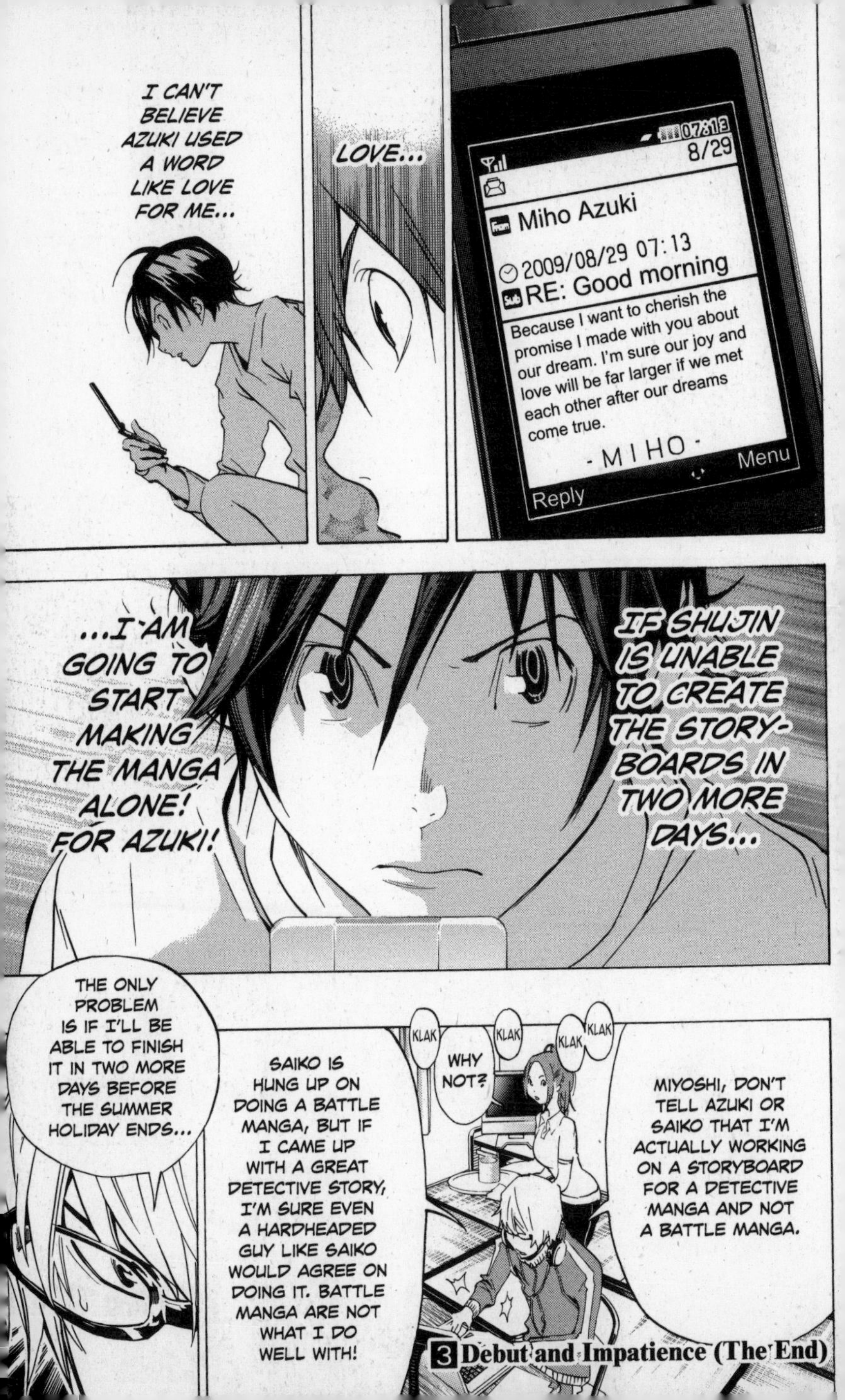
07:13
8/29
Miho Azuki
2009/08/29 07:13
RE: Good morning
Because I want to cherish the promise I made with you about our dream. I'm sure our joy and love will be far larger if we met each other after our dreams come true.
-MIHO-
Reply
Menu
LOVE...
I CAN'T BELIEVE AZUKI USED A WORD LIKE LOVE FOR ME...
IF SHUJIN IS UNABLE TO CREATE THE STORY-BOARDS IN TWO MORE DAYS...
...I AM GOING TO START MAKING THE MANGA ALONE! FOR AZUKI!
KLAK
KLAK
KLAK
KLAK
MIYOSHI, DON'T TELL AZUKI OR SAIKO THAT I'M ACTUALLY WORKING ON A STORYBOARD FOR A DETECTIVE MANGA AND NOT A BATTLE MANGA.
WHY NOT?
SAIKO IS HUNG UP ON DOING A BATTLE MANGA, BUT IF I CAME UP WITH A GREAT DETECTIVE STORY, I'M SURE EVEN A HARDHEADED GUY LIKE SAIKO WOULD AGREE ON DOING IT. BATTLE MANGA ARE NOT WHAT I DO WELL WITH!
THE ONLY PROBLEM IS IF I'LL BE ABLE TO FINISH IT IN TWO MORE DAYS BEFORE THE SUMMER HOLIDAY ENDS...
3 Debut and Impatience (The End)

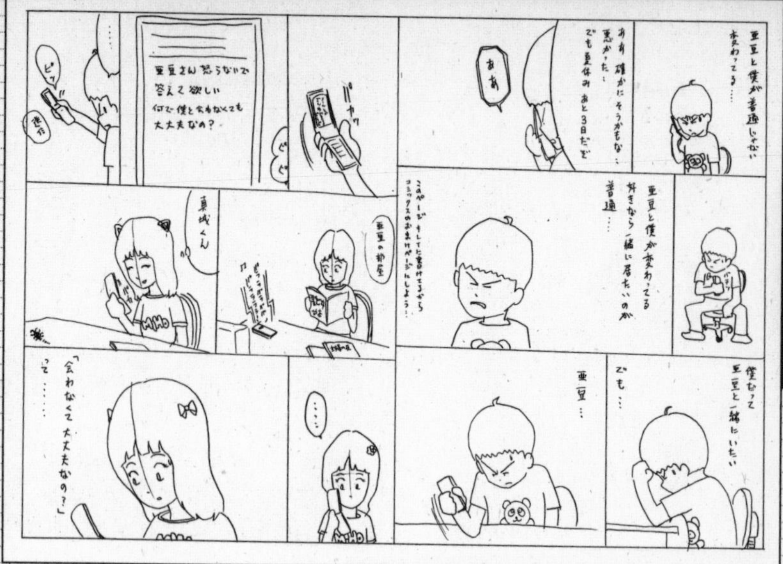
亜豆と僕が普通じゃない変わってる…
あぁ確かにそうかもな… 悪かった… でも夏休みあと3日だぞ
ああ
パカッ
ぐぐ
亜豆さん怒らないで答えて欲しい 何で僕と会わなくても大丈夫なの？
ピッ
送信
……
亜豆と僕が変わってる 好きなら一緒に居たいのが普通…
このページどうしても書けなかったらコミックスのおまけページにしよう…
亜豆の部屋
真城くん
僕なって亜豆と一緒にいたい
でも…
亜豆…
……
「会わなくて大丈夫なの？」って……

OHBA'S STORYBOARD

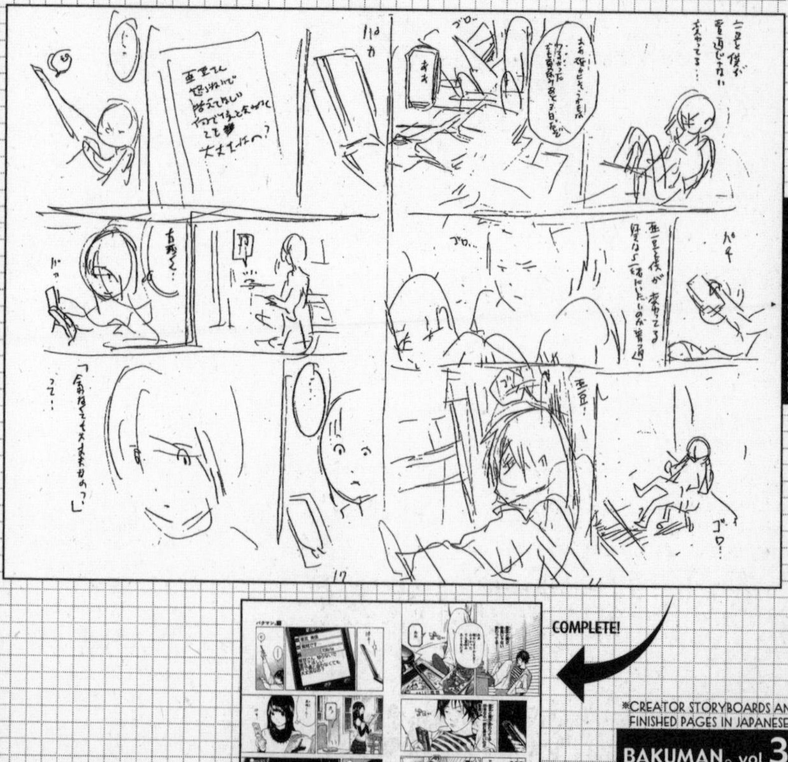
亜豆と僕が普通じゃない変わってる…
ゴロ
パカ
亜豆さん怒らないで答えて欲しい 何で僕と会わなくても大丈夫なの？
パチ
ゴロ…
亜豆と僕が変わってる 好きなら一緒にいたいのが普通!
亜豆!
ゴロ…
……
「会わなくても大丈夫なの？」って…

OBATA'S STORYBOARD

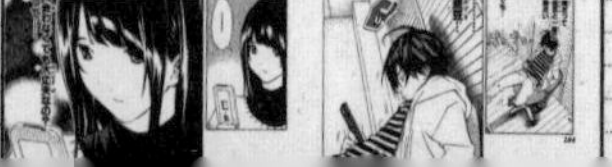

COMPLETE!

※CREATOR STORYBOARDS AND FINISHED PAGES IN JAPANESE

BAKUMAN。 vol.3

"Until the Final Draft Is Complete"

Chapter 25, pp. 184-185

BAKUMAN。

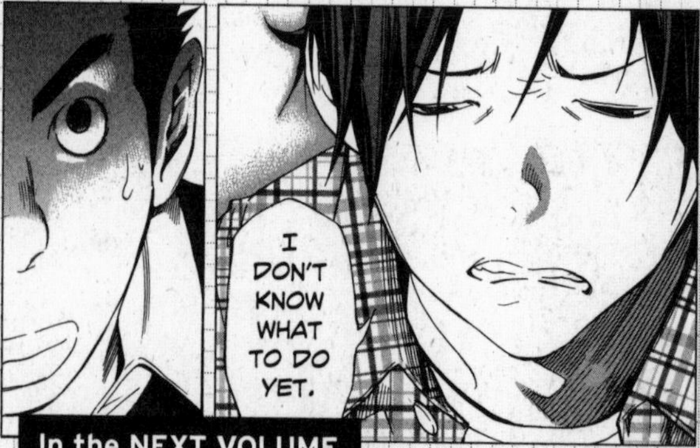
I DON'T KNOW WHAT TO DO YET.

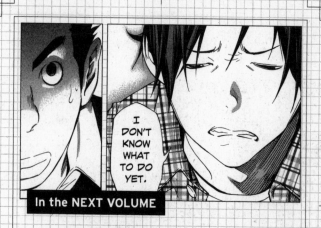

In the NEXT VOLUME

As summer break ends, Moritaka and Akito are in danger of breaking up as a manga creating team. It may be up to their editor, Hattori, to save the day.

Available May 2011!

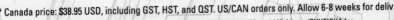